MURDER IN SHAKESPEARE'S ENGLAND

A MOST
EXECRABLE
ND BARBAROVS MVRDER,

done by an *East-Indian* Devil, or a Native of *Java-Major*, in the Road of *Bantam*, Aboard an *English* Ship called the *Coster*, on the 22. of *October* laſt, 1641.

Wherein is ſhewed how the wicked Villain came to the ſaid Ship and hid himſelf till it was very dark, and then he mudrdered all the men that were a Board, except the Cooke, and three Boyes.

And Laſtly, how the murderer himſelfe was juſtly requited.

Captain *William Minor* being an eye-witneſſe of this bloudy Maſſacre.

LONDON, Printed for T. Banks, Iuly the 18. 1642.

A Most Execrable and Barbarous Murder Done by an East-Indian Devil, 1642. British Library, Wing M2885. (*British Library*)

Murder
in
Shakespeare's England

Vanessa McMahon

Hambledon and London

London and New York

Hambledon and London
102 Gloucester Avenue
London, NW1 8HX

175 Fifth Avenue
New York, NY 10010

First Published 2004

ISBN 1 85285 422 7

A description of this book is available from the
British Library and from the Library of Congress.

Typeset by Carnegie Publishing, Lancaster,
and printed in Great Britain by Cambridge University Press.

Distributed in the United States and Canada
exclusively by Palgrave Macmillan,
A division of St Martin's Press.

Contents

Illustrations

A Most Execrable and Barbarous Murder Done
by an East-Indian Devil, 1642   ii

Plates

Between Pages 102 and 103

Abbreviations

CLRO	Corporation of London Record Office.
PRO	Public Record Office, The National Archives.
JP	Justice of the Peace.
n.d.	No publication date recorded.
n.p.	No location of printing recorded.

Preface

This book was inspired by the wave of books on gender and social history that were produced in the later part of the twentieth century. I applaud the efforts these fellow historians have gone to to include ordinary people in our stories of the past. I hope that this book will allow me to follow in their footsteps.

Many people have helped and contributed to this book, and I would like to thank them all for their kind words and constructive criticisms. In particular, I owe a huge debt to Dr Laura Gowing and Professor Justin Champion, who have read my work and guided me for many years. I greatly appreciate their efforts and their expertise. I would like to extend my gratitude to the seminar groups in 'Women's History' and 'Society, Culture and Belief in Early Modern Europe' at the Institute of Historical Research at which I was a regular member. These seminars extended my comprehension and allowed me to assess my work critically via other historian's ideas and projects. Having spoken at both these seminars, I would also like to thank those who attended for their prescient and thoughtful questions and comments, especially Michael Hunter, Alan Bray and Lyndal Roper.

I would also like to thank my colleagues for the interest and support they gave while I wrote this book, and I would like to especially mention the Engineering department at VSOE (where I worked while researching my PhD) and the staff and faculty at Richmond, American International University in London (where I completed this book). I am grateful to the following for permission to reproduce illustrations: Bodleian Library, Oxford, pl. 1; British Library, pls 3, 6, p. ii; Guildhall Library, Corporation of London, pls 4, 5; Lambeth Palace Library, pl. 2; Shakespeare Library, pl. 7.

Finally, I would have been quite unable to complete this study without the support and encouragement of friends, family and work colleagues. I would like to thank all who have supported me and assisted my work, especially Jane Ponder for her enthusiasm and cheerful discussion of my doubts, and Frances Maggs for her unflagging interest in and discussion of my ideas, and for her work (with her husband Michael) in proof-reading and critically assessing my writing. My thanks also extend to my family, and in particular my parents and in-laws who have been perennially intrigued by my studies. My love of reading and my fascination with crime stories were inspired and encouraged by my parents, and for this I want to express my particular thanks.

Most significantly, my husband, Tony Parkins, has been a source of humour and emotional support throughout the long research process. Without his assistance, this book would never have been possible; therefore I dedicate this volume to him.

Note on Quotations

The quotations used throughout this book are taken from original documents. The Yorkshire cases come from the Assi 45 archive at the National Archives, Public Record Office, and the London cases are drawn from the Session Paper Archive at the Corporation of London Record Office. Pamphlets and printed texts come from a variety of sources, notably the British Library.

The spelling and grammar used in the deposition sources has been modernised to make it accessible to readers. The original capitalisation has been retained, as have the original spelling of names. Words like 'ye', 'yf' and 'yt' have been modernised throughout (into 'the', 'if' and 'that'). Quotes from depositions have been left in the third person as this provides a sense of the original text and reminds the reader of the presence of the clerk and the judge in writing the text and questioning the witness. Repetitive phrases like 'this examinant' or 'this informer' have been removed unless this affected the sense of the content. Quotations from printed texts have not been modernised, however, and appear as they would have in the original, in line with literary conventions.

Introduction

In modern society we seem to be fascinated by murder. Detective fiction prevails in bookshops, on television and on film, while factual crime stories form a significant proportion of news reports, with distinctive or unusual killing still having the power to shock, even in our sometimes jaded times. Murders of children, contract killings, and multiple deaths can at times dominate the headlines and enthral and horrify us all. We are revolted by the extremity and horror of these crimes, while simultaneously we desire to know the details and immerse ourselves in the story of the killing. We wonder about the motive and about how such a crime could ever have come to pass. We are interested in the timing and ferocity of the attack. We are concerned about the fate of the killer, and continue to debate their level of guilt and the appropriate punishment for their crime, often for some years. Murder is one of the worst crimes imaginable, and as a society we are drawn to it and thoroughly engrossed by it.

This is not a new phenomenon. Indeed, people in the past were just as interested in extreme violence and homicide. Throughout time, all gratuitous violence has been consistently, roundly condemned and prosecuted, with murderers especially sought out. Of course, the process by which murderers were caught and the way in which they were tried and punished did vary. The crime itself changed over time, with new definitions, categories of crime and mitigation refining accusations and the process of punishment. One thing remained constantly true, though. Murder was perceived as disruptive and wicked, and no community could allow a murderer to go deliberately unpunished if it wanted to maintain its sense of law and order.

Murder was as intriguing a crime in Shakespeare's England as it was at any other time. It was not the most heinous crime on the statute books, as treason and heresy were always considered to be more serious by the state. However, aside from historical moments of overwhelming panic linked to plots to bring down the monarchy or forcibly alter the national religion, murder was usually far more feared by ordinary people and had a higher popular profile as it left tangible victims and caused visible harm. Homicide was not a crime only of the heart and mind; it was also one of bodies. Victims and their families and friends were said to cry out for vengeance over the blood that had been spilt: a vengeance that had to be pursued through the courts and resolved on the scaffold. Murder was a crime that ordinary people were intimately affected by and one in which they were expected to intervene, in terms of capturing culprits, giving evidence and witnessing the punishment. In addition, as homicide law was repeatedly re-interpreted in this period, this was a crime that was firmly historically specific and so one that is revealing of early modern beliefs and mores. In this book, I will discuss how ordinary people and the courts interpreted homicides and how these interpretations were often contingent on external factors like gender, race, religion and social status.

The legal system was constructed by the government and the crown to regulate disorder, to protect citizens and ensure communal harmony. However, these things were as desirable to ordinary people as they were to the state. In fact, ordinary people were regularly willing to investigate crime and prosecute their neighbours for homicide and for other crimes. These same neighbours were often willing to physically intervene in disputes to prevent a fight or protect someone from abuse. This was as true in petty theft cases as it was of violence. In fact, the legal system depended on ordinary people and would have been unable to function without them. Crime and the law were never just about the rich limiting and regulating the poor. The public identity of a community and the families within it was predicated upon notions of orderliness: homicide challenged this concept and threatened individuals, the community and the state. As such, killing was seldom seen as permissible and an uncaptured murderer was seen as dangerous both literally and figuratively.

It is not surprising then that stories of homicides both shocked and thrilled early modern communities and inspired long printed tracts, ballads, songs, popular prints and pictures. Courtrooms were packed for trials, vitriolic language was used to describe the crime in print and executions were always well attended. Although all crime was viewed dimly and perceived as dangerous, homicide struck at the heart of early modern communities. It disrupted order within homes and in communities, subverted law and called into question the role of justice. It is this combination of horror and titillation as well as the social and gender implications of the stories of crime that this book will assess. A focus on homicide is revealing of both the ordinary and the extraordinary: of everyday life, expectations and social and gendered attitudes as well as patterns of violence and disorder in communities that were more often orderly and law-abiding.

Both in law and its application, homicide was clearly defined as a series of quite distinct crimes. Differences in popular perceptions and judicial punishments were based on interpretations of the actions of the killer and victim, and on their gender. The law can be seen as having a tripartite classification: murder, which implied malice and led automatically to death; manslaughter, which was not premeditated, but was provoked and whose mitigating circumstances led to a lesser penalty; and excusable homicide, self-defence and other justified killings, in which the act was pardoned automatically. Such classifications were not entirely unique to this period, but the ways in which the crimes were discussed and prosecuted were quite specifically early modern. This was a crime as much determined by contemporary beliefs and mores as any other.

Murder was the oldest and most basic category of killing. All homicides were tried as murders in court. Any mitigation was applied by the jury or the judge during the trial and as part of their judgement. The key to a murder conviction was proving malice or *mens rea* (an evil mind). However:

> Malice was not easy to define, and even harder to prove; often it had to be implied from the facts surrounding the killing. So long as there was a general evil intent; an intent to injure someone, there was no need to prove a specific intent to kill the deceased.[1]

Although murder was the term popularly used to define all killings, it was actually a quite closely defined crime. The focus on intent legally excluded madmen and young children from culpability. A contemporary commentator and legal writer, Zachary Babington, argued that conflicts between good friends, sudden and casual violence, and provocation were also excluded from the full penalty of the law.[2] Clearly, not all killings were murders.

Murder was far from the only way of viewing unnatural death. Excusable and justifiable homicides generally led to automatic pardons or acquittals, and so were regarded as acceptable types of killing. They could include killings by an officer trying to legitimately arrest a suspect, accidents or self-defence. In each of these situations, while violence was present, the intention to kill was not. The actions were lawful and related to the pursuit of justice or the highly acceptable defence of self. These mitigations were carefully regulated, however, and all attempts at invoking such defences were closely monitored. To successfully plead self-defence defendants had to say they had been literally backed into a corner and had no other option but to strike out. As the action was still technically "a tort or 'contempt'",[3] and had deprived the king of a subject, the accused would have still been considered to be a convict and liable to forfeit all their goods and land to the crown. Such a sanction was generally considered to be unfair and was seldom practised. Most juries found the defendant not guilty as a way of avoiding this forfeiture.

The other principal category for homicide was manslaughter. In 1390 a distinction was drawn for the first time in common law between premeditation and spontaneity in killing. More thoroughly developed in the sixteenth century, this distinction formed the basis for the crime of manslaughter.[4] Unlike the pardonable acts of excusable and justifiable homicide, manslaughter remained a felony and so was technically subject to the death penalty. The general application of the ancient category of 'benefit of clergy' in these cases meant those convicted were seldom hanged, however. Benefit of Clergy was a standard defence, which was used to mitigate a range of felonies. Although designed exclusively for clergymen, by the sixteenth century it was used by all men, and was used by women from the eighteenth century. However, the mitigation could only be applied for a first offence and the convict had to prove they could read.[5] Punishment tended to involve branding on the hand with the letter 'M' (for manslaughter), and/or transportation.

As with self-defence, manslaughter was heavily regulated, although its main principles stemmed from sixteenth century judicial decisions rather than statute law. Nevertheless, the legal pre-requisites for manslaughter were well known. Firstly, the crime could not be premeditated. Manslaughter definitions were predicated on 'hot' anger, in which overwhelming passions dictated the deadly response. The second condition, provocation, related intimately to hot anger, and had become the abiding definition of manslaughter by the seventeenth century.[6] Provocation referred to an act that pushed a defendant beyond reasonable limits and led to them striking out at their victim. As such, under the law this provocation should not have been only verbal, but related to blows that angered the defendant. Even so, because of the freedom allowed to juries, in practise they could decide to accept verbal provocation in particular cases. The distinction between a provoked fight and one ascribed a malicious motive was a fine one, and relied on juridical decision in most cases. Defendants usually argued that the (invariably dead) party had struck first, using this blow (and any insults they were willing to repeat) as evidence of being provoked. The stakes were high. Although the difference was fine legally, in terms of the punishment inflicted it was of fundamental importance.

Despite the restriction of the definition of homicide to these three categories in most conventional legal histories, there were a further two categories actively applied in court. These categories were determined not only by the actions of the defendant, but by the nature of the crime and the gender of the killer. Petty treason and infanticide were forms of murder in which the punishment was distinctive or the rules governing conviction had been amended. Although both categories referred explicitly to murder, as they were clearly linked to malice and *mens rea*, these crimes had distinctive agendas and applications, which made them into separate categories of killing.

Petty treason was first defined in the 1351 Treason Act. Largely concerned with criminalising acts against the king, the killing of a social superior by an inferior was also defined as a treasonous act. Most commonly applied to wives who killed their husbands or servants their masters, the crime of petty treason was not subject to the mitigation of self-defence or manslaughter. Although not excluded by statute, the nature of the crime did not lend itself to any kind of comprehensible or allowable killing. No inferior could be given legal sanction to kill their superior, and so this crime was always regarded as murder. Wives and female servants convicted of petty treason were sentenced to burn at the stake, while male servants were hanged, drawn and quartered. Although petty treason was not limited to women, rebellious wives caused far greater public consternation in this period than servants. A wife who killed defied her gender and her status. She was viewed as unnatural and a domestic traitor. This made her one of the most invidious killers in the early modern imagination. A wife's actions were both thoroughly constrained by the law and critically received in public. Petty treason was seldom prosecuted, as these kinds of murder were rare. However, it was always considered more distinctive and shocking than ordinary murder.

The infanticide statute was a later development. Passed in 1624, it referred more directly to women as the prime and (under this law) the only culprits of this type of killing. The killers targeted were the unmarried mothers of illegitimate children, who killed their offspring on or soon after birth, and hid the dead bodies. Everything about this crime was secret. The pregnancy, the labour, the murder and the burial were all hidden from the community, making it an intensely difficult crime to police and investigate. It was a crime conducted in secret, something which inspired additional invective from the lawmakers and judges. It was generally presumed that such infants were murdered to hide an underclass of bastard-bearing women, who were determined to continue with their illicit sexual behaviour. As I will show, this law was concerned with regulating the sexual activities of independent, unmarried, young women, and not with saving the young lives of their infants. Like the wives accused of petty treason, this relatively powerless group of women was targeted by the law to further constrain and confine them. This was despite the relative infrequency with which such crimes occurred and the greater likelihood that women would in fact be victims of crime, and homicide in particular, rather than its perpetrators.

The regulation of crime was both a basic tenet of the law and a means for ensuring order. Justice needed both to be done and to be seen to be done. A trial was about more than a specific wrong or individual punishment; it was about ameliorating a social dislocation, and righting a potent and meaningful social wrong. Such a grand remit received a suitable response. Outside London, the visitation of the assize court was a twice-yearly occasion, in which the judges, lawyers and clerks processed into town with pomp and ceremony. The basic impetus for justice came from inside the community, but was administered from without. The judges were not natives of the region, coming from another one of the six assize regions and having had the role allocated to them in London. The cavalcade would process into town, heralded by trumpeters, and joined by the sheriff and local gentry. Such magnificent display brought with it the 'awful remoteness' of royal justice, and was intended to awe and cow local people.[7] Although pay was generally low, the visiting justices were entertained in lavish style, and the Northern Circuit in particular was famed for its hunting and scenery. Unlike provincial assize courts, the Old Bailey sat several times a year. Plague, war or natural disaster only occasionally limited the sitting of the court; but these and other procedural delays could mean a defendant could be imprisoned for up to a year before trial.[8]

Once a crime was suspected, the first step in the process of justice was to gather informations (or witness statements), usually from volunteers. Witnesses often willingly recounted their evidence to a clerk in front of a JP, after swearing an oath to tell the truth and not speak maliciously. Further witnesses could be called and questioned on the constable's or JP's instruction. Once this process was complete, and clear evidence indicating specific suspects had been obtained, indictments were drawn up. An indictment was an official legal document recording the formal and formulaic accusation of a defendant. This record was often in Latin and sometimes annotated to record the outcome at the grand or petty jury stages. The indictment was read and the defendant was either gaoled or bailed until the trial.[9] Gaol was not designed to be a form of punishment, merely a restraint on prisoners believed likely to flee. However, grim conditions and the prevalence of fever, as well as a corrupt system in which prisoners had to bribe the gaoler for better accommodations, meant gaols had unforeseen punitive qualities.

A grand jury read and considered the accusation in private before a trial was undertaken. If this jury believed the case should be tried, they found 'billa vera', or a true bill. If not, they found it 'ignoramous' and the case was dismissed (12 per cent of all cases taken to the grand jury were found 'ignoramous').[10] The last stage of the legal process was the trial, overseen by the judge and the petty jury. This trial was an open and public occasion, held in a courthouse packed with legal officers, defendants, victims and their families, witnesses and curious locals.[11] A trial was considered a public entertainment for many and was certainly a theatrical event. It was the visitation of justice, encased in the pageantry of the state. The events were dramatic, the evidence potentially shocking, and the outcomes (in terms of release or execution) were spectacular and gripping. The sessions of the court began with a long sermon in which order, godliness and obedience were stressed. Ordinary days began less prosaically, although they were still packed with noise, drama and thrill-seeking locals.

Victims usually pursued their own prosecutions, paying court fees and ensuring the attendance of their witnesses. They could even face legal penalty if the case were dismissed by the court (for providing a malicious accusation). Of course, in homicide cases, victims could not prosecute, so the crown usually acted in their place.

Although defendants came to court in chains, after they had pleaded to the indictment and the trial could begin, their restraints were removed. This allowed them to stand as apparent equals to the jury and to speak freely.[12] Crown witnesses were heard first under oath, and then the examination of the defendant would be read, if it were felt to be incriminating. The only lawyer in court was the prosecutor and he was not trying to provide balance but to prove a defendant's guilt. The defendant was not felt to need legal representation as 'in order to convict a prisoner the proof must be so plain that no counsel could contend against it'.[13] Defence counsel was not universally allowed until the 1730s, although the first changes came after a series of treason trials in the 1690s. Defence witnesses were always presented last. Before 1703 these witnesses were not sworn in or asked to speak under oath, nor could they be forced to attend, unlike prosecution witnesses who were usually bound by a recognizance.[14]

Like the words spoken by the defendant, defence witness testimony was considered suspect. The court felt that as such evidence was more likely to be false; an oath would only force perjury. How significant such an absence was is unknown. A credible witness, with a good reputation, may well have overcome the explicit implication of dishonesty such an exemption made, or jurors may have been unaware of its significance. Whatever impact it may have made, it would probably have been at least partly disguised in the hubbub of the courtroom. As the prisoner had no prior notice of the evidence against him, the trial 'normally degenerated into ... an "altercation" between prisoner and prosecutor and witnesses'.[15] The judge, jurymen, prosecutor and defendant could all speak and question witnesses at any time. This often confusing and disorderly cross-questioning must have made many points obscure and certainly made complex evidence difficult to present at times. The judge had overall control and could dominate in court, but his influence depended on his personality and willingness to direct the course of justice.

Once the evidence had been heard, the short trial was over. The judge might sum up the evidence, but his opinion on guilt had usually been made apparent during the trial itself. The jury then retired to consider its verdict. If the defendant were acquitted, however perversely, double jeopardy prevented the crown from re-trying them. However, in murder cases alone, the victim's family could invoke the ancient law of appeal and demand a new trial. This was only infrequently used, but it could be effective in securing a different and more punitive result.[16]

Conviction rates further varied with the crime and the nature and gender of defendant. At least a quarter of all those indicted for felonies were found not guilty and freed.[17] Murder had a 63 per cent conviction rate, infanticide had a 53 per cent rate and miscellaneous felonies (not involving death or theft) had a rate of only 26 per cent. The average conviction rate was just 58 per cent.[18] These rates were marked by social and gendered decisions about the accused. Juries were partisan and, across all felony cases, favoured women over men. However, the distinctions were even subtler than that, as wives were favoured over widows and widows over spinsters, in a hierarchy of assumed culpability and sympathy.[19] In murder cases attitudes often differed, though. Fathers and masters were treated more leniently in court than mothers and mistresses, and their actions in killing dependants were more often reduced to manslaughter or accidental death. Although 75 per cent of female defendants were discharged across the board, so were 50 per cent of male defendants. Indeed, despite this leniency, women received the same proportion of convictions for murder as men:[20] and, for instance, execution rates for female crimes, like infanticide, were significantly higher than for ordinary murder.[21]

Legal histories of this period tend to be cynical about the effectiveness of the trial process and of the application of justice. Trials from this period in history have been called 'nasty, brutish and essentially short'.[22] Some historians accuse clerks, judges and even jurors of cynicism, corruption and hasty decision making. However, most trials were much fairer than these descriptions imply. People in the past were as concerned with justice as we are; and this meant they wanted to be absolutely sure that those they convicted were in fact guilty. As a consequence, many ordinary people, as well as judges and jurors, made significant efforts to ensure justice was done.

Witnesses were seldom passive victims of bullying officials or overbearing clerks. The evidence of deponents shows that testimony varied in content and implication, often dramatically. The evidence recorded was not limited to that necessary to prove a specific crime. Often the recorded testimony was full of ancillary details and asides that reveal much about the social situation of the violence, while not being legally necessary for a conviction. This suggests that any 'unseen hand(s)' directing proceedings were singularly ineffective in most cases. Given the large number of people involved in the trial process, from gaolers to clerks, judges to jurymen, as well as witnesses, victims and defendants, it is unsurprising that a percentage were corrupt and that records were sometimes incorrect. The law could be malleable at times, a point both sides used to their advantage. Stories could be manipulated to give certain impressions of guilt, as witnesses were very well aware. The court process was far from perfect, but neither was it systematically corrupt or cynically operated.

Apart from the addition of manslaughter, murder law was essentially static in this period. 1624 represents the last real change in the statutes governing illegal killings until the 1752 Murder Act: and even the 1752 act did not change the nature of the crime, as it was concerned with the treatment of convicts. It ensured that the execution of a convict would take place within two days of sentencing, and that the body of the dead felon would be made available for dissection by the new breed of anatomists.[23] In any case, the legal records do not reflect change well, as they were formulaic documents whose focus was on the immediate events of a crime. Although detail and background information are often apparent, depositions were not designed as social records, but as a means for assisting the prosecution to build a case and select valuable witnesses. That the crimes themselves remained unchanged in this period only exacerbated this issue. Judges, jurors and witnesses alike were aware of the law and nuances of each definition of killing. They clearly understood how to imply a certain crime and deny another. Only occasionally were the basic tenets of a law challenged in court, and this was in a piecemeal way (often only recoverable in long-term comparisons).

Although the murder statutes remained essentially static, the way these laws were applied changed significantly. While the legal system was largely formalised in the first part of the eighteenth century, many of these changes had their precursors in the seventeenth century, in the informal and individual protections offered by judges and jurors in court. In fact, it would be foolish to conclude that the law remained unchanged until the reforms of the eighteenth century, without examining its application and common interpretations. There were few rules of evidence in this period, but hearsay, unsubstantiated rumour or evidence from accomplices were all frowned upon by judge and jury, criticised in court and sometimes totally excluded.[24]

Such popular demands for informal legal vigilance led to the 1624 statute on infanticide being interpreted in the courtroom with unexpected leniency. The law demanded only proof of illegitimacy and hidden death to secure a conviction, but witnesses consistently provided additional, detailed evidence. This evidence was intended to provide some certainty that a crime had been committed. Conversely, juries presented with evidence of hidden birth and stillbirth could ignore the statute and acquit. Further, by the early eighteenth century at least, a new defence to infanticide accusations had been popularly framed and legally accepted. Termed 'benefit of linen', this referred to the mother's supply of baby clothes which appeared to negate her intention to kill. Acquittals were also common in such cases. Neither benefit of linen nor the additional evidence of murder were required by the statute, and so were not enforceable in law. Nevertheless, they represented common practice across the country.[25]

The law was not the only arena in which change was experienced. Stories of homicide shifted in this period in line with social and cultural concerns. Although generally causes of concern, the power associated with unruly women was somewhat diminished by the 1700s, and women were less often seen as systemic threats. It has been argued that disorderly women were 'taken less seriously, less feared, they [were] also perceived as less powerful and dangerous'.[26] While this is true of infanticidal women and witches, this was less true of murderous wives. The threat of secret, domestic treason/homicide remained a cause of concern. Even today, a killer-wife is seen as dangerous and somewhat unnatural.[27] Even so, pamphlets were more sympathetic to abused and murdered wives in the seventeenth century than in the sixteenth, and by the eighteenth century women were regularly cast as passive victims of male sexual and violent passions.[28] The change in actual crime was negligible; however, the way these crimes were interpreted varied greatly.

It was not only shifting views of gender that caused changes in perceptions of killers. The 'usual suspects' of the sixteenth and seventeenth century – witches, papists, foreigners, soldiers and robbers – were amended to fit the fears of the eighteenth. Witches, soldiers and papists lost some of their ability to terrify as their numbers declined and perceptions of their social threat diminished.[29] Robbers, conversely, persisted as prime sources of fears. Their crimes were linked to greed and evil as solidly in the eighteenth and nineteenth centuries as they were in the seventeenth. Social fears of foreigners depended on historical context, political manoeuvring and warfare. However, in terms of home grown prejudice, the Irish joined the Scots as people to be feared for their ruthlessness and propensity to kill, especially in the nineteenth century.

At the same time, some crimes were not feared until later historical periods. Sex crimes and serial killers, for instance, awaited the disciplines of psychology and psychoanalysis to become widespread sources of national terror. Although these crimes only preoccupied and terrified people from the late nineteenth century, the offences themselves predated this. These shifts in terror are significant. Perception of crime was always as relevant as its incidence; stories of killers, and their depictions of themselves, will be an enduring focus of this book.

Of course, many more people were orderly and law abiding than were criminal. These people are just as valuable to historical discourses as the disorderly, but they tend not to appear in criminal records (and when they do it is only tangentially, as witnesses). Any study of crime tends to swamp this silent majority, presenting a vision of the past enmeshed in violence, deceit and criminality. Although this study of homicide in many ways replicates this distorted vision of the disorderly past, I have attempted to redress the balance. Honest and law-abiding people can be found in the records and their voices can be recovered. The role of witnesses, in particular, was revealed in deposition statements and occasionally in print. In such scenarios, judicial regulation can seem the only way in which communities could order themselves; the formality of the court and scaffold the only means for resolving disputes. Ordinary people, therefore, played a significant role in justice. Indeed, 'By the time a felon was hanged, as many as three dozen men had participated in the decision-making process that sent him to the gallows.'[30] People like jurymen, clerks, prosecutors and gaolers were involved as well as significant numbers of witnesses. This book will examine the contribution these ordinary people made to justice.

I will use two main kinds of source document: depositions and printed material, including pamphlets, legal tracts, popular prints, pictures and ballads. In addition, a range of disparate sources from indictments and recognizances to coroner's inquisitions will be referred to.[31] These texts are highly complex. They often had multiple and sometimes unknown authors, as well as clear motives and agendas. Even witness statements cannot be seen as representing 'unvarnished truth'. They merely represent the witness's perception and what the witness chose to tell the courts. Depositions were not official court records, although they were taken in front of a JP, magistrate or coroner. All evidence given in depositions had to be presented orally in court at a later date. Due to restrictions on storage space, many of the early depositions were simply destroyed after the trial.[32] Those that remain were fortuitously overlooked.

Some depositions may have been simple recordings of a deponent's tale, but it is likely that the majority were more confused stories in which the

JP and clerk frequently intervened for clarification and to re-order the story. The final narrative would be produced from these disparate pieces of information. It would be written by the clerk, influenced by the judge's direction and provide a version of the witness's words. An acknowledgement of the presence of these other hand(s) in the formation of the tale is crucial. Indeed, the involvement of other 'authors' of these statements caused some contemporaneous concern. Sir Matthew Hale frequently referred to crafty clerks and expressed concern about truth in these records.[33] However, such distortions can also be viewed as part of the complete narrative: they can be seen as shaping the words and the story and placing them in a formal legal context rather than transforming the witness's words completely and unrecognisably. As it is impossible to know which phrase came from which party, all depositions will be considered as the words of the witness to whom they were linked. Nevertheless, we need to remain aware of the possibility of multiple influences on the language used, spellings and arrangements of the words.

The function of pamphlets and ballads was very different; it was to sell as widely as possible and therefore appeal to a large audience. Printed accounts therefore focused on the most salacious cases. In this way, they are unrepresentative of actual crime, but provided crucial evidence about how crime was popularly portrayed. The stories that sold well were those that tended to terrify and intrigue. These were not everyday tales of discord between neighbours in a public house, or unexciting (albeit fatal) fights. Despite such cases making up the majority of violent deaths in this period, they were often ignored or cursorily recorded. Pamphlets tended to focus on minority tales of robbers, wives, rebellious servants and murderous mothers. Print fed on and constructed communal concerns.[34] The stories were consumed in a variety of ways. Although many were bought and read directly, the story could also be passed on orally, and then compared to other tales of the same crime, or to direct experience of the trial. Some authors of popular print were professionals, but most had other jobs, with a large number only writing one account of a tale close to their hearts and experience.[35] Moreover, pamphlets only represented one perspective. Popular tales could be criticised in print by another story with a different viewpoint. Many of these competing tales have been lost, yet their existence is still discernible. No homicide story should be seen as an authoritative and uncontested account: all of these narratives were variously dismissed or supported in the courtroom, in public spaces and in private conversations.

Trials were not officially recorded in this period, so, although depositions are not records of the words spoken in court, they do represent the only extant version of the evidence that could have been presented. Not all witnesses would be called, and much trial evidence was far shorter than depositions. Therefore, the evidence presented in deposition statements was frequently more detailed, lengthy and (potentially) more under the witness's control than statements from court. Some unofficial records of proceedings were made in this period, in a pamphlet series that later became known as the Old Bailey Sessions Papers. Before 1729 printed proceedings were published on an *ad hoc* basis, under a variety of different titles. Many authors heavily edited the sessions they recorded, including only the most interesting tales, excluding many cases completely and only briefly recording others. These are valuable records as they provide information on conviction and on execution patterns; however, they cannot be considered more reliable than other printed texts or as more official records. The 'Proceedings' were as constructed and as piecemeal as all other homicide narratives.

Stories of crime in print differed from those told in court: the language used was more judgemental and the stories themselves could be more sensationally presented. It is often difficult to distinguish between the view of the court and that of those outside, as jurors were as subject to the media as anyone else and many local people would both attend the trial and read about it in print. However, throughout I make some distinctions between cultural attitudes and beliefs and legal actions and processes. We must remember though that courtrooms could be highly theatrical spaces as full of people, gossip and often innuendo as the streets outside and on occasion as condemnatory in the language used as printed texts. Many of the same attitudes existed in both the courtroom and outside: while court-room were by no means always unfair, we should not see them as spaces of uncomplicated or completely consistent justice.

Ultimately, the sources used can only be suggestive: we cannot know who was telling the truth and who was lying, and although we can guess at the events leading up to a death, it is not the function of this book to accuse new killers or absolve others of guilt. What this book is interested in are the stories told about crime, what people say and how they can phrase it, what they can say about some criminals that they cannot (or do not) say about others. These things are revealing of social patterns in the past. They allow us to effectively 'read' communities, scouring records for their concerns and their prejudices. Therefore, in many ways, abstract decisions about guilt and innocence are irrelevant. Rather, this book is concerned with how contemporaries decided on guilt and how they established innocence, and what they said about people along the way. This is what murder and crime in general can reveal – what it was *like* to live in the past, what it was *like* to be male or female, and the kinds of difference other categories, like age, religion, social status and ethnicity, really had on everyday life.

In this book, I am reconstructing the lives of people we otherwise do not know about and have few other points of access to. Therefore, the murder stories herein are presented to act as a reflection of ordinary people and ordinary lives through the extraordinary lens of violence and death.

Investigating Crime

In 1657 Jane Scape was murdered in an almshouse in Newcastle upon Tyne. Despite being old, lame and blind, her death was too sudden for most to accept as natural. No one doubted that she had been cold-bloodedly killed, and a likely suspect was immediately identified. A woman, 'upon pretence of kindness', was reported to have given Jane a drink, which witnesses later contended had been poisoned. Jane identified the woman on her deathbed as Margarett Galene, a former servant who had come to see her the day before. As Jane had spent several hours with Margarett before the killing occurred, we can be reasonably certain that her identification was accurate. Despite her blindness, Jane said she clearly recognised Margarett's voice, although she did say her accent had changed. In any case, their long conversation undoubtedly provided other proof of her identity.[1]

This should have been a simple case. Poison was suspected as soon as Jane grew sick, and its use was considered by many to be proven by Jane's violent vomiting and swift death. The link was seemingly clear. One witness said that 'Immediately upon the taking of which [poison] she took on violent purging, which continued with her till the time of her death'. For the majority, there was no doubt that foul play had occurred. The problem was that by the time of Jane's death Margarett had left the area and no one seemed to know where she had gone or how to find her. Significantly, Jane was the only person to admit to knowing Margarett. All the other witnesses said she was a stranger and an outsider, suggesting that she had left Jane's service some considerable time before. It was apparently a perfect crime.

Nevertheless, if Jane had been murdered, her killer would need to be caught and tried. To this end, a hue and cry may well have been called. As none was described in the depositions, this is purely speculation, but it was the most likely reaction. The hue and cry was the traditional means of apprehending suspected felons. In the early modern period local communities were still bound by the ancient law of amercement, which stipulated that felons who committed crimes in daylight had to be arrested, or the parish would face a hefty fine. All able-bodied men were bound to answer the call and pursue such felons. This system of apprehension worked well if the felon could be tracked or located nearby. However, due to the fragmented nature of the legal system, tracking people over long distances was often prohibitively complex. In any case, the hue and cry referred only to physical pursuits of criminals, not to investigations. Communities were required to apprehend known villains, but local people were not *obliged* to enquire into a crime or piece together clues to discover a hidden malefactor.

Jane's murder was actually quite unusual. Criminals, even killers, tended to be well known, with suspects quickly identified based on their reputations and on circumstantial evidence. In cases where the crime was eye-witnessed, the evidence would be simple and there would be little need for a broader investigation. However, such absolute certainty only occurred in a small number of cases. The majority of defendants were implicated purely by circumstance. Neighbours often gave evidence about the previous interactions of the protagonists or known enemies of the victim. Until the early part of the eighteenth century there were few rules of evidence and anything could be said in court, whether it was circumstantial or third hand. Testimony about the character of the defendant that bore no relation to the charge was also frequently presented and apparently welcome. However, it is quite clear that not all this testimony was believed. In most cases only a few witnesses testified in a short trial of a well-known or notorious defendant. The vast majority of trials did not involve clever deductions, investigations or intuitive leaps; most were not murder mysteries.

However, the murder of Jane Scape was clearly mysterious and required a proactive and involved investigation. In fact, it was such a complex case that no one was apprehended or tried for three years, and only then thanks to the determination and investigative skills of Jane's son, John, who was horrified at his mother's untimely death, and from the beginning had suspected that his father, William, had been involved in the crime. His parents were separated at the time of Jane's death and they were apparently hostile to each other. John claimed that a few weeks before the killing his father had openly said, 'that his Mother had not six weeks to live'. John was so alarmed at the implications of this statement that he required his father to promise, 'before witnesses, that she should have a safe hereafter'. However, despite his initial suspicion of William, no link could be made between the threat and the woman who actually killed Jane until 1660, when John accidentally came across his father, living in another village, under an assumed name, with a 'wife' called Margarett.

While most witnesses simply recorded what they had seen or heard about the crime and the relationship of the central protagonists, John actively investigated. In fact he collected and presented highly suggestive and extensively researched evidence. In this he was certainly not representative of the vast majority of early modern witnesses. He acted in an unusual (albeit by no means unique) manner. Only a small proportion of witnesses were willing to invest time and energy in seeking out wrongdoers and bringing them to justice. Their efforts went beyond their legal duty to present known felons, as the crimes they investigated were hidden homicides that had previously not been seen as suspicious. Although it is impossible to know why they acted in such proactive ways, such efforts had the effect of communally asserting their values, while ensuring that criminals did not escape justice.

In most cases, the specifics of the investigation are unrecoverable. After all, the investigative process itself was not evidence and so would not be presented to the court unless there were extraordinary circumstances. When Jane Barker told a Lincoln court that she had taken two years to track down her son's killer, butcher John Blanchard, she did not describe the methods she had used to locate him. All we know is that she successfully did so and presented him to the court in 1647.[2] Similarly, in a 1677 infanticide case from London, midwife Elizabeth Cellier gave evidence on the strange markings on a napkin found with the tiny corpse that might have helped identify the child's mother.[3] Both hinted at the methods that they had used to investigate, but did not place as much emphasis on their own role as John Scape did.

Although most did not act as amateur detectives, solutions to complex crimes lay squarely in the hands of neighbours and family members. Contributions could be piecemeal, with witnesses each collecting isolated fragments of evidence. These small efforts by several concerned neighbours often led to a solid case. Such investigations were not co-ordinated by the court but by ordinary people, some of whom could be quite tenacious. They may not have launched as full an investigation as John Scape had, but most witnesses were interested in trying to avert violence and attribute blame for criminal behaviours. Ordinary people actively monitored and judged their peers as they eagerly participated in the broader justice of the state. In part, this popular involvement in crime solving was an extension of the prime tenet of the legal system – the capture of known felons. Neighbours got together to discuss their suspicions and locate malefactors. Small-scale collection and interpretation of clues was clearly allied to this activity and must have been a natural development. From there, more active investigation, on a small or large scale, would have been a short step.

Whatever the motivation, without ordinary people becoming involved, the system of justice would have ground to a halt, since there was no distinct, separate police force to deal with crime. Most victims were expected to pursue criminal cases in court. In a theft case, for example, a victim would have to determine who the thief was, gather witnesses to the crime and to the repossession of the goods and pay for these witnesses to attend court. The victim would also have to pay the legal and administrative fees involved in a prosecution, and would suffer a penalty for malicious prosecution if they lost. Responsibility for prosecution and justice could not be completely handed off to court officials, the watch or constables, because the legal system was simply not designed around the state investigating crime. Trials continued to be perceived as private conflicts involving an accusation and defence. The court acted as an arbitrator in these cases, with the jury deciding which side was more credible and therefore 'innocent' or 'guilty'. The court avenged crime on behalf of the crown, but victims played a central role in initiating and pursuing this justice. Without their efforts, both financial and physical, most trials would have been impossible.

Of course, the victim of a homicide could neither be proactive nor pursue the killer in court. Victims could record an accusation while dying, by repeatedly telling one or a series of neighbours who had injured them and how, all of which could later be reported. However, for the most part, they were completely dependent on others acting on their behalf by prosecuting the case and testifying in court. While family members could pursue a complaint privately, due to the heinous nature of the crime and irreparable nature of the damage done, the crown willingly took on the mantle of prosecuting in the majority of cases. Witnesses were well schooled in this highly proactive legal system, in which a successful trial relied on their tenacity and ingenuity rather than the actions of paid police or other officials. They were aware that they needed to be involved for justice to be done.

This did not mean the state had no formal structures for monitoring order or co-ordinating arrests. Every parish had a constable and watchmen, who were supposed to patrol the local area nightly and assist in quelling disorder and arresting malefactors. The position was unpaid and was conferred each year on a different incumbent (usually a richer villager). It was an unpopular and onerous duty, and many paid fines to avoid it. The fine was usually in excess of £10, but unwilling constables could also produce a 'Tyburn Ticket' to secure an exemption.[4] Constables played a clear role in administering justice. Indeed, these officials occasionally appeared in depositions co-ordinating the hue and cry or administering the capture of a felon.

The constable system was respected and represented the official arm of the law, but it was not the only – or the main – source of order. All communities were expected to police themselves, with individuals ready to intervene at signs of injustice. Every householder was bound to provide occasional watch duties in their own street at night. Again, it was rare for such men to directly fulfil this role. However, the tradition of fine-paying associated with this reluctance provided adequate funds to pay professional watchmen. Even so, the watch system should not be interpreted as comprehensive policing: it was only ever moderately effective at maintaining order. Watchmen were underpaid, undervalued and considered to be unreliable and highly corruptible. This was far from a prestigious post.

Informal systems of justice were effective because of the involvement of the whole community. Ordinary people were acting in the name of their locality when they prevented and avenged disorder. In most parishes, this clear sense of law and a desire for order came directly from the people, who were consistently interpreting the criminal law, in the decisions they made about presenting others as criminals and in convicting them of crimes. A high proportion of people expressed their willingness to participate in the formal pursuit of killers. This was due more to the shocking nature of the crime than the traditional monetary penalty of amercement. Communities were determined to police themselves and would put significant pressure on anyone tempted to ignore the rule of law. Even family members were expected to act in the name of justice and to apprehend a felon they may be related to: the needs of the community were seen as more pressing than familial obligation. When John Robson was killed in a fight in an alehouse, in Northumberland in 1666, servant Isabell Read was asked 'Whether he or his wife [her master and mistress (and the parents of one of the killers)] did raise hue and cry'.[5] Despite the familial connection, they would be expected to reveal the killers' names and even assist in their capture.

This sense of duty to the community and to justice pervaded popular understandings. In Farringdon in London in December 1692 William Fothergill told the court that on learning that Theophilous Young was responsible for Charles Graham's death he called in the constable and the watch and helped them search for Young.[6] When he made this claim, and added that he had searched all day, he was demonstrating his understanding of his civic duty as well as underlining his own respectable nature.

John Scape's actions went beyond this, however. He acted not because of communal pressures, but because he had a personal interest in uncovering 'the truth' about his mother's murder, or, at least, about his father's culpability. John claimed that Jane Clerke had crucial evidence which would help establish the truth in court. She had been Jane Scape's landlady in the months before her death and had known her for seven years. The witness told the court that many years before Jane had been blinded by a blow from a shovel. She said this to demonstrate how intimately she had known Jane and so how credible any evidence she then gave would be. Of all the local women deposed, she clearly knew Jane Scape the best. Jane Clerke's deposition did not record the detail of her evidence, but John considered it to be dramatic and even decisive. She told John that his father had come to speak with her regarding her testimony, but John said she had told him that 'he should fare no better for it, and that if she were examined upon oath she would disclose the truth of her knowledge therein'. Disappointingly, the only record we have of Jane Clerke's words failed to deliver on this promise of revealing truth, although she may have given additional evidence that has been lost. Even so, 'truth-telling' was the professed motivation of many witnesses and a desire for justice seems to have inspired many to speak in the otherwise hostile and alien environment of the court.

Female witnesses in particular may have found the mantle of truth liberating as it allowed them access to the otherwise male courtroom and permitted them to speak publicly and affect the outcome of a trial. There were few public forums in which women were permitted to speak and in which their voice carried weight. Men exclusively staffed the early modern courtroom. The judges, clerks and prosecutors were all professional men, and juries, both grand and petty, were always selected from propertied male householders. Therefore, women appeared in an alien and, to some extent, hostile environment, in which men commanded proceedings and judged the credibility of their words. However, in homicide cases, legal officials eagerly listened to women who account for one-third of deponents.[7] These women played a central role in justice and were clearly unafraid to speak in the otherwise masculine courtroom. They gave evidence even when their words were quite unremarkable, and when a man could have told the same tale.[8] Although some historians have argued that female voices were less credible in court, in homicide cases at least, women were heard and, subject to their general reputations (or 'local name'), believed.[9] This was a valuable opportunity for some women to achieve momentary power and influence the judicial proceedings.

An excellent example of this desire to speak out in court comes from Susanna Fisher's evidence from Yorkshire in June 1653. Susanna testified about a murder case. However, this was not all she was saying with her words: she was also publicly presenting her own selfless pursuit of justice. Susanna told the court that she had overheard William Staveley and Mary Armstronge talking in a field about the murder of Robert Lauchester, for which Mary was the prime suspect.[10] In the first part of her evidence Susanna clearly described Mary as terrified by the prospect of arrest and of speaking before the court. William reportedly responded to her outburst by saying 'if thou be abashed to speak before authority, we are all utterly undone, and [he] bound it with a great oath'. He was angry and worried by her terror, all of which Susanna reported as it was suggestive of his own involvement in the crime. This was the sum of her evidence about the homicide. But it was not the only thing she told the court: she was determined to make the most of her role as a witness and so told a dramatic tale about her own bravery and quest for justice.

After giving her eye witness account, Susanna went on to tell an extraordinary story of the consequences of making this report. She claimed that shortly after she had overheard the conspirators, Mary Armstronge and Richard Walker came to her house. Richard reportedly asked:

> what was the discourse that you heard betwixt Mr Staveley, and Mary, she answered, he had no authority to examine her ... [and] when she came before a better man than Mr Staveley, she would tell it [Mary also asked her, but Susanna] would not disclose it, till she came before a justice, then replied Mary Armstronge I hope you will do me no harm, she answered, she would do her no harm, if that she did hear would do her no harm.

Susanna's determination to speak out in this case put her in jeopardy. After her doorstep defence of the sanctity of justice, she was threatened by Richard and Mary, and it was these threats that partly inspired her description of events.

Immediately after his plea for information had been refused, Richard Walker threatened Susanna, saying that 'If she ... went in against Mr Staveley he would plague her to her end, as no woman was plagued, then she answered, she did not fear what Mr Staveley could do to her, for speaking the truth'. Later that day Staveley arrived 'with a fowling piece' and the situation seemed to have spiralled out of control. Despite her earlier bravery, Susanna began to understand the danger she was in. As she rather anticlimactically exclaimed, she 'fear he [William Staveley] intend to do her some mischief'.[11] However, she was as clever as she was determined to testify. Instead of backing down, she recorded the threat in a deposition. By speaking out she ensured the court knew of the grudge held against her in case of her death, thereby attempting to protect herself from retribution. At the same time, Susanna was also demonstrating her own fearlessness and essential probity. Her character and name were as much on display as what she had overheard; she described the process behind her evidence as a form of insurance and to make herself look good.

Susanna's evidence provides a perfect example of how revealing a witness's evidence could be. Her testimony was circumstantial and would probably be regarded as inadmissible today, although such evidence was commonplace in the seventeenth century. Susanna was an eager witness, who clearly wanted the court to know that she took justice seriously, despite personal risk. Her bravery was apparent, as was her trust in the power of the court to protect her. Her professed integrity was impressive. However, the very nature of her credibility is itself uncertain and, from these sources, unknowable. It is unclear how she came to overhear the couple while they were in a lonely spot, presumably chosen for its privacy. She may have had a difficult relationship with Staveley in the past and was using her new knowledge and her obvious ability to tell stories to deliberately injure him. On the other hand, she may have suspected the pair for some time and had overheard them as part of a larger investigation. Susanna's bravery in taking such volatile evidence to court, therefore, can not be seen as purely altruistic. She may just as easily have been pursuing a grudge as abstract justice.

Nevertheless, even the most enthusiastic and proactive witness was forced into a passive role in the courtroom. Although undoubtedly crucial to the judicial process, with their voices significantly affecting the progress of a trial and, in wider terms, the general orderliness of their society, as today, a witness was questioned rather than allowed to make an uninterrupted statement. The prosecutor, judge, jury and defendants could all question the witness on any topic and, in most cases, in any order. There were few rules of precedence or hierarchies for questioning. Thus the courtroom could become a rowdy place with questions on myriad issues fired at the witness incoherently. Such testimony could be difficult to follow, especially if there were several aspects to an individual's evidence or if their words concerned a technical or otherwise complex issue. Although everyone would be familiar with this type of fragmented evidence and would certainly expect it, such disorderly testimonies could be confusing. In most cases, when the killer was witnessed in the act or when the evidence was uncomplicated, such interruptions would have made little difference to the outcome. However, in difficult cases of hidden or carefully plotted crime, or in cases involving technical or medical evidence, such theatrical trials must have affected the jury's understanding of the case and their subsequent deliberations.

Witnesses were relative newcomers to the legal process. Juries had been used since the thirteenth century, when they consisted of local men who had witnessed the crime or intimately knew those involved: as such, there was little need for independent witnesses to assist their decisions. However, as time passed, they had less and less personal knowledge of the crimes they tried and so relied more and more on witnesses.[12] The evidence witnesses provided included details of a crime and insight into local views on the credibility and reputation of the accused and victim. This allowed a jury to make complex judgements about the reliability of a protagonist, based on the everyday social assessments of the community. Their evidence was crucial and illuminating and was not determined by the state or the judge. Deponents frequently disagreed about the nature of a crime, and the culpability of a defendant, with testimony appearing to be an argument between people with different perspectives and types of information.

A desire for credible justice was only one motivation for giving evidence. Witnesses gave evidence for complex and subtle reasons, such as a desire for justice, fear, resentment and self-aggrandisement. After all, testifying in open court offered cachet and power. The courtroom was a theatrical space in which large crowds gathered to hear dramatic evidence, and to witness the execution of justice. Cross-examinations had the thrill of potential scandal, and witnesses with shady elements in their past must have been aware of the potential danger of testifying and the risk of having secrets revealed. At the same time, these actors were influential. Their words could shape the lives and destinies of their fellows. Witnessing could set them apart, give them a moment of fame and glory and allow them to influence verdicts that they may have cared deeply about. Equally, however, witnesses could act from malice, and accuse a pre-existing enemy. They could be bribed to speak or to be silent, or they could lie simply to help a friend.

The cross-examination of a defence witness, in the case against Henry Harrison for the murder of Dr Clenche, shows how hazardous a court appearance could be. Dr Clenche was killed by strangulation in a coach in London in 1691, after Henry Harrison had lured him into the vehicle. Two witnesses saw Harrison leaving the coach before the body was found, and further testimony conclusively linked the murder weapon – a handkerchief – to Harrison.

In his defence, Harrison produced several alibi witnesses. Defence witnesses were not examined under oath, but were subject to cross-examination. Mr Baker gave key evidence in Harrison's defence. He claimed that he had seen Harrison at a drinking establishment on the night of the crime. However, the prosecutor, Mr Darnell, presented evidence that undermined Baker's alibi. Darnell claimed legal records showed Baker had been convicted for cheating the parish of St Giles. Although Baker claimed he had in fact been acquitted, another witness confirmed the conviction, and the mark it had left on Baker's reputation. The prosecution further eroded Harrison's alibi, by calling witnesses to comment on the reputation of the house he claimed he was in at the time of the murder. A Mrs Whetstead gave the following testimony:

> My Lord, I dwell in Crown-Court in Chancery Lane, over against Mr Maccaffee's House; and he and she are very ill People's; and keep a very evil and Scandalous

House, and such as are reputed to be House-breakers, Pick-Pockets, and Lewd-Women, do use and frequent the House; and there is commonly at late hours in the Night, Persons calling out Murder, and Whore and Rogue, and such sort of Language, disturbing their Neighbours ... and the Neighbours do account it a House of an ill Fame, and do avoid going thither.[13]

The implication was clear: if Harrison was in a house of 'ill fame' then his own reputation was damaged. His witnesses were not to be trusted and his alibi lacked credibility. Harrison was found guilty.

Ultimately, we do not know what motivated individual witnesses. Occasionally a case summary revealed a suspect motive, but most motivation remains inaccessible. However, witnesses often did reveal what (they claimed) had initially led them to intervene in the crime. Their reasons ranged from 'disliking them [the defendants] by reason of their whispering', to a paranoid suspicion due to the Catholicism of a suspect.[14] When witnesses made such statements they were not doing so to illustrate how the judicial system worked. By stressing the sudden or accidental nature of their involvement in the crime, they were publicly affirming their innocence of any complicity with the killers. Explanations of why and how a witness had seen a crime were crucial pieces of testimony which could be questioned by a suspicious court or doubtful community. Crimes that occurred late at night or in doubtful settings were especially subject to query. Witnesses were determined to show their investigation had not been malicious and that their interest was justified.

Witnesses usually explained their involvement by stating that they had seen the crime while going about their lawful business. In London in March 1677 Joanna Dionys began her testimony by stating that she had been working industriously at warming her mistress's bed when she heard swords clattering 'which occasioned her to look out of the window'.[15] Although she was testifying about street violence, she carefully distanced herself from it. This was because, to be believed in court, a witness needed to be above reproach. In some ways this affected how their testimony was presented. Most evidence was given in a passive and non-judgmental manner. Witnesses seldom made direct accusations of culpability; an assertion that they 'verily believed' the accused to be guilty was often the most they would commit to. In fact, many deliberately underlay their evidence with uncertainty. They did not want to explicitly accuse, partly as they may have accepted that it was the court's role to judge. They may also have been cautious as they feared the backlash if the defendant was acquitted. Deponents were usually both highly conscious of the legal hierarchy in which they operated, and were constrained by it.

Other witnesses were simply reluctant to speak and said little about what they may have seen. Witnesses were challenged according to their probity, their malice towards the defendant and their social status, with their role fraught and potentially dangerous. Depositions were occasionally so short that it is difficult to say with any certainty that the witness had in fact seen anything. Some witnesses may have been too frightened to speak, while others seriously limited their evidence for financial gain or to protect friends and neighbours. Whatever the reasoning, by their reticence, these witnesses alienated themselves from the crime and its consequences for their neighbours. They chose their own needs over those of wider society and, although their individual choices seem explicable, the broader distinction between them and more proactive witnesses is unclear. It may have been that they felt sidelined in their communities or even disenfranchised due to a lowly status or tarnished reputation. Certainly the division does not seem to generally relate to gender or status, but rather to an individual's personal priorities. By not giving evidence these locals showed a profound disassociation from justice.

On occasion, the motive for silence may have been more tangible. Although successful bribes would be concealed, cases in which bribery was attempted can be found. In these cases, witnesses were paid off to prevent them accusing someone publicly. In London in 1697 several witnesses gave explicit evidence about George Gadsby's public murder of his wife. Further witnesses corroborated this testimony and then gave extraordinary evidence about attempts by the defendant's mother and an unnamed man to bribe them into 'forgetting' what they had seen. Henry Cobb described the attempted bribery to the court. He said a man approached him 'and told me that I was not obliged to own [stand by] what I said before Sir Robert Jeffrey when I came to the Old Bailey'. Robert Randle further described the strange man as offering 2d., 6d., 8d. and finally £100 to ensure his silence in court. At first glance, £100 sounds an excessive amount, and this may simply be an exaggeration on the witness's part. It would certainly have been a lot of money to the ordinary working people it was offered to.

Randle claimed that Gadsby's mother accompanied this man 'to Endeavour to stifle and take off the Evidence against her son'.[16] This desperate act was doomed to failure. Witnesses could not deny in court what they had admitted in a deposition. The recognizance they had sworn to ensured that witnesses could not easily change their evidence. A recognizance was a method of legally obliging witnesses to attend court and provide testimony on pain of a financial penalty. The sum was frequently large and guaranteed by up to two family members or acquaintances. Failure to attend or to provide evidence previously attested to could lead to financial ruin for the witness and up to two others. This may explain the large bribe offered in this case – as an attempt at recompense for financial losses to come. However, the loss of face and standing in the community that would be suffered if evidence was proved false could not be so easily recompensed.

To a degree, the exchange of money to compensate for injuries was a commonplace activity. The payment provided necessary subsistence for the family of the injured party, especially if it was believed that they would never fully recover. Murder should have been exempt from this popular form of negotiated justice, and money exchanged purely for accidents, temporary wounds or to prevent prosecution in a number of minor crimes. However, the practice of financial compensation was not unknown in homicide cases. In 1646, a Yorkshire court asked William Binks why he had not made a complaint until a year after his son's death. He replied 'they were in hope Wilson [the defendant] would have given the wife something but he refused to give anything'.[17]

Such private agreements were usually well hidden: the exchange of money for an absence of prosecution depended on silence, after all. Such an exchange was also considered shameful and illegal. In Yorkshire in 1653 Thomas Taylor sent a representative to the Michael Badkin's household after his death, 'to know of this Examinant [Michael's relation, Marke Badkin] whether he had any thing against him concerning his father's death'. By pointing out that Michael was commonly thought to have been diseased, Taylor's representative attempted to shift the blame for his death away from Taylor. However, an agreement was finally reached between the parties, involving a sum of money being transferred to the widow. No one openly admitted what that money had been for, with Marke saying 'Thomas Taylor offer[ed] his mother forty shillings by way of gift to relief her because she was poor and had been sick long, but not in reference to his fathers death to keep them from prosecuting against him'.[18] Such negotiations had to be undertaken with care. Accepting money and covering up a capital crime implicated all parties in the killing. In extreme cases, such collusion could leave family members liable as accessories to the murder and therefore subject to the same penalty as the murderer: death by hanging.

As we have seen, not all witnesses were reluctant to give evidence. As with Susanna Fisher, some were proud of their involvement in uncovering crime. Only a small proportion of witnesses can be described as 'detectives', however. Even Susanna made no claims to have actively investigated the crime she spoke about. Most testimony centred solely on what the witness knew or had learnt. In any case, it was the outcome rather than the process of investigation that mattered; the facts of the case rather than the trail followed in collecting evidence. Most ordinary witnesses did not extensively discuss the process they had undergone to collect evidence, usually because they were relating something they had seen by chance.

John Scape, though, clearly acted as an amateur detective and was in fact quite proud of his investigative skills. He keenly related how he had captured his father and his father's new 'wife', and how he had pieced together evidence and collected testimony. Although his initial discovery of his father had been fortuitous, the rest of his actions were deliberate and purposeful. He discovered that his father had moved to Durham from Newcastle upon Tyne and had changed his name to William Calverley, and that he was 'cohabiting' with a Margarett Greene as 'man and wife'. He questioned the neighbours and they told him where the pair lived and that they had 'so done for eight or nine years'.

Both William and Jane Scape were probably quite elderly at the time of Jane's death. John deposed that he had been married to Jane for twenty-seven years, but that he had been divorced from her for an additional eighteen or nineteen years. His time references may not be accurate, and as no ages were recorded we cannot know for sure. However, if, as with most first marriages, William and Jane had married in their mid-twenties, both William and Jane would have been in their seventies. Even if William's dates were inaccurate, the couple were likely to be over fifty years old, which was still quite elderly in 1657. Whatever his age, William was not described as frail, and he certainly had no trouble travelling. In any case, his crime would (and could) not be ignored.

As Jane had been dead for only three years, the marital status of Margarett and William was of especial interest to the court. William was questioned about his first marriage and how he came to be married again before his wife's death. Divorce was not permissible in this period. The only legal remedy to an unhappy marriage was a form of legal separation, which did not allow either party to remarry. William claimed he was 'divorced' by preacher Dr Hennryson, but the preacher would not have had legal authority to do so, a fact he and William may have been unaware of. William testified that he had married Jane twice, once in London and once in Newcastle. Despite the inviolable legality of the first marriage, William and Jane had 'married' each other again, possibly following their relocation. They may have acted so to ensure their respectability in the new parish. The local community would want to be convinced of the legitimacy of a marriage, and such legitimacy would also affect the inheritance rights of any subsequent children. A public display of legitimate marriage was something all parties understood and respected.

William may have felt that by asserting his divorce, in the same way that he had asserted his marriage, he could publicly end what he had publicly begun. Ritual wife sales have been recorded in this period, in which a new lover 'purchased' that wife from her husband, and the 'payment' was used to buy drinks for all to seal the deal.[19] Whether William believed in the legitimacy of this act, as others clearly did, is unknown. However, after his divorce, he went through a marriage ceremony with Margarett, in front of a number of witnesses, and lived with her openly for nine years as man and wife thereafter.

Margarett could (and did) name the minister and the witnesses to her nuptials; after all, her marriage was her badge of honour, proof of her legitimate married status and so central to her identity. She did not mention whether she knew of her husband's previous marriage or the continued existence of William's first wife. Indeed, she may have been quite unaware of the illegitimate nature of her marriage. All of those involved may have believed in the legality of the new marriage arrangements. However, as William had changed his name and moved some distance from his earlier home, it is more likely that he was aware of the fragile legal status of his second marriage (although perhaps not of its absolute illegality). None of the witnesses discussed possible motives for Margarett's purported murder of Jane. Nevertheless, we can speculate that the illegitimate marriage and continued existence of the first wife may have incited William and Margarett to plan and execute a secret homicide.

John was far more interested in proving culpability than in considering his father's motivations. On learning of the marriage he travelled to Newcastle to speak to Jane Clerke, his mother's former landlady. John was told that Jane 'would speak something materially to the death of his said mother'. William had apparently learnt that his son had uncovered his new identity and life. On John's arrival, he was told that 'his father had been lately with her, and spoke something to her condoning it'. Unfortunately, Jane did not reveal how William had justified his crime, and as William formally denied any involvement, we can only guess why he and Margarett may have committed the crime. Nevertheless, John believed he had made a crucial connection and wanted to confirm evidence he had probably heard at the time of her death. When the crime occurred, no trail could be found leading to the Margarett his mother had identified and no connection could be made between her and William Scape. John believed that the Margarett his father lived with was the same one who poisoned his mother and had worked for her years before. When he had discovered his father's new life he clearly believed that he had stumbled on the vital clue that would allow him to pursue this case.

From this point, John's case grew more difficult. Now, rather than being a physical pursuit of a culprit, his case pivoted on establishing and proving identity. John Scape was concerned with both finding out his father's new identity and establishing the past identity of his new wife Margarett. After Jane's death, William had disappeared from sight, clearly distancing himself from his former wife. When John linked his father with the woman he believed committed the crime, he was convinced of his father's guilt. However, the firm identities of the pair had still to be established. William clearly denied a connection between Margarett Galene (the ex-servant who killed Jane) and his wife Margarett Greene. He said 'That he knoweth not that ever she was servant to her [Jane], or that he ever saw her [in] his former wife's life time to his knowledge'. Margarett too denied having worked for William's former wife or having ever met her, saying 'and if ever it can be proved that she was ever in her company, she will be willing to suffer for it'.

From their perspective a denial was crucial. If the link could be made then the jury would undoubtedly convict. Margarett Galene could be placed at the scene and had handed the (probably) poisoned cup to Jane Scape. Although circumstantial, this would have been enough to allow most juries to convict of murder. Likewise, William would be at risk due to his unlawful marriage and potential culpability. Both had to cast doubt on the link between the Margarett's identities. By the same measure, John Scape was eager to establish the connection and would have attempted to persuade the jury of its plausibility. Margarett seemed certain of the court's inability to firmly prove that her identity and that of Margarett Galene were the same.

Margarett's optimism was by no means misplaced. The jury would only be able to decide according to probability; there was none of the certainty of fingerprints or DNA. People were frequently mobile and so could not be expected to live in any one place continuously. In any case Margarett had been a servant many years before, and in terms of her lifecycle could be expected to have married and changed her name, residence and occupation many times. None of Jane's acquaintances on her death had remembered Margarett, and no one could even name her with confidence. The decision would rest on her credibility under cross-examination and on the jury's impression of her and William's guilt.

No verdict was recorded in this case, and so we cannot know whom the jury ultimately believed. However, in many ways, it is the process of the trial that is the most interesting and revealing aspect of this case. The killer(s) had to be publicly pursued and prosecuted if all were to be satisfied that justice had been done. In order to be effective, justice had to apply equally to all, with all suspicious cases thoroughly legally pursued and all credible suspects tried openly. Any subsequent trial may well have irrevocably damaged all parties involved. If the accused were found innocent, John Scape's pursuit of his father would seem bitter and inexplicable. Even if innocent, William and Margarett Scape would be marked by the questions over their own marriage and William would possibly be liable for prosecution for bigamy. Certainly their standing would be tarnished. If guilty, the pair faced death, and John would have found his reputation in jeopardy as his father was marked as a notorious felon. The only real winner would have been the noble concept of truth and justice: public order would have been served – and Jane Scape's murder would have been avenged. Despite the personal tragedies, this alone was the concern of the court.

2

Supernatural Sleuths

Witches, ghosts, demons and spirits were all part of people's mental worlds in the early modern period. Not everyone believed in all these beings, but even those who did not would recognize a description of a supernatural being and would be able to interpret its meaning. We need to accept the cultural context of pervasive supernatural and magical belief when we consider the early modern period.

England was as profoundly religious as the rest of Europe, with ordinary people relying partly on God to explain epidemics, bad weather, strange diseases and sudden death. The Reformation stirred up religious conflict and led many people to challenge and reform their views on God and magic. For many, this process heightened their beliefs. New enemies were created. Catholics – papists – were widely feared in England and believed to be plotting the overthrow of the nation and return of popish 'tyranny'. In this period, Protestants identified the Pope with the devil and priests were frequently perceived as wicked and dangerous. Other agents of the devil were also commonly feared. Witches were actively prosecuted in the sixteenth and (albeit far less frequently) the seventeenth centuries. Their powers (and other magic) were still considered to be very real. Things we consider to be intangible and incredible were part of the mental world of the majority of the population.

Although never a dominant form of criminal evidence, ghosts, witches and God all feature in testimony. For instance, when Marie Hobson accused Jaine Kinley of causing her son's death by magic in Yorkshire in 1649, her only evidence was an instinctive dislike of Jaine and some strange words she had heard her utter. Even so, Marie's evidence was persuasive. It was cleverly presented and made up for its essential lack of tangible evidence with highly suggestive implications. Marie said that one night Jaine had laid hands on a pig before a crowded room and stated the pig would go mad. The pig consequently did so, and then died. Having made Jaine's unusual abilities manifest, Marie went on to describe the killing of her son. She contended:

that Jaine Kinley ... about a year and a half since did follow him the said Abraham

Hobson, with an apple and a piece of bread and would not part with him, till she forced him to bite both the apple and the breads as he told her.

After he had bitten Jaine's offerings, he brought up blood. He died over a year later.

According to Marie, Jaine had killed her son using only supernatural powers and malicious intent. Marie's words were the only evidence presented in this case. She could not prove guilt, but could use her testimony to implicate Jaine in this intangible and magical crime. Even apparently innocuous actions were given sinister meanings by Marie. For example, she contended that, after the initial assault, Jaine was asked to visit and touch Abraham. Along with scratching or otherwise injuring the witch responsible for the curse, the touch of the magical assailant was something commonly believed to assist a victim's healing.[1] Jaine refused to visit or to touch Abraham, and her refusal was presented as additional evidence of her guilt. Marie's narrative was especially skillfully constructed. Indeed, it seemed to rely on associative literary connections for its impact. The use of the apple and the bread as the means for Abraham's ultimate demise linked this deposition to stories of Eve and the Fall and to transubstantiation. The apple also echoed popular fairy tales in the method utilised to convey an evil intent. Her words used deep symbolic resonances in place of 'factual' evidence.

Only the depositions of Marie and her son Abraham have survived in this case. Abraham gave evidence just before his death. After a long illness, he had become convinced he would soon die and wanted to be sure to implicate Jaine. He described the events preceding his death as dramatically as Marie had done. However, his reconstruction of the crime was quite different. In fact, Abraham's story used sexual references to display the unnatural nature of Jaine's impact on his body. In his tale, the injury was magically inflicted but its impact differed. He claimed Jaine used her special (feminine) magical skills to attack his masculinity. He said that she had sat next to him at a Christmas feast, spoken of love and touched his knee. The next day this knee became very swollen, and he claimed it proved impossible to cure. The harm, he then contended, spread to other 'parts of his body', with the implication being his sexual potency had been affected and his masculinity harmed.[2] Her magic struck first at his virility and then at his life.

Both stories were powerful, and it is unfortunate that Jaine's deposition has not survived. As it is we cannot compare her tale to her accusers' or look for alternate explanations for the crime. Both witnesses probably believed that the magical process they were describing could occur and that it was the probable cause of Abraham's sickness and death. Their evidence powerfully encapsulated these beliefs and effectively depicted Jaine as a real threat. Although they could provide no tangible proof, their suggestion of unnatural practices was comprehensive and resonant. Moreover, their words assisted in almost dehumanising Jaine. She became a witch in their stories, and thus her crime required different and less rigorous kinds of proof. Cases involving magical assaults were never expected to leave the same kinds of tangible evidence as other crimes. In these cases, suspicion, a local name for wickedness or scolding and a reputation for magical ability were usually all that were needed. As this case was prosecuted as a homicide rather than under the witchcraft statute, the jury should have required clear evidence of guilt. However, a pervasive general suspicion of criminality was enough to initiate a trial, and although not tangible proof, this suggestive testimony was certainly an effective means of portraying someone believed to have been a deliberate murderer.

Abraham Hobson and his mother could not explain his year-long debilitating illness and subsequent death. They were shocked and frightened by his deadly ailment and sought explanations in the supernatural. Such beliefs were not unusual, although other witnesses may have been less willing to believe that magic had caused his death. These witnesses may have blamed disease, or attributed the death to poison (perhaps placed on the apple Jaine had 'forced' Abraham to eat). Despite widespread belief in God and magic, the probability was that they would have relied on rational rather than magical interpretations for her death.

In fact, although God remained a general explanation for good fortune and religious belief continued to predominate, by the end of the seventeenth century ordinary people generally preferred rational and logical explanations for death to divine and magical ones. A small proportion did continue to rely on magic, the supernatural and divine intervention to explain the process of a killing or the capture of an elusive felon, but such beliefs were being replaced by a desire to medically and tangibly explain death and by an acknowledgement of human agency in the capture of criminals.

This shift from the supernatural was depicted differently in court records and in printed tales. In court, a demand by jurors, judges and communities for tangible evidence emphasised the role the witness and the detective played in solving crime. Indeed, by the end of the seventeenth century, the courts were often reluctant to give credibility to witnesses telling supernatural stories. Courts wanted tangible proof of a crime – evidence of poison, of injury and a physical link to an accused. They seldom credited inference, and stories of witches, demons and God that had seemed reliable in the sixteenth century were increasingly doubted by the eighteenth. The witness who presented tangible, credible and directly witnessed testimony was favoured. In print, this shift was less clearly defined, however. Although by the seventeenth century God and the supernatural were less frequently discussed, human agency never became a prime concern of pamphleteers. Unlike modern stories in which the detective is central, in these tales the writer was concerned only with establishing guilt, telling of the wickedness of the crime and condemning the killer. The witness, the detective and investigative amateurs were little discussed in commercial tales.

Nevertheless, in many ways, the divine was never satisfactorily removed from homicide tales as wickedness remained central to all stories of crime. God and the supernatural may have been losing their place as specific explanations, but they maintained their role as the overarching contexts in which crime and justice existed. Indeed, references to God and the devil remained part of the formal structure of the courtroom. Witnesses and jurors were sworn in on oaths that relied on their belief in the dominant conceptions of God and definitions of the sin of perjury. In addition, religious language pervaded the formal process of law and, in particular, the language of the courts. Malice was defined as an absence of fear of God and, in the formal documents of the coroner and assizes, as the 'instigation' of the devil. This did not remove culpability from the accused. Rather, their shunning of God and goodness acted to compound their sin and their crime.

Under the law, all the worst crimes were felonies, and all felonies were defined as being done with *mens rea*, or an evil mind. This verdict could be mitigated in court (for example in manslaughter cases), but it was the basic assumption of English criminal law. Likewise, God and sin were omnipresent in printed texts, albeit usually in the introductions and post-scripts. Sixteenth century pamphlets had repeatedly made reference to supernatural and divine assistance. These kinds of story were still apparent in the seventeenth century, existing in concert with newer ideas on empirical evidence and assertive witnesses.[3] A tale of murder was prefaced by an exhortation to end wickedness or a biblical quote. These references framed the tale but they did not determine how the story was told. A murderer chose to kill and chose to defy God, and printed texts continually asserted that the action had been of their own free will.

God can be found in nearly all stories of crime, but his presence had meanings in addition to the personal beliefs of individual witnesses. Judicious use of God in a story could absolve a witness from explaining how they had acquired their evidence and why they had investigated a crime. Stories of divine providence could even be used instead of tangible facts. By invoking providence, storytellers and witnesses could gloss over contradictory or implausible evidence and bury their role as accusers behind ghostly voices or fortuitous events.[4] In these cases, providence provided a cover for nervous witnesses and implicitly validated their evidence. The invocation of divine sanction allowed a witness to act as mere conduits of godly judgement. The divine was seen as ordering the cosmos and imposing justice. Such beliefs had a special link to homicide: popular belief dictated that 'murder would out', that is, that providential evidence would appear if man failed to avenge the crime. Many believed that if human endeavour proved insufficient, then God would ensure a felon was captured, either by throwing obstacles in the way of their flight (like terrible thunderstorms) or by intervening more directly.[5]

A murder and horrific assault from 1602 illustrates this enduring interest with providence, and its use as a means for explaining the extraordinary. According to printed accounts, a young girl called Elizabeth James and her brother Anthony witnessed ten unknown robbers break into their home and kill their parents. The children were then kidnapped and taken from their home in Essex to the house of Annis Dell in Hatfield. Although Annis had not been involved in the original crime, she apparently accepted money for 'dealing' with the children. Annis's son George killed Anthony and dumped his body in a pond. Elizabeth was spared death, but Annis acted quite viciously towards her and cut out her tongue (to prevent her speaking) and abandoned her in a wood (presumably to die).

In this story, providence immediately intervenes, if in a low key and implicit manner. Elizabeth survives due to the fortuitous kindness of strangers. Although severely injured she was helped out of the forest (by an unknown stranger), given free medical assistance (by a kindly surgeon) and fed by a plethora of people over the next four years. At this point, Elizabeth (again fortuitously) arrived outside the house of Annis Dell. She immediately recognised her assailant and used charades to indicate her relationship to the murdered boy and the identity of the killers. In this, she showed extensive resourcefulness. However, on its own, this evidence was not enough. The court needed her to verbalise her accusation – to tell the court what happened and persuade them of her reliability and truthfulness.

This was when God was perceived to intervene more directly and more miraculously. Although his presence had been implied in all the preceding fortuitous events, from this point he directly intervened in the apprehension and prosecution of the killers. One day, while playing with a friend, Elizabeth began to speak. Her tongue had not grown back, and she should have been unable to say anything, so her new ability to speak was interpreted (by this early modern audience) as having been facilitated by God. This Godly intervention allowed the killers to be tried and condemned. Annis and George had long been suspected but no one had been able to prove their guilt (in this or in any other matter). Elizabeth's testimony was therefore decisive. Her (miraculous) words had led to their conviction.

Although Elizabeth was a crucial witness, she always presented herself as an agent of God. A sceptical aid to the judge did try to test Elizabeth. He dressed as a devil and jumped out on her when she was alone. Instead of showing fear, she calmly told the terrifying demon that, 'I speak nothing but the truth, and what the thing within me instructeth me to speak'. The 'thing' was undoubtedly God. Elizabeth's persona as young, innocent and seemingly good made her the perfect agent of God. At the same time, Annis Dell was the epitome of dangerous femininity in that she was old, disliked and sexually corrupted. God had obviously made a choice between these two women. They were presented as diametric opposites, one an image of acceptable and desirable femininity and the other of the wickedness of a woman who was unrestrained. Elizabeth's goodness and potent godliness could not have been more underlined in this account. By the end of the tale, good had triumphed, despite none of the original killers having been caught, and the goodness of innocent femininity had succeeded over the wickedness of an old evil woman. Annis and George were duly condemned and executed in 1606.

Such references to the supernatural need to be read in a complex and sympathetic manner. The presence of otherworldly images cannot be reduced to literal interpretations in which witnesses are seen as uneducated and easily led. In fact, witnesses seldom viewed crime and legal retribution solely in divine terms, especially after 1640. Whenever the supernatural is referred to, it should be viewed with subtlety, as reflecting both belief and a passive means of presenting testimony. Images of God and the supernatural should be partly read as metaphors, with ordinary people using easily recognisable and colloquial images to express their convictions. Historian Alexandra Walsham described providence as 'part of the mental furniture of the early modern mind, an explanatory tool which contemporaries could employ at will'.[6] It was a belief that happily co-existed with other, contradictory views, and was used eclectically. Natalie Zemon Davis has argued that 'the artifice of fiction did not necessarily lend falsity to an account; it might well bring verisimilitude or a moral truth. Nor did the shaping or embellishing of a history necessarily mean forgery'.[7] It seems likely that supernatural references were made because such images corresponded to popular ideas about the world. They were not deliberately untrue, but acted as a reflection of the personality, confidence and belief of the witness.

When divine assistance was noted, it was in a context largely devoid of anything other than formulaic religious references. God and the devil seldom provided the entire explanatory framework in court. References to the providential that can be found were both commonplace and conventional. Witnesses were comfortable with these forms of expression, emphasising the evidence itself rather than its purported source. Audiences were aware that when a knife turned up at a murder site with the name of the killer etched on it, they were hearing a tale in which God had directly intervened to assist the judicial process as well as a legal fiction in which positive proof of guilt was being supplied. In this way, the divine did not replace the secular, but augmented it. Nevertheless, such evidence could easily act to efface agency, as on occasion the supernatural provided shape to a tale and was used instead of more complex tales of human deduction and action.

At times, supernatural solutions to crime provided more exciting stories than those of human ingenuity and hard work. The drama provided an incredible (albeit familiar) story for public consumption. Tales of ghostly assistance in the finding of corpses were particularly popular. In 1662 in Yorkshire, Isabel Binnington was described in print as discovering (with ghostly help) the body of Londoner Robert Eliot. The pamphlet described Isabel as first seeing the spirit at night. Initially, she claimed not to realise she was seeing a ghost. This was unsurprising as the figure was remarkably corporeal. Isabel said it had 'long flaxen hair in green clothes, and bare-footed, and without a hat, She conceived that it was some wandering person that might have come for lodging'.[8] However, she quickly determined she was seeing a spirit, and began to fear it, claiming that she grew frightened when it later approached her. Instead of acting herself, she communicated the matter to the JP, passively asking for his advice. Isabel did not describe herself as speaking to a priest or as seeking religious advice, despite the supernatural nature of her problem. Both she and the JP took a practical approach and used the spirit as a source of information. The JP instructed her to go home and question the spirit, asking its name and that of its killers. Isabel then presented the ghost's responses in her deposition, as clear evidence of the crime and of the guilt of the killer.

However, the supernatural was not enough to secure a conviction, even in this highly dramatised printed account. The tangible still had a role to play, and in particular a body was required. The body was the ultimate proof that a crime had occurred and without it the case would probably have been considered to be a fantasy constructed by Isabel. Although people were willing to hear evidence originating from a ghost, they always wanted other proof of the crime and of the culpability of the killer. But, in this case, the spirit was even given credit for locating the body, making it the entire source of information and of truth in this murder. When Isabel claimed she saw some mould on the floor, she made no claims of intuitive leaps or resourcefulness on her own part; rather, she meekly followed where the ghost led, dug a hole and found the dead man's bones. This meant that Isabel was (apparently voluntarily) robbed of her agency in solving this crime, with the story focused on the unnatural sleuth, who was the only source of knowledge. This did not mean that she had not uncovered the crime, just that she was unwilling to admit to it.

For some, belief in the supernatural was quite pervasive. Indeed, as with Marie Hobson, belief in the supernatural could lead witnesses to construct convincing and creative evidence. In a culture in which magic played an everyday role as part of legitimate religion as well as of healing, it was perfectly plausible to some that certain individuals could use magic to kill. Even so, most cases of English witchcraft referred to minor harm, or *maleficium*, rather than murder. English witchcraft prosecutions were never as numerous or as dramatic as continental or Scottish cases were. By the later seventeenth century, prosecutions were waning and philosophers and judges alike frequently expressed scepticism. There were cases of supernatural harm or death in the mid-seventeenth century, but such accusations were losing credibility by the end of the century, with judges acquitting or refusing to proceed. The belief in witches may have persisted but judicial acceptance of this belief was diminishing. Hence, prosecutions declined both in incidence and in ideological potency:[9] the role of magic declined in the everyday lives of judges and some ordinary people, so magical forms of killing disappeared from the courts. To achieve conviction, a crime had to appear plausible, and as belief in witches declined, this method of murder became untenable in court.

Conversely, and as with the Jaine Kinley case, some sudden deaths seemed inexplicable, and, at these times of strain, supernatural methods of killing sometimes appeared credible. Belief in such possibilities depended not on tangible evidence, but on individual ways of seeing the events. The witch was a compound of all 'antisocial, treasonous and diabolical threats', and so a natural suspect when the apparently inexplicable occurred.[10] In Yorkshire in 1646 four women were accused of causing the death of infant William Cockcroft. The father of one of the young victims, Jonas Attley, interrogated the women using violence to elicit a confession. He said he 'did give the said Mary [Midgely] some strokes whereupon she did confess herself to be a witch and that Elizabeth Crosley Sarah her daughter and Mary Kitchinge were all witches'. However, in her deposition Mary claimed she confessed as her 'head [was] sore broken [and] did confess unto them what they required in hopes to be freed from further blows'.[11] Her claim of coercion seems convincing to modern ears, but it may also have convinced an early modern jury. Such a case should not be seen through the prism of the European 'witch-craze'. Despite accusations of demonic power, Mary's voice was still audible in court. The court accepted supernatural evidence, but did not automatically believe witchcraft had occurred. As in any other case, further evidence and testimony about her reputation would be required for a conviction.

Despite the intensity of witch beliefs, cases of murder were unusual. Although witches were tried and convicted into the eighteenth century, I have found none prosecuted for murder later than 1661, although other historians have found examples as late as 1682.[12] Belief in magic existed side by side with more rational beliefs, and as investigative methods developed so magical explanations decreased. By the end of the seventeenth century, magic had largely disappeared as a viable explanation for death. In its place came evidence about the body and expert testimony on the cause of death and identity of the killer. In the eighteenth century world of empirical, tangible justice, the supernatural villain was unwelcome. People still believed in magical powers, but the courts no longer pursued such accusations.

In any case, from the mid-seventeenth century, the supernatural existed as only one part of the complex legal narrative of a trial, in which thoughts, impressions, rumours and tangible facts were collectively presented as evidence. References to God, demons or ghosts often had discernible logical implications as well as reflecting contemporary popular belief. The devil was both real and metaphorical to most contemporaries. Despite his clear wickedness, when referred to in stories, the devil did not remove the killer's culpability.[13] His presence instead acted as shorthand for senseless wickedness, in which the killer acted in a strangely inexplicable manner. When Richard Foster threw his baby on to a fire and grievously injured his wife in Northumberland in 1664, he said he had done so because the child was 'a devil'.[14] Likewise, when Nicholas Grice killed his wife Elizabeth in 1676 in Leeds, one witness said he cried 'I am the devil, I will overcome thee if I can'. He told another witness that in killing his wife he had 'overcome the devils serpent'.[15] William Keath exhibited similar psychosis when he killed Margery Brambery with a knife in Yorkshire in 1658. William was found near the body, pulling off her shoes. Edward Humphrey deposed that he was too fearful to approach Keath but he did watch and listen. He said that Keath threw a stool down the hill from where the body lay and said 'devil gather up thine own' before leaving the scene singing.[16]

In all these cases, the killers were reported as mentioning the devil after they had acted in an inexplicable manner. In part, this was a reflection of popular belief. However, it was a use of language that also reflected contemporary forms of accusation with references to the devil used as a means for establishing the instability, if not the madness, of the perpetrator of the crime. When yeoman John Jarratt reported the words of John Benington after his killing of Barnitt Maltby, he made a salient comment on Benington's words. He deposed that he had found his servant beating Maltby 'and had beat his brains out of his head and his face all beat in pieces'. He asked his servant why he had acted in so vicious a manner and he replied that 'he took it [his victim] to be an evil spirit.' Jarratt, however, was suspicious of his claim and clearly told the court 'but this deponent did believe that he was not distracted then or at any time before'.[17] He wanted to refute the implication of madness such a reported phrase conveyed.

Many supernatural references can be read as symbolic presentations of suspicion related to the court as they framed intuitive leaps by witnesses. However, evocative stories did provide witnesses with an additional means of psychologically testing suspected killers. Such methods always existed in tandem with more rational approaches to crime solving. One infamous early modern belief was used to dramatic effect: cruentation, or the touching of a corpse by its supposed murderer, still occurred in this period, albeit infrequently. It was believed that if the true murderer touched the corpse of their victim, its wounds would start to bleed again, thus providing positive proof of their guilt.[18]

Despite its drama and colourful representation in testimony, only a few examples of this magical practice can be found in this period. Samuel Pearson was made to touch his wife's corpse in 1658 in Yorkshire, and John Horne, Edward Ranyne and John Wade all described what they saw. John Horne said that the coffin was opened and a woman bared Elizabeth's face, and 'He could not see any blood about her and Samuel Pearson was called to lay his hand upon her, and so soon as he had touched her he did see the blood bubble in her mouth and some run down at the left side ... of her mouth fresh'. Edward Ranyne concurred, but John Wade qualified his sighting by stating that although he had seen blood it had only been a drop. Such comments would probably have had quite a dramatic impact if repeated in court, but they were not enough on their own to convict.[19] On the other hand, a refusal to participate in the touching of a corpse may have been highly suggestive in itself. In Kingston upon Hull in 1669, Thomas Fysher, aware of the potential danger agreeing to touch a corpse could involve, sought to protect himself. William Ward said that Thomas told him he was innocent, but may be forced to touch the body 'and if he were forced to go to touch her body he would have other two or three persons to do the like besides himself'.[20]

In a similar way, a timely ghostly presence could allow insubstantial evidence to be confidently reported and could even force an abandoned case to be reconsidered. However, there is little evidence to suggest that apparitions alone influenced judgement. In 1660 in Westmoreland, Robert Hope told the court that:

> a vision appeared in the form of a man like Robert Parkin [the victim of a murder a year before] ... and when he ... charge the spirit; What was the reason it did so molest him, it replied I am murdered I am murdered I am murdered, his answer again, was it by any man, it replied no, and thereupon he desired it to go to its rest for when he came before the Justice he would divulge it to them.

Robert said the ghost showed him his wound and said a woman had killed him. His ghostly identification of a female culprit seems particularly incredible in this case, as seven deponents had, some months before, provided evidence that solely implicated John Lawson, a prominent local man (although it is unclear whether he was tried at this point or not). Robert may have been deluded, or this may have been a cunning attempt to direct suspicion away from John Lawson. Whatever his motivation, he did not initiate a new enquiry.[21] Indeed, it was striking that no one else mentioned supernatural assistance in their evidence. Whether or not Robert truly believed he had seen a ghost, for the other deponents tangible evidence was far more effective than ghostly hints.

There is no doubt that belief in the supernatural was pervasive in the early modern period. Ghosts, witches, fairies, demons and God define how people considered their world and how they explained any number of large and small scale problems, from crop failure to infertility, lost fortune and lost lives. However, despite these clear beliefs, the supernatural was never the only explanatory framework and by the seventeenth century it was losing power as a credible cause of human problems, notably sudden deaths.

God, wickedness, ghosts and witches were referred to well into the eighteenth century and certainly remained part of the belief system of certain people and part of everyday language. Some people believed such things to be wholly truthful, while others accepted these references as part of a more complex depiction of events, in which the supernatural had meanings outside the literal. Ghosts could hide a reluctant witness's agency, devils could indicate an inexplicably wicked act, witches could be killers whose methodology was otherwise unknown, and God could represent innocence and goodness facing up to clear wickedness. Magic and the supernatural need to be seen as part of a broader context and, on occasion, as shorthand for what was essentially human agency. Most people acknowledged that the majority of killers were corporeal and, although wicked and possibly inspired by the devil, acted at their own volition. For some, magic was a comfort and provided a language through which they could express their evidence and concerns. For the majority, more traditional eyewitnessed evidence or personal investigations made up almost all their testimony.

It should not be surprising that there are often several readings of one set of events, nor that sometimes these readings reflected supernatural beliefs and concerns. What we must never do, however, is allow these readings to be privileged over a rational viewpoint, especially as rational explanations greatly outnumbered the irrational. Supernatural beliefs need to be viewed in context and seen as complex interpretations with layers of meaning. Otherwise we will lose what is distinctive and revealing about these kinds of stories of crime – how they demonstrate popular beliefs and tactics to explain the inexplicable, and how they allow witnesses to efface their role in solving crimes.

3

Bodies

In Hertfordshire in 1699 Spencer Cowper was accused, along with three others, of murdering a Quaker woman, Sarah Stout, and disposing of her body in the river.[1] The subsequent trial became an epic battle for truth and justice and at the centre of the dispute, and the prime source of evidence, was the body of Sarah Stout. In this and other cases, the body dominated the entire proceedings, defining the nature of the crime and providing the key proof for conviction. Although it had always had a role in the courtroom, the body was increasingly becoming an important source of evidence as well as a symbol of the wickedness of the crime.

The coroner initially recorded a verdict of suicide in this case, and Sarah's neighbours apparently believed she had killed herself over an unhappy love affair. Gossip about her death was intense. In fact, a rumour that Sarah's death was precipitated by an illegitimate pregnancy quickly gained ground. The Quaker community were horrified at the slurs to their faith her purported suicide, illicit sexuality and pregnancy implied. Six weeks after her death (and the suicide verdict) Sarah's mother could bear it no longer. She publicly declared her daughter had been murdered by Spencer Cowper and demanded her daughter's body be disinterred and dissected.

Spencer had certainly been an acquaintance of Sarah's and had even dined with her before her death. Sarah's maid claimed he had intended to stay the night at the house, and that she had last seen her mistress alone with Spencer. Spencer countered this by asserting that before dinner he had reserved a room in a local inn and that he had slept there. He claimed he left Sarah alive and well at her home shortly after dinner and had not seen her again. His story changed during his trial, when he suggested that Sarah had been infatuated with him and had sent numerous love letters to his London home. This was not substantiated by other witnesses, however. In any case, as she was dead there was no way of knowing what Sarah may have felt, and the court was eager not to further stain her reputation in speculation.

The trial was further complicated by the local prominence and political aspirations of those involved. In this staunchly Protestant and Puritan county, the Quakers were isolated but determined to do everything they could to protect and maintain their reputations. At the same time, Spencer, the younger son of the local Whig MP, was a respectable, married lawyer with his father's wholehearted support. The scandal of his involvement with Sarah was used by local Tories against his father. Indeed, the Tory group joined with the Quakers to push for prosecution, while the Whigs stood behind the Cowpers.[2] The entire community was thus caught up in this contest over justice, local name and political power.

The debates surrounding this case continued long after the trial was concluded, with Spencer frequently popularly condemned despite his having been acquitted in court. He was damned as a Lothario well into the eighteenth century and even after his death. At the centre of the dispute was the body of Sarah Stout; in fact, Sarah's body was the main evidence and impetus for the case and the later accusations. She was literally viewed and probed by her neighbours, and then, after burial, by scores of surgeons and doctors. The persistent focus of the trial was on the varying and damning medical interpretations of the corpse, which was hotly contested in and out of court. Indeed, the debate continued in pamphlet accounts long after the trial and led to considerable contention and controversy. It was Sarah Stout's body, rather than traditional testimony, that was key evidence for both sides. She could not speak in court and yet she was crucial to the progress of the trial.

By the seventeenth century, bodies were providing sources of forensic medical evidence in suspicious death cases. Although similar evidence had been used for hundreds of years on the continent, such testimony was largely new and innovative in England. Indeed, the use of bodily examinations represented a transition in jurisprudence and in ideas about evidence. The collection of such evidence was motivated almost exclusively by private individuals rather than the court or professional bodies like the Royal Societies. Forensic medicine did not become professionalised until at least the mid-eighteenth century, and the seventeenth century should be seen as a transitional period, in which new and old forms of testimony existed in tandem. That is, the new medical interpretation of the body co-existed with popular impression, hearsay and circumstantial report. By the end of the seventeenth century a significant number of homicide cases pivoted upon bodies – the dead body of the victim, the incriminating body of the accused and the probing and inquiring bodies of witnesses. Indeed, the body generally played a pivotal role in court throughout this period. It provided some certainty in trials that were often otherwise uncertain; it allowed solid, provable evidence to replace hearsay and circumstantial report. The body of the victim hinted at a cause of death, while the body of the putative killer, especially in infanticide cases, provided evidence suggestive of culpability.

If the power of the body in court was increasing, the tangible evidence it offered was frequently contested. Expert witnesses were not the only sources of bodily evidence, as lay and professional witnesses alike comprehensively surveyed the corpse and the suspect. In most cases the word of a medical professional would have been more credibly received, due to their proven medical knowledge and experience in diagnosing bodies. While professionals were paid for their testimony, often by the relations of the victims, lay people tended to investigate voluntarily. This division should be seen as largely based on skill rather than gender. Women could be surgeons, although there were relatively few of them, and they could give medical evidence in court. While they were increasingly overlooked in the eighteenth century, these women were usually considered as skilful in the seventeenth century as male surgeons.

Lay witnesses were somewhat constrained in their evidence-giving, but they were far from silent, especially when they disagreed with the professional verdict. When professional evidence was absent or limited, lay witnesses frequently chose to fill the gap. In infanticide cases, the special authority of married women meant they played an equal role with midwives in monitoring the births of their neighbours. As such, they deposed on equal terms with midwives, presenting themselves as just as skilled and knowledgeable. Although such evidence was later exclusively male and professional, in this period claims to authority came from men and women, professional and lay, the expert and the amateur. Evidence was weighed individually, and the court decided on its respective meaning in a piecemeal and sometimes contradictory manner.

Although bodily testimony was the clear forerunner of modern forensic evidence, this was not yet a solely professionalised, male field. Nevertheless, at least part of the impetus for change came from professional men, whose structured testimonies increased the value and acceptability of bodily evidence.[3] This was especially true in the capital, and probably other urban areas. While 78 per cent of bodily testimony was given by (mostly) male professionals in London, this figure dipped to 44 per cent in largely rural Yorkshire.[4] Both convenience and fashion can explain the distinction. Doctors and surgeons were more plentiful and easily accessible in urban areas, meaning they were more likely to be called to treat a serious injury and consequently give evidence if the patient died. At the same time, there was a growing interest in post-mortem examinations in this period, especially in notorious or difficult cases. Official organisations of physicians and surgeons were reluctant to institutionalise dissection in training or practice, and were therefore not the direct instruments of change. It was individual doctors who were innovative in the consideration of bodies, and it was these professionals who actively constructed new knowledge in court as they tested theories on the cause of death.

Professional men did not control all bodily discourse in the courtroom. Lay witnesses willingly provided bodily evidence in cases where professionals were absent or unwilling to act, and so often dominated in rural areas. In Yorkshire, unpaid and unregulated volunteers alone provided 56 per cent of all bodily evidence.[5] Such witnesses responded to and encouraged popular desires for tangible proof in court, and worked to establish the truth by freely appropriating information from other peoples' bodies. Women, in particular, eagerly collected bodily evidence, especially (although not exclusively) in infanticide cases. As their distinctive expertise concerned the reproductive body, this was the arena in which they had repeated opportunities to speak authoritatively. Even so, lay and professional women played a role in other kinds of homicide, drawing their expertise from their roles as mothers/nurturers and as skilled professionals. Female witnesses testified in 84 per cent of Yorkshire cases containing bodily evidence, while in London, where professionals dominated and opportunities were more restricted, the figure was 47 per cent.[6]

Despite a general eagerness to use this testimony, the precise meaning of many bodily signs was hotly disputed, as professional and lay witnesses alike struggled to interpret the often ambiguous evidence before them. The courtroom became a forum in which bodily symbols were weighed and their meanings determined. Bodily evidence came in a range of shapes and sizes, from early dissections of corpses and professional opinions derived before or after death, to marks, wounds and suggestive bodily changes noted by neighbours and relations. All these types of testimony, regardless of their source, can be termed 'forensic', since those witnessing had similar intentions – to provide tangible proof in court, by giving evidence that contained biological and medical information about the corpse and, in infanticide cases, the accused.

Descriptions of the body were like ocular post-mortems, in which witnesses described in detail and with some relish how they had watched, listened, viewed and touched both live and dead bodies in pursuit of evidence in a criminal investigation. These proactive witnesses did not just discuss events they had fortuitously witnessed, but actively immersed themselves into a case after the first seeds of suspicion were sown by examining bodies and discussing and actively interpreting the resulting information. In doing so, witnesses deliberately investigated deaths and actively policed their communities. But not all bodily witnesses willingly testified: some were reluctant and limited their evidence; others were hesitant about the implications of their words and ensured their doubts remained in their evidence.

Nevertheless, their words could be heard in court and formed part of the process by which bodily evidence was weighed and judged.

Although clearly described in depositions, bodily evidence only infrequently appeared in pamphlets. We learn of the Sarah Stout case from a printed text, but most pamphlets were concerned more with the presentation of a *fait accompli* than with the process of detection or evidence-gathering. Guilt was presented as self-evident or as providentially proven, with ingenuity and human endeavour seldom recorded. This means that with the exception of courtroom transcripts, pamphlets tended to record the outcome with an abridged story of capture alone. However, this tension between the depositions of witnesses and pamphlets relates to the form and intention of the relative documents, and does not reflect the everyday endeavours, experience or involvement of ordinary witnesses.

In fact, the ever-increasing prominence of bodily evidence can be directly related to broader shifts in witnessing. By the seventeenth century the court was increasingly demanding credible and provable evidence of all kinds over hearsay, rumour and reliance on providence.[7] As juries grew distant from the cases they tried, they sought certainty and privileged evidence that was not circumstantial or reflective of local prejudice alone, but was universally acceptable. Eyewitness testimony had always been valued, but, increasingly, guilty verdicts also relied on reported interrogations, logical investigations and solid facts, like bloodstains or footprints. Change was slow and incomplete in this period, but juries, judges and witnesses alike all showed varying degrees of interest in defining truth and reshaping justice into a more objective tool. Although the body had always played a part in homicide cases, the increasing desire to prove a case rather than relying on local name or less verifiable report led to a steady gain in its evidential popularity. Dissected and analysed, the body became more than a symbol of the wickedness of homicide: it was transformed into universal and solid proof of the crime and the culprit.

Such evidence was very much a work in progress in this period. Although, as noted, autopsies had regularly been performed on the continent since medieval times, and continental courts could appoint, instruct and pay medical professionals for their opinions, such evidence had never before been a feature in English courts.[8] External examinations had always been performed, but dissection was still treated with great suspicion throughout the seventeenth century and only slowly filtered into the mainstream.

The dissection of a corpse, even to establish a cause of death, was popularly seen as additional punishment to which only particularly heinous criminals were sentenced. The invasion and dismembering of bodily integrity was universally feared, post-mortem examinations viewed with suspicion. Most were reluctant to dissect a body unless necessary, with some concerned that such bodily penetration endangered the soul's external rest.[9] In addition, the dissected corpse was usually pictorially depicted as effeminate:[10] penetration by a medical professional could be seen as emasculating male corpses, laying the private open to public view. In the same way, bodily exposure for women appeared erotic and thus could represent a post-mortem assault on reputation.

While in the eighteenth century the mass dissection of executed felons by surgeons led to riots, this disaffection was not apparent in earlier dissections. There was always some popular and legal hostility towards dissection, but autopsies of homicide victims were never explicitly opposed. Indeed, family members often requested the invasive examination, with the pursuit of justice outweighing concerns with the hereafter and with every successful presentation of evidence this type of testimony increased in value. But according to the law, dissection was considered unnecessary. A murder was supposed to be self evidently visible to such extents that even a lay jury was sufficient to establish a crime had been committed. This common-sense approach continued well into the eighteenth century, with some cases attracting little or no bodily evidence.

Another reason for the stunted development of forensic evidence lay in the adversarial system of English law. On the continent trials were longer and private affairs, in which the prosecutor and judge worked in concert with witnesses to jointly agree on a suitable verdict. The continental legal system required definite 'proofs' to convict. In the absence of a confession, the words of several witnesses counted as part proofs, with medical and physical evidence providing additional confirmation. Such trials were more like private investigations than the displays of public justice seen in England. English verdicts were based on the best possible evidence on the day and, unlike the continental system, a trial would not be halted to allow medical witnesses more time to prepare or to conduct further tests.[11] English juries were free to make any decision they chose, they could disregard even large numbers of direct witnesses, choosing to believe the single one who saw the events differently, without having to discuss or defend their verdict. Although the judge could harangue them for an 'incorrect' verdict, he could not change it. Such a system did nothing to encourage medical testimony or the development of a body of expert witnesses.

The legal system underwent changes in the last half of the seventeenth century, which were formalised via eighteenth century amendments to laws on procedure and evidence. Ordinary people, influenced by broader philosophical and legal shifts, were increasingly determined to present credible proof in court.[12] At the same time, the status of coroners rose, and as their prestige grew so their ability to demand precise and truthful evidence increased. In fact coroners became indelibly tied to bodily evidence, as in presenting it their status was elevated, which in turn raised the profile of forensic evidence. All this led to a fundamental change in attitudes towards evidence. By 1729, the body had attained clear prominence, with around 40 per cent of all homicides having an autopsy performed under the direction of the coroner or presiding JP.[13]

Such testimony brought some certainty into trials and allowed an element of proof into complex cases. Although the efforts of unqualified lay witnesses may seem flawed to modern eyes used to the certainty purportedly presented by science and to the expertise of the qualified witness,[14] if a broader under-standing of the nature of medical evidence is employed, we can see that, despite occasional reluctance, witnesses providing bodily testimony were at the forefront of an evidential revolution. Lay witnesses, midwives and sur-geons, along with the more qualified physician, were appropriating both the ideas and the methods of elite thinkers. Such witnesses were reinterpreting natural philosophy in the pursuit of justice, using their expertise and em-pirical research. At times, as with the trial of Spencer Cowper, the relationship with natural philosophy was overt, with courtroom conundrums being replayed in print and the forensic evidence challenged. The contributions of bodily witnesses formed part of a far broader intellectual tradition.

Even so, bodily evidence was highly nuanced and not every witness played an equal role in its delivery. It was presented in an explicit attempt to clarify the murky waters of a criminal accusation, to augment other testimony and provide the courts with a much-needed means for establishing the truth. Reliable evidence was consistently being demanded in seventeenth century courts.[15] The ideological shifts of the seventeenth century, followed by the legislative changes of the eighteenth, played a role in making experts more desirable as the source of objective truth in the courtroom, pushing bodies to the forefront of the legal process. However, not all such evidence was seen as the same. Complex hierarchies of skill and knowledge were apparent within testimony. All professionals from doctors, surgeons and midwives down to those who nursed the sick or wrapped the dead, clearly stated the experience from which they drew. Likewise, married women, experienced in the ways of female bodies and pregnancy, spoke on related matters and on infanticides, while single women and men remained silent. It was unusual for the completely unqualified to speak on bodily matters in court, but when they did it concerned the bodies of those close to them. The courts would have been aware of such witnesses' lack of status and judged their evidence accordingly, as it was the credibility and reputation of the witness that dictated their believability.[16]

Simply by determinedly presenting tangible evidence to the court, witnesses initiated debate and encouraged other deponents to future excellence. It did not matter that their conclusions were sometimes wrong. The repeated presentation of bodily evidence led to its becoming a regular and expected fixture in such trials. It was the investigative process itself that provoked innovation and change, rather than the accuracy of their results, and the process had a momentum distinct from individual investigations. Witnesses' actions in the overt pursuit of truth had wide-reaching consequences. By the mid-eighteenth century the lower echelons of the medical hierarchy and lay people no longer participated in this type of evidence giving, which became a paid and appointed duty. As English procedures began to mirror those of the continent, women were systematically excluded.[17] However, the beginning of this modern scientific pursuit was as much in informal and popular testimony as specialist evidence; inspired as much by women and lay people as by medical professionals.

There are other explanations for the popularity of this evidence. Depictions of the corpse had always made a lasting impression in the courtroom, providing evidence of the fact of the crime, with the bullet hole, the stab wound and the discoloured skin acting as the focus of attention. On occasion the corpse was even present during a coroner's inquisition, making the body not only palpable but tangible. Details of the wound added to the drama and excitement of a trial. The early modern court was a highly theatrical space, and so the necessity for creating an instant and indelible impression in any witness's evidence was crucial. Moreover, the verdict was final and not subject to appeal. The best a convicted defendant could hope for was a pardon. Juries made fast and binding decisions, and so descriptive, and even gruesome, evidence concerning the nature of the wounds was surely influential. In this atmosphere, the dramatic potential of a described body must have been enormous. Bodily evidence added to the theatre of the courtroom, providing titillating and colourful detail.

A case from Yorkshire in 1651 perfectly illustrates this point. William Lupton gave evidence concerning his attempt to save the life of James Slater after a stab wound 'with gods help'. He vividly described the wound, leaving little to the audience's imagination. He said he 'saw his [Slater's] Bowels come out of his belly as much as his hat would hold'. He gathered up these intestines and sewed up two holes in the bowel 'and then put them again into his belly and sewed the wound up also'.[18] His evidence swam in dramatic detail, of which a prosecutor may well have made profitable use. In the absence of photographic evidence, such testimony would have had a sensational impact on a thrill-seeking court audience.

It was in this climate of intense interest that Sarah Stout's body was literally dissected, figuratively deconstructed and imaginatively reinvented in court. While some witnesses noted the lack of bruises and mentioned froth around the nostrils, others clearly described a crease around her neck as if she had been strangled. Her chastity and sexual behaviour was physically tested and publicly discussed. A midwife was called in to examine the corpse to see if Sarah had been pregnant.[19] She declared she was not and added that Sarah was in fact a virgin. Nevertheless, her sex life remained an area of contention between prosecution and defence. The prosecutors argued that Sarah's resistance to Spencer's advances may have caused the murder. The defence argued that her pregnancy or her yearning for a sexual relationship with the uninterested Cowper were both motives for suicide. The midwife's testimony satisfied Sarah's mother, who was keen to assert her daughter's chastity in the face of increasing gossip. Indeed, by 'proving' Sarah's virginity, the midwife effectively limited speculation about her relationship with Spencer. Gossip was then forced to focus instead on Sarah's desire to have an affair. This was by no means the limit to which her body was probed and discussed: Sarah became a collection of parts, all potentially offering proof of a felony, all relying on the correct and credible interpretation of professional medical men and a series of lay observers.

Bodies had always provided clues to crime, especially when they carried large, externally visible wounds, which were usually noted and mentioned in court as the obvious cause of death. In addition, the body had been used historically as a crude diagnostic tool, as according to folklore the touch of the killer would cause the corpse to bleed afresh. Cruentation, or the touching of corpses by the purported killer, was linked more to suggestion and fear than to bodily reality. Nevertheless, the belief had been very popular, and although this practice was seldom recorded in court in the seventeenth and eighteenth centuries, it may have been more informally employed to encourage confessions. It was not so much that blood actually flowed (although some did believe this); rather that the fear that blood *might* flow led some guilty parties to confess.

As mothers and the prime carers of the family, women had always been prolific givers of bodily evidence in all kinds of criminal trials. Feminine knowledge and experience in these matters had long been respected, and women had historically held various court-appointed roles that involved the examination of bodies. Women acted as the searchers of corpses during plagues, when they were trusted with the vital, if low status, job of assessing the cause of death.[20] Respectable matrons were also formally instructed to act in groups to find a witch's mark or establish pregnancy and male sexual potency. As mistresses and mothers, women policed the sexuality and sexual behaviour of their servants and children. They were held socially and communally responsible for the actions of such girls, a role they took very seriously. Girls' beds and possessions were searched and they were questioned about their activities.[21] This type of evidence did not completely disappear in this period. Women continued to provide such details, albeit occasionally augmented with newer kinds of facts.

Lay evidence remained important, despite the concomitant professional interest in the evidence of bodies. Some lay witnesses embraced rational methods and used bodily knowledge to investigate crime. In Skipton in 1679 a series of witnesses told the court how they had followed tracks in the snow, noting their size and direction of travel, and used this information to arrest Edward Barrow for shooting his friend.[22] Similarly, bodies were often treated with detachment and considered in terms of the clues they could yield, even by those inexperienced in dealing with murders. Corpses were seldom referred to as fear-inducing, and few recoiled from their duty to assess the body and glean information. In fact, in 1690 in Yorkshire, labourer Thomas Jackson eagerly examined a corpse found while undertaking building work at the home of a poor woman. He stated that as he had worked in a graveyard he had swiftly recognised the bones were human and so proceeded to interrogate the householder as to whose they were and how the person had died.[23]

Some arenas of assessment remained staunchly lay, as they were considered to involve legal rather than medical decisions. Diagnoses of madness continued to be collectively determined by respectable laymen. A doctor's opinion was not required, since in law the symptoms of madness needed to be plain to the whole community. A mad person could not commit a crime, and so assessment of this state was vital, particularly when a felony charge was involved.[24] Such evidence continued to be based on colloquial, highly subjective and practical considerations. Madness was primarily about the social acceptance of an individual as incapable of malice. When gentleman Charles Jackson killed his friend and servant with a shovel he expressed great sorrow for his actions. Under examination he was asked 'whether he was then ... in one of his melancholy fits or no To that he saith, if he was not in it, he was entering into it, or else he would never have struck at or hurt Jamye Browne'. A letter from four gentlemen and the justice of the peace to the judge attested his innocence. They claimed to know 'Charles Jackson to be at the time of the said stroke and many years before to have been *non compos mentis*'.[25] Their testimony was anecdotal. They were not medical experts, but they were prominent local citizens: their words relied entirely on their social status and their reputation for credibility.

With the exception of infanticide cases, it was doctors and surgeons who gave most medical evidence, as we have seen in the Sarah Stout case. These men leant heavily on their professional reputations, working alone or exclusively with other professionals. A doctor would sometimes employ several surgeons, or consult with other doctors to discuss his findings or explore new ideas. However, doctors did not consult with lay witnesses; a hierarchy was present which constrained and defined their work. Doctors, in particular, ensured that they clearly identified themselves as experts from the beginning of their testimony. In 1688 Michell Tallbott was referred to as a 'Practitioner of phisick gentleman', and in 1653 John Conset identified himself as a 'Dr of Phisicke'.[26] In both cases, the men were identifying themselves as qualified medical practitioners. This meant they had been university educated and were considered experts. They were also expensive to hire. Members of this all-male profession usually considered themselves to be gentlemen.[27]

Language played a crucial role in constructing and emphasising superior medical knowledge. Most physicians described at length their exact diagnosis, making copious use of technical terms, even though it is possible that many of the words used were incomprehensible to the jury. Their words implied the authority with which they spoke. In 1687 in Cumberland Doctor Jameson said he found Lancelott Graham 'in a very sad condition'. The evidence he subsequently gave did not stint on detail, and he clearly expected it to be unquestioningly accepted. He described his thorough examination of the wound and its effects, stating that it had not penetrated the bowel 'so far as he could judge', but that the skin of the victim was flat and fleshy and some stomach muscles 'seemed to be grievously injured'. He further noted that:

> By the shortness of his breath, and sibillation or hissing accompanying it always after, By which a rupture of some vein or Artery in the intestines has followed for about seven weeks after he did void a quart of blood by stool at a time [for] several days (yea once a Flagon) ... But by his violent coughing through his Asthma hurt received in his Lungs by bruises it burst out unexpectedly and so continued till it killed him.[28]

This description was far more detailed than many other surveys of wounds. Dr Jameson wanted to be seen as an expert. His ideas were presented as certainties, his examination objective and his conclusions exclusive.

Unlike physicians, both men and women could act as surgeons, and, although women were always in the minority, reference to them appeared regularly in the archives. Surgeons were not university educated and learnt their profession by apprenticeship. Consequently, their status was lower than doctors, but they were more numerous and much more affordable.

Indeed, it was status and profession rather than gender that determined a surgeon's credibility. Female surgeons gave evidence both voluntarily and as paid, professional witnesses. Despite their minority status, the language they used was identical to that of their male colleagues, as was the authority they tried to assert. Male and female surgeons expressed themselves more colloquially than physicians but both clearly asserted their skill and authority. They identified who had employed them, and thus firmly indicated their authority. Surgeons were proud of their knowledge, and constantly established their credentials in their testimony to ensure their searches of corpses were perceived as legitimate. Much surgical evidence was brief, often including only a cause of death statement. William Beever moved swiftly to the point when, in 1695, he simply stated that 'the wound that Josias Eaton had given [to] him above his right eye on his face was mortal'.[29]

Some deponents did provide more detail of the injuries they had seen, although not with the linguistic excesses of doctors. Thomas Fyner deposed 'that Thomas Wildsmith was so mortally wounded that he was run through the vulva of the Bladder and also the Gaul, so that his very excrements and his Gaul came up at his Mouth'.[30] His description was precise and had a vivid power. In a case where no other witnesses existed, such an assertion of the non-accidental nature of the death could have made quite an impact. The words of a professional had potency even without the confidence and status of the physician: in 1676 a report concluded that 'the Surgeon cleared him of that guilt, who supposed it a natural death, therefore he was acquitted'.[31]

The credibility women enjoyed as experts in this period was lost during the eighteenth century. Female professionals and lay witnesses of both sexes were gradually excluded from positions of reputable authority with regard to bodies. As the medical profession become more exclusionary and as forensic evidence became a more regular and paid requirement in court, so male professionals dominated this field. However, in the earliest days, women spoke as confidently and as readily as men. There were fewer female surgeons and no female doctors, but some of these women were unafraid to speak in court. In the early days of this evidence at least, their words and their expertise were considered perfectly acceptable. In 1661 surgeon Margarett Norcliffe confidently told the court that she was sure the victim's wound had been mortal, as his brains had 'piple [come out] out at the orifice'.[32] Anne Heath recalled how she was initially sent for by Thomas Smyth and his wife to act as George Wood's surgeon. When he died the next day, her role evolved into that of expert witness. She said 'being entreated by the Coroner and Jury empanelled and sworn to enquire after the said death [and] to search the wounds which she did accordingly before them'.[33] Midwives too made an impression, albeit rarely, in non-infanticide cases. When midwife Anne Hampstall and surgeon Henry Smalley were deposed about their joint examination of rape victim Mary Bush, their evidence appeared to be remarkably similar. Both confirmed that a rape had occurred and that Mary had become fatally infected as a consequence.[34]

Far more women gave evidence as low-status workers on the periphery of the medical profession. There were clear gender divisions in the kind of medical work most women were called on to do, although this did not necessarily stop such women speaking in court, and women clearly presented themselves as experts in specific contexts. Women were deposed for instance as nurses of the wounded, and washers and wrappers of the dead. This was essentially unskilled work, but in general women's long experience of tending to other people's bodies gave them a kind of expertise. They claimed to know what injuries should look like and what marks on the body suggested. Elizabeth Croswicke deposed in 1672 that she had been sent for to dress William Barnesley's wound. She was identified only as a widow, and so may have been an informal surgeon, or as some kind of care assistant. However, her evidence clearly displayed her skill and experience. She confidently deposed that:

> she searched the said hurt, and found that about an Inch deep, and dressed the said hurt, and saith that that was no mortal wound to her judgement, and thought that the cold did him more hurt, than the hurt that this did.[35]

Her evidence concerning the detail of the wound was precise, and the opinion that followed was clearly, forcefully and credibly expressed.

Other women reported their observations of the victim's distress or the scale of injuries with dramatic flair. Beatrix Eastwood said she nursed Henry Illingworth for six days and nights, and provided hearsay evidence of his accusation of three men. In addition, she added that he had been half throttled and:

> that he was so sore inwardly in his throat that he could let nothing down but sometimes some drink and sometimes water and sugar but no meat and said that he sometimes desired this deponent to put her finger in his mouth to take out something that stuck in his throat which she did but brought nothing out but caused blood and bleeding.[36]

This description of suffering cast the victim in a new light, shifting him from a brave manly protagonist to victimised and gravely injured. Beatrix's evidence was descriptive but also creative and theatrical. Ann Linfit used similar horrified language after winding John Dokeson's beaten body. She declared that 'his Back and Thighs were very black. And his privy members red and black and very much swollen. And that she had wound very many corpses, but never wound the like before'.[37] Her assertion of having 'wound very many corpses' indicated her expertise. This, when linked to her powerful description, made her evidence highly suggestive.

A plethora of similarly skilled professionals willingly spoke at Spencer Cowper's trial. In this, the trial was highly unusual. Forensic evidence at this time was seldom placed at the centre of a case, and was even less often disputed or debated in court. Usually the evidence presented conformed to the other facts in the case and was not a cause of contention itself. But Sarah Stout's body was at the heart of Spencer Cowper's trial. Lay witnesses, a midwife, surgeons and doctors examined the body and disagreed about the medical evidence. All the testimonies relating to Sarah's body proved highly uncertain. The debate at the heart of this case was over how drowning should be defined. A dispute emerged between the prosecution and defence involving prestigious local and metropolitan doctors and surgeons, all of whom made internal and external examinations of the body. The first autopsy was conducted six weeks after death and another occurred even later. The body had decomposed, so the debate pivoted upon how such inadequate evidence could be interpreted. This unstable body linked with general confusion about the meaning of identifiable signs made the tangible evidence so desired by witnesses and jurors very uncertain.

Although most professionals in this and other cases gathered their evidence exclusively from external examinations, autopsies were increasingly being undertaken, albeit irregularly. Physicians and surgeons tended to perform these procedures collectively, using pre-existing knowledge and a willingness to experiment. Bodies were not always fully dissected. However, in complex cases, or where one of the parties was willing to pay for the privilege, they were at least partly opened (usually in the vicinity of the wound). The body was probed for obvious signs of trauma, such as large wounds or blood clots, and the organs were examined for abnormalities. Signs were still read at a basic level, with little absolute certainty coming from these early analyses. David Shevill and Charles Clerke provided an intriguing view of the developing science of autopsy in what may be the earliest recorded dissection in a homicide case. In 1662 these surgeons jointly deposed that they had been appointed by the mayor of Newcastle upon Tyne to ascertain the cause of Anne Mennin's death in gaol. They said that they were 'ordered to open the body of the said Anne Mennin', although they provided no detail of how this was performed or of the precise nature of the consequent examination. The surgeons merely stated that they had found poison in her stomach 'which was absolutely the cause of her death as they conceive'.[38]

Autopsies were more regularly performed towards the end of the century in urban areas, especially the capital. Even then they were far from commonplace. The professionals involved in such examinations were invariably appointed (and paid) male experts. Two cases from London provide more detail about post-mortems and the kinds of testimony produced. The examination conducted by surgeon Andrew Firsland confirmed the circumstantial evidence of other witnesses in Aldgate in 1677. Several witnesses told the court how Ellenor Toms had been violently shoved by Constable John Dodd in a quarrel over his right to seize her goods. Firsland:

> saith that ... he together with other Surgeons opened the body of Ellenor Toms and made search in her lungs her heart Liver, spleen, stomach and kidneys: and that in her stomach he found coagulated blood: agreeable to what she had vomited formerly up only not stinking: and that her spleen was all putrid from some external bruise or violence but all other parts were well: and further saith that he never found such a spleen without violence offered.[39]

Although an apparently detailed exploration had occurred, the surgeons failed to uncover any new evidence.

Not all medical evidence backed up existing beliefs. Some acted to challenge, albeit in a hesitant manner, the words of circumstantial witnesses. In London in 1690 the professionals who conducted a post-mortem spectacularly clashed with the eyewitnesses to an alleged beating, each providing very different stories. Eyewitnesses contended that Peter Howseley, a drawer at the Sun Taverne was beaten by two gentlemen, one using a cane and the other a sword. Witnesses described the attack, while other deponents told the court of Peter's constant complaint of severe head pain after the incident. They emphasised his words, quoting him saying 'that he believes he should not live a Month to an end'. He died a month later. This was all highly traditional evidence, involving witnessed attacks and a dying man's accusation of his killers.

In a break with usual practice, however, two doctors and six surgeons were instructed to conduct an autopsy in this case. Although we have no way of knowing who instructed them, it seems likely that the doctors were employed by the defendants, who as 'gentlemen' probably had the means to pay for this help. Rather than giving individual evidence, the professionals gave a joint report in which they said:

> We whose names are underwritten being present at the opening of the Body of Peter Howsly upon our Oaths certify that upon inspection of the head both outwardly and inwardly we did not observe any bruise depression crack or breach in the skull nor any corrupt stinking matter nor any blood out of its vessels, nor any sign whatsoever of any external violence or injury.

The report listed the organs of the body and pronounced them to be sound.

At the end of the statement the professionals clearly concluded that 'Peter Howsley did not die a violent but of a natural cause of death'.[40] Although it was unsurprising that their testimony was favourable to their probable employers, it is still significant. In this case, tangible, medical facts were being used in law to contradict traditional forms of evidence. The weighty reputations of the medical men involved meant their evidence would have been influential and authoritative, albeit not necessarily decisive.

The Sarah Stout case was more thoroughly contested and contentious than any of the other cases mentioned above. The prosecution claimed that Sarah had been murdered by being hit on the head and strangled, even though bruises could not be found on the decomposing corpse. They argued that she had too little water in her lungs and few of the expected signs of internal putrefaction to have drowned. Despite their efforts proof was difficult to locate. So, in order to make up for the deficiencies of the post-mortem, they introduced novel and creative evidence. Dr Clement used testimony drawn from battle-experienced sailors, who argued that having watched scores of watery deaths, both drowning and burials at sea, they 'knew' that dead men floated and drowned men sank. Such evidence was not the result of laboratory tests, but it did represent an attempt to construct truth using empirical data. This was a plausible alternative when little other certainty existed – the jury had to be able to make the best possible decision on the evidence available on the day.

Nevertheless, the doctors for the defence strongly contested these conclusions. Although the refutation was successful in court, the evidence presented by the defence was systematically challenged in print. Lengthy medical debates and speculation continued long after the trial had finished. In particular, the medical evidence was rigorously examined in several pamphlets, most notably in one entitled 'The Hertford Letter'. While two defence doctors said that only two to three ounces of water was needed to drown, the author of the 'The Hertford Letter' rebutted this, quoting Boyle and contemporary ideas on putrefaction. It also described an experiment on a dog thrown into the Thames in which twenty-seven ounces of water was found in its lungs.[41] The defence said sailors were unreliable witnesses as they were superstitious, and contended their own canine experiments had proved that drowning victims could float. Another experiment, using a convict recently hanged, was also described in court. In this case, the convict's corpse was taken out of its grave on the night after its burial and was thrown into the river as an experiment on the buoyancy of a dead body. It sank on entry, and the defence claimed that this indicated that just as the previously dead did not always float, so those drowned may not always sink. 'The Hertford Letter' again dismissed these claims, arguing that the body had been overly compressed while temporarily buried, and this removal of air led directly to its sinking.[42]

The uncertainty surrounding Sarah's body and of the body of knowledge about drowning meant, ultimately, that the case was unproven, and although Spencer was acquitted some people were never convinced by his acquittal and rumours and gossip plagued him throughout his life.[43] However, the case did push forensic medicine further into the limelight and encouraged debate on its merits. The arguments surrounding Sarah's body were learned, detailed and at times resourceful. Evidence was presented as fact, even when it was pure supposition or was openly contested. The medical men who gave evidence were professionals who were seldom willing to concede fallibility. Not all the debates took place in the courtroom, as many experiments preceded and antedated the trial; however, the court was the fulcrum around which this investigation pivoted, inspiring medical professionals and spurring on their work. This was cutting-edge medical testimony in which proofs were not only presented but professionally constructed and tested.

While forensic medical evidence was growing in popularity, its impact in court was uneven in this period. Juries often could not understand the testimony given, or were hostile to it as it contradicted existing beliefs or knowledge. Some may have felt its value was limited and chose instead to rely on circumstantial report. Ultimately we cannot know how influential such information was in early cases, as jury deliberations have always been secret. However, by using other sources we can speculate on the likely reaction to this evidence.

Most medical professionals were unwilling to completely abandon traditional reported evidence in favour of purely 'scientific' or bodily testimony. With the exception of doctors, their testimony tended to be as much a mixture of the highly traditional evidence of hearsay and eye witnessed account and the new evidence of the body. Hybrid testimonies were given which included elements of both old and new types of facts and mixed bodily information with circumstantial evidence and deathbed reports. Dying accusations were valuable sources of evidence, although in order to be fully valid the court had to be convinced that victims were cognisant of their forthcoming death and therefore of the impending heavenly judgement on any false accusation. The presence of a medical professional, who had informed them of their fate, would have acted as a confirmation to the court that the victim was aware of their approaching mortality. In fact, this was a crucial part of a surgeon's legal function. Surgeon Anne Whitwood deposed that she had plainly told George Dixon that he could not be cured, before enquiring who had injured him. She then recounted that he replied that Thomas West, Nicholas Spence and 'a trooper' assaulted him and pursued him with a sword and 'stroke him from the wall', thus breaking his leg.[44] Although proponents of forensic bodily evidence, these professionals seldom ignored an opportunity to supply incriminating non-medical information to the court.

At the same time, doubt and uncertainty were apparent in professional testimonies, as were words of challenge from lay witnesses. At this early stage in the history of forensic medicine, few rules existed and all witnesses could speak freely on a range of topics. In fact, medical professionals were frequently willing to acknowledge their own shortcomings. In the case of the death of Mathew Laidley in 1698, two surgeons deposed that Mathew was 'Labouring under an Imperfect palsey', which could have occurred from either a fall, a bruise or 'as likewise from Inward Causes'.[45] In other words, they could not tell with any certainty what had caused his death, and their confusion was their only evidence.

Even physicians were not always treated as the sources of certainty they purported to be, and their diagnoses and their actions were constantly monitored by the public. As jury deliberations were not recorded, it is difficult to quantify individual juror's doubts. However, doctors were critically assessed and viewed by their communities, which implies that jurors could be just as sceptical of their authority and skill. Indeed, in an unusual case from London in 1674, physician William Blackbury's treatment of his own child was seriously doubted and he was eventually tried for his murder. Despite William's profession, the neighbours insisted on viewing the boy's body and they found it to be 'strangely discoloured' and bruised. Two women searched the body and claimed he had died a violent death, despite the parents' assertion that he had simply died suddenly.[46]

Medical testimony was repeatedly probed, and its value assessed on a case-by-case basis. In this context, providing evidence in a homicide case posed clear risks to a medical professional's reputation. While attracted by the power and authority such a role could offer, professionals were keen to avoid public questioning of their skills or blame for the death. Doctor Joseph Thornton made clear statements in 1686, first about the cause of death and secondly about his own role. Joseph had treated the victim for his wound and clearly told the court that he was recovering and would have lived if he had avoided further conflict and subsequent injury.[47] Anthony Kirton similarly distanced himself by arguing that 'he verily believes if the said Ralph Featherstone had applied himself to a skilful Surgeon in any reasonable time ... the said wound might have been cured'.[48] Kirton was clearly stating that the death had not been his fault.

Although Spencer Cowper's trial clearly had an impact on the professionals involved, their ideas and even possibly future research, it may not have directly influenced the jury. Like their counterparts today, the jurors were not medical experts and they may have found complex evidence confusing. In the face of so many eminent men who disagreed it would have been difficult to rely on status alone to decide who was correct. Although jury deliberations were sealed, comments made by the judge in the Sarah Stout case provide insight into courtroom confusion. He reportedly said 'the Doctors and Surgeons have talked a great deal to this purpose, and of the Water's going into the Lungs or the Thorax, but unless you have more Skill in Anatomy than I, you won't be much edify'd by it'.[49]

Spencer Cowper was acquitted of Sarah Stout's murder, despite many continuing to believe in his guilt. The bodily evidence at the heart of this case was highly nuanced and not every witness played an equal role in its delivery. It is, of course, unknown whether the medical evidence influenced the jury. Nevertheless, this case revealed how medical evidence could be accepted in court and how keen both sides were to assert their version of the 'facts' provided by the body. In contrast to the sixteenth and early seventeenth centuries, when such evidence was seldom seen, by the beginning of the eighteenth century, medical evidence had become fundamental to the decision-making process and central to the verdict of the jury. Bodily testimony, with all its faults and inconsistencies, was increasingly becoming a crucial component in early modern trials. Despite its fallibility, tangible proof was increasingly demanded by, and helped to determine, early modern justice.

4

Infant Corpses

In Kingston upon Hull in 1668, widow Susanna Vales was suspected to be pregnant with an illegitimate child. As a result, she was subjected to months of surveillance. One of her neighbours, Susanna Doughty, deposed that she had watched Susanna Vales and discussed her suspicions with Magdalen Stockwell. Magdalen reportedly told her 'that she thought that Susanna Vales was with child if ever she the said Madalen Stockwell had had a child'. Doughty then reported this opinion to Mary Harrison, who commented that 'she could not tell, but wished it were not so'. Doughty was approached later that day by a solider named Parkinson, who asked her why she had discussed Susanna Vales in such a way. To this 'she answered she told it to a friend as a friend might tell her and this said Mr Parkinson was very angry with her and said he would make her pay for it'. At this point Susanna Doughty had not discussed the matter with Susanna Vales, despite having broadly elicited opinions on her possible pregnancy. When she did meet Susanna she was forced to apologise and agree she now believed 'it is not so'. However, she concluded her testimony by again remarking that Susanna was 'very grown'.[1]

We learn of this suspicion and surveillance because Susanna was later suspected of killing her newborn infant. In this case the source of the suspicion came not from an infant corpse (as indeed no body was ever found) but from her own body: Susanna was watched and her size and shape discussed by local women. She was suspected to have had illicit sex and then to have killed her child to hide her shame. Her own body was the cause of suspicion and it became the prime evidence used against her in court.

Throughout the seventeenth century, regular and inspirational use was made of bodily evidence in infanticide cases. This testimony made forensic evidence a generally visible, practical and desirable means for establishing truth in difficult cases. Even experts found it difficult to distinguish between stillbirth and murder. In fact, so worried was the state by the possibility that murdering mothers were escaping justice that an act was passed in 1624 that made proving murder unnecessary in cases involving unmarried mothers. Criminal innocence could only be established if a credible witness testified that the infant had been stillborn. No further proof was needed, although neighbours often went beyond the law and sought additional evidence to prove that a crime had in fact occurred. This made bodily evidence essential to the forming of a case and infanticide cases some of the most frequent and prominent arenas for forensic and bodily evidence. The corpse of the infant and the body of the putative mother were central to proving a homicide had occurred; and to the development of modern forensic medicine in general.

Forty-one per cent of all bodily evidence related to infanticides, despite such cases representing only 19 per cent of all homicides.[2] Forensic evidence was frequently the main, and sometimes the only, kind of testimony given in these cases. In total, 71 per cent of cases included some kind of physical testimony.[3] If we exclude confessions and make allowances for lost records, this means only a very small percentage of infanticides were prosecuted without bodily testimony. Such evidence was presented for a range of reasons, not least because it allowed matrons to assert their respectability and expertise. Along with other forms of forensic evidence, it dominated court cases by the eighteenth century and became part of a professionalised, male domain from which women were largely excluded.[4] However, one of the principal origins of this science lay in ordinary women using their traditional knowledge to testify about other women's bodies. The science was as much rural and feminine as it was urban and male.

The murder of newborn infants by their unmarried mothers was a distinct type of crime in the seventeenth century. A statute was passed in 1624 that defined a new type of murder in circumstances in which the mother was unmarried and had hidden her birth. The law was anomalous and in many ways can be considered to be a hysterical reaction to (largely false) perceptions of rapid increases in illegitimacy and the ineffectiveness of previous legislative restraints. Yet the law was not universally embraced, and increasingly witnesses and juries demanded more compelling evidence than the statute required before convicting. Infanticides were complex and difficult to prove, as stillbirth and murder were barely distinguishable medically. In these challenging cases bodily evidence was especially necessary. Over the course of the century infanticide law was popularly reinvented with proof of murder and live birth pushed to the forefront of prosecutions.

There are a number of explanations why infanticide trials proved so inspiring. The statute, passed in 1624, came into effect in a society in which the body and tangible proofs were seen as increasingly important. In this context, the new law was seen as open to interpretation as ordinary people sought to mould its application. Many lay women and midwives chose to interpret the new law in ways not intended by the statute, albeit demanded by local sensibilities. As the statute inverted the presumption of innocence, the courts could infer guilt, leaving the mother-defendant to prove her innocence in draconian circumstances. This seemed to motivate ordinary people to act in spite of the law, to prove a crime had occurred in addition to a concealed death; yet neighbours were often reluctant to convict an innocent (and often young) girl unjustly. This provided the perfect setting for new types of evidence. Traditional testimonies from hearsay, local name and reported reputation all continued to be provided in these cases, along with eyewitness accounts about the sexual activities of the woman accused. However, physical evidence provided substantive proof to confirm these reports. Infanticide should be viewed as a crime defined around the body, displayed in gestation on the body and prosecuted via the body.

Despite this concern with truth, bodily evidence was not always used to secure acquittal. The evidence was not used exclusively by either the prosecution or defence: testimony was malleable, and could be applied to proving either guilt or innocence, a live or stillbirth. These testimonies had opposing functions, with the body contested and open to interpretation and witnesses conflicting in their intentions and in their readings of meaning. By proving maternity in cases where no infant could be found, witnesses placed a woman squarely in the frame for murder with few options for a defence. The law stated that a hidden death was enough to prove murder in cases where the mother was unmarried.

Testimony that aimed at establishing live birth deliberately had a different effect. Such evidence was unnecessary under the law, but as witnesses were concerned with protecting the innocent, their evidence of stillbirth or life helped establish that a crime had in fact occurred. This shifted the application of the law from its original remit, forcing the courts to publicly prove guilt rather than presume it. Examination of the records shows that the impact of this evidence was clear. In London in 1690 Martha Nook was acquitted in spite her free confession to hiding the death of her illegitimate child. The midwife and other matrons had all testified that the child had been stillborn, not murdered. The statute was read out to the jury, but they chose to acquit on the credible evidence the matrons had supplied.[5] The words of such witnesses were influential and could make the difference between life and death in these felony cases.

In the Susanna Vales case, while neighbour Susanna Doughty was not alone in either her suspicion or her confusion, the case proved difficult to resolve. Unlike other suspects, Susanna successfully refused to allow the women to examine her, which she was able to achieve possibly because of her age and status as a widow. Young spinsters in the same position were often maidservants who had little privacy and seldom felt able to refuse others permission to search either their bodies or their property. In addition, being a widow Susanna undoubtedly lived alone (or had more independence at least). She certainly had enough personal authority to thwart local desire to examine her.

Generally, however, unmarried mothers were in a difficult position in court. The matrons who gave evidence were respectable, sometimes professional, often of the middling sort, with experience of authority over others. The women they targeted were usually young, poorer and single. The matrons acted in groups, while the mother was often alone. As unmarried women the mothers were considered to be sexually and morally suspect, and so further alienated from respectable, married women. Much about these mothers was demonised and isolated. The majority of unmarried suspects were subjected to numerous examinations and verbal interrogations. They were watched, probed and discussed at length by hostile and suspicious neighbours, employers and family members.

The majority of suspected women presented little defence, either against the investigation or during the subsequent trial. Most of those who confessed to pregnancy claimed the child was stillborn. Their testimony was short and often unconvincing, however, their defences resting almost exclusively on protestations of ignorance of how to care for a child, or simple misfortune. In 1670 in Kirby Dorothy Snawden blamed her newborn's death on her falling into a swoon immediately after the infant was born 'and as soon as she came out of it she took up the said child which was then dead and cold'.[6] Her implication clearly was that she was not responsible. However, the law argued that she was. Simply by having the child on her own as an unmarried woman and having no one to confirm its natural death, she was considered to have effectively murdered it.

Nevertheless, as in the Susanna Vales case, not all suspects were completely silenced. Proactive and determined defences were difficult to find under such a closely defined infanticide law. Neglect and ignorance of the pregnancy or of how to bear or care for a child were never acceptable defences. Even so, some suspect mothers battled to control their identities in this intensely hostile environment. Matronly declarations of the signs of pregnancy, in the form of body size, milk or blood, could be countered. In 1674 Margarett Glanes reported that she 'and several neighbours observed the said Jane Browne very big on her body'. Jane was Margarett's lodger, and Margarett claimed she questioned Jane about her size three months previously, but had been told by Jane that she had dropsy. Two weeks before her deposition, however, Dorothy Cowper, a neighbour, came to Margarett 'and acquainted me what notice the neighbours had taken of her [Jane]'.

This unnerving neighbourly interest galvanised Margarett to search Jane's room, where she found the bed to be full of blood.

Other witnesses repeated similar observations to Margarett's, with Mary Bovill speaking first of the 'greatness of [Jane's] body' and then of her fear when it was 'lately much fallen'. Jane, however, was not willing to allow such evidence to damn her. She refused to allow a physical examination, claimed that the blood had been 'occasioned from other causes happening [to] women', and blamed her size on a combination of a blanket she wore around her waist to keep warm, ill keeping, ill lodging and wet feet, all of which she claimed had 'puffed up her belly'.7 The gossip and rumour remained, but Jane at least made an attempt at controlling and shaping her own image, and at influencing the meanings others derived from her body.

In their capacity as knowledgeable women, midwives or wives were almost ideal sources of truth within the context of a criminal accusation, as they were independent, unrelated to the accused and in part disinterested. Their credibility in court was based on their status, and their evidence judged as it related to their local name and their persuasive ability. The majority of bodily evidence in infanticide cases came from married women and midwives. Indeed, in the Susanna Vales case all the women were married and referred to their own knowledge and experience of pregnancy: they were experts on the reproductive body and could make authoritative decisions about bodily signs. Their gendered authority meant that they could speak as experts. Midwives, in particular, were proud of their professional standing. Katherine Lawson began her testimony by stating 'That she is a midwife by profession', referring to her own ability by saying that she had reviewed the body 'to the best of her skill' before coming to any conclusions.8

Much infanticide evidence focused on interpretations of directly witnessed bodily details. Deponents told compound tales to the courts describing how they had watched suspected women, collected information, and searched the suspect's homes and bodies. These proactive investigations involved local women repeatedly intervening in crimes, using traditional feminine wisdom laced with sceptical inquisitiveness. In this period knowledgeable women could be powerful and the consequences of a matronly pronouncement were serious. The credible words of such a witness, even in the face of doubt and contradiction, could lead to a conviction.

In most cases the power matrons wielded came not from always being right or even from a formal structure (as indeed most women acted independently and without official sanction); instead, it came from their ability to define their knowledge as superior to others and their words as more credible. Co-operation was a key feature of lay bodily evidence, with women frequently choosing to work together. The potency of the bodily evidence such witnesses supplied was significantly bolstered by collective presentation of their opinions, as they clearly informed the courts that they had shared and discussed their evidence before reaching conclusions. When the court did appoint women, it was always as a group. Although sometimes lacking any formal structure, these groups of experts were commonly referred to as a 'Jury of Matrons', and had traditionally operated for hundreds of years to cloister pregnant women in inheritance disputes, or decide on the pregnancy of convicted felons.[9] These women revelled in their rare formal role, often announcing their expertise at the start of their evidence. One deposition preamble recorded that the JP advised the constable to 'summon and charge several grave matrons to enquire after and search all women within there constabularies that they should any way suspect to be guilty of the late private bearing of a child'.[10] This was an official and important role in uncovering truth and pursuing justice.

As with all other expert witnesses, the matrons who testified about bodies protected their own status by constructing exclusivity. Not everyone could publicly comment on bodies. The accused mother, spinsters and men were all effectively silenced on these matters. Notable exceptions did occur, but in the main only respectable matrons with skill and experience would have enough credibility to speak in court. The most significant foil against whom the matrons repeatedly identified themselves was the accused mother. Witnesses referred to the lies she told to deny her pregnancy or to any insults she may have heaped on the investigators. The evidence presented in court represented a summary of accusation, rebuttal and the search for damning evidence that had occurred over several months. The defendants and the witness had been engaged in a profound struggle, from which only one side could emerge unscathed. By giving evidence the matrons were policing the sexuality and criminality of these young women, but they were also defining themselves as different to these immoral young women, with separate and even opposing identities.

Not all accused women passively accepted accusations, though. Unmarried mother Anne Pearce challenged an accusation of murder by claiming she had had a premature stillbirth. She acknowledged the bodily signs others had identified, especially the milk found in her breasts, but re-interpreted their conclusions. Ann disclosed the location of the corpse and admitted to sexual impropriety. Her reputation had been a significant factor in local suspicion, with John Hill commenting that she 'lived a very suspicious and lewd life and was expected to be with child'. Ann claimed that she was pregnant but that the child had never moved inside her, and was therefore at an early stage in her pregnancy. She gave birth when going to the toilet and initially hid the baby. However, the infant's body was the most persuasive evidence of her innocence. Ann claimed that she bore 'a thing' and two matrons agreed calling the body a 'half Birth'.[11] Their evidence, if considered credible, should have confirmed her innocence.

Spinsters were excluded from the authority claimed by married women. Although they gave evidence in infanticide cases, their testimony was restricted by their limited knowledge and credibility, and by their fear of admitting to what may be inappropriate information. Most stuck to the same kinds of story. Susan Smith declared in 1671 that she 'did not know any thing' of her sister's pregnancy despite spending a lot of time with her, and Dorothy Hornby said she was so 'frighted' at the sight of a newborn that she fell into a swoon.[12] Expressing knowledge as a spinster could be dangerous. When spinster Martha Popple examined an infant's corpse and gave evidence on its wounds, other witnesses implied that the child was therefore probably her own.[13] Although this was only a rumour, rather than an accusation of murder, Martha's unexpected knowledge had left her open to suspicion.

The evidence most spinsters gave carefully separated them from complicity. A clear example is provided within the testimony of Barbary Gowland, who gave evidence against fellow servant Mary Greene in 1674. Barbary began by saying she had worked with Mary for three weeks:

> And during that time (although this informer lodged in the same bed with her) did not know the said Mary Greene to be with Child: for she did work and spin without trouble and eat her meat and victuals and complained not of pain or distempers.

Although she was her bed mate, Barbary explicitly avoided referring to any bodily signs that she might have noticed, and referred instead to Mary's work and eating patterns as evidence of her good health. Work and food were signals a spinster could reasonably be expected to notice and comment on. This avoidance of bodily topics pervaded Barbary's words, and throughout her evidence she made her spinsterly innocence apparent, even though, in some ways, it limited her capacity to demonstrate Mary's guilt.

Barbary continued by stating that she did not question Mary's claim to have had a headache the previous evening, saying that she went to sleep and later arose 'and all this while ... [she] was ignorant of any child'. Later, when Mary tried to leave the house with the concealed body, Barbary deposed that she refused to allow her to. However, she claimed this was not due to a conscious suspicion of Mary, but rather to an unspecified fear 'the cause thereof she knew not'. Barbary concluded her evidence by describing the search of Mary's clothes and the discovery of the corpse, but her evidence made it clear that she only witnessed this search and had not participated in it. From start to finish, she depicted herself as incredulous, innocent and unaware. As a spinster, Barbary simply did not have the personal or legitimate authority to admit to noticing such things.[14]

Although men occasionally instructed women to investigate, they were seldom directly involved in infanticide investigations. Women carried out searches and their evidence was delivered independently. Even when not instructed to do so women grouped together informally to examine suspects. The co-operative nature of much female evidence provided additional credibility as well as removing the burden of accusation from individual women. Legal officers directed evidence collation and masters could instruct women to search. In most cases, their role was to provide status and add an air of officialdom to what was essentially women's business. In London in 1692 mistress Deborah Daniel sent for the midwife and constable when she strongly suspected her servant. Her testimony noted 'but before the constable came' the midwife had obtained a confession and located the body.[15] His presence was symbolic (if indicative of the formal trial to come); hers was crucial to the investigative process.

Male testimony concerned issues other than the bodies of those involved. Men dug up corpses or retrieved them from wells (or other depositaries) and collected rumour and reports of suspicions or sexual misbehaviour. Their testimony tended to be brief and limited to the reporting of conversations the witness had overheard or participated in, or to their own role in finding an infant's body. Men seldom referred to the bodies of the women involved, and when they did they did not present opinions or make deductions. Yorkshireman Benjamin Green, the self-claimed father of a dead infant, said he questioned the child's mother, Hannah Allen, several times about a possible pregnancy. He lived in the same house with her throughout, though he never admitted understanding the events he witnessed. He was obviously suspicious of pregnancy, but her denials seemed to convince him. Even finding her 'sick' with 'some wet under her' did not convince him she was in labour: he said he accepted her reply that 'she had made water'.[16]

Female witnesses had many reasons for investigating and testifying. Bodily evidence could provide a voice in, and influence over, a prosecution. Medical evidence was generally given from choice, with the majority of witnesses respectable and married and so only tangentially privy to the illicit sexual activity of young unmarried women. It was the determined pursuit of tangible bodily evidence that allowed respectable matrons access to this less salubrious world, in which they could discuss elements of other women's lifestyles in order to condemn unacceptable activities. However shockingly conservative the actions of these witnesses now seem, we have to view them in context. Women with illegitimate children threatened the economic stability of often poor local communities, while also psychologically endangering sexual order. As such, the young unmarried mother threatened to subvert the very building blocks of a respectable woman's identity, marriage and status. There was little female solidarity in such cases, and women swiftly sought to identify and distance themselves from the malefactor. So, although most such women were acting out of a genuine belief in the wickedness, immorality and profound disorderliness of the accused women, their actions tended to reinforce negative, patriarchal images of femininity as dangerous and threatening.

At the same time the patriarchal status quo was implicitly challenged and subverted simply by women speaking in court. As a *feme covert* a married woman's legal role was theoretically constrained, but such technical restrictions seldom prevented women speaking publicly and having at times a strong legal presence.[17] Indeed, female witnesses frequently spoke in court in numerous cases, especially homicides. By bolstering their own power they extended everyday definitions of femininity and have presented historians with a distinctive view of early modern women. Whether they were conscious of it or not, when respectable matrons gave evidence they constructed powerful new identities for themselves. Although they acted to effectively damn other women, they presented themselves as reliable and resourceful women and their search for proof led them to reveal truths about their own lives. Acting as expert witnesses in infanticide cases gave these women a legitimate legal voice and the ability to substantially influence a binding verdict.

The evidence female witnesses provided was often predicated solely upon their personal credibility. They did not lay their evidence out for the jury to decide upon; instead their decision about the facts *was* their evidence. The witness's word was frequently all the information the jury had, because the reasoning behind an accusation was repeatedly left out of the evidence. The conclusions women drew were from secret female knowledge to which only married women and midwives were privy. This information was not for public consumption, and many female witnesses, unlike doctors and surgeons, kept their reasoning veiled. Sara Garthwaite said she had accidentally happened upon Frances Webster and reported that 'by some symptoms or signs that she saw about the said Frances Webster [she] did suspect that either she [Frances] had borne a child or had had a miscarriage'. Likewise, Londoner Rebecca Edwards coyly noted only that 'by some signs she did suspect,'[18] while in 1729 Jane Howden from Pontefract claimed that Mary Falkner 'had all the outward visible signs imaginable'.[19] Matrons could be confident that the source of their knowledge would not be investigated, probably as they had developed an unassailably legitimate role. As the evidence they presented concerned feminine bodies and the reading of other women's intimate signs and indicators, the position they occupied was one in which they could speak confidently and with little fear of contradiction.

Female witnesses' deliberate obliqueness may have a range of explanations. Some of the stated unspecified signs may never have existed, being added later into the witness's narrative to spice up a story or legitimate an invasive search. Or, it may be that some women enjoyed the secrecy afforded by imprecise phrases and wished to remain the only arbiters of the physical evidence they had provided. If the essence of the evidence remained undisclosed, it could be neither assimilated, understood nor queried. However, it may have been that these female evidence-givers, or indeed the clerks who transcribed their words, did not have access to acceptable kinds of language with which to discuss the specifics of their bodily evidence. In a pamphlet from 1673 a mistress's investigations were recorded in unusual detail. The wife was called 'inquisitive' and as 'seeing some things, which for modesty sake I shall omit'.[20] Despite her successful investigation, the process of her actions remained veiled as the court was unwilling to hear specific details of intimate feminine processes. Additionally, these women may not have had access to specific, known or commonly understood words for certain feminine functions or by-products, even if they desired to be more precise in their evidence.

The infant's body, if indeed one could be found, was undoubtedly crucial to a murder case. Locating the body was a prime objective of searchers as it not only proved a crime had been committed but often provoked a confession. Midwives monopolised examinations of these small bodies. Indeed, matrons seldom gave evidence about the corpse when a midwife's testimony could be secured. Although few tests were performed on infants and no dissections were recorded, the body was meticulously examined for external signs of the cause of death and to determine its relative size on birth. Midwives did not necessarily give damning evidence.[21] When Mabell Stephens described a body she found as 'sore bruised and wounded on the sides and head and had both the arms broken',[22] this was clearly a murder. However, bodily evidence could just as often help secure an acquittal. In 1696 in London midwife Hannah Gardine and wife Judith Manlon both clearly deposed that the corpse recovered from the toilet was 'not above five month gone'. It had not gone full term, and its extreme prematurity indicated it had been miscarried. In fact, Hannah Gardine went further and claimed 'it had been Impossible to have saved the Childs Life', even if women had been present at the birth.[23]

As in the Susanna Vales case, it was the body of the live mother that was the prime focus for female lay witnesses, and their deliberations about its nature and meaning dominated infanticide accounts. Matrons watched, discussed, examined and interrogated their suspect in an attempt to secure evidence and a confession. Their investigation often lasted a considerable time since even in the face of constant denials and threats suspicious women continued to press their point. A mixture of skills was used to elicit the truth, with matrons relentlessly alternating interrogation, physical examinations and the searching of the suspect's things. In 1690 in Sheffield two midwives interrogated Hannah Allen over a suspected birth. The first midwife physically examined her and questioned her about pregnancy. A second midwife arrived the next day, and 'asked her [Hannah] what she had done with it'. Hannah denied having given birth, but midwife Isabell Machon was undeterred and returned later to question her again. This time Hannah confessed to having had a miscarriage, claiming that she had wrapped the foetus in an apron and thrown it into the cellar.[24] Her confession had been secured due to the pressure exerted by the midwives during the three interrogations (and at least one physical examination). However, it was Hannah's responses and confession that were then presented as evidence in court.

Physical examinations were often forceful, despite being essentially informal and generally occurring before official legal action. Suspected women were monitored closely for some time for signs of birth. After the supposed birth occurred, searchers quickly moved in. The resulting physical examinations were essentially a means of confirming suspicions when interrogation had failed. In 1669 wife Jane Wilson said that although she had long suspected her servant, her questions had achieved only absolute denial. When Isabell later disappeared into a cow shed Jane followed and examined the area. She found the dead child, and conducted a thorough search of her servant's body.[25] Mistresses were always especially alert for signs of pregnancy or of birth, and were often the first of the neighbours to question servants or to search their bodies. In fact, mistresses often defended their policing of a servant by arguing that they had long been suspicious but had been unable to prove pregnancy until after the birth. In 1673 Elizabeth Dowson of Cumberland explained to the court that although suspicious of her servant, Mary had been two miles away when she gave birth. Elizabeth was clearly informing the court that she had not sheltered Mary knowingly, and would have exposed her if she had been able to.[26]

Most suspicion arose from observation of external signs as a host of respectable married women carefully monitored unmarried women to seek tangible evidence of their illicit sexual activities. Body size was a prime indicator since it was difficult to disguise. Although it by no means constituted solid proof of pregnancy, expanded (or suddenly contracted) bodies crystallised suspicions, hinted at sexual misbehaviour and even murder. Londoner Elizabeth Daniell said in 1682 that she and her husband often visited Rebecca Dod 'and they did observe her to grow bigger and bigger and she did suspect her to be with child'.[27] A shift in body size was suspicious, but only in conjunction with other factors. Margaret Spicer claimed that although Ann Man's body size changed, Ann was 'a woman of Good Reputation [so she] did not think of her being with Child'.[28] Size was certainly contentious and provoked overt debate. In 1671 in Rotherham Gertrude Law was suspected of pregnancy. Ann Ekroid supposed her to be with child because of her body size. However, 'afterwards it was observed by several women that the said Gartrude did grow less in her body who said they thought they were deceived in adjudging her to be with child'. Gertrude also argued that a mistake had been made, saying 'her swelling was occasioned by something else'. She said she had not had a child for over three years and had swollen due to an interruption in her menstrual cycle. It was the discovery of the corpse that broke this deadlock and indicated that Gertrude had lied.[29]

Although most of the intimate signs of pregnancy were kept secret, the presence of milk and blood was frequently revealed, though even these signs were contested in court, with matrons and mothers openly disagreeing on the meaning of bodily signals. In 1673 in Yorkshire a midwife admitted to some confusion about whether Issabell Browne had had a child recently or not. The searchers had found milk in her breast 'in a reasonable measure' but an intimate search led them to declare 'that they do not think her to be with child now'. However, the presence of the milk troubled them and led them to question their own conclusions, as did her body size (they argued that 'her petticoat was much of it drawn together'). It was only when the corpse was found and Issabell confessed that the case became clearer.[30] Excess blood was also suggestive and far more difficult to hide than milk, especially for young female servants who were occupying someone else's house and whose movements were constantly monitored. Although blood could have alternative interpretations, in conjunction with body size or milk, it became yet another piece of bodily evidence indicating wrongdoing.

In the Susanna Vales case neighbours demonstrated their willingness to believe the worst of their peers. In many ways women expected and understood this situation and in other circumstances may well have participated in the accusation process. All single women were potentially vulnerable. Even a good reputation and social standing did not prevent suspicion. Susanna Vales was a widow, probably of previously good character (certainly no one suggested otherwise in their evidence). However, her neighbours were quite ready to believe her capable of sexual and criminal misdeeds. One act of illicit sex was considered to be enough to condemn a respectable woman and ruin her reputation forever and some neighbours relished this opportunity to judge their peers. Margarett Hell reported seeing Susanna in church and said that she had passed her suspicions on to two others and that they discussed it together several times. They agreed that her body had grown considerably and declared that this led them to suspect pregnancy. Mary Harrison ominously recorded that 'if she be so, she hath much disgrace her self'. Susanna's claim of having had colic was generally disbelieved, and she was at a loss to know what to do. She clearly knew of the women's suspicions. Her friend, Sibell Walker, told her to speak to the women involved, but she reportedly replied, 'she should only get an ill word of them' and that she was 'scandalized' by their suggestions. Susanna was later found not guilty, but she had had to maintain her denials under enormous pressures, and it is, of course, unknown whether she ever regained her former unsuspected status.

Susanna's refusal to be examined was risky, and ultimately did not stop rumours of her pregnancy. Agreeing to an examination may not have condemned her either: even quite large groups of women often could not decide on the meaning of bodily signals, though they could clearly identify them. Although they strove for unassailable professionalism, witnesses were aware of the limitations of their knowledge. Many clearly stated how confident they were in their evidence, others freely admitted to confusion or to doubt. Diagnosing pregnancy was problematic and the records indicate that women regularly disagreed over what constituted proof and what kind of evidence was solid and incontrovertible. Body size, milk or blood could all be explained away. Matrons therefore ensured that any doubts were explicitly presented in court, along with alternative scenarios. This may have damaged any sense of overarching authority, but it did allow female witnesses to present a clear picture of what they saw as the truth.

In the absence of a body, many women made it clear that their pronouncements were based on supposition alone. In 1664 in Northumberland a strange disagreement occurred over the suspected pregnancy of Dorothie Bates. Dorothie claimed she had been pregnant but that the child had not stirred in her womb and was stillborn. However, no baby materialised and the two matrons admitted their own confusion. A physician had examined Dorothie and informed her that she was not pregnant but had wind and ague. Without a body little further progress could be made.[31] In this case, the witnesses' lack of conclusion was their only evidence.

Matrons were not infallible and neither were they universally believed. They did not always agree, and on occasion lively debates occurred in the courtroom, although few extended their disagreement over interpretation into personal attacks on the credibility or knowledge of the other party. Indeed, few women made explicit claims of superiority. As coalitions of female deponents usually existed without formal hierarchies, jury decisions were based on reputation, name and experience alone. Debate and disagreement was a central feature of lay testimony, and the judgements made were freely admitted to be interpretation rather than fact.

A particularly good example of such disagreements can be found in Yorkshire in 1662, when Elizabeth Chadwick, a widow of two years, was accused of secretly having borne and killed a child. Elizabeth denied pregnancy and claimed that her neighbour, Elizabeth Atkinson, had accused her wrongfully because of 'some differences' between them. Elizabeth Atkinson had involved her neighbours in her search of Elizabeth Chadwick's body, seeking to bolster her own evidence through a forum of supportive opinions. The court, therefore, gained the distinctive evidence of five knowledgeable women, one of whom was a midwife. Elizabeth Atkinson said her physical inspection of Elizabeth Chadwick had provided confirmation of her earlier suspicions, as the searchers had found Elizabeth Chadwick to be unwell and 'that her body was much settled, from what it was the day before And searching the house further, they found that much water had gone from her'. Later in the week the women returned to search Elizabeth again, and this time Elizabeth Atkinson contended that they 'found signs that she had a child lately And further I did find her breast to be full of milk'. Elizabeth Atkinson further claimed that Elizabeth Chadwick had admitted to her that she had engaged in illicit sexual activity with a man who had since gone to Ireland. Another searcher, Alice Sinyth, also claimed she was convinced that Elizabeth Atkinson had had a child.

However, three of the participants in the search of Elizabeth's body and belongings disagreed with Elizabeth Atkinson's findings. Midwife Isabell Cotton said 'she could find no sign, or other cause to believe, that she [Elizabeth] had lately had a child', and the other two women concurred. Hellen Roberts stated that she had been with Elizabeth Chadwick when the child was supposedly delivered 'and found no cause to think or believe, that she either was with child, or had lately had a child but was satisfied that her illness proceeded from some other cause.'[32] Only Isabell Cotton possessed any formal medical skills, and yet her evidence was not presented as more reliable (nor was her opinion necessarily completely persuasive, as the other witnesses had all volunteered their information regardless of her presence). All the female deponents – whatever their diagnosis – gave their considered opinions, and felt themselves to be skilled and their interpretations valid.

There were significant constraints on female power that limited a witness's ability to speak effectively. The power to judge did not come without risk. In fact, to speak publicly about another's sexual activities could prove dangerous, especially to the witness's local name. Witnesses therefore viewed their own role cautiously. Matrons were sophisticated witnesses who could actively choose the level of their involvement in a criminal case. Some deponents limited their testimony or chose not to speak at all, probably as they feared their interest in corpses and their knowledge about biology may have been misconstrued and even considered to be inappropriate. Some may have even avoided giving medical evidence due to the potential stains on one's standing that such an action could leave. In 1754 Elizabeth Mayle, a London midwife, refused to examine a rape victim, even in the face of her mother's pleading, by saying 'I never was before the face of a judge in the Old-Bailey in my life, and I did not care to be in dirty work'.[33] Clearly, despite the opportunity to wield power over their neighbours, not all women found the giving of bodily evidence to be worthwhile. Many potential witnesses made an active choice between justice and a possible increase in their status and the concomitant risks to their reputation.

A woman's personal reputation was fundamental to the credibility of her evidence. If proved false (or when a history of suspect testimony existed), her status was indelibly eroded. Often such detail is unrecoverable, but on occasion evidence exists of the kind of doubtful testimony that could effectively destroy a woman's reputation. The best example of self-under-mined evidence can be found in the dramatic case of midwife Elizabeth Lawman. Elizabeth gave three separate statements concerning her role in the birth and death of Susanna Watkins's infant. The first two statements were dated on the same day and so it is unclear which came first. However, it appears that she first denied all knowledge of the birth and said she was not present. She then claimed she was called by Andrew Waterlow, Susanna's master and the infant's father, to assist with the labour and that as she entered Susanna had given birth to a dead infant. She took care of Susanna and helped to bury the infant. Her final statement was taken four days later and her story had changed again. Elizabeth claimed she had not called in, but had been under a window, for an unspecified purpose, and heard Susanna calling for another midwife. She entered the house and as she did so the infant was stillborn. She then said Andrew Waterlow refused to allow her to call in other women as witnesses. Elizabeth seemed to be struggling to ensure that the tale told of her actions allowed her to retain some of her credibility, which had been undoubtedly damaged by the four and a half month delay in reporting the birth. Elizabeth's initial denial may have stemmed from a desire to keep out of the whole affair. However, she was placed under extreme pressure and constantly re-examined until it became clear her initial story was untrue.[34] Although she may have been previously credible, Elizabeth was represented as deceitful in her depositions, which may have discredited her in court.

Although matrons had authority locally to investigate in almost all infanticide cases, at times they could come up against a greater force which prevented both investigation and testimony. Indeed, little could protect them against capricious and powerful individuals. In 1681 witnesses told a tale of a thwarted investigation two years earlier. Mary Clapham said she and others had 'vehemently suspected she [Anne Wright] was with child by reason she was not like other young women unmarried'. Mary claimed she had also suspected Anne to have been pregnant since this time, but could give no information on either delivery. Richard Hardishly and John Burne repeated similar tales of suspicion. Thomas Duckett, however, provided the clearest information. In his deposition he claimed to have seen Ann apparently in labour and then later with a small naked child. He said he:

> Told several neighbours of the matter and what he had seen that night. But neither I nor any other neighbour durst at all meddle to search or busy themselves about the matter by reason the said William Wriglesworth her master was a troublesome man.

He suspected that Ann had been pregnant since that night, because her size had increased and she had milk running from her breasts. Despite these suspicions, no physical or verbal examinations were made. The local investigators obviously feared her master and felt too constrained to act effectively.[35]

All these women played a role in making forensic and bodily evidence a regular feature in criminal cases. In infanticide cases bodily evidence was vital to the pursuit of a case and provided some certainty that a conviction was just. In terms of the larger process, it is unimportant that witnesses were sometimes wrong or that they often forced the courts to rely on their word alone. It was the process of collecting and employing bodily evidence that made the real impact. Simply by consistently providing such testimony about infant corpses, these witnesses made this evidence an expected and necessary feature if infanticide cases. The same desire for truth and justice underlies similar tests today; such concerns are as much a modern as an early modern obsession.

Of course, witnesses were not always wrong, although it is difficult to make a judgement in individual cases, not least because much of the evidence was hidden and opaque, leaving us (and the jury) to rely on words alone rather than on a witnesses' reasoned chain of evidence. Nevertheless, the women who gave evidence were at the forefront of a broader demand for tangible proof before conviction. In the eighteenth century such desires inspired 'scientific' tests (like the hydrostatic lung test for infants), which could also be flawed. What is important, though, was that despite the formal process that emerged in the eighteenth century, the origins of forensic medicine were as much in the informal and the feminine as they were in the male and the professional. Women, without formal status or remuneration, played a vital role in this evidence-giving persuaded often only by a desire for justice and the potential power the public giving of evidence afforded.

5

Husbands and Wives

I know not which live more unnatural lives,
Obedient Husbands, or commanding wives.[1]

In London in 1687 Marie Hobry killed her husband Denis, thus becoming
a celebrated and notorious criminal. The couple lived an ordinary life in
St Martins-in-the-Fields. Marie was a midwife by profession, and Denis was
frequently away from home, working as some kind of trader. Both, but
especially Marie, were well known in their community. However, they were
never on friendly terms with their neighbours or truly accepted, probably
because of their nationality: Marie and Denis were French, and Marie was
commonly referred to as the 'French Midwife' rather than by name.[2]

The couple had been married for some years by 1687, but according to
Marie's testimony had always been miserable together. She claimed that
Denis beat her very badly and regularly abandoned her, leaving her destitute. When he returned to her the cycle of abuse would begin again.
Marie claimed she was frequently tempted to commit suicide, which was
both a deadly sin and a felony in this period. Marie also admitted that her
thoughts regularly turned to homicide, and she told her neighbours that
she had threatened to kill her husband and had almost done so on several
occasions.

After years of abuse, Marie finally issued Denis an ultimatum in 1687,
telling him that if he continued to treat her badly, she did 'not know what
Extremities you may Provoke me to'. As was the pattern of their life together,
Denis promised her and then broke his promise. The incident that precipitated the homicide came after a night of drinking. It was described in one
text in great detail. Marie went to bed at ten o'clock, only to be awoken
at five by her husband's drunken entry. He came in:

outrageously in Choler [anger], and more than half Drunk. This Examinate was
a-sleep, till her Husband waked her with a heavy Blow with his Fist upon her
Stomach, and said to her, *What are you Drunk?* This Examinate Answering, *No,*
you are Drunk, you'd never come home at five a clock in the Morning else; you have
been among base company He made this answer, *I have been among ... Rogues,*

that have made me Mad, and you shall pay for it Whereupon he gave this Examinate another violent Blow upon the Breast.[3]

The violence continued for a while. Marie claimed she was squeezed until she could not breathe and blood came out of her mouth. She told a tale of rape in which Denis forced 'the most Unnatural of Villanies' on her, leaving her bleeding copiously and crying for help which never came. He then threw her violently across the room and bit her.

Marie was obviously in dire straits. The violence was depicted as excessive and showed little prospect of ever reducing. Her despair was complete, and one pamphlet captured this by imagining her thoughts as, 'What will become of me? What am I to do! Here I am threatened to be Murdered, and I have no way in the world to Deliver my self, but by Beginning with him'. So, as he had passed out, she took off his garters, tied them round his neck and strangled him. She claimed she immediately regretted her action and tried to revive him with brandy, but to no avail. He was dead.

Although already an exciting and dramatic tale, what happened next was extraordinary. Marie's thirteen-year-old son (who lived away from home as a servant) advised her to flee. However, Marie had no money and was disinclined to leave. Instead, she acted scandalously: she dissected her husband's body with clinical precision and great calm and disposed of the corpse, piece by piece, in a variety of locations, most prominently his limbs in Houses of Office (public toilets) and his head at the Savoy. With the assistance of her son and two other men (all of whom were later acquitted of being accessories), Marie spread a story amongst her neighbours that Denis had left her again to go travelling. She was obviously determined to get away with her murder. Nevertheless, she was caught when the pieces of the body, notably his head, were displayed and recognised. Marie was apprehended and charged. Despite her attempts at cunning she did not deny the crime and pled guilty at her trial, being duly convicted and sentenced to burn at the stake, guilty of murder and of petty treason.

Marie's terrible crime quickly made her infamous. Ordinary people were fascinated by the balance of power in the home, making domestic homicides sensational and even celebrated. The household was the epitome of order in the early modern world and orderly homes were generally equated to a stable and easily governed state. Domestic rebellion or disruption could therefore unsettle the whole community, although in fact domestic killings formed a relatively small overall percentage of prosecuted homicides in early modern England. However, the statistics fail to reveal the full impact of these domestic crimes: domestic homicides inspired interest quite out of proportion to their incidence.

As today, husbands killed their wives in far larger numbers than wives killed their husbands. Eighty per cent of all cases of killing involving couples were of men killing their wives. In view of the fact that many of these crimes were preceded by years of non-fatal abuse, it seems clear that certain early modern husbands constituted a significant threat to their wives. Nevertheless, it was wives who were considered the epitome of treason and disorder in the home, and who were disproportionately subjects of public printed condemnation. This was partly due to cultural conceptions of women as naturally non-violent and common ideologies that linked good wives to acceptance, passivity and silence. An ideal wife was supposed to endure her husband's violence and passively agree to his commands, however unusual or difficult. She should be the opposite of the scolding, nagging wife who attempted to 'steal' the breeches and 'command' her husband. Her silence meant she did not complain or question his commands. In metaphoric terms, he was her king and she his obedient country. Rebellion was never acceptable.

Indeed, wives were constrained legally. Since the home was of prime interest to contemporaries, the harshest penalties for murder were saved for domestic crimes. 'Petty treason' referred to the killing of a superior by an inferior, usually a husband by his wife or master or mistress by a servant. This law would ensure a wife could not make a self-defence or manslaughter claim: her act was always indefensible and always murder, however the husband had acted and whatever she had endured. Husbands could argue that they acted to correct their wives or had been provoked into beating them, but a wife could never mitigate her crime.

A wife who killed was generally characterised as malicious and evil, beyond redemption until execution. She could not exonerate her actions by claiming to have been provoked by her husband, or physically protect herself in any way. In prescriptive terms, she could not even leave the home without his permission, meaning she had no right even to flee. In practice, wives did flee violent men. Indeed, it was the most often used tactic in defence of their lives when faced with a violent and intransigent husband. Neighbours and local officials could speak out on the wife's behalf to try and temper the husband's violence, but he could quite legally demand she return to the home without making any promises to reform his own actions. At the same time, petty treason carried the extraordinary penalty for wives of burning at the stake. When the husband killed, he would only be hanged. The meaning attached to the different penalties applied should not be dismissed. Burning or quartering were public declarations of the heinousness of the crime committed, and invoked shock and salacious interest in the community who came to watch the execution.

In fact, husbands were not only allowed to beat their wives, under certain circumstances they had a duty to do so. Social rules dictated that household members all lived under the direct authority of one man, whether husband, father or master, and he had the power as well as a legal and social responsibility to correct, guide and police his dependants. A husband was legally responsible for the actions of all in his household and was bound to 'correct' them with physical violence to prevent their wrongdoing. Blackstone's *Laws of England* described a man as legally entitled to beat his wife with a stick no bigger than his thumb. He could also make unlimited use of his fists and feet when he beat her. He could not maim her or permanently harm her, but he was given a wide remit when it came to everyday domestic violence.

Literature, from prescriptive texts to bawdy ballads, instructed early modern men and women in the hierarchies and relationships of the family. Simply by ensuring the obedience of lesser members of the hierarchy, order should have been guaranteed. Even so, at times wives were perceived as needing lawful, violent correction. At these corrective moments power in the household was firmly linked to a responsibility to ensure order. This power was by no means limitless. Excessive violence represented a new kind of disorder, and one which was, in many ways, far worse than the infractions the correction was supposed to police. These tensions between power and responsibility, and correction and culpability can be traced across early modern households.

Tales of domestic discord were fundamentally concerned with defining the roles played by husbands and wives, over and above all other household members. Violence had always played a role in household order, as superiors physically policed their dependants. However, disorder also played a key narrative role, as stories of unlawful violence (and especially murder) were repeated as cautionary tales, whose function was to demonstrate the outcome of lax discipline or injudicious use of power. Although the former was theoretically easy to correct, with stern discipline and the enforcement of household hierarchies, the latter remained unresolved and problematic in this period. Superiors who abused their power were reviled, and if they killed they were prosecuted and condemned. However, such violence was difficult to prevent because communal intervention would challenge and curtail one of the key rights of the early modern world – the right of husbands to police their own households. Although intervention was possible, it was fraught with danger and constrained by popular conceptions of power and duty.

Marie Hobry's story was not just a stereotypical tale of a wicked wife, however. It was a complex tale full of reversals. None of the central characters was clearly or consistently portrayed. Marie, in particular, was described as married, then her marriage was questioned; she was beaten, then abandoned; she was powerful, and self destructive; she killed, and regretted her actions immediately; she hid the body, and then she confessed; she was a passive, enduring wife, and a wicked, brutal killer. Denis was a lesser focus for the writer, but he too was described as having little consistency: he was vicious and a victim; a domestic tyrant, while also a victim of domestic betrayal. Despite one author's assertion that his was a 'Plain and a Naked Narrative', all parts of this tale were clearly deliberately constructed. Authors were writing in order to tell 'the truth', but also because the tale was salacious and scandalous and so sure to sell well.

Marie's story provides crucial information about how early modern people perceived marriage and gender issues in relation to violence. In all early modern homicide tales, women were constrained by their gender. In prescriptive terms, their identities were limited to 'good' and 'bad'. A wife – and indeed any woman – was either passive and silent (and thus under male control) or dangerous and potentially threatening. Women were the metaphoric epitome of both order and disorder. They were simultaneously described as obedient and passive, while also being damned for refusing to be controlled and seeking illegitimate power.[4] All violence committed by women was seen as wrong, but homicides committed by women were generally perceived as thoroughly malicious. Wives' dangerous insubordination was depicted as destabilising the family, undermining legitimate male power, and could even imply the ultimate destruction of the state itself. Women were potent images in the arena of power and control. When she ruled, a woman was presented as creating a nightmare world-turned-upside-down.

A murderous wife was generically depicted as malicious and scheming. No explanation or mitigation was legally possible and few defences were ever offered. Wives generally had their individuality erased from the record and their personal motivations hidden from sight. They did not attack with either the openness or legitimacy of husbands. In this context, husbands had a narrative advantage over wives. As most male domestic violence was socially acceptable, husbands had greater freedom to discuss and explain their actions. Often a husband's ability to blame his wife for his violence was only limited by concerned neighbours with contradictory tales. Without the public statements of neighbours, a husband was free to cast aspersions on a wife's chastity, sanity and innocence, presenting himself as blameless. Wives had no such freedom of self-expression, as their roles were limited to rigid conformity or unnatural malice. A wife was seldom depicted as casually violent; she was always portrayed as determined to kill. Her words were seldom recorded and her voice was deemed unnecessary to the making of a judgement.

Narratives about independent, good women who lived outside male control did not exist in this context. The conventional tale of a wife-killer was of a woman acting out of wickedness to betray and kill, sometimes because she had a lover or else as an expression of her nature. It was only as clear victims that women could be positively presented. Victims of husbandly violence could be portrayed as virtuous – albeit after their death. It was generally true that, in terms of protagonists, in early modern homicide stories, the only good wife was a dead wife.

On the other hand, male violence replicated hierarchies of power, gender and marital order. To many commentators the conjugal relationship was the prime site for the exercise of male authority. Male violence existed on a continuum, in which attitudes towards violence ranged from acceptable and expected to criminal behaviour. Unlike the simple equation in which violent women were considered malicious, male violence was seen to be more complex and easier to excuse. The line between acceptable and unacceptable male violence was often blurred. In moderation, a man could legally beat his wife, children and servants, which made the distinction between permissible and criminal actions rather less than straightforward. Some male violence was always seen as acceptable. At the same time a man who could not control his wife or the members of his household was a laughable figure, and one on whom scorn would have been poured. The marital relationship was often portrayed as fraught, with an uncontrolled woman often depicted as violent, scolding and adulterous. The husband's failure to control his wife inverted familial power, allowing the wife to wrest control and demand that her husband do the demeaning feminine tasks she usually performed, often while she openly cuckolded him. Therefore, at times, male violence was seen as a necessary means of ensuring social order.

The tale we are told in the case of Marie is distinctive, though. Although an acknowledged killer, and, as the titles of the pamphlets recording this case constantly remind us, considered hellish, miserable and barbarous, Marie's identity was expressed in terms which differed from other early modern tales of a killer-wife.[5] Marie had a voice, if only in one tale, and she spoke in the first person (something seldom seen in other printed stories or depositions), with a clear identity as a victim as well as a killer. Hers was a distinctive and complex tale within which a paradox existed. Marie's killing was described as an act of desperation rather than pure malice. In part, she was depicted as a good wife – as she had endured beatings, desertion and abuse over several years with few complaints. She had stoically accepted Denis back, despite repeated betrayals, and had acted as passively and obediently as wives were expected to do. Hers was a tale with which it was possible for all to empathise at least in part.

Such willingness to explore Marie's motivation left the authors of these pamphlets with a problem. By publicising a wife's defence, this story made her actions appear comprehensible. There was apparently nothing else that Marie could have done in the situation the tale described other than kill her husband. However, this was an unpalatable narrative for an early modern audience and one they ultimately could not accept. Even so, as Marie had been evocatively presented, it was not so easy to dismiss her as simply wicked. This tension was simply resolved in the text by her execution and her own affirmation of the justice of this action. However, in terms of the story itself, such an ending failed to deal with the idea that Marie had been victimised and had no options other than to kill or to die.

This discussion of her motives, though curtailed, is unique in early modern homicide stories. Most other killer-wives were unable to speak freely about why they had been violent; they were effectively silenced by legal and cultural hostility. Throughout the assize records these women scarcely recounted their evidence in depositions or had their words recorded in print. As depositions were primarily constructed for the prosecution it is not surprising that most defendants said little. However, the silence of wives was quite pervasive. Although many men were roundly criticised for their violence, such violence could be legitimated, either through their own statements or those of other witnesses. Wives did not have access to these forums. Whether innocent or guilty they could not freely represent their violence in the same way that men could, which was a reflection of institutional gender inequality in court.

An example of the constraints imposed on killer-wives can be found in the detailed depositions from Yorkshire in 1671 concerning Margarett Pinchbecke's murder of her husband John with an axe. Margarett was discovered with the axe in a blood-soaked room and confessed to the crime, and so it is unlikely that she had not killed him. However, it is her access to a defence (or lack of it) that is of interest. The majority of the evidence came from Elizabeth Pinchbecke, the couple's young daughter who witnessed the events. Elizabeth claimed that early in the evening her parents had 'fallen out' and 'after some ill words there was some strokes betwixt them and her father took the stick from her mother; And several strokes was given'. Elizabeth claimed she was uncertain who had given and who received the majority of the blows.

When her mother retired to bed Elizabeth saw her take an axe with her and conceal it, but she did not tell her father of this. In the early hours of the next day, she heard her mother rise and:

she heard a great stroke given which she believes was upon her fathers head by her mother with the axe: And upon the first stroke her father gave a great shriek and after that she heard a stroke or two more but her father cried no more.

Elizabeth then proceeded to tell the tale of her involvement in the crime, saying that:

her mother caused her to get up and put on her clothes And her mother then took her father on her back with one of his arms above her shoulder and the other of his arms under her other arm and commanded her to carry his feet which she did as well as she could but she was scarce able to bear them but was forced several times to let them fall.

The mother and daughter carried the body through the village to a stream and left it there.

When they returned, Margarett swore Elizabeth to secrecy, saying 'if she ever spoke of it to any one she would kill her'. Margarett attempted to clean away some of the blood, but when neighbours came to the Pinchbeck house the next day they found an axe by the door 'very bloody and found blood on the longsettle and seat by the bedside and upon the bed and chest and in several other places of the wall and other parts of the house'. Although Margarett had tried to conceal her crime she did not deny the murder when questioned by her neighbours. In contrast to the loquacity of her daughter, though, she said little of her crime, commenting only that she had done it as 'he had done her a great injury and did deserve it'.[6]

The most striking element in this story is the way in which Margarett was depicted as a killer. She was defined in the statements as a cruel wife who apparently murdered her sleeping husband on a whim. Elizabeth described her mother as dominating her and orchestrating her involvement, which along with the threat of violence she had described made Margarett appear to be a cruel mother as well as a wicked wife. This material can be read in a series of ways. It could be that Elizabeth's testimony was shaped to replicate the central concerns of the court. The initial quarrel between John and Margarett was sidelined in her text, as it would have been irrelevant to the prosecution. Male juries rarely considered female violence in the context of manslaughter, and as she was a wife it was even less likely that a jury would concur with an assessment that Margarett had been provoked by her husband's actions. Her crime would have been petty treason whatever she may have said in the courtroom, and everyone would have been aware of this.

At the same time, Margarett's own economy of speech bolstered the impressions created in Elizabeth's text. Her words may have been deliberately excluded from the record, being considered unnecessary or distasteful by those taking her statement. Alternatively, Margarett may have censored herself knowing that any comments relating her husband's behaviour to provocation would be unhelpful in her defence. Or, indeed, she may have adopted a cruel persona, and encouraged such a narrative in Elizabeth, in order to draw all the blame onto herself and protect Elizabeth from execution alongside her. Her telling and meaningful silence is a feature found repeatedly in the depositions of murderesses. Whatever her motive, Margarett was thoroughly constrained by cultural perceptions of her act. There was no possible defence. Words could no longer help her.

To an extent all women were sources of fear and concern in this period, despite their relative lack of power. Popular belief implied that if women were given licence or freedom they would abuse it and endanger others. A subtext underlay all female characterisations in this period: unrestrained femininity could be dangerous – and, for some, even fatal – and special laws (for witchcraft, infanticide and petty treason) were in place to categorise this behaviour and severely chastise it. The severity of the punishment, of course, acted as a warning to other women. This was, however, only one of the ways in which women were represented. Women fulfilled a multiplicity of daily roles and occupied as wide a variety of identities as men. Women were respectable wives and mothers and pillars of the community. These virtuous women can also be seen in homicide records – and indeed in the story of Marie Hobry (albeit tangentially). They acted as key witnesses, collecting evidence and presenting it to the court. In this, and other contexts, respectable women spoke as experts on the female body and on the lifestyles of other women.

However, Marie's identity was complicated by factors other than her gender alone. As a papist, a foreigner and the perpetrator of an especially heinous crime she was marked out as extraordinary, untrustworthy and stereotypically bad. She was always presented as an amalgam of these identities, which made her the worst and most notorious of killers. Indeed, out of a set of fifty-two cards in a series entitled 'Rebellion', Marie appeared three times in the acts of killing her husband, disposing of the body and being executed.[7] The other cards in the pack depicted national scandals and threats to the state, and no other person was depicted so often except the Prince of Wales.

Despite being an ordinary woman from St Martins-in-the-Fields in London Marie's crime had made her an infamous and immediately recognisable personality. She was quickly demonised, as a generic threat to her husband and all husbands, to the state and even to the king. She was partly depicted as an 'Everywoman', but was not named in the cards, being called the 'Popish Midwife' throughout. This namelessness allowed her to become generic – an everywife and a general example of femininity. Likewise, few of the pamphlets or the witnesses they claimed to have quoted refer to her by name, and when they do there is confusion over what to call her. On occasion, she was called Madam Hobry; while at other times she was called Marie Desermeau, her pre-marital name. Questions over which name to use revealed local doubts about the legitimacy of her marriage. Suspicions about her sexual behaviour added to her reputation as a bad and suspect woman. Marie's lack of name also indicated her social alienation. One wife said Marie lodged with her for three months, but referred to her only as 'the French midwife', as she claimed she was unsure of her name.[8]

Marie's role in these cards was as a representation of the nefarious nature of Catholics, foreigners and women. These were the enemies within.[9] All were perceived as untrustworthy while remaining integral parts of society. They threatened national and household stability and were constantly feared for their potential to commit treason. A wife who killed her husband was acting as dangerously in metaphoric and social terms as a Catholic plotting the overthrow of the king. Both were treasonous, both dangerous and neither accepted nor conformed to their prescribed, humble social roles. Marie's Catholicism and foreignness were palpable parts of her identity and even her name. She may have been so distinctive because of her limited English: one pamphlet refers to her using a translator to plead in court. This may be artistic license, since as a midwife she would need to be able to communicate, at least in simple terms. However, this does indicate how isolated her foreign identity made her. Papists and foreigners were the ultimate scapegoats, believed to have dangerous ideas and tendencies and perceived as uniformly mad, bad and dangerous to know. Although they played only a peripheral role as killers, the perceived threat such individuals posed was omnipresent in this period. Marie was damned as much for being a papist and a foreigner as she was as a wife. In fact, it was these broader elements that made her a more notorious killer than any other husband-murderer.

Marie's actions only served to magnify these stereotypical depictions of her identity. The stories about her were told to indicate how truly wicked she was. One of the most significant events of the case was her cool dissection of the corpse. The dismemberment caused a shock that was registered in print and ensured her notoriety. Even Marie's friend Margaret Vasal exclaimed, 'O thou wretched creature, art thou not content to murder thy Husband, without cutting him to pieces!'[10] The dissection was depicted in print, pictures and on playing cards. In one print Marie was assisted by her son and egged on by devils as she defiled her husband's idealised body.[11] The dissection had broader meanings than hiding her crime. Although common on the continent, few autopsies were conducted in England. Dissection was viewed ambiguously: it was used as an additional punishment to be inflicted on the specially wicked after execution, but at the same time was gaining popularity as an investigative tool. Bodies were examined to discover the cause of death as well as to learn how they worked. Such investigation was reviled and encouraged according to individual perspectives and beliefs.

In this case, Marie had been trying to conceal rather than reveal and to escape punishment rather than ensure justice. She was the antithesis of the new science. When she dissected her husband she was acting wickedly, and by cutting him to pieces, she literally 'disembodied' him, tearing apart his form and with it the power he had exercised over her. Dissection was also somewhat emasculating, as it involved male bodies being penetrated and thus inverted marital order, leaving Marie standing over Denis, with his whole body under her illegitimate control. Marie did not just kill her husband; she violated his physicality and his masculinity. It was not a coincidence that just after she had successfully asserted her own identity, the value of her life and her own will to live, she then deliberately (and literally) deconstructed her husband. The household could not cope with two active identities. It was prescriptively ordered around one alone – the husband and the master.

A further metaphor for the abhorrent nature of this crime can be found in Marie's disposal of the corpse. Whether wittingly or not, she chose a highly degrading ending for her husband's deconstructed body. As we have seen, she separated the parts and placed them without ceremony in different toilets, his head at the Catholic Savoy. The equation of Catholicism, waste and dung was clear. Her action was also uniquely feminine. Women traditionally used dunghills and houses of office to dispose of bodily waste and of mis-carried, stillborn or murdered infants. The dunghill can be perceived as a space that women could easily access and that offered concealment and some protection from prying eyes. These spaces can be seen as partially sexualised – as they were occasionally the recipients of illegitimate bodies (in the form of murdered newborns). Such a public and cavalier disposal also negated Marie's religious beliefs, which would require a decent, Christian burial for the corpse. The act seems incongruous when we compare it to her later remorse and passivity. At this stage in the tale, Marie was purely wicked, purely selfish and concerned with escape. Only when she renounced this, by accepting – and even welcoming – death, would she, and any other treasonous wife, start her social rehabilitation, finding forgiveness only in heaven.

Regardless of the impact of Marie's startling murder of her husband, the vast majority of violence was enacted upon wives by violent husbands. Such assaults were far more common than a wife killing her husband, although they were also less well publicised. A husband's violence was scandalous but never as shocking as a wife who disobeyed or assaulted her husband. In fact, disobedience and resistance legitimated husbandly violence and even encouraged it. After all, it was his duty to both police and correct her.

Marie's actions were extreme but they highlight the problems of domestic violence and the difficult position it left women in. Nevertheless, relatively few cases ended in death and most domestic violence was considered moderate and appropriate by the neighbours and even the abused wife. Any examination of homicides will always overstate the role abuse played in the home, as domestic abuse only rarely caused death. It is clear that order was always more prevalent than excessive abuse. Most violence was considered minimal and acceptable. In most cases, harmony and obedience were only occasionally disrupted by moments of violence.

When domestic violence did take place, it usually took the form of consistent and long-term assaults, rather than quick murders. Husbands who beat their wives to death did so over long periods of time. They coupled their attacks with explicit threats to their wife's life or limb. Beaten women consistently reported that their husbands had threatened to kill them while they were beating them. Revealing the husband's threat allowed the beaten woman to firmly establish that his violence had been excessive. This information could then be used by neighbours to pressure the husband into more reasonable behaviour towards his wife or, in the cases discussed here, be repeated in court to show a pattern of unnecessary violence on his part and even a desire to kill. There were no guarantees with this type of evidence giving. Juries could be capricious and choose to interpret the information differently. Indeed, the prosecutor did not always allow the evidence to be presented in court. However, such evidence was recorded in depositions, was known about by the local community and would affect the husband's reputation and social standing if nothing else.

As with most wife-killings, the murder of Anne Feales in Yorkshire in 1641 was prefaced by years of abuse. Anne and her husband Marmaduke lived in Gleadles and had been married for several years at the time of her death. Anne was regularly beaten and threatened with death by her husband before finally being killed. Her body was found hanging in the centre of the room by her husband, who claimed he had been away from home for several hours. He inferred that Anne had killed herself, which was both a mortal sin and a felony. Marmaduke claimed that he had argued with his wife that morning and said he had threatened to leave her. He deposed he went out to buy butter and found her dead on his return. He told the court that he thought 'she hanged herself'. The implication was plain: his threat to leave her had caused her to commit suicide. His explanation made it clear that he was in no way involved in the crime. He concluded that 'he was neither of consent nor counsel of taking her life away, but left her quick [alive] in the house when he went'.

However, Marmaduke's voice was not the only one heard in court, and several neighbours willingly spoke out to contradict his claims of innocence. His violence was well known in the community, not least because Anne had reported instances to her neighbours. She told several that she feared for her safety, and after her death several of these neighbours came forward to report her fears. Anne Bradbury claimed that Anne had 'said unto her she know not what to do, for her husband would either kill her or hang her, he having a knife in one hand and a rope in the other, and that he had put a rope three times about her neck'. Although this assault had taken place in private, her reported words acted as evidence of his threat to kill his wife on an earlier occasion. Not all the assaults were unwitnessed, however. Anne Bradbury also told of an incident she witnessed directly, in which Marmaduke 'gave his wife diverse strokes with a balke staff of two yards long, and said he would kill her and she said she stood in fear of her life at all times'.

Anne's neighbours took her in when she fled acute attacks and sheltered her from her husband. The day before her murder Anne had gone to neighbour Mary Dolfyn and asked for sanctuary from her husband. Mary later reported that Anne had said that 'she feared her husband would kill her that night, and said that life was sweet and she would faine [like to] save it'. Mary added that Anne had told her that a week before her death Marmaduke had struck her 'over her loins with a ... staff two yards long'. Anne Bradbury confirmed this assault, saying that the day after Anne had come to her door and told her that her wounds were so bad she felt she would die. As well as being told about this abuse, Mary and Anne (and Anne claimed 'several' others) examined her and took note of the bruises.

Her neighbours did try to intervene in what they clearly considered was unwarranted violence. Although a husband could legally beat his wife, his violence was legislatively and collectively policed by the community. A husband's moderate violence could be as open and public as he wished, as it was broadly socially acceptable. A man could legally physically chastise his wife when he chose, for even the mildest infraction,[12] although his violence was always limited by law and by convention. Such rules tended to be subjective and somewhat difficult to enforce, and some studies have shown that early modern husbands could be brutally violent. Nevertheless, husbands could not use unreasonable weapons, and they were not permitted to permanently disable, disfigure or otherwise irreparably harm their wives. They could not legitimately kill them.

Domestic assaults and disharmony were sources of intense theoretical and literary interest in this period. Domestic violence was regularly condemned in print, with husbands repeatedly urged to temper their fists at home. Husbands were required to control their wives, while tyranny was condemned. William Heale defined wife-beaters as 'gangreened members of an unhappy state ... [infecting] the whole Body with such fatal distemper, as will prove mortal and destructive to all human societies.'[13] In an earlier work he had argued domestic violence was neither natural nor necessary and only bad husbands resorted to such tactics.[14] Extreme domestic violence was far from socially acceptable behaviour and was regularly criticised from the pulpit, broadsheet and chapbook.

As wives were considered the spiritual equals of their husbands, his abuse of them was especially criticised. A wife held a prominent position of authority. She could instruct servants and train children, and could legitimately use violence to correct them. She was also the principal consumer of the household, ran a complex budget and assisted her husband in his business matters.[15] Wives were supposed to be obedient to their husbands, but assertive and responsible in the market and often in the household. The tension between a wife as a responsible and somewhat powerful mate and a wife as without rights and a potential victim of domestic assaults was difficult for early modern legal and social theorists to resolve. It was this tension that led to repeated calls for husbands and wives to live in harmony, as well as to intense popular interest in domestic murders.[16]

At the same time, domestic violence had some popular legitimacy and was frequently presented as the only way of controlling so-called unruly women. All violence committed by wives was seen as unacceptable and so popular depictions of assaults by women were confined to shocked prose. However, male violence could also be presented more lightly as comic and amusing. Ballads repeatedly used humour to show wilful women as socially and sexually shaming their husbands. Marriage was depicted as a constant power struggle, in which men had to assert themselves to prevent rebellion from their wives.[17] These tales were told in carnivalesque and overtly humorous ways. They show wives consistently plotting to escape control, subvert male authority and replace it with their own illegitimate rule. In the 'Couragious Anthony' stories, for example, the hapless husband described his life as a subject of his wife:

> She flew in my face and called me a fool,
> Then combed my head with a three legged stool,
> And furnish'd my face with so many sad scratches,
> That for a whole month it was cover'd with patches.[18]

In addition to physical assaults from his wife, Anthony, and other put-upon men in ballads, was forced to perform demeaning feminine chores, like cooking and cleaning. These wives were inverting social hierarchies, assuming power and abusing it.

In 'A Hen Peckt Cuckold', an extremely violent wife forced her husband to do the chores she should have undertaken:

> She makes me to sweep the house
> And dishes to wash also
> And ev'ry foot gives me a Douse,
> It is but a word and a blow.[19]

In the eternal fight for the 'breeches' these literary wives were determined to achieve and maintain power. One female protagonist [20] carefully listed her approach to husband management:

> A husbands a Rampant thing,
> Unless you do keep him low,
> He'l like a mad man fret and fling,
> And never his Duty know.

Later in the ballad she claimed that if he disobeyed her, she would punish him further. She said:

> for I'll get a lusty Rod
> My words they shall be but few,
> But I will Jerk, and sick his cod,
> And make the Rogues Buttocks blew.[21]

In ballads, wives were usually physically able to beat and brawl as often as husbands were. In wielding a 'rod' she was literally taking on masculine genitalia and characteristics. When a wife wrested power, however, her rule was described as overly harsh and even tyrannous. She was often portrayed as worse than any man or husband could be.

These comic projections of the disorder of female rule were didactic. It was clear that these extreme examples of female tyranny were primarily about encouraging men not to allow women to gain any kind of control or authority in the household. Ballads stressed that men were violent because of their wives:

> A good wife makes a husband glad,
> Then let him not distast her,
> But a Scold will make a man turn mad,
> If once she proves his master.[22]

Popular printed tales implied that a good and well controlled wife would make a man's life a joy and the household run smoothly, while a shrewish, adulterous and uncontrolled wife would attempt to (mis)rule her husband and the entire household would suffer. In these stories, a man's domination of his wife was clearly equated to domestic bliss.

The violent repression of wives seen in ballads was often depicted as both funny and somewhat heroic. The men were described as acting in unchar-acteristically violent ways after intense provocation from their wives. In 'Couragious Anthony' Anthony snaps when his wife 'pisses' on him and then calls him a liar. In one ballad, his revenge for this act was a beating with a cudgel of holly in lawful correction. In another version of the same tale, the husband's response was somewhat more extreme: his wife asked him to apply eye drops for her, and he used his own mixture to do so, blinding her. He gleefully said:

> Then blest be the henben and mercury strong;
> That made such a change in my wifes tongue
> For it is a medicine both certain and sure,
> To bee cured of a scold, but I'll say no more.[23]

According to these tales, a put-upon husband could only become a real man again when he physically asserted his masculinity and violently re-pressed his unruly woman. The men who did not periodically act in a dominant and violent manner became fools and cuckolds in literary rep-resentations – portrayed as figures of fun for their fellows and as receiving only contempt from their wives.

Sometimes the desire for dominance over a wife led to murder, and on occasion a husband could use his role as the household head to justify his actions and mitigate his crime. In 1673 in Yorkshire John Holden was forced to explain his violence towards his wife Mary. Several witnesses gave evidence that he had severely beaten his wife in public on the street and that she had died the next day. When John came to be formally accused he claimed that he had been sorely provoked. He said he came home and asked his wife for 6d., but she refused to give him the money and left the house. He pursued her and asked her again, and she hesitated. Thereafter, 'he said he gave her a cuff on the ear ... and she then went away [again] and he had nothing but a piece of bough [available as a weapon] that he took up with which he struck her'. John was claiming that he had legitimately asked her for money, and when she refused that he had rightfully beaten her using the only weapon to hand. Onlooker Susan Brayden described his violence differently. She said that after he had initially hit Mary, she had 'said she would not be killed for sixpence and so she gave it him and he thrashed her sever[er] after then he had done before'. Even when his wife obeyed him his violence did not decrease. John's neighbours contended that he had acted with unnecessary brutality, notwithstanding his protestations of legitimacy.[24]

Despite mixed messages on the acceptability of domestic violence, husbands were seldom allowed to brutalise their wives unchecked. This was an area of widespread concern, with neighbours consistently monitoring husbands to ensure that they did not contravene the limits of their authority. These (mainly female) observers willingly watched for and noted the cause of domestic disputes. They assessed the severity of the wounds inflicted, intervened when they could to prevent the worst of the violence and occasionally allowed beaten women to hide in their homes. Indeed, neighbours successfully controlled abuse and limited the worst excesses of husbands in most cases.[25] These (mostly) women were proactive monitors of other people's homes. They translated any suspicions firstly into gossip and then into evidence in court.

Such diligence means that we now have extraordinary information in many vivid testimonials on the kinds of domestic violence that led up to a wife's death. As death could not be ignored by the courts, and as death from serious physical injuries was often a matter of chance in the early modern period, a cross-section of extreme domestic violence has been recorded. In 1696 in Sheffield, Ann Reynes witnessed Robert Maud beating his wife severely. Ann told the court she had 'heard the said Robert call his said Wife Bitch and bid her get him some meat ready but she did not go about it speedily so he took a staff now showed, and bid her rise or he would be her death'. Ann 'desired him not to strike her his wife with that staff for it was an unreasonable weapon to strike withall'. However, Robert was not deterred and fatally wounded his wife. Ann concluded her testimony by saying she had frequently seen Robert beat his wife and threaten her life.[26]

Wives whose husbands repeatedly beat them had little recourse. Although neighbours could act to ameliorate situations, men simply controlled so many aspects of everyday life that some wives were unable to escape abuse for long. Indeed, in 1678 Mary Wilson told a Halifax court about the drunk John Bicholls' attack on his wife Diana. 'He got her [Diana] by the arm and pulled her up being set on the bedside and let her fall suddenly upon the bed again several times and she prayed him to let her alone she was so full of pain'. Diana had previously run away and hidden with Mary saying that 'she durst not abide in the house without her company', and that her husband had broken two rods upon her back. However, the 'hard usage' Diana suffered did not consist only of physical violence. John periodically refused to allow Diana to come home and would not 'allow her money to buy her coals nor victuals'.[27] Although flight was a well-used and frequently successful tactic, without another source of support Diana's ability to escape was significantly constrained.

Legal separation offered a more long-term solution, but it was a lengthy, expensive and arduous process in which a wife would need to prove excessive violence over a considerable time. In any case, a wife who requested a separation on the grounds of violence could easily be counter-sued with accusations of adultery, and there was no guarantee that a jury would interpret the acts of violence as unwarranted.[28] Establishing that a husband's actions had shifted from legitimate to criminal was far from easy. In Yorkshire in 1658 neighbours testified that Elizabeth Pearson had regularly told them of the abuses she had suffered from her husband. Elizabeth reportedly told Jane Raynes that she was in a 'very sad condition' and detailed a beating she had received after a quarrel about geese, saying that 'if he had given her [Elizabeth] one blow more she thought she had died there at the door'. She then pleaded that she 'durst not' go home. When questioned, Samuell, Elizabeth's husband, denied having beaten her on many occasions, confessing only that 'he gave her a tip with his toe'. A male messenger mirrored Samuell's downplaying of his beating of Elizabeth when he was quoted as commenting (of the wounds that later killed Elizabeth) that 'he thought there was more made of it than it was'.[29] These men, in common with many others, considered their violence to be moderate. In this case even the wife's subsequent death did not convince them otherwise.

Definitively linking male violence to malice could be problematic. The records show that many wife-victims had often reported that their husbands had beaten them. However, violence alone was insufficient to suggest male culpability for murder, as it could be interpreted as spontaneous and so classifiable as manslaughter. In fact, a murderous man had to be defined as especially brutal and as having carefully planned the crime. Although the motivation had to be plain, to successfully characterise such a killer the wife's good character also had to be convincingly presented. Indeed, many stories depicted the (dead) wife as thoroughly obedient, passive and silent, even in the face of extreme attack.[30] In so doing, the husband's brutality was underlined, as the text made it clear that he had in no way been provoked.

Passive wives were especially prominent in printed material. In a 1675 pamphlet George Allen's murder of his estranged wife was described as a killing 'aggravated to the highest degree, by being perpetrated on a poor innocent of the weaker sex, and the nearest relation in the world'. George apparently lured his unnamed wife into a field in Islington and knocked her on the head. No one was surprised by his crime, and his wife's family was recorded as receiving the news of her death at his hands with 'a kind of prophetical apprehension'.[31] She had been specifically constructed in this tale as an archetypal good wife and was presented for public consumption as the perfect victim. She was a bland character, without even her own name. More importantly, she failed to act in any way to save herself from a man she must have mistrusted. In this tale, George was clearly a tyrant, in the face of his wife's sweetness and obedience. His crime would, therefore, have remained unmitigated murder.

The Anne Feales' case was as enmeshed in these concepts of a husband's right to beat his wife as these other tales. Marmaduke was portrayed as persistently unresponsive to the pleas of his neighbours with regard to the treatment of his wife. Although Anne had pleaded for assistance and her neighbours had responded, they had been unable to prevent her death. Thereafter, they did the only thing they could do, and presented a self-consciously piteous tale to avenge her death in court. These neighbours contradicted Marmaduke's convenient tale of Anne having hanged herself by repeating Anne's tales of abuse. Anne Chortley claimed Marmaduke had even boasted to her of beating Anne, saying 'from the crown of the head to the sole of the foot I have not left one [unbruised] spot on her'. Anne was presented as a good, silent and much abused wife who had endured her suffering well, had only asked for moderate and necessary assistance, and had always returned to her husband when she could. She was repeatedly depicted as being completely unable to help herself or to avert her subsequent death. One deponent described her as appealing to all her neighbours for help and as pleading with Anne Bradbury's husband, saying 'unto him you are the man that must save my life, or else I die'.[32] Anne's neighbours described her as a helpless victim of Marmaduke's extreme behaviour. She was repackaged in death as the ultimate, virtuous and undeserving victim.

Such wives needed to be presented as undeserving of violence if a husband's protestation of provocation was to be nullified. Although women in depositions had more rounded characters than those appearing in print, witnesses were still keen to depict assaulted wives as blameless. Passivity was perceived as a natural role for women as it fitted well with prescriptive notions. Natalie Davies has argued that fear was a language very much available to wives, as it mirrored prescriptive notions of women as passive non-agents.[33] So although the victims of mortal violence did passively resist their husbands in an acceptably feminine manner, by temporarily running away and pleading for help, they were not described as actively avoiding harm.

Many similar testimonies aimed to convey impressions of innocence.

Repeatedly, witnesses implied that a beaten wife had acted to defend her husband from prosecution or censure. When Edithe Jagger died in 1653 Alice Ambler clearly told of her sister's abuse. Alice claimed to speak on her sister's behalf and with her explicit authority, reporting Edithe as saying that her husband took her to Colely Milne at night hitting her 'with scuttles and his hands and feet and knocking her down over 40 times'. Edithe told her sister of the incident, but remained with her husband.

However, Edithe also ensured that her sister understood that she was loyal to her husband, unless he crossed the crucial line bounding her loyalty and killed her. Alice claimed Edithe:

> wished her [Alice] not to speak of it to him [her husband] so long as she was alive for if she did he would strike her again and kill her to which she replied and said he deserves a Rope, but her sister ... wished her to let him alone until such times as she was dead.[34]

Despite her husband's consistent brutality, Edithe had acted in a dutiful and selfless manner and tried to protect him from the law. When she reportedly instructed her sister not to accuse her husband 'until such time as she was dead', she was being depicted as a woman terrified of further assault but placing her duty before inappropriate ideas of revenge. She accepted her husband's everyday brutality but wanted to ensure that unwarranted and unlawful violence was properly punished. However, there was another reason for her reticence. If she had spoken out and then had not died, she could have been suspected of shrewishness and thus of deserving her beating. Only the passive presentation in her sister's deposition would have been appropriate and suggestively potent enough in court, especially when linked to her death, for her husband to be effectively condemned for his brutality. He may not receive a murder conviction, but the chances of some sort of conviction would certainly be better.

In these scenarios of domestic danger a good wife made a compelling and dramatic victim. A stoic acceptance of husbandly violence could easily be seen as virtuous and godly. A victim presented as being dutiful would have made a favourable impact on early modern communities, as a saintly woman and a martyr to wifely values. Such tales had the moral authority to multiply exponentially the horror and disorder of the husband's assaults. With the exception of children, abused wives were treated far more sympathetically than other dependants in this period. Indeed, early modern audiences were quite receptive to narratives of defenceless and wronged wives. The bond of matrimony was very difficult to break, making the abused wife a poignant figure, as little could be done to help her against a truly intransigent man.

Katherine Sprackling was abused over a period of twenty years by a drunken husband in Thanet in Kent. According to a printed record, in 1653 Adam Sprackling had his servant tied up and 'Then he began to rage against his wife, who sate quietly there: her words to him were full of loving and sweet expressions; but he on a sudden drew his Dagger and struck her with it on the face'.[35] He tormented her all night before finally killing her, apparently enjoying inflicting the abuse. He was convicted and later executed with 2000 people in attendance. But it was not his actions alone that were the focus of the story; rather, his wife's extreme obedience was the main interest of the text – albeit depicted to demonise his violence. She, not he, was the deciding factor in the audience's decisions about his violence. Her suffering was saintly and appropriately feminine, and it was this that prevented his actions being portrayed as legitimate.

The stories told by proactive neighbours induced sympathy for wives, which dependants (other than young children) otherwise seldom received. Without the extensive narrative efforts of opposing witnesses a husband could easily construct a tale in which he was justified or highly provoked. When John Brunton killed his wife in Leeds in 1647 he argued that his wife had repeatedly attacked him one night and that he had killed her to save his own life. John claimed that his wife had:

> drunk with a soldier all the day until night then until the middle of the night after which at the same time she went with the said soldier into a house where nobody dwelt where they continued so long as they both well liked yet upon the next day his wife came home again.

John's wife was far from the innocent and passive wife Anne Feales. He claimed his wife was so violent he was forced to throw her out of the house twice. When she returned for the third time he claimed that she 'broke open the door with a hedge stake ... and fell upon him and pulled him down to the ground by the hair of the head'. At this point, John stated that he reached out, picked up a random object and struck his wife on the head. The implication was that he had not intended to harm her and had, in fact, tried to integrate her back into the household. It was her disorderliness that prevented him being successful. Strikingly, neighbours concurred with his version of events, with one adding that his wife gave John 'very bad language'.[36] No one was willing to tell a different tale, and so John's words stood uncontested.

Killings by husbands and wives were sources of voyeuristic interest in this period. Neighbours and strangers were eager to learn the details of a conflict and the method of the attack. Domestic violence of this kind was interesting because those involved were familiar figures. Most people had some experience of a marital partnership – either their own, their neighbours or their parents. Many may also have known couples where there was violence. The conjugal couple was at the centre of early modern society and everyday experience. People were interested in the violence and passions within. However, there was no sexual equality in stories of domestic violence. Male violence was frequently permissible while female violence was not. Each of the parties was defined by specific rules and associations; each was given gender-appropriate public identities which framed their stories in court. This was the ultimate battle of the sexes and men were always supposed to win. Early modern communities disapproved of male violence and censured it publicly and criminally, but it also defined their concepts of order. As such, male dominance, even when expressed physically, was always preferable to any kind of female disobedience.

Women were far less constrained when they played roles other than wives. Prescriptive texts emphasised silence and passivity as ideals for wives to pursue, but other women could be proactive and could speak publicly and forcefully. Of course, there was always a gap between prescriptive demands and the every day reality of being a woman. The neighbours who spoke out in court were usually women, who not only took an active interest in policing the households of their neighbours, but were determined to be the ones to stop violence or prosecute a crime. They did not rely on their husbands to act, despite the fact that in most cases they too were wives and supposedly as tightly bound by the prescriptive limits of passivity and silence.

6

Disrupted Households

In 1677 Hester Que accidentally killed herself. She fell to her death while trying to escape a violent beating from her mistress.[1] Although most households were orderly and peaceful, on occasion they could be disruptive and unpleasant places to live in and very difficult to leave. This was not just the case for wives with violent husbands, but for a whole range of other household members. The duties and responsibilities of the household went far beyond the central conjugal couple, despite early modern preoccupations with the relationship and behaviour of this pair.

Any kind of abuse of power or lack of appropriate deference caused communal disquiet in this period. Indeed, notwithstanding the accidental nature of her death, Hester's neighbours spoke out to ensure that her mistress's role in her death was thoroughly investigated. No crime had been committed and yet the actions leading up to Hester's death were a source of avid local discussion and eventually a public court case. Although a death could not always be prevented, many neighbours would be keen to posthumously defend the abused servant. Masters and mistresses, as well as being in charge in their household, were bound by broader duties of care; they were responsible for policing their homes, but they were not expected to act unfairly or abuse their subordinates excessively. A coroner's inquisition decided that Hester had fallen because she was 'in great fear and terror of mind, to avoid the cruel usage and violent beating of her said Mistress Jane Shute'. This was not explicitly defined as a crime, and we have no evidence that Jane Shute was ever prosecuted for her actions. However, as the case was discussed before the coroner, the resulting public attention and criticism would have been humiliating in the extreme. Of course, this was the reason her neighbours had spoken. They could not change her actions, but they could be relied upon to publicly expose them.

One witness reported that two weeks before her death Hester had told him of her terror. She claimed her mistress had beaten her with an iron rod 'because she had not cleaned the house so clean as she would have it'. She then pleaded with a male neighbour for assistance, saying 'she wanted food and came to him for relief and that she would not go home to her mistress for that she laid rods in piss for her'. In total, ten women testified to the court concerning the violence Hester suffered. Jane Shute was being publicly labelled as cruel and extreme. One witness said that:

> Hester Ques mistress did cruelly beat her till her head was soft with blows and her Mistress whipped her with several rods and that she was black and blue and that she kicked her and pinched her and heard such screeches from her as would pierce ones heart.

The witnesses were unwilling to see such a cruel woman escape public censure. Despite their clear knowledge of her suffering, they had not intervened to prevent Hester's death. However, these neighbours were galvanised into action by her suicide. They attributed her despair – a mortal sin – to her mistress's abuse and they used their evidence to ensure that everyone knew about the latter's tyranny.

Lawrence Stone famously punned that the family who slays together, stays together.[2] However, in early modern England an individual was in more danger from family members than from strangers. Fellow householders, friends and neighbours were in day-to-day contact, and most lived happily and peacefully with their peers. Nevertheless, these friends and acquaintances constituted the greatest threat to any individual's life and limb. Whether through accident, rough play or malice, neighbours and fellow household members represented as much of a danger in the past as family members do today. Those one prayed and played with were the most likely to assault, injure and even slay.

At the same time, the household was the basic social group of early modern society. Groups of households, rather than of individuals, made up communities. Most of these units were peaceful, orderly and non-violent. In fact, households were prescribed as regulatory systems for broader society. Communities were expected to police and order themselves, under the broad umbrella of state control and national law. They did so by placing the responsibility for domestic order on the prime male of the household, the husband and the master. It was collections of households that made up the wider state, and so their order in theory directly affected the stability of the nation. At its most basic form, a household centred on the conjugal couple – the husband and wife. However, it always encompassed more than this pair, and its meaning in this period frequently diverged from more modern conceptions of 'the family'. In addition to family members, the household also included servants and apprentices (who may or may not have been related) and other live-in dependants. It was a social and domestic unit of people linked by proximity and by loyalty.

In many ways the household was a physical space, defined by the walls and area of the home in which all members lived. However, its meaning was always broader than this. Individuals represented their household when they acted publicly. The maidservant who was shamed for fornication spread her shame to the master and mistress who had failed to police her activities and who were responsible for her misbehaviour in a more direct way than her biological family. Every act committed by a member of a household reflected the order and status of the broader unit. Wherever the disorderly act occurred and whoever was directly responsible, blame could simply be transferred to the conjugal couple and be used to diminish their standing. While in theory the master was responsible for all those within his household, with the right to physically correct those subject to him came a duty to keep order, prevent sin and crime and morally instruct those he dominated. Orderly household members could be a credit to the master and mistress, but the disgrace of misbehaviour threatened the household and the community and so ensured the constant vigilance of the conjugal couple.

The household was never exclusively private. As the prime social building block of society, its members were policed by other households and its legitimacy, potency and authority were criticised or upheld by those who existed outside in other households. The home was never considered to be a private space purely for the family. It often doubled as a workshop, and a proportion operated as unlicensed alehouses for neighbours and strangers alike. Hospitality also dictated that food, rest and assistance be offered freely to those in need, although this was by no means an obligation always fulfilled in this period.

The entire household was as enmeshed in the interplay of power, rights and duties as married couples were. On many levels the hierarchies of power and deference were clear. Both the master/father and mistress/mother were forces of order in the home and were owed allegiance by servants, children and sometimes even elderly parents. The central couple had authority over those lower in the hierarchy as well as a duty to maintain order. But despite this clear hierarchy, the household was neither static nor stable. In fact, servants were disproportionately suspected of resentment and of violence. The fear of rebellion underlay discourses of household power, with servants constantly suspected of planning secret assaults on their superiors. This interplay of rebellion and control dominated interaction within households, and was carefully monitored by outsiders. A disorderly household threatened to disrupt the community and thus the state. While a master's authority had to be upheld, tyranny could not be tolerated. In the century in which national rebellion led to the king being executed and the monarchical line being disrupted, the discourse of fair rule and passive obedience had particular resonance.

Masters had the most genuine authority in the household, but they were by no means the only individuals with access to legitimate power in this context. Although subservient to her husband, a woman had power as mistress and as mother. In a large number of households, women had sole authority. These 'master-less' homes caused prescriptive disquiet, but they should not therefore be seen as disorderly. Women successfully exercised authority in the household every day, despite the fact that a wife was always considered to be less able to order the home as she was a victim of her sex. Women were generally considered to be unable to control power equitably. They were commonly believed to be prone to unfairly treating those subject to them. Female sexuality held further dangers for the household. Mistresses were felt to be vulnerable to sexual overtures from male servants and so could endanger the family by cuckolding their husbands. Although the mistress held a powerful position in the home, her role was frequently questioned. Female servants were likewise considered untrustworthy, forming a sexual danger to the home in relation to potential liaisons within the household and without. Their actions directly reflected on their mistresses and the reputation of the entire household.

Responsibility and duty did not just apply to those lower down the hierarchy. As the Hester Que case showed, masters and mistresses were expected to take care of their servants and to police them, but never exploit or abuse them. This balance of responsibility was the same as that expected of a husband and even of the monarch (especially during and after the civil wars of the seventeenth century). Their superiority and rule was predicated on their fairness. Tyranny undermined this rule and even legitimated revolution. However, this philosophy always had limitations. Even in the face of a tyrannous husband, a wife would not be allowed to kill or assault him in any way; in fact, she could not even legally flee. Servants were more protected. Unlike wives they had legal redress and an avenue of escape, even if those like Hester Que did not or could not use it.

Indeed, servants had several sources of potential protection from unscrupulous and abusive employers. They were under the protection of their family but also neighbours and guilds. Most local people were interested in what went on in their community. They felt it was their business to monitor other homes for any signs of wrongdoing or disorder. This meant they diligently watched for the abuse of servants. Family members and neighbours alike could intervene informally to request moderation if they felt a master was acting abusively. This was a delicate balance as masters and mistresses were supposedly the monarchs of their own homes and so should have been able to train and chastise their servants as they wished. As these informal efforts were seldom recorded, it is difficult to assess how widespread the problem of abuse was or how effective the informal intervention of family and neighbours could be. However, as with wives, the law stated that a servant could not be abused unreasonably, nor could they be permanently disabled or killed by any form of 'correction'.

If the concerns of neighbours were not heeded and the abuse continued, the community could act more formally to chastise the master or mistress and demand they act more reasonably. The case could be taken to the guild or it could be prosecuted in court. These were extreme actions that many were loath to take though. Neighbours put off pursuing formal proceedings, as did servants. Informal measures would have been pursued for some time as no one would have wanted to unnecessarily disrupt the household. In extreme cases servants could petition to break the contract that bound them to their master. However everyone, including the courts, was keen to maintain the status quo and preserve the bonds of the household where possible; and it was likely that the abused servant would be sent back to the abusive home after the master had been censured.[3]

It was the youngest, weakest and lowest members of the household hierarchy that were most often at risk. Unlike older, male servants, young boys and maidservants were often unable to defend themselves and deflect violent abuse. They lacked the physical strength of older male servants and would have found it difficult to individually deter a master. They were also less independent and may have felt more constrained by notions of the passive behaviour appropriate to them. Servants had few rights beyond the amorphous right not to be excessively abused or injured. At the same time, as with the beating of wives, it was difficult for neighbours and guilds to judge whether a beating was reasonable or excessive. Often the distinction depended purely on opinion. Therefore the law offered little practical relief from all but the very worst and most deadly of beatings – small comfort to the (dead) servant involved.

As with the Hester Que case, John Dokeson's family complained of excessive violence when John died in 1681. They argued that John's master, James Shemeild, had deliberately killed him. John's stepmother, Sarah Parkin, said that John had told her that James had beaten him:

> very cruelly several other Times particularly That he beat him once with a knotted rope up and down the chamber where he wrought: Another Time he beat him with a Lath, That had a nail in it, which made Two holes in his head, and two in his arm.

John said the bruises from this beating were so bad that 'he must feel his punches on his Belly, while he lives in this world'.[4] This young man would not have been expected to defend himself. Social convention dictated that his master had a right to punish him, and he a duty not to retaliate but to obey, endure and persevere. An older servant may well have hit back, leading to a fight between men of similar age, physical strength and inclination. He could have been heavily censured for his act, but in many ways his master would expect such behaviour. Developing and displaying a violent masculinity were facets of growing up for boys. As they got older, the risk of a violent response would have increased. Despite being theoretically inappropriate, such actions were largely expected and to an extent tolerated. However, the pervasive subtext to descriptions of assaults on young servants would be that they had no way of hitting back or protecting themselves from harm.

We must be constantly aware that mistresses and masters had positions of overwhelming legitimacy when it came to beating their servants. They could easily defend their violence by arguing that the servant had been disobedient and disrespectful. Nevertheless, when these authority figures killed, their act was never as feared as that of a treasonous servant. As their violence was acceptable to a degree, it was more difficult to wholeheartedly condemn. In 1729 Charles Jackson defended his actions as reasonable when he killed his servant James Browne. Charles was reportedly a victim of terrible bouts of melancholy, which may have influenced his actions, but he still spoke of being angered as a master by his servant's actions. He said 'some language fell from the said Browne to him ... which was not pleasing to him'. Charles further added that otherwise they 'loved each other well because they frequently took tobacco together'.[5]

These attitudes were well ingrained in early modern society. Cornett Ereskine's claim that his servant was wilful and unpleasant was actually supported by another servant who witnessed the exchange. Henry Wakefield was a good and obedient servant who appeared shocked by the extremity of John Deane's misbehaviour. He said John quarrelled with his master and:

> seemed very abusive of his master, that the said Cornett thereupon declared, that to prevent his said servants doing any further mischief that night, he would put him to bed and tie him down, and ordered him to fetch a cord, which he did.

While Henry was elsewhere, Cornett claimed he had accidentally mortally injured John. However, from his deathbed, John told a very different tale, arguing that he had been unsuccessful in evading his violent master. John did not believe his lateness, rudeness or drunkenness were appropriate reasons for such severe violence.[6]

Stories of violent employers were not only linked to men. Very occasionally certain women were also identified as powerful and as violent in household murder stories. In theory, masters and mistresses were jointly responsible for all the lesser members of the hierarchy. However, in practice, power was divided along gendered lines, with wives/mistresses primarily responsible for the actions of female servants and the husband/master for male.[7] This was the only time that women had legitimate access to power and to acceptable narratives of violence. As with husbands, a mistress's chastisements were theoretically limited only by convention and the monitoring of neighbours. However, women never had the same freedom as men to act violently as their violence was associated with the abuse of authority. They were seen as unsuited to power and innately unjust. Nevertheless, women did successfully exercise power and threatened, coerced and beat their servants and their children as part of their everyday lives. Again, despite my focus on disorder, the vast majority of these women did not kill or maim but exercised power equitably.

As a mistress had a similar kind of authority over the servant as the master, and had the legal right to correct them, the same kinds of narratives applied to their violence as to those of their husbands. Mistresses lost their passive, victimised gender identity that they had as wives and daughters when they took on a more powerful and responsible role. Indeed, masters and mistresses could be portrayed as acting in unison, with no distinctions made between their merged identities. In 1646 a 'poor friendless boy (about twelve years of age)' was cruelly tortured with whips of wire by his master, Miles Lewis, and his wife.[8] The couple was of good reputation, but reportedly treated the apprentice badly from the start. In addition to beating him severely, they limited his food and gave him hard and unreasonable work.[9] Friends of Margarett Colling also complained of excessive treatment when they told a Yorkshire court that she had been severely beaten by her mistress while very sick, and that her master, Robert Blow, had repeatedly tried to ravish her. After hearing reported evidence from Margarett's friend of her misuse, and after viewing her bruised and black body, the coroner's jury concurred with them that both master and mistress were culpable.[10]

Female cruelty was more apparent when women acted alone. Mistresses were especially responsible for their female servants' sexual behaviour and reputation, as well as controlling their other social relationships.[11] After all, a misbehaving female servant could significantly affect her mistress's local standing. Susan Duffin beat her servant Thomasin Robinson while she lay in bed (possibly pregnant or recovering from childbirth). When she died two hours later neighbours were unsure of the exact cause of her death, but were angry at the extremity of Susan's behaviour. Susan had entered the house where her servant lay 'went into the room where the said Thomasin lay sick in bed and said she would have her pennyworth of her and then fell a beating the said Thomasin with her hands.' Elizabeth Bartheby watched as Susan struck Thomasin and later said she repeatedly hit her about the head and face with her hands. Then she took up a staff and 'hit her across the body and with violence of the stroke the chirnstaffe broke but she did it so suddenly she had not time to prevent her'. Although Elizabeth stood by and did nothing when Susan used her fists on the prone and sick servant, when the mistress used a wooden staff she was shocked enough to want to intervene.[12] This violence was entirely feminine. The protagonists were female and their violence was publicly described by other women.

These images of female violence could be exaggerated in print since pamphlets particularly emphasised cases of outlandish women. Violent women were nearly always depicted in simple terms as excessively cruel, and despite their legitimate authority in these cases, their violence was seldom mitigated. When an unnamed London scalemaker's wife was portrayed attempting to murder her servant, her behaviour was shown as larger than life, and even carnivalesque, in its illegitimacy. The wife was far from a good wife or mistress. The author defined her character simply, saying 'she was of light carriage, and used to frequent Taverns and Playhouses'. The implication was that she was an entirely inappropriate wife who drank and was probably conducting a number of illicit affairs. Her husband was said to be a good man, but he was not in control of her, and she was unruly and licentious. Her apprentice had reportedly seen her in a 'suspected' house and had told his master. The wife fobbed him off with a story about visiting the sick, but when he husband left again she turned her wrath on the boy: 'Sirrah, said she, I will make you an example to all telltales ... [and that] he should die the cruellest death that ever could be thought of, or devised'.[13] The wife, using two male friends (probably her lovers), stripped the boy, bound him to a spit, stopped his mouth and roasted him over a fire. Fortunately, he pushed the gag out and cried for help before he could be killed. In her unruly sexuality, her defiance of her husband and the wickedness of her attempt to kill him, this mistress was marked out as especially and uniquely femininely wicked. She was the ultimate unruly woman, in that her limited domestic power was blatantly misused.

Despite the intensely hierarchical and prescriptive structures which supposedly enforced order, dependants were quite widely feared. They may have lacked real power, but for many a dependant's lack of social power was inversely proportional to their perceived threat. That household members were prescriptively subservient did not prevent them from being threatening in narratives as the dominated were depicted as violently resentful of their status. Conflicting stories were told in court and in print about the relative dangers of household rebellion and domestic violence.

While some pamphlets told disproportionate tales of dangerous inferiors, session papers and deponents told of excessive correction and abuse. This was a society obsessed with notions of order, with elaborate rules and conventions dictating everyday conduct and duties of deference. Such concern was constantly overshadowed by a spectre of disorder, and the disruption of carefully delineated duties and responsibilities was pervasively feared. The real bogeymen of early modern thought were those who undermined order and spread chaos: however provoked, whatever their good reasons for acting so, their defiance of authority was a threat to all. This threat was therefore heavily legislated against.

In early modern terms the most feared betrayal was that which came from within the household – a secret attack from a hidden and unexpected assassin. This tension was largely played out in the drama of the central couple, but fear of disorder embraced the whole social unit. Servants were widely perceived as resentful of their subordinate role. All who were prescribed to defer to the master could offer a potential threat if they managed to express their true feelings and kill those with power over them. Wives and maidservants were repeatedly suspected of trying to poison the master and it was feared they would use their domestic duty, the provision of food, to kill him unawares. Male servants were suspected of acting secretly to seduce the master's wife, cuckolding him. A popular murder scenario of the time saw the mistress persuaded by her journeyman-lover to murder her husband and then to marry him. In this way he killed his rival and usurped the business, increasing his own social status as a result. There is little evidence of either significant numbers of poisonings or of killings by wives and their lovers. Nevertheless, the suspicion of betrayal underlay most domestic relationships, as the stories of perfidy amongst household members persisted in the consciousness of this society.

The most scandalous tales of violence in this period were those that inverted prescriptive ideas of order. The socially powerless were consistently feared. Although an unruly master or (especially) mistress could be seen as wicked, a servant who killed a superior was acting treasonously. There was little sympathy for such wicked malefactors, as a rebellious servant broke a sacred trust and obligation when he chose to be disobedient. Servants who killed their master were guilty of petty treason. This alone was enough to condemn most, with little interest displayed in explanations.

Servants were always more likely to be killed than to kill, despite this cultural focus on their resentful and dangerous natures. Indeed, apart from cases of poisoning or hidden assaults, few killings fit the narrative of the resentful and untrustworthy servant who acted secretly. Nevertheless, such stereotypes were frequently repeated. One of the most popular involved a (male) servant who was seduced by a 'whore' with whom he consequently planned to rob and kill members of their household. Thomas Savage's assault on his home and murder of a fellow servant provides an excellent example of this kind of perfidious story. Thomas was tried at the Old Bailey in October 1668. His crime was subsequently described in print, where he was publicly labelled the 'bloody apprentice'. Thomas was described as 'blinded by lust', which incited him to rob his master's house. The cunning and perfidy of his crime had a feminine source: the story declared that he was 'deluded thereunto by the instigations of a whore'. Thomas had come from a good family and had been gradually tempted into wrongdoing. He had been made wicked by circumstance. However, the whore was described as purely and unambiguously (and perhaps even naturally) wicked. The pamphleteer said she 'seldom leaves a man till she hath brought him either to the hospital or the Gallows'.[14]

Thomas's crime was the main focus of this account, since the woman's wickedness was viewed as devilish temptation rather than action. Thomas actually committed two crimes – burglary and murder – but they were seen as intimately connected. He entered his master's house at night with the intention of stealing his goods. When a maidservant questioned his activities she was killed with a hammer, although she managed to accuse Thomas with her dying breath. He was quickly captured with the money he had stolen. As both a thief and a murderer his perfidy was complete. Although the family had been previously unaware of his resentment, he had struck them a terrible blow. It was this kind of potential danger from servants that many feared.

This was a terrible crime, but it was not representative of violence in the household: most was violence between two men and was viewed as natural and normal, unless differences in status were apparent. Indeed, most battles of dominance between male servants and their male masters can be seen as extensions of the workplace conflicts that were a common feature of early modern masculinity. Although still far from permissible, conflicts were often about reordering the workplace and defining power and position. In these cases, male servants were far from helpless. Isaac Lister reacted ex-cessively to a taunt from his master, William Robinson, in 1724 in Yorkshire. Isaac quarrelled with his master while at work and in front of other tailors. William threatened to strike Isaac to make him be quiet, and threw his shears 'moderately' at him. This enraged Isaac, who responded by 'threw[ing] them back with great violence'.[15] As in other all-male conflicts, although the fight was unequal it was uncommon for either man to be defined as passive or unwilling to fight.

Age, maturity and social position dramatically effected how violence was considered by contemporaries, if not the courts. Indeed, in narrative terms, it was difficult to describe an adult male as a helpless victim. Older men were expected to fight back, even though they were subject to the same duties of obedience and acquiescence as young boys and girls. Violence was entirely appropriate to their gender and to their nascent position in society. They would one day become masters themselves, so it was to be expected that they would want to assert their social and physical muscles.

Occasionally a case appeared in court in which passivity was linked to an adult male servant. In these cases, collective presentations were made of past abuses, similar to those used by the neighbours of murdered wives. However, these tales were told less frequently as such narratives sat uneasily with contemporary views of adult male masculinity, making these stories unconvincing. In 1669 ship's mate Samuel Hogg was frequently thrown off the ship by his master Thomas West, before being finally thrown overboard and killed in waters outside Limerick. Three witnesses told of Thomas's repeated assaults on Samuel, from which the crew repeatedly rescued the unfortunate Samuel. They deposed that Thomas:

> drew his knife and swore he would cut off the nose of the said Samuel Hogg or slit it ... and so abused him that he was not able to abide in the same ship but was forced to leave the ship and for his safety went on board a London ship.

Samuel was described throughout as a loyal servant who had patiently born his master's excessive abuse. Samuel fled only when his life was put in very real danger, and he returned to his fulfil his duty onboard the ship when the 'masters fury was over'. Samuel was finally killed a few weeks later, after another argument and further threats. Despite the master's declaration that Samuel was drunk and had fallen accidentally, the history of unfair treatment and unreasonable assaults indicated foul play may have occurred.[16] Nevertheless, Samuel's passivity was strange as his behaviour was unlike that of most adult men. This may well have been questioned in court.

Violent assault by a servant was never really permissible. Servants were an integral part of early modern households and were tied to their masters with firm bonds of mutual obligation.[17] In prescriptive terms, servants were more subject to a master's and mistress's authority than to their biological families. The master and mistress were responsible for them and for their mistakes. Servants and apprentices lived at close quarters with their masters and intimately interacted with them and their businesses. Theirs was an ambiguous role, as both subject to their masters and vital to the household economy. Like an unruly wife, their misdeeds could greatly impact upon the household tarnishing reputations and providing a source of destructive gossip.[18] These intimate workers protected their employers from menaces, while also representing a significant threat to everyday financial and sexual order. The balance of power shifted in response to the age and skill of the servants themselves. It was also gendered with dramatic variations in the potency and narrative identities of male and female dependants.

Older male servants may have been clearly identified with violence, but it was not acceptable for them to assault their master. They were neither expected to endure abuse nor to physically remedy it. Rather, their physical presence and their invaluable role in the running of the business should have been enough to deter any violence. A servant in dire straits because of the violence of a master or mistress – whether young, old, male or female – would be expected to rely on the intervention of neighbours or the guild to defend them from intransigent violence. Violent men may have been a fact of life, but their behaviour was not acceptable. Their violence was always criticised, albeit sometimes excused by whatever circumstances they had endured.

Even the most passive members of a household would have been subject to suspicion and have their behaviour monitored. Young female servants, for example, were seldom a physical threat to other household members. Young women were more often associated with the wicked but passive killings of newborns. The illicit sexuality such an act was intended to conceal could severely damage the local standing of the whole family unit, and question the role of the mistress. However, young women were seldom a physical threat to family safety: their violence was usually aimed at themselves or at the infant who was evidence of their misconduct. These women had their sexual activity monitored due to the threat it potentially posed to the household and reputations of their superiors.

Any assault by a servant on their master or mistress was technically petty treason. Like wives, servants were supposed to endure mistreatment. However, unlike wives, they could leave the household if they could no longer stand the abuse. Although both were bound by contract and obligation, servants were able to dissolve their tie to a master and take up employment elsewhere. This could be difficult and require strength of character and familial, economic and emotional support, but the possibility of dissolution underlay all such agreements. Marriage was never considered to be imper-manent. Divorce was impossible and the duties and responsibilities of both parties remained constant. The servant-and-master relationship was fun-damental to the social system, but designed to be finite and constantly in flux. After all, servants could eventually become masters or mistresses in their own right. Patriarchy was predicated, however, on the relations between wives and husbands remaining unchanged, with husbands in ascendance. With all these options available to them, servants who chose to kill received little sympathy. This is not to say that wives were permitted to harm their husbands, but on (very rare) occasion sympathy could be expressed for their unenviable and unending role as a victim of an abusive and intransigent man.

Servants by no means always directed their violence towards their employers. Not all violence was treasonous or regulated by complex conventions of duty and obedience. Servants frequently clashed with each other, but in these cases the special crime of treasonous murder was obviously not applicable. Although often not closely related, servants were in the position of siblings in the hierarchy of the household, and their violent responses to each other were part of a larger tapestry of household relations. Even here, gender dynamics defined primary relationships. In 1689 Richard Rawsby killed Elizabeth Huggit with an axe because she refused to obey his commands. Richard demanded that Elizabeth prepare his dinner, but she countered by asking him to assist her with a calf first. When he insisted on his authority, she apparently boxed his ears. This behaviour was unacceptable to Richard. He picked up an axe and hit her with it several times. Unlike the wives described earlier, Elizabeth had no duty to obey Richard, and his authority to instruct her to act was certainly unclear.[19] However, even without the legitimacy that existed in other relationships of subservience, popular attitudes towards gender structured and defined this and other interpersonal household relations.

Danger could also come from accidents or from rough play. Servants often had access to weapons that they had little control over, and could cause death by misadventure. In most cases, the court would decide that the action had been unfortunate. However, even young children had to be examined in court to decide whether they had acted with malice or without intent. William Blaynners accidentally killed his fellow young servant Mary Jackson when he toyed with a fowling piece. He said 'as he was pulling the cock up it slipped from him ... [and] it went off'. When he saw that Mary had been hit, he ran from the house terrified by the consequences of his act.[20] Likewise, in Cumberland in 1671 John Wildrish explained his violence towards a fellow servant by saying that they had quarrelled 'and cursed several times and being both drunk with Brandy'. Unlike most other defendants, he tried to further excuse his actions by claiming that 'he was so drunk that he was not sensible of what he did'.[21] His action would not have been excused but the court, and the community, would have clearly understood the context of the battle, and may have limited his culpability for the act to manslaughter.

Servants could be legitimately violent on occasion as long as it was not directed at their household superiors, especially if the violence was part of their duty to defend the household from strangers and malefactors. In fact, the defence of the property of the household was part of a servant's general social obligation. The act of protection was about more than defending wealth; it was also about reinforcing the inviolate power of the household unit. The violent defence of property asserted their master's right to own things unmolested as well as protecting the goods themselves. Most such conflicts would have concluded without injury of any kind. However, those we can easily access involved court action because of an unnatural death. Even so, the courts would have been somewhat sympathetic. The jury was made up of land-holding males who would clearly relate to the need to police and protect property and the household's good name.

Indeed, in 1654 when several male servants engaged in a lengthy running battle with several self-proclaimed yeomen, their acts can be seen in this broader protective manner. Groom John Lapidge was accused of striking George Wood with a blunt instrument and causing his death. The tale told in a myriad of depositions was, however, of a series of running battles involving staff members and several young men, whom Lapidge and his fellow servants believed were encroaching on their master's property, using his resources, and possibly poaching on his land. Such an encroachment could not be permitted if local credibility and authority were to be maintained.[22] One servant said to another, 'John you must go home to the well, Swan the housekeeper hath sent me for you For there is hunters come into the house and they are unruly'. Other servants confirmed that the men had arrived uninvited, were noisy, demanded beer, and claimed that they had called back Lapidge and two other male servants from the village to defend the household. However, the potentially poaching yeomen said they had been invited in by the housekeeper to drink beer when three men attacked them and caused Wood's death. Perceptions of the rights and duties of the two parties (or at least in the stories told in court) were obviously seriously at odds.[23]

Although the tensions between husbands and wives, masters and servants formed the main constituents of communal concerns with household disorder, household violence had other manifestations. Tensions, duties and responsibilities were elements in a number of other instances of disorder. Children were instructed in their duty to their parents by social convention and biblical command. Parents were expected to strictly instruct and police their children to ensure their orderly conduct before they reached adulthood. However, as children grew, their relationships to power, authority and obligation shifted. When a son came of age his duty to his parent remained, but his obligations had often fragmented. Most sons would become a servant or apprentice (with new obligations), and then, when independent, his own

A Horrible Creuel and bloudy Murther,
Committed at Putney in Surrey on the 21. of
Aprill laſt, 1614, *being thurſday, upon the body*
of Edward Hall *a Miller of the ſame pariſh,*
Done by the hands of *Iohn Selling, Peeter Pet* and *Edward Streater,*
his ſeruants to the ſaid *Hall,* each of them giuing
him a deadly blow (as he lay ſleeping)
with a Pickax.

Publiſhed by Authority.

1. A Horrible, Creuel and bloudy Murther, Committed at Putney in Surrey, 1614. (*Bodleian Library, Oxford*)

Murther, Murther:

Or,

A b'oody Relation how *Anne Hamton,*
dwelling in Wetiminiter nigh London, by
poyfon murthered her deare husband Sept.
1641. being affifted and counfelled
thereunto by *Margeret Harwood.*

For which they were both committed
to Gaole, and at this tyme wait
for a tryall.

Women love your owne husbands as Chrift doth the Church.

Printed at London for *Tho: Bates,* 1641.

6. Murther, Murther: or A bloody Relation how Anne Hamton … by poison murthered her deare husband, 1641. (*British Library*)

A true Relation of a barbarous and most cruell Murther,

mitted by one Enoch ap Euan, *who cut off his owne* naturall *Mothers* Head*, and his Brothers.*

The cause wherefore he did this most execrable Act: most remarkeable the warning of others; with his Condemnation and Execution

VVith certaine pregnant Inducements, both Diuine and Morall, to Men from the horrible practice of Murther and Man-slaughter,

Ouid. Fast: Lib. 2.
Ah nimium faciles, qui tristia crimina cædis
Fluminea tolli, posse putatis aqua.

LONDON,
Printed by *Nicholas Okes.* 1633.

---

7. A true relation of a barbarous and most cruell Murther, committed by one Enoch ap Evan, 1633. (*Folger Shakespeare Library*)

8. William Hogarth (1697–1764), 'Cruelty in Perfection', 1751. Tom Nero being apprehended in a country churchyard, where he has just murdered Ann Gill, whose body lies on the ground. Around her are watches and other objects which Tom has persuaded her to steal. A figure to the left of the murderer holds the knife used to kill her. Above, an owl and a bat fly across the night sky.

man. A daughter, however, shifted from her father's authority to that of her husband. When children married, they entered different households with new relationships of authority and power. Although unusual, the previously dependent child could threaten their parents, especially if the lines of dominance and power had not been sufficiently redrawn. Households were never static; they changed and shifted depending on the identity of their members. This dynamism was an accepted part of social order, but the consequent changes could signal disorder.

Excluding newborns, assaults on children were relatively rare and were generally impersonal attacks centred on rage or concern for the family's well-being. These killings will be discussed elsewhere, however. Attacks by older children on their parents occurred precisely when hierarchies were confused and old systems of deference and obedience had been eroded. Such cases were also very rare, but are indicative of the strain that shifting hierarchies of power and deference could place on violent or unstable individuals. In 1690 in West Ham Juliana Mosse petitioned the court for protection from her grown up son, as she feared he would kill her. To substantiate her claim she described the cause of her fears, saying that she:

> maketh oath, that she doth go in fear of loosing her life or receiving some bodily harm by Henry Mosse her son, because the said Henry hath heretofore assaulted and wounded this deponent by stabbing her in several places in her body with a penknife.

She further claimed that he had demanded money from her by threatening her life and that when she recently saw him in the street and 'for fear of him did conceal her self'. Her daughter, Dorothy, corroborated her story, saying Henry had threatened to 'rip up his said mothers Belly'.[24]

In a similar case, in 1653 John Hopkinson, 'a very old man', went missing and was later found dead. His son was immediately suspected of the crime because John had taken out a warrant in the weeks before his death against both his children, as he feared they would kill him. Witnesses at the trial listed the previous occasions John had been assaulted by his children. Elizabeth Wood described two aborted assaults on the old man. Four years previously she said William Hopkinson, the son, had asked her father to poison John Hopkinson for him, and, even more evocatively, she described a scene of violence she stumbled on to. She said that a year ago she had:

> found the said John Hopkinson upon the Ground and Susann his daughter … lying upon him, and holding him so hard by the throat that he was black in the face.

Elizabeth's arrival prevented the abuse continuing, and she said John blessed her for saving his life. This testimony proved insufficient, however, as William was found not guilty.[25] Both Juliana and John were seemingly helpless in the face of constant assaults from their children. Both turned to the law to protect them from the overwhelmingly frightening threats and deeds of their own children. They were no longer in control.

Older parents who lived in the same household as their grown-up children were the most vulnerable to physical abuse. In these cases, the elderly parents presence was perceived as a threat to a master's or mistress's power and authority at home. As such they became a target for bullying. In 1667 in Sheffield, John Shore viscously beat his mother-in-law to death, loudly abusing her in a witness's hearing. Alice Webster said that John laid Ellen's beaten body on a dunghill, saying, 'I have laid thee to sleep let them take thee up that will, for I will be at the ... Head in the morning'. Ellen had been subjected to a terrifying beating with a stool and iron tongs, after she saw John beat up his wife.[26] He had beaten her to remind her of his physical and social power as head of the household.

Margaret Clarke also received brutal treatment from an in-law when her daughter-in-law, Margaret Kempley, 'crushed her about her breast and sides'. The attack left two bones sticking out of her chest, which were noticed by several neighbours. One witness saw the blows that led to the death, and others repeated in court the victim's own accusation of her daughter-in-law. Margaret Kempley did not deny the assault, but justified her anger by claiming that Margaret insisted on lying in the same room as her and her husband, even after she had physically lifted her up and removed her. Margaret obviously felt that her mother-in-law was seriously encroaching upon her household authority, and so deserved the blows.[27]

Irrationality or madness was the only acceptable explanation for such an extreme and extraordinary act as killing a parent. In 1694 in Long Cliffe in Yorkshire Matthew Hargreaves admitted that he had killed his mother with an axe. However, he claimed 'it was in his own defence, or else she would have killed him'. Matthew was found outside the house covered in blood, by curious neighbours who had heard shouting. Another witness said that he had seen Matthew bound in his mother's house, but as Matthew had refused to speak to him about the intimate affairs of his household, there was little he could say in Matthew's defence in court. Violent madness was more openly identified in 1725, however. Several witnesses stumbled upon the bloody bodies of Sarah and Ralph Waddey after an assault by Ralph's son Richard with a stick. Sarah was conscious enough to immediately accuse her stepson of the violent attack, but even she agreed with the general consensus that Richard was 'out of order in his senses'.[28] Such terrible crimes could not be legitimated. They were either due to madness or to evil. There was no good reason to assault elderly parents, no other possible ways to excuse this crime.

These were not the only cases of abuse within the family. The list is very long indeed, with occasional sources of violence found among aunts, uncles, brothers and sisters. Not all these relations were members of the same household, with some travelling considerable distances to attack and kill their relations. Sometimes the motive was money, but at other times it was less clearly attributed to resentment or to devilish influences. Even so, most families and households remained orderly. Their order may not always have matched to strict prescriptive regulations of total obedience and passivity, but it was close enough for domestic harmony to reign.

At some level there were informal and perhaps even unspoken negotiations, with good and valuable workers allowed more opportunity to resist the strict regulation of their masters and to be somewhat (though never wholly) independent. However, in general terms, it remained the case that 'good' wives and servants were silent and passive, while 'bad' householders were oppressive, wilful and violent. Communities tried to protect those who were abused, but ultimately they were far more interested in preserving the order that shored up the household. After all, order in the household reflected on wider society. By protecting the family, the community was ultimately protecting itself.

7

Poison: A Woman's Weapon?

When Mary Bell was accused of killing her husband in Yorkshire in 1663 the case against her was predicated upon the popular cultural stereotype of a murderous wife.[1] According to prosecution witnesses, six years earlier she had placed poison in her then husband's food. This was not a hot-blooded or spontaneous crime: she was accused of cold-blooded and malicious murder – a uniquely feminine kind of crime.

It is unclear whether Mary had been previously accused of this crime, or even if she was aware of earlier suspicions. However, some of her neighbours had clearly been waiting for an opportunity to accuse her. Even those who had not known her at the time of the crime were suspicious of her. As a consequence, they had overtly monitored her day-to-day behaviour long before the case became a matter for public record and legal redress. Poison and husband-murder were big news, with suspicions openly discussed well before official action was initiated.

Mary's evidence was disappointingly limited, consisting solely of a denial. However, in many ways, this was unsurprising. Depositions were taken only to assist the prosecutor in planning the trial. Most defendants therefore chose to limit the evidence they gave to those trying to convict them of a crime; after all, anything they said in this forum could be used against them later in court. Other witnesses had far more scope to speak and accuse, and eagerly did so. One neighbour, Margarett Armestronge, laid out the details of the purported crime with clarity. She said:

> Mary Robinson [as Mary Bell was then] made his [her husband Cuthbert's] breakfast ready and gave it her husband which meal was made of oatmeal, rather a hasty pudding, And she … did see him sup some of the meal, and in the mean time he was eating of it he fell very sick and did fall a casting and vomiting and so continued till about night and then he died.

Although there was no direct accusation, this description made it plain that Cuthbert had been poisoned and firmly indicated that Mary's oatmeal was the means of conveying the poison.

If a weapon can encapsulate a crime, then poison was the perfect expression of the malice and deliberation of the murderer. In fact, poison was the archetypal murder weapon, as it allowed a silent assault on an unwitting victim. Unlike the cut and thrust of a brawl or a beating, poison was often used against someone otherwise completely uninvolved in the action. The intentions of the poisoner were also apparently clear in the mode of killing, perceived as striking not in hot anger, but in a cold and malicious act of deliberation. The killing could not be described as accidental, an act of self-defence or even manslaughter; on the contrary, the planning and consideration involved meant it could only be murder. After all, most poisons had to be purchased or specially acquired, and their effectiveness considered and even measured. Poison was used secretly (often over a considerable time frame). In terms of most spectators, jurors or other commentators, there could be only one outcome of the act and one intention – to kill.

Spectators consistently classified poisonings as cold-blooded, stealthy and hypocritical crimes. They were considered to be the worst kinds of killing, as they did not allow the victims a chance to defend themselves. Poison was unfair and unsporting, and in early modern terms any inequality in a crime, especially violent crime, greatly exaggerated popular perceptions of its magnitude.[2] Poisoners would not be treated lightly in court, and their killing was unlikely to be mitigated. Rational expressions stating why this crime should invoke horror were almost unnecessary, as the wickedness of the act was usually quite clear. While violence from hot anger was mitigated in the form of manslaughter, a planned killing could never go unchallenged. Sir John Coke's address to a jury in 1614 summed up a range of popular and legal perceptions of the crime: he said that, 'of all murders poisoning is ye worst and more horrible 1 Because it is secrett 2 Because it is not to be prevented 3 Because it is most against nature and therefore most hainous 4 It is alsoe a cowardly thing'.[3]

As the Mary Bell case demonstrated, this 'sneaky' method of murder was considered a 'weapon of the weak'. Those without social power were perceived as eager to use this weapon to kill and thereby 'overthrow' their social superiors, which was why poison was so widely feared. Anyone – whatever their strength and however meek or loyal they appeared to be – could be conspiring against and slowly killing their betters. The least socially powerful in society were the prime suspects in poisoning cases, and wives, maidservants and women generally were believed to exploit the opportunities poison offered to assault and kill men. In literary terms, poison was the much feared and often discussed weapon of the disgruntled wife who arbitrarily attacked her husband without his knowledge. It was, quite simply, consistently perceived to be a woman's weapon.

Poison was a perfect weapon for a wife as she could use it without her husband's knowledge to pollute his food and drink. As a wife's prime duty was household provisioning, and her main concern was supposedly her husband's well-being and care, she was defying her central domestic duty to act treasonously and kill her husband and master.[4] The petty treason she was committing linked well with her cold-blooded method of killing. Poison compensated for her physical weakness, more than levelling the playing-field. Throughout the early modern period, and into our own time, poison was strongly culturally linked to femininity. In fact, it was seen as allowing a wife to effectively usurp her husband's legitimate marital power; to steal his authority via her secret rebellion.

The stereotype was in many ways self-perpetuating. Wives and female servants were more often suspected of the crime than anyone else, closely followed by other women, and so any signs of poison found on a victim were attributed to them. However, not every wife or maidservant was under constant suspicion. Those known to disagree with their husbands or to have cursed or threatened their master or fellow servants were always far more suspect. Printed texts reinforced the stereotype by concentrating on these 'assaults from below'. The threat of wives and servants had a cultural resonance that pamphlets exploited. Conspiracy theories and threats from unlikely sources were eagerly consumed in a period in which papists were continually suspected of misdeeds and the female witch was a popular and recognisable image. In such a mental world, it was not difficult to imagine disaffected wives and servants biding their time before a murderous assault. The hidden nature of the crime increased its threat. How could a husband protect himself from an assassin he was unaware of and a deadly assault he knew nothing about? These wider considerations meant the public responded well to published accounts of these stereotypical threats. Such stories terrified and titillated men and women, who consumed them in equal measures.

That the link between poison and women was a stereotype should not imply that women did not commit these crimes. Poison was a weapon that even physically (and socially) disadvantaged women could make use of. Those unable to act violently, but determined to punish or kill another, could poison, and in fact had little choice other than to poison – especially if they wanted to 'get away' with the crime. Nevertheless, there were relatively few cases of poisoning in this period, and of these we must remember that poison was not just a female tool: stories of female poisoners dominated print and popular memory, but the reality of the crime was somewhat different. This was as much a male as a female crime.

So, although men universally feared being poisoned by their wives, only a very few such cases can be found in the records. Wives seldom killed their husbands, and when they did it was not always with poison. Poison was often suspected and bodies were scrutinised, but relatively few cases were ever proven in court. Indeed, despite the prosecutions claim of a simple and directly witnessed murder committed by Mary Bell, the jury cannot have seen this crime as so straightforward. If they had, why else was the case still unresolved after six years? Margaret Armstronge's evidence replicated common perceptions about how such murders occurred. Her desire to present convincing evidence probably led to her exaggerating her testimony. She may well have been trying to boost her role in the crime and as the bringer of justice. After all, her words had a dual role: they implicated Mary but also emphasised her own role in the proceedings. However, despite her damning accusation, Mary was still free six years after the crime. She may have had powerful supporters, or Margaret may never have spoken out before or had previously had her words dismissed. This is something we can never know. However, these women were essentially fighting over the truth in court and both their reputations – and Mary's life – were at stake.

Whatever Margaret's motivation or credibility, her accusation was quite resonant. By claiming Mary had poisoned her husband's breakfast, Margaret accused Mary of domestic treason by misusing her prime wifely duty – the provision of food. This act of petty treason inverted the traditional organisation of domestic power, by challenging and overthrowing her husband. If believed, this accusation of deliberate and presumably planned killing should have clearly led to a verdict of murder. The witness statements made it clear that Mary should be viewed as a cruel and unfitting wife. She was presented as sexually voracious and disobedient by a range of other witnesses, the majority of who knew nothing about the original crime. They spoke in court to give 'evidence' about Mary's character, blackening her name in the hope the jury would look more favourably on their otherwise flimsy evidence. By making Mary into a 'bad wife', they hoped to imply she was also a murderous one.

Servant Elizabeth Lowes spoke in court, despite knowing nothing of the crime itself. She said her master (now Mary's second husband) had called Mary a 'whore and forsworn whore' and that 'upon which the said Mary did assault him and offered to beat her Master'. She then contended that 'it was suspected that her Master Henery Bell and the said Mary did bear a Bastard child to him'. Such comments were rumour, yet this was perfectly permissible in court. Hearsay was not forbidden as evidence until the early eighteenth century, and such 'background' information was welcomed until the end of the seventeenth century, although it was cautiously examined and carefully judged. It would not necessarily have been believed, but it did give the jury insight into the 'common fame' of the person concerned. It allowed them to hear, if not the truth, then local beliefs about the accused's character. By suggesting that Mary was unruly and unchaste, Elizabeth sought to undermine Mary's status as a wife. She concluded her narrative by claiming she had heard Mary confess to the murder. The evidence effectively stripped her of any claim to good wifely qualities. Indeed, the juxtaposition of two separate husbands within one narrative series gave the (perhaps unintentional) impression of almost adulterous, and certainly sexually voracious, behaviour on Mary's part, even though in fact there were six years between these husbands.

This was not the only evidence to be presented. Both Elizabeth Lowes and Henery Bell (another servant from the household) testified that Mary had spontaneously confessed. Servant Henery apparently goaded Mary by saying he feared she would poison him 'as thou did thy husband'. Mary reportedly wept at that and clearly declared that she had indeed killed Cuthbert and regretted it. This implausibly sudden confession could have been damning, especially if delivered along with other accusations about her character. The jury would carefully assess the credibility of all the witnesses, with their evidence subject to challenge and rebuttal by Mary as part of her defence. Even with their carefully constructed image of a quintessentially bad wife, Mary may have escaped conviction. After all, she had survived six years of rumour and local suspicion. She obviously had enough standing and credibility to avoid early accusations, although the years of suspicion must have damaged her previously good name. Nevertheless, her status and demeanour would have been used to challenge her accuser's characterisation of her as a bad wife, and their concomitant accusation of murder.

Poisoning linked well with that other early modern preoccupation with intangible female powers – witchcraft. Witches used words and devilish contacts to harm or occasionally murder from a distance. Killing was far from common and was only infrequently cited in witchcraft cases. Like poison, witchcraft was secretive and pervasively linked to femininity. It was linked to disgruntled and 'masterless' women who lived on the periphery of society and who attacked their own communities. Witches derived their power from the devil, who permitted them to harm and overthrow legitimate power using illegitimate witchcraft. Their methods were intangible and hidden. Maleficium – harm associated with witchcraft – was associated with muttered words and the curses of old women, who had often been snubbed or refused aid or assistance. Popular fears about the potential dangers of these words infused these old women and their curses with power. Witches were feared and avoided, although the muttered curse could be an effective means of securing assistance and relief as neighbours voluntarily helped and provisioned the 'witch' to prevent her employing her potentially destructive powers.[5]

Like poison, witchcraft was a 'weapon of the weak'. It gave illegitimate power to those who were naturally considered to be inferior and legitimately subservient. It was this that turned tales of poisoning by otherwise passive and apparently benign subjects (usually female) into excellent copy for pamphlet accounts. A 1677 pamphlet recorded a tale of a seemingly innocent sixteen-year-old girl, who had admitted to poisoning her mother eighteen months previously. This 'unnatural' girl was discovered only when she tried to poison her new guardians.[6] Despite her age, she was clearly presented as wicked. Her actions had been deliberate and were neither mitigated in the tale nor in court. The brutal assault and killing of one's parents was not a form of petty treason, but it was certainly a horrific crime, recorded as unnatural and usually attributed to pure wickedness, it was the antithesis of expected familial relations. The girl's motives were not discussed but, as with witches, she was assumed to be acting out of pure, unchecked malice.

In some cases the link between witchcraft and poison was more overt, and the distinction between the crimes was at times blurred. In 1649 in Yorkshire Jaine Kinley was accused of killing Abraham Hobson. In this case the method of the killing was obscure and contradicted even by the two principal (and related) witnesses. Abraham Hobson hinted that Jaine had used supernatural powers, since she harmed him with her touch alone. Abraham's mother, Marie, accused Jaine of killing using an apple. She implied that this method of killing was supernatural – but it could equally be explained by poison. Biting into the apple had supposedly killed Abraham, but Marie did not explicitly say how this had been achieved.[7] However, the two accusations – of poison and of supernatural witchcraft – sat easily together. Poison and witchcraft were perceived as similar in methodology and intention: they were seen as uniquely female crimes in which harm was done from a distance via stealthy malice. Whichever explanation for Abraham's death the witnesses individually believed, they had clearly identified whom they considered to be the killer. Their uncertainty about the actual method of killing merely illustrated how cunning and secretive the crime had been. However she had committed the crime, if she was found guilty, Jaine would have been considered to be malicious and crafty as well as wicked.

Wickedness, rather than innocence, was always a more credible narrative when a woman was accused of murder. Implications of unnatural assistance or extreme malice always tallied with definitions of female killers. Men were expected to be openly violent and to act in hot blood on the spur of the moment. Their anger was frequently inappropriate and often condemned as excessive, but it was also entirely appropriate to their gender. Silence, obedience and cold malice were likewise culturally linked to women. Women were repeatedly classified in binary opposites – in terms of sexuality and character they were defined as 'Madonna' or 'whore'; in terms of general behaviour they were meek, passive and good or resentful, vengeful and wicked. Women had no legitimate outlet for violence in this society. They often lacked the strength to physically challenge and such a response was usually repressed by extensive custom and education. A disobedient woman was made all the more dangerous for this absence of a violent outlet. Women were also considered to be more prone to wickedness and to listening to the devil than men. Thus despite the overwhelming statistical link between men, violence and homicide, it was women who were pervasively feared and continually considered as malicious.

Just as wives were frequently suspected, so to were women who lived without men, as spinsters or widows, often on the edge of poverty and of society. As in the case of Jaine Kinley, these women could be suspected of a killing, even if the method of killing was unknown and other evidence circumstantial. Defending against such amorphous and unproven accusations could prove difficult indeed. In 1654 Jane Scales was accused of killing a month-old infant using a complicated form of poisoning. Jane was reported to have killed the infant at the home of wet-nurse, Alice Lund. In fact Jane was described as using a perversion of the female desire to nurture by feeding the babe a substance taken from a piece of white paper. After this the infant grew suddenly sick 'and presently the said child did purge both upwards and downwards very Filthy matter both white and yellow'. Jane claimed she had fed the child some sugar. However, several witnesses used their evidence to implicate her as they felt that she had deliberately poisoned the child.[8] Jane was not ascribed a motive for her act. It was apparently just random wickedness.

Although they were supposed to be subservient, servants were seen as harbouring intense resentments for their masters and mistresses. It was felt that these passions had to be held in check by strong discipline from the master or mistress, just as a wife needed to be kept in check by her husband. In order to prevent social dissolution the master and/or mistress needed to constantly assert their authority and, if necessary, physically chastise their servants, beating them into obedience. Contemporary books, pamphlets and church sermons abounded with lessons on the necessity for keeping firm order in the home, a concern underpinned by an intense fear of the disorder that a failure to control the servant, child or wife would unleash. Order and disorder always existed in tandem, with the fear of one underlying the drive for the other.

The threat of the maidservant was identical to that of the wife. Female servants were responsible for provisioning the household. They took part in purchasing goods for consumption, preparing foodstuffs and delivering drinks when asked to do so. The resentful servant, therefore, had the same opportunities to strike against their master or mistress as a wife had. Again the threat lay in the secret and unpredictable nature of any assault. Such power could make others in the household suspicious and uncomfortable. Fear, of what may be done and what had been done, underlay many accusation of poisoning. It is impossible to know how many cases of poisoning did occur, and whether some cases of natural causes were wrongly attributed to poisoning (or vice versa). It was very difficult in an era before forensic tests and scientific 'certainty' to be sure of identifying all cases (as indeed it is even now). Depositions about this crime, therefore, represent evidence about the fear of poison and the dread of secret attack as much as they provide reliable stories about the incidence of such killings.

Female servants fitted the stereotype for this crime perfectly. At times, they occupied an even more passive role than the wife, lacking even the limited power she had over lower members of the household hierarchy. In fact, in terms of hierarchies there was no one below the maidservant: even wives had more authority as they instructed the servants and had status from their marriage and children. Maidservants did have internal hierarchies, and so some maids could have influence over more junior colleagues, but this influence was relatively small.[9] As both women and servants they were expected to be passive, obedient and silent. They were not expected to resist instruction or to react violently if disgruntled or to challenge the authority of the master or the mistress, either verbally or physically. Women were not usually considered to be naturally violent. Unlike male servants who sometimes acted violently towards their superiors, a maidservant would be expected to be entirely passive and non-violent.

This did not mean she was beyond suspicion. In fact, as with wives, this expectation of repression meant she was actually more suspect in many cases. Although a female servant had no legitimate outlet for her rage and disaffection, she was not considered immune from these passions. Although female servants had little real power in the household, they were never seen as helpless and were frequently depicted in stories as insidiously dangerous. Young female servants could be seen as silent threats, making use of their domestic role to quietly and maliciously attack. A female servant represented a risk in the household, and in many cases a more dangerous and fearful one than male servants. She was forced by social conventions to be crafty and cunning and to hide her disaffection. Indeed, many may have believed such cunning and wickedness were endemic to her sex. In universal terms, women were feared for their potential to plan and commit cold, malicious murder.

Poison was perceived as the perfect weapon for the stealthy female servant, as it easily permitted calculated domestic treason. Few would have been interested in her motives, as her wickedness alone was the focus of the narratives. In Selby in 1667 Liddy Wilson poisoned a large pot of food in her mistress's house and was described as watching and openly laughing as guests fell violently sick. Liddy had ingested some of the food herself, and so was as ill as some of the others, but even so she was immediately suspected because she had made and served all the food. Further, Liddy had recently purchased the poison ratsbane for the household, and attempted to hide this fact by asking the seller, John Watson, to lie. When a portion of the poison was 'found' in the remains of the food, witnesses stated that Liddy tried to destroy this evidence. However, Liddy's mistress, Mary Sposforth, instantly suspected that Liddy had been responsible, crying on discovery of the act that 'there was *treason* amongst them for they were all poisoned'.[10] Her use of this word is significant. By killing her superiors, Liddy would have committed petty treason, and from the description of the crime it seemed the act was well planned. Despite her relative lack of power, Liddy had been swiftly transformed into a dangerous and treasonous enemy, who had plotted the downfall of her mistress and her neighbours.

While wives managed to direct the poison to husbands alone, the few servants prosecuted for this crime instead poisoned large groups of household members and neighbours. They attacked indiscriminately, with even their fellow servants targeted, as the case of Liddy Wilson clearly showed. This matched popular beliefs about servants' and wives' resentments. Wives were believed to resent the power of their husbands, and so naturally attacked their spouses. Servants were thought to resent both master and mistress and potentially all of those above them in the social hierarchy, including married, female neighbours as well as superior servants. In such cases, it was easy for neighbours to believe they could strike more broadly and still be attacking people they resented. The mass potential of their assaults was not discussed in depositions, however. Witnesses did not decry the more extreme crime of multiple murder. All poisonings, even those that did not lead to death, were considered to be wicked and heinous crimes regardless of the number of people affected. As with other mass and serial killings, these crimes were not considered to be different from other murders, nor were the motives or characters of the killers differentiated. The perceived heinousness of the crime depended only on the intention of the killer, not on how many victims were accrued.

Murder was seldom abstracted from the personal. Individual quarrels provoking violence were the norm, with multiple killings proving a real conceptual problem for early modern people. When Mary Taylor poisoned an entire pot of ale for general consumption in Samuel Fish's house, her action was certainly intended to have a random and mass impact. However, the coroner's inquisition limited her crime by concluding that her intention had been the murder of Samuel alone and that the tabler, George Braviner, was actually killed in error. Nevertheless, one deponent declared that the beer pot in which the poison was placed was 'for the use of the family' and that at least two other people had drunk from it and become very ill. Another deponent stated that Mary had spoken to her in the street before the poisoning and said 'she hoped to see (within a short time) some of her enemies fall'. The coroner's inquisition concluded that Mary had acted with malice, but failed to fully present the possible mass nature of the killing. The punishment would have been death whatever implication had been drawn, but the coroner was obviously keen not to speculate about Mary's potential to have caused mass deaths.[11]

As the association between poison, femininity and social subservience was so strong, men were seldom considered to be poisoners. Even male servants were expected to act in a more gender appropriate manner and kill or injury violently. The records back up this cultural assumption. Just as male servants were seldom imaginatively linked to poison, so few such men were actually prosecuted for this crime. When male servants were linked to poisoning, it was often in unusual circumstances when they may have felt they had few other options. For example, in London in 1691 Edward Francis confessed to callously poisoning the entire household in an attempt to kill his master. Described as a 'blackamore' servant, he was probably a black slave, and as such, he could not choose to leave his master, or in any way avoid abuse. Unable to retaliate physically or simply leave his master's employ, in many ways Edward was in a very constrained position.

Despite his constrained and unenviable circumstances, Edward would have received little sympathy from his neighbours. His race would have alienated some, and his status as a slave would have prevented any legal recourse. As a slave he could not simply leave his master if he disliked his correction or wished to live elsewhere. For a servant, although the ties of service were binding, legally and socially, they were also breakable in extreme circumstances by legal petition, or simply by fleeing. A slave was not so easily released, because, like a wife, he was compelled to remain with his master whatever the circumstances. It was probably this very intensely constrained social position that provoked his crime. Unlike male servants, Edward could never have expected to be of an equal social status to his master. He was in an indelibly inferior position and may have felt unable to be violent in the way white servants could be because of this. In fact any action he took would be considered all the more murderous and treasonous because of his menial racial and social status. This may explain why he did not physically assault his master, although it may be that in acting secretly Edward was pursuing a cunning plan to kill his owner without being detected, hoping to thereafter secure his own freedom.

Whatever his motive, by using poison, Edward displayed his quite unusual and inappropriate masculinity. He swiftly confessed to the killing, apparently uninterested in denying his role, claiming that he had bought the rat poison eight or nine months earlier as he had been told that it caused sickness and vomiting. His crime was carefully planned. He had been plotting for some time, making him the epitome of early modern fears of social rebellion. Edward admitted to widely distributing the poison in milk drafts, in ale and in gruel. He successfully killed his mistress and a cat and made several other household members violently ill, but failed to kill his master.

In fact, the master took a key role in interviewing and ultimately accusing his slave of homicide. Another household member, Rebecca Dymock, re-counted that:

> His master asked him whether he put in the poison into his victuals to kill him, the Black answered yes, his master then Asked him what hurt have I done to you that you should be so bloody to me to kill me, he was silent, his master said what did you think to get your liberty by killing me, The Black said yes.[12]

If repeated in court, this statement would have had a powerful impact on the jury. Whatever he later said to deny or justify his act, Edward's heavily witnessed confession to planning and carrying out this crime would have gone against him in court. It was clear evidence of deliberation, and enough to convict him.

Such a crime was always considered to be petty treason. If convicted, Edward would experience an extreme and unpleasant death. In these cir-cumstances, it is not surprising that neither his desperation nor his treatment was discussed. None of the deponents felt sympathy for him (possibly because all the witnesses were poisoning victims). Edward's voice was muted and he did not explain his actions, but the difference between his status and that of a servant may have played a role. These constraints were never made apparent, but they pervaded the story and would have been plain to the contemporary legal audience and the local community. Like a wife, Edward was expected to be passive, but unlike a wife, his spiritual equality and legal status were seriously questioned by emerging concepts of natural racial hierarchies.

It is clear that Edward's case was anomalous. Most violence by male servants was overt and physical, especially when the servant involved was no longer a child. In the context of early modern England, men were expected to be violent and to display their violence in public for their peers and their superiors to see and judge. A male servant would intend to become a master himself one day, and so although he would be expected to be obedient, he would not be expected to be entirely passive. A male servant with no spirit or strength would ultimately make a poor master. In conceptual terms, he had to be appropriately obedient in the context of his service, and then switch to being strong and independent later on. The overlap in these roles created a sort of tension, although in reality the shift was gradual, with the assertiveness and status of the male servant changing with age and experience. Masters would have been aware of the potential for adult male servants to violence and would have directed their expectations and correction accordingly.

Indeed, unlike women, men were *never* consistently linked to poisoning. In fact, the supposed *modus operandi* of the poisoner was alien to early modern conceptions of appropriate masculinity. Men were, and are, presupposed to act with hot and sudden anger when aroused, which could lead them to beat, tear or rend their victims. Violent masculinity was rarely linked to cold deliberation, and since poisoning required planning and calculation, it was simply not a crime most contemporaries felt a man could or would commit. Contemporary beliefs in the gendered nature of the link revolved around what each sex was thought capable of doing. Men were perceived to be naturally violent and to respond to their anger by lashing out. So men were believed to kill their wives without resorting to secrecy and cunning, using knives, axes, blunt instruments and their hands to openly injure and kill them. As I have argued, wives (and other women) were thought to be naturally cold-blooded and malicious and so poison fitted their stereotyped characters. Indeed, in relative terms, women did make frequent use of this weapon. One-quarter of all husband-murders were by wives using poison. However, as instances of killing by wives were generally low, in absolute terms few women ever committed this crime.

On the other hand, poisoning by husbands was not subject to as much press attention, and was seldom an issue of genuine popular concern. However, it is clear from the archives that many more men *actually* poisoned their spouses than wives did theirs. The numbers are still low but exceed killings by wives both absolutely and relatively. The disparity between the reality of poisoning by husbands and the imagery which firmly linked the crime to wives is intriguing. When we consider popular discourses of fear in relation to poisoning this figure becomes significant. Despite being seldom linked to poison, and despite poison being generally considered to be feminine, some husbands made deadly use of this means of killing. Apart from proving malice and therefore murder, the passivity poisoning suggested challenged a man's masculinity and physical dominance of the home. However, the attraction of poison lay partly in the opportunity it offered to kill secretly without being caught. As with all poisoners, therefore, the absolute number of poisonings committed by men – including those committed in secret and remaining undiscovered – can never be known.

In psychological terms, poisoning could effectively effeminise a killer, solidly linking the crime to cunning and silent deliberation. It was not a stereotypically masculine act. In order to poison, men had to take on the quiet passivity more often attributed to wives, and to get away with the crime they had to pretend it was not happening. This did occur, albeit infrequently. For example, in December 1692 Londoner Katherine Austin was instantly convinced her husband had poisoned her when she drank a drink he had made her. She consistently accused him and demanded his arrest for the crime. Katherine apparently told her female friends that she:

> put her fingers into the pot [that he had given her to drink from] and felt something at the bottom of the pot that was white and gritty and asked her husband what it was and he told her it was egg and sugar, but all along till she died she charged him with poisoning her.[13]

Like the generic accused wife, her husband denied he had participated in her death. Few husbands willingly took on the mantle of passivity and cunning, however. Indeed, it is unclear if the court would have believed Katherine, so unusual and counter-intuitive was her accusation.

Even though poison was not solely a female weapon, the perceived link between femininity and this weapon was pervasive, and it could even be used to deny or divert suspicion from a male defendant. In 1662 in Yorkshire John Mennin used gendered assumptions about poison to bolster his denial of any involvement in, or knowledge about, his wife's death. Anne Mennin had been held in a local prison for over two years on suspicion of witchcraft at the time of her death, and arsenic had been found in the last meal that John had sent her. He claimed they had lived 'lovingly together' for thirty years and that his housekeeper, Janet Akaman, had dealt with the food. When questioned, John 'Saith he used no Arsenic in house, neither doth he know, that his wife was poisoned and if she were he think that if any did it it was (naturally) the woman that brought the meal than any other'. His denial of culpability centred on redirecting suspicion on to a more comprehensible, feminine murderer. He was arguing that it was simply more natural and explicable that a woman would have killed in this way.

Both John and Janet were indicted for Anne's murder, but the grand jury dismissed the case, and neither was ever tried. So it seems that John's gendered rebuttal of the accusation had been effective.[14]

In the majority of cases, husband-poisoners did not mirror the poisoning style of women. Rather, they acted in a more distinctive and 'masculine' manner. Their creative use of this weapon could, of course, help to explain why men were so seldom associated with poison. Although their killings were deliberate, they were seldom cunning. In fact, husbands often mixed poison with other kinds of offensive assault and explicit threats to kill their wife. Such an approach was not stealthy and this mixture of mental, physical and pharmaceutical assault was never associated with wives. It was exclusively and specifically male.

Thus poison became one part of a long-term attack by a man on his wife. In most cases, the husband openly administered the poison after beating his wife and clearly telling her that he intended to kill her. The poison allowed him to watch while his wife was pharmaceutically assaulted, remaining distant but in control. These men told their wives about the poison partly to add to her terror and possibly partly to allow them to reassert their masculinity. This was not the secret crime of a weak and desperate wife, but of a powerful and uncontested husband. In telling his wife of his plan, a husband did not jeopardise the killing as a wife would have done. A husband who knew he was being poisoned had the physical and social authority to stop her and chastise her. However, even a wife's awareness of a husband's intention to kill could not always save her life. These husbands were exploiting their powerful position in the home to terrorise and then eliminate their wives.

Anne Archer suffered an explicit threat of death from both the poison ratsbane and her husband's fists. She had related the history of her domestic abuse to her neighbours in Yorkshire in 1694, including an incident when he 'kicked her out of naked bed and put her out of doors'. Anne frequently told neighbours that she suspected her husband was trying to kill her because he had made few attempts to disguise it. When Mary Pitt ingenuously asked her how 'she durst have such an ill thought of her husband, she replied that she had great reason'.[15] Such husbands may have even enjoyed the terror their overt homicidal behaviour could induce in their wives, gaining as much power and pleasure from her fear as her subsequent death. These husbands used poison as another means of torturing their long-suffering wives and so they made no attempt to keep their abuse secret from the victim. Indeed, some of the pleasure of the assault lay in the wife's knowledge of her fate. Nevertheless, the poison was usually kept secret from neighbours, who would otherwise have almost certainly have intervened; and if they did not know about the poison, the husband could still claim his innocence at any future trial. The only evidence against him would be a reported accusation from his wife. This could be damaging, but it was far from a conclusive or definite case.

In fact, poison proved to be an evidential problem in all cases. One of the biggest problems lay in identifying the cause of death and naming the poison used. This could be crucial later in proving culpability. It was the nature of poison to be administered secretly, and once digested it was difficult to detect. Even if a wife knew her husband was poisoning her, only her reported accusation could be repeated by neighbours as evidence of the crime. In most cases the courts wanted more tangible proof of murder and of the defendant's guilt, but, unlike other forms of homicide, poisoning cases seldom offered the courts measurable or visible wounds to the body. The existence of the poison could often only be surmised from previous health or the rapid and suspicious nature of the death. To overcome this problem, witnesses and juries had to be flexible and creative. Bodily evidence and autopsies were successfully used in other kinds of cases to establish the incidence of homicide, but without access to modern toxicological tests 'certainty' was beyond the technical abilities of early modern practitioners. However, this did not mean that dissections could not be successfully employed to augment other evidence and provide the quite desirable physical 'proof' of the crime.

Some signs of poison were believed to be 'written on the body' and were therefore available for identification and testimonial purposes. In suspicious death cases bodies were always examined to see what they could reveal about the crime. As external examinations were favoured over autopsies, the job of identifying 'signs' of poison was not one left exclusively to physicians or surgeons. In fact, it was the suspicions and testimony of ordinary people that led to the investigation of most poisoning cases. Witnesses were inextricably involved in the investigation process and it was not until the mid-eighteenth century that such lay evidence declined in popularity.

Women gave the majority of such evidence, probably because their knowledge of food led them to recognise strange ingredients, and their knowledge of bodies (drawn from their caring function) meant they could also comment on the corpse's colour, bruising and other visible wounds.[16] The poisons tended to be generically identified, usually as arsenic or ratsbane, since although other poisons were probably used, without the facilities or ability to conduct chemical analysis, distinctions were difficult to make. This should not diminish the value of the evidence given. Witnesses in these cases strove to identify something well hidden. Indeed their endeavours in this respect should reveal the difficult circumstances in which witnesses were acting as well as demonstrating the limitations of early modern forensic knowledge. Even so their intention was to prove a crime had been committed, using whatever methods of 'truth' and proof they could.

External signs were used as indicators of hidden occurrences. Witnesses who swore they had seen unusual bruising, for example, were often using their words to indicate foul play and even poisoning. Altered skin colour was often used to indicate a poisonous or foreign substance in the body. Victims were described as vomiting copiously or breaking out in strange reactions. Sarah Langhorne was described as having nine wounds on her body, all of which, witnesses concluded, were the result of poison.[17] Anne Hamton's husband was presented as reacting even more violently in 1641, when his body erupted in boils, his nails peeled off and his visage was horribly defaced. In this case, a surgeon was involved, but his intervention merely confirmed popular suspicions, as he claimed that when he opened the stomach he instantly found the poison.[18] The means of killing should have been difficult to establish with certainty, so witnesses described it as having visible side effects. Such symbols could have been perceived as a direct effect of divine intervention, as God was believed not to want a murderer to go unpunished. Some of the wounds may, however, have been real: bruising could, after all, indicate internal bleeding. However, in most cases, the wounds described as indicative of poison were probably fictitious. These fictions were often repeated to aid the cause of justice and to provide certainty in cases where little other direct evidence existed, although on occasion they may have been repeated to spice up a tale by making the case more dramatic. These descriptions may have been compelling, but, without other circumstantial evidence of a dispute or a reported complaint from the victim, were seldom solely enough to convict.

These were not the only highly fictionalised 'proofs' of poison to be used in court. In Mary Bell's murder trial, Cuthbert Robinson was described as having vomited immediately after he had eaten the oatmeal his wife Mary had given him. Margrett Armstronge then provided 'tangible' proof to the court of his murder by telling a (probably) apocryphal tale. She said:

> And she hath heard it reported and doth believe that there being some chickens about the house did take up and eat some of what the said Cuthbert did vomit and did suddenly die.

Although Margrett had to admit that she could not swear that Mary had killed him, she said no one else ate the same food as Cuthbert, because Mary had quickly taken it away. The death of the chickens was described as a way of proving that the food had contained poison. The birds acted as a creative legal fiction that made up for the medical inability to 'prove' the crime, and the fiction then became apparently tangible evidence that could be used against Mary in court.

Lay witnesses were not the only ones interested in finding a way to 'prove' that poison had killed. Medical professionals also made extensive use of external examinations to distinguish poison from natural deaths. It was a complex process in which their expertise was challenged and stretched to the limit. In many ways, the professionals identified poison in the same way as lay witnesses. They relied on extreme and unnatural features appearing on the surface of the corpse, which would simply indicate that an alien substance had been used. Increasingly, however, dissection was used to try to incontrovertibly identify the poison. The stomach was the focus for these explorations, with undigested pieces of the poison searched for and used as proof of culpability. In 1662 David Shevill and Charles Clerke made one of the earliest recorded dissections in a homicide case for precisely this reason. The surgeons jointly deposed that they had been appointed by the Mayor of Newcastle upon Tyne to ascertain the cause of Anne Mennin's death in gaol. They said that they were 'ordered to open the body of the said Anne Mennin', although they provided no detail of how this was performed or of the precise nature of the consequent examination. They then recorded that they had found poison in her stomach 'which was absolutely the cause of her death as they conceive'.[19]

The location, shape and their identification of the poison found was not discussed in their evidence. It could be that their identification of poison also represented a 'legal fiction', as the providential location of an undigested piece of critical evidence was somewhat unlikely, especially in the context of surgeons substantially inexperienced in dissecting human bodies to provide such forensic evidence. Although the desire to secure tangible evidence encouraged and inspired forensic techniques, in these early cases it seems unlikely that the autopsy alone could provide such clear and irrefutable proof of guilt. In the case of Anne Mennin, a search of her food from the jail apparently led to a clear discovery of poison. Ultimately, however, the grand jury was unconvinced by this evidence and the case against Anne's husband was not formally pursued. It seems that in some cases poison remained intangible despite the best efforts of witnesses. In this it achieved the aim of the putative poisoner, as it allowed the killer to murder without facing the legal consequences of the crime.

Poisoning was considered to be the worst kind of killing and, despite the infrequency of its occurrence, it was often anticipated and broadly feared. The act itself was a clear representation of murder: as it was secret, cunning and innately malicious. That this worst of crimes was usually linked to femininity was not accidental. Women were perceived as more easily wicked than men: they were believed to plot and plan against those they were prescribed to obey because they were naturally wilful and lacked any sense of justice. That husbands committed this crime more often than wives did not change this perception, probably as men used the weapon differently in ways that did not suggest the secrecy and cunning that contemporaries pervasively feared.

Although poison was difficult to locate in bodies, this did not deter witnesses from searching for it. The 'legal fictions' they presented as the outcomes of their searches may not have always been correct and on occasion may have been presented maliciously to accuse someone against whom no other proof existed. However, as with other early forensic endeavours, the search for credible proof and the pursuit of techniques that could provide this proof ultimately assisted in the development of the science of forensic medicine and in establishing its value in court. The creative evidence of bruises and vomit eaten by otherwise healthy animals was as much part of this noble endeavour to understand the world as a dissection by an elite doctor. Anxious not to allow a murderer to go unpunished, ordinary people made use of ingenious evidence to prove guilt when few other options existed.

8

Murderous Mothers

In Oxford in 1651 22-year-old Anne Greene was convicted of killing her child. Anne had been a servant in the household of Sir Thomas Read, and was described in a pamphlet as 'of middle stature, strong, fleshy, and of an indifferent good feature'. Despite her lack of physical allure, Anne reportedly seduced her employer's grandson, Jeffrey, who was a youth of sixteen or seventeen, 'but of a forward growth and stature'. She admitted that she had 'often solicited [Jeffrey] by fair promises and other amorous enticements'. The subsequent illicit sexual encounter led to an illegitimate pregnancy and the secret delivery of a male infant. The body of the infant was found dead in the toilet soon after birth. Although members of the household claimed not to have known about the pregnancy or birth, suspicion immediately fell on Anne. She was then tried and convicted for the murder of her child.[1]

The pamphlet recorded that Anne had committed the murder to conceal her shame – she had acted, it was claimed, to prevent her neighbours and her master learning that she had had sex outside marriage. In terms of seventeenth century attitudes, young immoral women were believed to have killed their infants in large numbers to circumvent popular chastisement and the enduring shame of having an illegitimate child. Anne was representative of this stereotype in that she was portrayed as sexually voracious, potentially immoral and coldly malicious. Not all young women gave in to sexual desire; indeed the vast majority did not. However, all young women were considered capable of acting immorally and killing any subsequent child. The young women who succumbed were seen as licentious, as insatiable and as lacking all maternal and natural feelings towards their children. In this period, young, unmarried women became a focus of intense legal and social hostility. They were perceived as potential monsters, capable of killing their infants without conscience and without shame.

Today, we consider that there is almost no crime worse than the killing of a child. For that child to be killed by a parent is shocking and for it to be killed by a woman is more horrifying still. If the child is killed by its mother, the disbelief expressed in the media is even more extreme and is eloquently represented in vitriolic assaults on the mother's unnatural character. In addition, although we no longer consistently expect unmarried mothers to be cruel to their children, as a society we still question their appropriate maternity. Single mothers are blamed for broad social problems, such as crime and the degeneration of society, and are often condemned for their lack of morality. Even today, society finds the sexual activities and choices of young girls to be socially reprehensible and even dangerous.

In early modern terms the killing of a child or infant was just as horrifying and illicit mothers were just as reviled and condemned. Stories of innocence destroyed and of the wickedness of the killer abounded. Mothers were – and are – supposed to love and cherish their infants and to be ready to die for them rather than kill. However, there was a codicil to this early modern belief. Unmarried mothers were suspected of unnatural and un-maternal feelings and proclivities. Unlike married mothers, they were morally suspect as sexually lascivious and wanton women. These women were not expected to cherish and care for their infants. They were part of a broad cycle of sin and wanton misbehaviour, having broken early modern mores and ecclesiastical law by their illicit sex act. By the seventeenth century they were widely suspected of being prone to disguising this sin at all costs – even if it meant killing their infant.

Mothers were the most frequent killers of children, and children formed the largest group of victims of female homicide. Even so, the absolute numbers were low. Women may have been actively suspected of killing, but in reality they seldom did so. This group was by no means undifferentiated, with unmarried mothers considered the most prolific killers and certainly the most vilified. This relationship between mothers and murder pivoted on marital status. It was not that married women did not kill their children – for indeed they did. It was not even that they were not prosecuted or executed – they were, albeit in the small numbers one would expect from so rare a crime. Rather, it was that they were given the benefit of the doubt in terms of the law and in terms of the attitudes of their contemporaries.

A married woman with a dead infant was presumed innocent, an un-married woman was not. Married women had an opportunity to speak in their defence, to present themselves as good mothers acting out of desper-ation, madness or from a misguided desire to protect. Unmarried women were always more constrained by law and convention. A statute passed in 1624 codified this distinction. It clearly described unmarried women as immoral, sexually promiscuous and wicked. The law stated that an unmar-ried mother acted purely to defend herself and to hide her illicit and sinful misbehaviour. An unmarried woman's connection to maternity was downplayed and even ignored. She was considered to be an unnatural un-mother who could be dealt with only by the harshest application of the law.

Neonaticides in seventeenth century England have created more historiographic interest than any other kind of murder for this very reason. I will refer to such killings as 'infanticides', despite this term not being in contemporary usage. It is important to clearly define this crime linguistically, as it was entirely legally distinct from other murders. Historians have discussed infanticides at length, using them as evidence in debates about the legal responses to illicit sexuality, gender under the law and the for-malisation of sexual persecution in the early modern period. The debate has been rich and fruitful, with studies tracking the incidence of the crime as well as the narratives of individual cases and discussion of the motivations of all participants. Much of the debate has been concerned with identifying who instigated prosecutions and who was therefore responsible for the persecution of (invariably) young, unmarried women. Historians are divided between laying the blame for this harsh pursuit of unmarried women on the law and on local communities.[2]

Let's take a moment to review this balance of responsibility for infanticide prosecutions. Ordinary people, often the neighbours and family of the accused, provided the evidence to try a case. They raised suspicion, inves-tigated, collected evidence and proved culpability in court. Without local people, prosecutions could have been impossible to pursue. At the same time, however, the law which allowed these prosecutions came from above. The 1624 statute was a national act, applying equally in communities that welcomed it and those that were unsure about it. A case could be prosecuted despite local resistance, although the verdict was always the product of the (local) jury. Without this law, infanticide would have continued to be prosecuted under ordinary homicide law – where the onus of proof was on the prosecution. As it was difficult to distinguish between stillbirth and murder, such crimes would have gone largely unpunished. Therefore both the law and local co-operation were necessary. Each case became a nego-tiation between individual judges, neighbours, jurors and witnesses, in which innocence and guilt were actively constructed.

The murder of neonatals was certainly taken seriously throughout this period. The 1624 act was not repealed until 1803. While it was active, it was well used. Around 20 per cent of all homicide prosecutions involved mothers who killed their newborn infants. Although women were acquitted at higher rates than in other homicides, at least 72 per cent of those convicted of this type of murder were sentenced to hang – well above the normal homicide rate.[3]

Unlike any other homicide law before or since, the 1624 statute reversed the presumption of innocence in cases of unmarried women who concealed their infant's death. It stated that if a woman had a child who:

> by the laws of this realm be a bastard ... whether it were born alive or not, but be concealed: in every such case the said mother so offending shall suffer death as in the case of murther [murder], except such mother can make proof by one witness at the least, that the child ... was born dead.[4]

As infanticide was extremely difficult to prove by medical means, the statute circumvented the whole troublesome process removing the burden of proof from the prosecution and placing it on the defence. The law aimed to prevent infanticide by further demonising illicit sexuality, rather than by providing unmarried mothers with alternatives to killing, like homes for unwanted children. Unlike other murders, the attention of the court was seldom focused on the act of killing itself but on the events that occurred before or after the birth/death (in particular the concealment of the pregnancy and the dead body) which was believed to define the character of the killer. Indeed, the crime was both a sin and a secular taboo, as it involved murder preceded by illicit sex. It was the act of hiding the body, and thus the illicit sexuality of the killer-mother, that was the focus of the law. Consequently, in infanticide cases, unmarried sexually active women were seldom seen as entirely innocent. The invariably young, female defendant stood in court without legal representation, was presumed guilty, and had very few options for her defence. This inversion of judicial concepts of guilt and innocence left her in legislative terms the most demonised of killers.

However, the law was always about more than protecting infants. While the law reflected a fundamental concern with murder, it also represented a reaction, on the part of legislators and the populace alike, to the perceived rise in rates of bastardy, despite no concomitant rise being recorded. The infanticide statute was passed as a culmination of a growing sense of concern with patterns of illegitimacy and economic and social fears of the consequences for early modern society. Law makers and ordinary people collectively feared illegitimacy, as it threatened their moral structure and imposed unwelcome – and sometimes heavy – burdens on a community's finances. The parish was responsible for providing poor relief to those in need. An unmarried mother was likely to impose herself and her child on the parish, forcing it to provide (meagre) amounts of money to house and feed the family and, for example, to pay for the child to be apprenticed. Although the mother and child would live in poverty, the financial burden was resented by members of the parish who may also have been on the cusp of subsistence.[5] This aid was a cause of major contention and probably inspired countless people to investigate suspicious pregnancies.

Concerns also centred on morality. From the mid-sixteenth century, legislators were increasingly concerned with punishing men and women who acted outside social norms and pursued what were perceived as dangerous sexualities. Where earlier laws against illegitimacy had focused purely on infants who could be chargeable on the parish and were therefore economic threats to local people, the 1624 act targeted all illicit pregnancies. In fact, the statute referred to unmarried mothers as 'lewd', and as being inclined to kill 'to avoid their shame, and to escape punishment'.[6] As such, these women were demonised in print and in court. Bernard Mandeville in 1714 said 'She who can destroy her child, her own Flesh and Blood, must have a vast stock of Barbarity, and be a Savage Monster, different from other women'.[7]

Such comments litter infanticide tales. In 1700 in London Margaret Spicer was recorded as saying of Ann Man that she was a 'wicked creature',[8] while Mary Banke said of Isabell King 'Thou Murdering quean hast thou murdered thy child'.[9] The wickedness of such women was a fundamental part of their identity in these tales, and as such was difficult to excuse. Stories of wicked mothers were partly about constructing images of acceptable maternity by criticising the 'perverse' opposite.[10] So, even while acknowledging their youth and inexperience, the stories persisted in condemning. In 1690 in London a maidservant killed her newborn and the pamphlet account stated 'She had little to say for her self, being a very Ignorant Silly Girl'.[11] She was, nevertheless, convicted and sentenced to hang.

Although there is evidence of limited casual promiscuity,[12] most early modern women were respectable and sexually cautious. Although most of the women accused of infanticide had not previously had an illegitimate child, some women did fit the legal stereotype. Anna Boardall provides an unusual example of an unmarried mother of several children tried for murder. Anna had had two bastards before the suspected murder. She claimed that she failed to disclose her pregnancy because she was concerned about the reaction from local women, but stated that she had prepared for the infant's arrival. In fact, she blamed the infant's death on external factors, claiming she had begged Abraham Ryleye for some beef collop 'and because she had none she thinks that did her hurt'.[13] Her neighbours suspected she had killed the child, while she asserted that she had no reason to. The implication of her evidence was that she had not killed as she had no (good) reputation left to protect. This assertive, unashamed woman was the exception. Most of the other accused women minimised their sexual experience in their narratives and claimed they were mortified by their subsequent pregnancies. No legal distinction was made between these naive girls and more habitual offenders, however. One illicit sex act was seemingly sufficient to transform a previously innocent woman into a wicked killer.

Such focused hostility has led some historians to speculate that society felt threatened by young, unmarried women.[14] Like older women who were accused of witchcraft, an expectation of infanticide from women outside male control was a patriarchal fantasy of dangerous, unrestrained femininity. The focus of this anxiety is perplexing, though. How could young powerless women, often without their own homes or any close familial support networks provide such a threat, especially when the incidence of infanticide was relatively small when compared to killings by men? These women were often close in age and experience to the innocence of childhood, and had almost no economic or social power. In fact, such women were more threatened than threatening, and more vulnerable than powerful.

In addition, they were running a real risk of discovery and consequently of mortal punishment. The constant supervision of their neighbours and their own lack of privacy made illicit sex and pregnancy very risky events, which could easily be discovered and lead to their reputations being destroyed.[15] Infanticides formed a sizeable portion of prosecuted homicides throughout the seventeenth century.[16] Large numbers of women were caught and tried for this crime – possibly even comparable to the number prosecuted for witchcraft in England. However, in real terms, infanticides were only sporadically experienced by individual communities. We must always remember that 95 per cent of unmarried mothers did not kill.[17] Contemporaries may have feared them and prosecuted relatively high numbers, but these women were never a real source of absolute danger in terms of the number of killers and the numbers killed. They were certainly not as big a threat to social harmony as male violence was.

One of the statute's prime aims was the control of illicit sex and, in particular, sexually active unmarried women. Because of this, criminal innocence and illicit sexuality were almost impossible to reconcile in narrative terms. Once guilty of the sin of sexual incontinence, few could present a persuasively innocence façade. The Anne Greene case provides an excellent example of this. By luck and a twist of fate, Anne survived her execution for infanticide, reviving after she was cut down from the gibbet. She had hung for thirty minutes, and her friends had pulled liberally on her legs in an attempt to speed her death. Hanging in this period was essentially slow strangulation. Death usually took between half and three-quarters of an hour, quite unlike the sudden drop and swift death of the nineteenth and twentieth centuries.[18] Few would have survived such a drawn out execution. Indeed, the assembled crowd had believed Anne to be dead.

After being cut down, Anne was placed in a coffin and scheduled for dissection. To be given (by judicial instruction) to surgeons for anatomical study was a heinous punishment indeed. The penetration of her corpse after death was believed to endanger the immortal soul, and so only especially wicked criminals were sentenced to this additional degradation. However, once Anne was placed in the coffin, an onlooker claimed to have seen her breathe, and so another witness tried to ensure she was dead by stamping on her breast and stomach several times, 'with all the force he could'. At no time was she actively revived, with her 'corpse' placed in a dark cold room to await dissection. However, the doctors due to dissect her could not ignore the signs of life she exhibited after they arrived, and instead of cutting her open, these medical men carefully tended to her recovery.[19]

Anne's recovery was extraordinary and caused widespread interest and wonder. Although questionable in law, she was popularly considered to have been divinely rescued. Her execution was believed to have failed due to divine providence. Many felt her to be innocent despite her criminal conviction. However an unquestioned link between her criminal innocence and her admitted sexual immorality proved impossible for some to accept. In the long preamble to this remarkable story, several Oxford scholars used poetic forms to muse on her newly found state of innocence. Most found it difficult to reconcile her apparent innocence, demonstrated by providential intervention, with her sexual sin. Considering her innocent of her actual crime – murder – was less of an issue. Traditionally, surviving the hangman's noose was popularly considered the direct intervention of God to prevent wrongful execution. The law took a different view and blamed incompetent hangmen, but the popular link of divine intervention and criminal innocence was well established, if not always a precursor to release.

Anne was clearly sexually guilty, and so the question the scholars and other contemporaries had to ask was, how could such a guilty woman be a target for divine intervention? As one scholar declared:

> Strang wench! What character may fit thee best
> That still canst Live, though Thou art Hang'd and Prest?[20]

The intervention of divine providence in such a clear case of guilt must have seemed mysterious to these observers. Puns on her sexuality littered the pamphlet, with one poet remarking:

> Now we have seen a stranger sight;
> Whether it was by Physick's might,
> Or that (it seems) the Wench was light.[21]

Her 'lightness', with its physical and sexual implications, was paradoxically used to explain her escape from death, although it would more usually act to condemn her. Her sexual guilt did not sit well with her providential innocence.

The pamphleteer made an effort to logically prove her criminal innocence by arguing that the infant had been stillborn, and that she had not known she was with child, giving birth quite suddenly to an imperfect infant. These were oft-cited defences in such cases, which had no legal efficacy under the statute and were usually dismissed by the court. That they were used here shows how difficult it was to establish credible criminal innocence in light of sexual guilt. Indeed, as one of the poets argued:

> Thus 'tis more easy to recall the Dead
> Then to restore a once-lost Maidenhead.[22]

Anne's redemption remained anomalous, as her lack of sexual innocence hampered most attempts to portray her as legally innocent of the murder of her child. The conflation of sexual and criminal innocence was replicated in verdicts and testimonies (albeit less eloquently) across this period. Her illicit loss of virginity was enough to damn her. Indeed, after admitting to illicit sex and pregnancy, a suspect's criminal innocence became immediately doubtful.

The sex act itself, although one of the core events in many infanticide stories, was largely denied and left implicit in defendants narratives. Even in the story of Anne Greene where her illicit sex was the focus of so much interest and concern, the sex act and relationships of the parties was not the subject of extensive interest. The act was referred to obliquely with the prime focus being a condemnation of the lust rather than detailed descriptions of love affairs or passion. Depositions tend to replicate this pattern, but some provide a limited insight into the illicit sex that was at the heart of events. Even so, these tales force love and sexual desire onto the sidelines, with witnesses concentrating on condemning and sermonising.

Most tales of sex were told in matter-of-fact ways with limited details. In these stories the women were passive and the sex disassociated from desire or anxiety. In Yorkshire in 1661 Isabell Truit described the conception of her child thus:

> shortly after Martinmas last she having been at Huton Bushell and going over the moor homewards towards her master Robert Storr his house, a stranger who named himself John Dickson of Midleton did meet her and did begett her with child.[23]

It is unclear if the act was consensual or not, although to an early modern mindset conception indicated that a female orgasm had occurred, which negated later claims of rape. Even so, in her tale of the conception, Isabell did not talk of passion or of a relationship with the child's father. His only connection to her was the sperm he supplied and the unfortunate pregnancy that ensued. Otherwise she depicted herself as entirely passive and uninvolved.

That emotional involvement and physical pleasure were absent from these tales is not surprising as depositions were hardly the place to express such feelings. In fact, many defendants sought to minimise and deny pleasure, as it would surely have weakened their case and destroyed their credibility. When, in 1663 in Brompton, Yorkshire, Isabell Barton was accused of infanticide, several witnesses presented evidence to the court of a seemingly long-standing affair between Isabell and William Grange. Servant Edmund Barton told the court and several other witnesses that William often lay in bed with Isabell. However, Isabell used her testimony to deny her illicit relationship by telling a tale of reluctant sex. Instead of describing her affair, she claimed that last summer in Scarborough 'a man that she did not know, did pull her off her horse, and did ravish her'.[24] She deliberately replaced the passion of consensual sex with an unlikely story of physical assault.

Anne Greene's case illustrates how illicit sex could effectively destroy reputations. As a consequence, the narratives a female defendant could use were limited by her concern to present herself as innocent. Communities did not forget allegations of illicit pregnancy or infanticide and brought up even unproven accusations time and again. Ann Wright was accused in 1681 of an illicit pregnancy and suspected child-murder that occurred in 1679.[25] Londoner Elizabeth Atkins likewise answered charges in 1704 on a case that was eight years old,[26] while Marie Ryley was questioned at length about a ten-year-old crime. Marie claimed she had had the child alone and it had died:

> And had her trial at the Assizes at York, where she had the sentence of death pronounced against her, but by some means she saith she was after reprieved by the Judge there being till the following Assizes; And then she saith she was acquitted, but doth not know well by what means.

Marie was described as 'of evil fame by reason of her former miscarriage, and bad deportment', by one of the seven women who gave evidence after examining her. Her earlier crime was used to undermine her credibility and provide a reason for current suspicions.[27]

It is unsurprising, then, that denial and secrecy were the central themes in defendants' statements. Jane Mewers claimed she had left her bedroom when in labour because she did not want to disturb other occupants. She explained her resort to having the child amongst coals by saying 'she was in such a distraction she knew not what she did'. Jane was clear about her desire to keep the matter secret, however. When 'asked why she denied she was with child she saith she thought to have got to her sisters at Kenton and there to have borne it'.[28] Her actions were based on the need to deny rather than explain. Londoner Anne Jurejon claimed she had kept silent about her pregnancy as 'she did not think she had been so near her time but that she had 2 months to go'.[29] The implication was that she would have let someone know nearer the time.

An admission of illicit sex was often enough to destroy a woman's credibility in court, and, in more personal terms, it forced women to face up to something they had probably denied even to themselves. Isabell Sowden went to extraordinary lengths to conceal the birth of her child, despite her mistress's intense suspicion. Mistress Jane Wilson deposed that she had long suspected Isabell but that she had 'absolutely denye[d]' it. Her suspicion was heightened when she saw Isabell go to the stable, but she still only discovered the truth after the birth and death of the child.[30] A sense of desperation pervades the stories of women faced with the ultimate degrading admission. When Sarah Hibberd was accused by her sister and another woman in London in 1677 of having had a child, she 'a first cried no, no, in a slighting manner but sometimes afterwards being charged by the Midwife she then confessed she had a child.'[31]

The battle to preserve an acceptable sexual identity was so crucial to establishing innocence in infanticide cases that it frequently became the main focus of depositions, while the act of killing was barely discussed. Epic battles occurred between prying neighbours, who were determined to publicly expose shameful actions, and isolated women, who denied the charges and hid the evidence of their own bodies in an attempt to retain control over their lives. Jennett Young tenaciously deflected her mistress's accusations of pregnancy by claiming she had a fever in her belly. Her display was apparently convincing, as midwife Ann Waugh claimed that although she examined Jennet, she was in such a bad condition she did not suspect pregnancy. Jennett clearly felt under intense pressure, with one deponent claiming that when questioned, Jennett 'answered by her with cursing and swearing'.[32]

Unmarried women were consistently monitored in this period. Neighbouring women – even family members or members of the same household – watched young unmarried girls in an attempt prevent sexual immorality and to prevent illicit sex being successfully hidden. In particular, neighbouring women were concerned with identifying pregnancies. Although a source of joy for married women, an illegitimate pregnancy was a source of shame and a financial threat to the household and the community. In Germany, although illegitimate pregnancies were reviled, a pregnant woman would be begged not to commit infanticide.[33] Such reassurance in the attempt to protect the innocent did not exist in England. Witnesses were not interested in offering support or alternatives to these women. They were waiting to punish the unmarried mother for her sexual incontinence and her flouting of communal norms. Midwives and other women even withheld their services during labour, while they questioned the mother repeatedly about the identity of the father. Once they knew who the father was, they could legally oblige him to financially care for the child.

Nevertheless, the pressure to confess often occurred over a considerable time span. When widow Susanna Vales was suspected of pregnancy in Kingston upon Hull in 1668, she was subjected to months of surveillance. Susanna Doughty deposed that she had watched Susanna Vales and had publicly speculated with a fruit seller about her condition. When she gossiped further she was confronted by Vales and forced to apologise, but her suspicions persisted. Margarett Hell reported seeing Susanna in church and said that she had passed her suspicions on to two others and that they discussed it together several times. Susanna was later found not guilty, but she had had to maintain her denials under enormous pressures, and it is, of course, unknown whether she ever regained her former unsuspected status.[34]

Unsolicited physical examinations were useful tools for determining the truth. In 1672 Elizabeth Ivoor said she had 'diverse times' examined Mary Bradley, as she had been suspicious for several weeks. Mary withstood these examinations until she was threatened with a warrant. Elizabeth reported with relish that:

> Mary Bradley having been told (as I heard) that a warrant would be pursued against her and she the said Mary had before Authority to answer such things as could be alleged against her touching the bearing and bringing forth a child.

In the face of such enormous pressure, Mary's resolve collapsed and she disclosed the corpse to her questioners.[35] Grace Child exerted similarly intrusive pressures on Jane Lockwood, when she repeatedly questioned and examined Jane until she felt sure birth had occurred. Then she called for a thorough bodily search to be conducted, during which the necessary evidence to indict was located.[36]

The act of murder was often peripheral to the story of guilt in these cases, and only briefly described. Sexual immorality and proof that the foetus existed were all that were needed to secure a conviction. An implicit link was made between the woman's sexual immorality and her propensity for wickedness and murder. The law explicitly connected these women with homicide and declared that an assumption of murder could be made in these cases. Unlike all other instances of homicide, even those involving men known to be violent, it was only women such as these who were to be presumed wicked. In many ways, these women were conceived as the most natural and wicked of all killers, and so little actual proof of the crime was necessary. Details of the violence served, therefore, only to confirm the wickedness of the action. Indeed, most violence was inflicted in a desperate attempt to keep the child silent and hidden. In 1728, eighteen-year-old Ann Milburne told Mary Barber that the child had cried when it was born and that she had tied a rag around its neck 'to hinder it from crying out'.[37]

Even so, the majority of infant murders were committed through neglect. Dorothy Snawden attributed the death of her newborn child to her falling into a swoon immediately after the infant was born 'and as soon as she came out of it she took up the said child which was then dead and cold'.[38] A lack of violence did not indicate innocence according to the statute, but it certainly swayed opinion in court as it fed into stereotypes of passive femininity. Therefore, witnesses determinedly noted this lack. In 1667, Margaret Bankes said of Grace Robson's child that 'so far as she could judge upon her viewing of the said child it was neither wounded nor bruised'.[39] An absence of violence could introduce doubt into the proceedings. Homicides were traditionally identified as such when clear wounds were visible on the body, and an absence of clarity (despite the lack of legal necessity) led neighbours to question the validity of the conviction.

In fact, women often denied homicidal violence by telling tales of natural deaths, despite the scepticism of the courts regarding such claims. Such stories are difficult to uncover due to the hostility of the pamphleteers and to a consistent absence of such testimony in depositions. However, a few voices are audible. Defendants and witnesses consistently related stories of stillbirth in court. These comforting tales allowed the mother to continue to deny her crime (to herself and to others). The defence had little legal merit, however. Martha White told the Yorkshire court in 1671 that her child 'came dead into the world', while Dorothy Tinsley disassociated herself even further by claiming she was 'delivered of something, she knew not what.' Sarah Peele likewise dehumanised the infant by calling it a 'mention of a child or shape'.[40] The entire birth process was experienced very differently by unmarried women: married women described long and arduous labours, whereas unmarried women claimed their labour was quick and unexpected often dismissing the infant as a waste product or lump of flesh.[41]

The claim of stillbirth was not merely a negation of maternity or a psychological distancing from the corpse. Women were eager to prove they had not killed their child violently. In 1675 Sarah Whitfield said of her female infant that 'she did not do any harm to it and that it was dead when it was born'.[42] Such defences relied on a sympathetic jury to be effective. Not all juries were willing to hear extenuating circumstances, as a printed text from London in 1673 illustrated. A midwife and surgeon judged a servant girl's infant to be stillborn:

> but the law doth pronounce in such cases, by a statute of the 21th of King James, That if any child be unlawfully begotten, and born dead, without one witness at the least, and concealing the same to hide their shame (or words to that effect) it shall be accounted as murder, so this woman being delivered of a bastard child (by her own confession), and concealing the same, the Jury found her Guilty of Murder.[43]

As such judgements made clear, mounting a plausible defence for this crime was extremely difficult, especially if the judge or jury were reluctant to interpret the law generously.

Infanticide stories need to be read on many levels, since they were about much more than telling tales about a putative crime. Their imagery was not accidental. Explicit references linked murderous women with all that was sordid and inappropriate, referring to contemporary images of femininity, in which marriage and maternity played a joint role in defining personal standing. Illicit mothers were portrayed as the very antithesis of maternity and acceptable femininity,[44] as anti-mothers who had illicitly conceived, borne and killed their children. Narrative innocence was alien to these women, but images of social, sexual and moral degradation were not, and such images pervaded texts. Mothers were generally differentiated by their marital status into discrete groups of good and bad.[45] Illicit sex and the absence of a husband were considered to permanently change women, even those who had previously enjoyed a good reputation, such as widows.

As with the Anne Greene case, the very language of infanticide stories conspired against the female defendant, alienating her from the broader world of acceptable femininity and assisting her criminalisation. In addition to being tried for murdering their infants, women were judged on their social and gender identities. The language of the texts and the focus of the stories displayed the social judgements that were being made about the women being tried. Although illegitimate pregnancy may not have been a deliberate choice on the woman's part, the illicit sex that preceded it was perceived to be one. This act of immorality – even if it only occurred once – ineffably marked the woman as wicked and tainted. The sin and social stigma involved led to popular hostility and an absence of sympathy. As well as being anti-mothers, these were anti-women whose lives were defined with degraded language and scenarios.

It was in the disposal of bodies that the imagery of degradation was most visible. The disposal of the infant's body was a key part of the crime as defined by statute, as it formed a deliberate attempt to conceal the shame of the woman's illicit sexual behaviour. A large proportion of corpses were concealed in the mother's bed, under her pillow or hidden in the small, locked trunk in which a female servant would keep all her worldly possessions. Such locations were often the first place that suspicious neighbours or mistresses would look for bodies, and so were highly ineffective in distancing the mother from the crime or hiding the illicit infant from sight. It would be easy to attribute such actions to psychological causes, arguing that the mother had separation anxieties or that she could not accept that she had killed her child.

Such arguments do, of course, have merit, but such concealments are also revealing of the social realities of young women's lives. The majority of the killers of newborns were young maidservants, who gave birth in houses that were not their own, in often hostile environments, in which their movements were heavily circumscribed and in which privacy was minimal. They had nowhere else to put the tiny corpses. Their options were further limited by female neighbours who watched their every move. Any unusual activity would have sparked interest and inspired nosy neighbours to investigate further. As most women acted alone, it was not surprising that many found the effective disposal of the infant impossible to secure.

Legitimate maternity was clearly presented and regulated in this period. Married motherhood represented a coming of age and a fulfilment of women's marital and gender roles, and pregnancy was a public event that involved whole groups of local women.[46] Illegitimate pregnancies, on the other hand, lacked the ritual and symbolism of legitimate pregnancies. As well as being hidden in gestation, the birth itself was solitary, often unplanned and seldom assisted. When plans were made, they concerned concealment and were born out of fear rather than customary expectation. Even the act of birth itself was distinctive, as it was presented as fast and silent, with a number of bodily disposals taking place outside of the home, often in fields or ditches.[47]

In 1725 Martha Broadbent said she miscarried about halfway through her pregnancy and threw the body into a snow drift. Although she apparently hoped that no one would ever find it, the corpse was later discovered by a dog. Likewise, Margrett Walker said she had suddenly gone into labour while outside, and had a stillborn infant whose body she threw into a ditch. Such births, like many conceptions, took place in inappropriate spaces. The subsequent infants were defined as disposable. They were not treasured, but were symbols of wrongdoing, and, for the unfortunate mothers, precursors of doom. Significantly, Richard Moody told a Yorkshire court in 1671 that he was 'raking some rubbish upon his land' when he saw a dead child in a ditch.[48] These were anti-births – denied by their anti-mothers and conducted in inappropriate spaces.

Maternal dysfunction was underlined in the stories told about killing in court, in extreme tales to emphasise the inappropriateness of the act. Mary Willan from Kirby told the story of her labour in 1683, saying:

> She laboured about two hours in great pain upon her knees and then after brought forth the said child standing and that the fall of the child from her body broke its navel string but she forgot to take care to tie it up from bleeding.[49]

Her lack of care was probably deliberate, but it was also an example of her lack of preparation for being a mother. It was likely that some such women really were ignorant of the signs of conception or the appropriate actions during birth. As most unmarried mothers were spinsters, they would have been excluded from the formal rituals of legitimate birthing, and would have little experience of common practice.

Degradation was even written into the language the courts used to define and discuss these crimes. In London cases, excrement became a defining feature of infanticides, and was used as a weapon, cause of death and metaphor for immorality and wrongdoing. In several inquisitions, the legal record referred to the disposal of bodies in toilets. Such records briefly recorded the charge, the salient evidence and the verdict of the coroner's court, all of which would then be passed on to the assizes for the trial of the guilty party. In other homicides the manner of the bodily disposal was seldom recorded, which makes the frequency of such references in infanticide cases all the more significant. References to excrement served to underline the degraded aspects of the case and the unnaturalness of the mother.

In 1718 in St Gyles Jane Flintoff told the coroner's court that she had miscarried and 'she not having were with to defray the charge of Burial did put it into the house of office'. However, the formal record presented Jane's action quite differently. The coroner's jury were recorded as deciding that Jane had had a live child and that she had taken it 'into a certain house of Office filled with excrement and other filth feloniously wilfully did cast and thrown wherein the said male bastard infant did then and there Instantly become choked'.[50] Instead of being a coda to evidence describing the disposal of a corpse, the house of office was the place of murder and the excrement therein the means of suffocation, making the act one of unparalleled baseness. Jane was found guilty, as were all the other women who were described as murdering in this way.[51] The link of bodily waste, dunghills and illegitimate infants was clearly made in these stories, all of which became a potent metaphor for the sexual and social degradation the crime implied.

Dunghills and houses of office were, of course, more than metaphors: they were also a logical point of disposal. For women who had little privacy and restricted access to hiding places for corpses, a dunghill must have seemed a rational place to conceal an unwanted infant. Some women may have (at least partially) experienced labour in privies; they may even have mistaken the pain for other bodily functions or have used the space to conceal themselves during part of their labour. In these cases the privy would be a convenient place for the disposal of the corpse. Likewise, dunghills facilitated secrecy and could physically conceal bodies. In 1661 Sarah Fawcett confessed to hiding her infant's body on a dunghill, saying 'she take up the said [dead] child and put it into her apron and carried it and buried it in a dung hill and covered it with dung and never confessed to any'.[52] The smell of the dunghill or privy may also have assisted by concealing that of the decomposing corpse.

Even in an age when unbaptised newborns were commonly buried in unconsecrated ground or at the side of the road,[53] the dunghill would not have been an appropriate place for a burial. In 1724 in the West Riding of Yorkshire Joan Fountain claimed she had had her stillborn child on the dunghill and had buried it in the waste matter, but added that she 'could not be easy till she had taken it up and laid it upon the said Dunghill that it might be seen and buried decently'.[54] Despite pervasive stereotypes, not all unmarried women were unmaternal or unconcerned with their infant. In this case, Joan was determined to have her child properly buried, whatever the risk.[55]

Metaphors of cleansing and renewal can also be read into infanticide texts, since water and fire were recurring locations for the disposal of bodies. Such locations were secure and secret, but the association may also have helped to purify the bodies of the mother and infant. References were not explicitly made to cleansing, but it seems unlikely that the sophisticated audience, well schooled in the imagery of pollution and restoration, would not have interpreted such reports at least partially in this way. In 1642 in Yorkshire Elizabeth Stonas disposed of her newborn in the fire. A fellow servant described her discovery of the corpse: Anne Garbat said she was cleaning the chimney and 'she then and there did see a little thing amongst the ashes and taken the same up she found it to resemble the likeness of a child'. Elizabeth then confessed it was her child and that she had covered it in hot ashes. She did not say whether it had been dead or alive at the time.[56] Anne Giles likewise made use of fire for concealment in 1695. While she claimed she had flung her infant into water, crucial evidence of her act was found in the fireplace. Anne Johnston had searched for a body 'but could not find any child, But in the Chimney corner of the said house, they found a fresh after birth hid under the Ashes'.[57] The hot fire had notably failed to conceal the evidence of her crime.

Water was a more common hiding place, especially popular in rural Yorkshire, but cases can also be seen in London. Wells and rivers were convenient locations for disposal, and were effective forms of concealment. When Gertrude Law from Rotherham disposed of her infant in a well in 1671 the corpse was only found by chance by William Husband after he glimpsed something and prodded about with a rod.[58] Fire and water disguised and distorted the body of the infant, a point deponents emphasised. When, in Brightside in Yorkshire in 1656, Thomas Mathewes saw an object in the water, he initially imagined it to be a 'pig in a poke' and only later realised it was a child.[59]

Despite the vitriolic condemnation of women believed to have killed their infants, the 1624 law was far from universally accepted. Although designed to ensure conviction of the guilty, many believed the statute also convicted the innocent – women who had their child in secret and alone, but had not murdered it. This popular concern to protect the innocent and fully prove culpability in the guilty transformed the application of the law by the end of the seventeenth century. To prove that women had secretly had an illegitimate infant was, for many witnesses, not enough to make a conviction just, and juries displayed their displeasure with such limited evidence by consistently acquitting. A determined jury would acquit even when the evidence clearly matched the legal definitions of guilt. Conviction rates were actually lower in infanticide cases than in any other type of homicide, despite the assumption of guilt which should have made the process much easier. Execution rates for infanticide were higher though.[60] Such evidence is difficult to interpret. As we have already noted, convicted women were more likely to be executed. Juries could be capricious and wilful, and not even the obvious displeasure of the judge could prevent them giving a contrary verdict.

In some cases the law was rigorously applied. In 1675 a pamphlet recorded an infanticide case and stated that 'it being questioned as the Law requires in such cases, whither she cried out at the time of her Delivery, she affirmed she did [but no one heard her]'.[61] The writer made clear what had been apparent in court, that judgement was not to be limited to killing alone, but extended to the mother's failure to declare her pregnancy. Effectively, the mother was to be judged on events that occurred before the putative crime, when she had failed to disclose she was pregnant. However, other juries defied the statute to acquit. In a London case from 1690, Martha Nook was tried for murder, although she claimed the child was stillborn. Her defence did not impress the pamphleteer, as he commented that 'she made several frivolous Excuses' and admitted to hiding the truth about the child. She did not seem to have had a witness who could speak in her defence. Nevertheless, when the statute was read to the jury she was found innocent. This was a clear act of legal defiance in the face of what was obviously considered to be inappropriate justice.[62]

Stories of infanticide were interpreted against a background of fluctuating economic and political climates and of personal testimony about the past character and name of the defendant. These crucial details are unavailable since no record of jury deliberations exists, but anomalies in individual cases and fluctuations in the frequency of convictions remind us of the specificity with which each case was judged. Although, the wider context was one of broad criticisms of transgressive motherhood, cases were never considered as generic or interchangeable.[63] Context was everything. The application of the inflexible 1624 law was subject to the decision of a jury; and as we have seen this law could be popularly disputed and amended.

Interpretations of the 1624 statute shifted during the seventeenth century, and new defences for the crime developed. The beginning of the eighteenth century saw a dramatic decline in convictions for infanticide. Both the legal system and localities underwent varying degrees of change, though neither was wholly responsible for shifting attitudes towards murderous unmarried mothers. These changes in acquittal rates and prosecutions cannot be linked to a decline in the incidence of crime. Although we cannot know how many were killed, we do know there was no significant decline in illegitimacy rates at the end of the century. The decline in prosecutions related to a change in how the crime was perceived rather than to declining incidence.[64] As in witchcraft cases, the courts were increasingly willing to give the benefit of the doubt to the accused.

In narrative contexts, by the end of the seventeenth century notions of innocence were being extended. Instead of presuming guilt and needing only a lack of witnesses to effect a conviction, juries increasingly sought additional proof that the murder had occurred and a clear idea of the intent of the killer. Decisions about a case came to be based upon stylised proof of a mother's intentions towards her child before it was born. Questions at trial increasingly focused on how prepared the mother was for the birth and on establishing that she had been ready to care for a live infant. Acceptable maternity was being redefined and unmarried women treated as more credible mothers. The 'benefit of linen' defence, as it has been termed, came to rely on women proving they had prepared clothing for their unborn children, in anticipation of life. Although they can be found throughout the century, these stories were beginning to dominate by the end of this period.[65] This defence meant that unmarried mothers could present themselves as caring even if they lacked a husband. In 1691 in London an unnamed woman's trial was recorded in print. In this case the infant appeared to have suffered great violence, possibly strangulation, but the pamphlet observed that the court could not certainly establish that the infant was born alive or that its mother had been violent. In addition, they clearly noted that the mother had made provision for her lying-in, and so had planned to keep the child alive. She was acquitted.[66]

As the century progressed, unmarried women regained their voices in the courtroom and presented reasoned explanations of their plans in an effort to disprove any murderous intentions. In Yorkshire in 1681, Elizabeth Armytage told of her sudden, painful labour, which prevented her from gaining assistance, claiming that 'she had had a night would have killed a horse'. However, she added to her statement carefully constructed testimony designed to ameliorate perceptions of her hidden birth. Elizabeth claimed she had told two women of the pregnancy and that she 'had provided some Linen clothes for her child and had an intent to have borne it at her sister Armytages when she had come to her full time where of she wanted a full month'.[67] By the eighteenth century, this shift in attitudes was being replicated in print, with unmarried women increasingly seen as passive victims of sexually obsessed men.[68] These widespread changes in popular and legal sensibilities created an opportunity to replace the earlier silence of female defendants with credible defences. Juries and witnesses were calling for tangible proof of crime. Most defendants embraced the legal changes readily, redefining themselves as good mothers even in the absence of husbands and in the face of social disapproval. Nevertheless, as long as the law existed, the possibility of a conviction remained, and up to the early eighteenth century extreme cases and distinctive circumstances led to the conviction of young unmarried women.

In London in 1670, married mother Mary Cook killed her 21-month-old child, Betty. Mary cut Betty's throat in one stroke and then admitted her crime to her husband and neighbours. At the time Mary was thirty-seven years old and married, with eight other children. She was quite unlike the stereotypical unmarried and licentious mother who killed her newborn to protect her sexual reputation. And yet while Mary's crime was quite different to Anne Greene's, it too revolved around early modern ideas of maternity.

Despite the focus of the law and local communities, not all murderous mothers were unmarried. In many ways a married woman's crime was as notorious as that of an infanticidal mother, in that it was hidden – disguised by a layer of appropriate maternity. Such stories were eagerly consumed in print – not only for the horror they induced, but also for the ambiguities at their heart. These killer-mothers were wicked, yet this overlaid their maternity rather than effaced it. Unlike the unmarried woman who became an anti-mother on conception, the married woman moved from possessing an appropriate, nurturing maternity into wickedness. It was this transition that ghoulishly attracted and repelled readers.

Married women were expected to be maternal and caring. Pregnancy and childbirth were joyful times for married women, albeit fraught with the danger of death and disease. Mary Cook was described as being devoted to her children, which most would clearly expect in this period. So in killing her child she acted inexplicably. Rage or correction could never adequately explain the killing of someone so young, and such violence never sat well with common interpretations of maternity. Mary was described as deranged, but also as wicked. The preamble stated she had tried to commit suicide several times and chose to kill her child because she was concerned about what would happen to Betty after she had killed herself. Suicide was considered a felony and a mortal sin, not just an expression of anxiety or mental illness: Mary was thus dangerous and sinful, the focus of the tale and the only real agent in the crime to come.

On the other hand, the child Betty was presented as endearing and charming and far from inciting or encouraging the forthcoming violence. The child's innocence was displayed in a few lines of text. Mary spoke to Betty 'unto which the Babe answered, Ey, crying, Aha, aha, as it used to do when it was pleased, and put forth her hand to stroke her Mother'.[69] These events must have been imagined, as only the mother and child had been present. However, by providing the child with a recognisable and sympathetic identity, this text neatly conveyed how undeserving she was of such cruel maternal attentions, and the depths of barbarity that her mother had sunk to in subsequently killing her. She was presented as the epitome of innocence wronged.

Evocative though they may be, stories like those of Mary Cook were extraordinary. Very few married women were prosecuted for the murder of their children. Indeed, they were seldom suspected of the crime that was seen as pervasive amongst unmarried mothers – the murder of newborns. According to the law, a married woman would have had no motive for such killing, as she had no shame to hide. When a married woman was suspected of killing either her infant or an older child she was tried under conventional homicide legislation. Proof of killing would, therefore, be required and so conviction rates were concomitantly lower.

Only when the legitimacy of the infant was suspected did the married woman's trial appear to mirror the stories told about unmarried mothers. Nevertheless, the legal reality was always fundamentally different. In such cases, the suspected adultery of the mother challenged the married woman's respectability. Mary Browne was accused of killing her newborn in 1669 in Yorkshire. Although she presented herself to the court as a married woman, her putative husband denied that he was the father of the child or that he had ever had 'carnal knowledge' of Mary. Mary was also questioned about an abortion she had previously procured with the help of some drugs from another woman. In both cases, she told the court that the infants had been 'quick', that is that they had stirred in the womb.[70]

Accusations of adultery could be used to slur a previously good name. Alice Dyson was posthumously accused of murdering an infant begotten in adultery. It is unclear how Alice died, but even after her death blame for the infant's death had to be attributed to reassure the community that the killer was no longer at large. Her husband, John Dyson, claimed he had found a naked man in with Alice and had made him pay £20 in compensation. He refused to lie with Alice after this, and claimed he did not know she was pregnant with the child whose body was later found by accident. Katherine Rychardson, Alice's servant, tried to refute the accusations by claiming she had not found incriminating evidence in Alice's bed nor seen her ill. However, the suggestion of serious sexual immorality may have been enough to sway the jury and imply Alice's sexual and criminal guilt.[71]

In the absence of suggestions of impropriety, cases involving married women seldom made it into court. Those that did were hampered by a lack of motive, although the core questioning bore a remarkable similarity to cases involving unmarried women. In Yorkshire in 1650 Anne Jackson was accused of murdering her newborn. The story she told of a solitary and hidden birth replicated those told in infanticide cases. Other women gave evidence concerning the physical evidence of the birth, and Anne was questioned before she publicly admitted to the child. The reason for her secrecy was unclear. However, it may be significant that her husband was away when the baby was born, and that when he returned he refused to look at the child.

Anne's own story shifted this narrative away from those told by the unmarried. Anne presented herself as a concerned mother who endeavoured to act in the child's best interests in an effort to save its life. She said that when the infant was born it whimpered once. However, unlike unmarried mothers she did not describe herself as trying to mute its voice. Instead she said 'she used all the means she could to preserve it alive (but it forthwith died)'. She claimed she called for help and, when her husband returned:

> acquainting him with it desiring him to see it (and laid it upon a table wrapping it in a cloth And she asked him what she might do with it if she might call in

neighbours, and where she might bury it, and he gave her no answer at all, so that she being destitute of help, After buried it in a garden.[72]

No mention was made of illegitimate sexuality, although it is possible that not all depositions for this case survive. Certainly Anne's actions were suspicious enough for her neighbours to present her for prosecution.

The fact that a defendant was married could be used as a defence. When Ann Armstrong was accused of murder in London in 1719, the description of her actions was identical to similar cases of infanticide. Ann said the infant had 'dropped' from her suddenly and that she had put the body in a box and fled from service the next day. She said her master's family pursued her and accused her of the birth publicly. However, Ann then presented a threefold defence. She said 'That the family knew she was with child, That she had made provision for the unborn infant and that she's the wife of William Armstrong now at sea'. Ann's claims addressed the principal concerns of the statute. She insisted she had not hidden the pregnancy and had wanted the child. Her marriage also negated any claims that she was immoral.[73] The accused's marriage was convincing evidence, and had a significant impact on a trial since, if believed, it re-instated the presumption of innocence for the accused. When Alice Sawbridge was accused of murdering her newborn in 1693 in London, she refused to explain why she had had the infant alone and disposed of its body in a clay pit. Despite this the court concluded that, as it was not a bastard, she had to be innocent.[74]

Married women were given more freedom in contemporary narratives, although they were still constrained by broad, gendered notions of appropriate behaviour. In particular, they could express themselves as maternal and moral, both crucial elements in constructing innocence. Unmarried women did not have access to such narratives of innocence until the early eighteenth century. Nevertheless, innocence was difficult for any accused woman to portray convincingly, and there was a narrative tension between married mother and child killer that most texts found difficult to fully resolve. Married women still experienced the duality of characterisation that affected all women involved in violent crime. The concept of the co-existence of femininity and violence was not acceptable in this period and so few positive images of violent women can be found. Femininity was conceptually constructed around nurturing and passivity and was linked to violence only in parody or in condemnatory texts. Public reactions to mothers who killed were almost overwhelmingly of instinctive horror.

There were a few grey areas, however, such as provocation, justifiable chastisement and mental instability. All were difficult to establish and few offered the certainty of extenuation. It is worth remembering that although a married mother was less conceptually constrained in what she could say about herself, any mother who killed would find herself in a position that was almost impossible to justify, and reliant not on the persuasiveness of her tale but on the mercy of the court.

A particularly interesting example of the duality of characterisation experienced by married mothers can be found in a case from Yorkshire in 1662, when Elizabeth Atkinson was accused of beating her stepdaughter to death. Evidence in this case was divided between Elizabeth's persuasive defence of herself and three representations of her violence from other witnesses. Elizabeth used images of maternity to construct a narrative of justified violence. In her deposition she claimed that she had asked Margarett, her stepdaughter, to fetch a pot of water, to which Margarett replied 'that if she would have the water or her she should fetch them [her] self'. Elizabeth said she responded to Margarett's disobedience by giving 'her a stroke or two therewith but not more'.

Having admitted to a level of chastisement acceptable by contemporary standards, Elizabeth went on to portray herself as a devoted mother who later cared for Margarett when she complained of feeling ill. She gave a lengthy description of how she put Margarett to bed and fed her after 'she this Examinant took her and carried her into the house in her arms'. Elizabeth clearly stated that Margarett 'had been sickly and weak for diverse weeks together'. She thereby implied Margarett's death had not been due to her moderate blows. Finally, she added as a codicil that Margarett's uncle had refused to get her water in the night 'he thinking it to be one of her usual tricks', a tactic obviously designed to show Margarett to be difficult, and emphasise that Elizabeth had not been the only one to think so. She concluded by stating that she had alerted her husband, the child's father, to her weakened state, expressing fears for her life. Clearly, her care of the child was the focus of her tale: she managed to both minimise the violent aspects of the hours before Margarett died and direct attention on to her maternal devotion, despite Margarett's unpleasant nature.

However, the remaining evidence diametrically opposed Elizabeth's cosy construction of domesticity. The other three witnesses told tales in which the violence of the beating was emphasised, while the familial relationship of the core characters was underplayed. John Lodge said he heard Margarett 'crying until (as they thought) she could cry no more for her Stepmother Elizabeth Atkinson [beat] her very sore with some kind of stick or staff'. He added that he had seen Elizabeth 'punching and dragging of Margarett Atkinson her husbands daughter'. He told the court that he advised Margarett to go home and be a 'good girl'. Margarett responded by telling him she greatly feared her violent stepmother.[75] In these witness statements, Elizabeth's persona was removed from its domestic context and was described in stark language as unreasonably violent. Without claim to passive femininity, Elizabeth's actions qualified as murderous. Whereas she had tried to present herself as only minimally violent, the witnesses aimed to undermine this view.

In fact, so difficult was it to present a coherent story of married maternal violence that madness was often invoked to explain such rage. Stories about killer-mothers played on the inconceivability of maternal violence, its unnaturalness and inversion of all female, and especially maternal, popular imagery. A London session paper of 1674 used the combined imagery of the devil and madness to explain the actions of a married woman's brutal slaying of her infant. The unnamed woman was referred to as 'the unnatural Mother'. Despite this condemnation, her motives in killing were clearly outlined in the rest of the tale. The story told of how, after her delivery, the mother had been tempted by the Devil to become 'discomposed and distempered in her mind'. She instructed the nurse to build a fire 'pretending she was cold', and sent her on an errand. Then 'she cruelly thrust the poor Innocent into it; and then threw the Coals upon it, where it was burned to Death'. This was a horrific and seemingly deliberate crime. However, the declaration of madness excused the act, as the jury declared the mother was not of sound mind and acquitted her.[76] An unmarried woman acting similarly would have had her wickedness rather than her mental incapacity emphasised.

When mixed with contrition and a martyr-like determination to die, a plea of maternal madness made a compelling tale. In the murder of Betty Cook, none of the gore or pathos of the crime was edited from the text; instead the killing was clearly placed in the context of maternity gone bad and possibly mad. According to the preamble Mary Cook had 'a very civil and sober life and conversation, living in the neighbourhood very inoffensively'. However, she was melancholy and repeatedly attempted suicide. Her maternal instinct led her to worry about 'what should become of that child, which she so clearly loved, after she was dead; upon this she concludes, she had better rid that of life first, and then all her fears and cares for it would be at an end'. Mary's maternity had been warped by her melancholy, but it was still apparent in the text.

Unlike the cold-blooded acts of illegitimate mothers, Mary was purportedly acting in her child's best interests and had to overcome her natural feelings towards the child before she could kill it. Her husband made every effort to have Mary released as mad, but the court refused and the pamphlet recorded that Mary approved of this decision. As in many such cases, Mary reportedly supported her own execution as a public atonement for her crime. According to the preliminary sermon, Mary hoped her death would 'outcry the loud cry of innocent blood, shed by her for vengeance'. She used her final act to construct herself as a martyr, with her contrition and resolve to die inverting her crime and allowing her to publicly restore her status as a good and self-sacrificing mother.[77]

In fact, the madness of married mothers was often presented in a very edifying manner. In a few cases, the mothers who killed their infants described themselves as acting in the child's best interests, protecting them from hunger or sin. In this way, the killer-mothers were depicted as nurturing and caring for their children when they killed them. In all such cases, the women were described as desperate and as regretting their acts. But desperation was a mortal sin, and showed a significant lack of faith in God. However, these mothers became martyrs, as their desperation did not concern themselves, but their children. In 1666 Emett Kithon confessed to killing her daughter 'for her daughters own good to free her from sin'.[78] In 1640 Dorothy Crason was affected by more tangible concerns for her child. She said her youngest came to her and asked for 'some victuals of her to eat, and she having no victuals at that time to give unto him ... took up the same [a knife] and cut the throat of the said Michaell Crason'. Dorothy clearly stated that this was the only reason for her actions, and added that 'she is heartily sorry for the said fact and wisheth with all her heart it were undone'.[79]

The pathos of these tales appealed also to pamphleteers, as an account from 1690 clearly shows. Katherine Fox killed her two children and her husband, because her husband had frittered away a large fortune with 'riotous living', leaving Katherine and the children wanting. After being publicly beaten by her husband, Katherine returned home to her hungry children. The pamphlet depicted her thoughts and actions as:

> Alas! Poor Babes ... Your Father hath lost his Patience, with his wealth, and we our Hopes, with his Mishaps: Alas! Alas! What shall become of me, or who shall succour you, my Children? Better it is to Die in one Stroke, than to languish in a continual Famine.

Katherine's motives for killing her children were portrayed as a last act of motherly compassion. This was carefully distinguished from her murder of her husband, in which she had acted from fury, due to his selfish 'ill Government'.[80] The tales of these murderous mothers were of maternity distorted but also of maternity as enduringly all-encompassing. As long as the women died at the end of the tale, they were almost admirable because of their extreme maternal devotion.

In a final irony, impending motherhood impacted on trials in a distinctive manner by legally allowing the suspension of an execution and a *de facto* reversal of a guilty verdict. Although not eligible for 'benefit of clergy' on account of their sex, convicted women did receive mercy in certain circumstances – if they claimed pregnancy. If substantiated, this secured them a respite from the sentence until after the birth, although in practice a decision of pregnancy often allowed these women to go completely free.[81] Impending motherhood was a powerful image, and although the women were not returned to innocence by a legislative decision, they were no longer publicly held accountable for their actions. Pregnancy needed to be credibly ascertained by a jury of matrons, and the infant needed to be thought to be 'quick' in the womb. The accused's release was contingent on this decision. Nevertheless, pregnancy provided married and unmarried women with a defence for even the most heinous of crimes – a unique opportunity for women in this period.

Pregnancy was a dangerous time for women. Maternal and infant mortality was high, with post-partum infection a real fear for all women. Suspicion of murder and the vilification heaped on an illegitimate pregnancy only added to the pressures on unmarried women. Although not similarly suspected, married women were then constrained to fit stereotypes of maternity and they were forced to be perpetually good, nurturing and selfless mothers. Whatever strain they were under – financial or mental – they were supposed to nurture their children. Despair or momentary violence could not be excused. A father could be violent, regret his act and be convicted of manslaughter. A mother never had her violence defined in this way. Women were not supposed to be violent, despite their role in policing the household. Although married women were sometimes given the benefit of the doubt, all mothers were supposed to act according to rigid guidelines of behaviour and morality. By stepping outside these constraints, even for a moment, women risked alienation and the full force of the uncomprehending and unforgiving law.

9

Child-Killers

In a pamphlet from 1694 concerning a series of murders in Devonshire, an unnamed father was reported to have killed four of his children in one savage bout of anger. The father's actions were undeniably brutal, but his young children whom he had killed 'by beating out their Brains with a Mattock, while they were on their knees begging for their lives', had not been the initial focus of his rage. He had wanted to kill his wife, but when she fled from his violence he took out his frustrations on the children, aged between nine and twelve years old. This act struck even him as wicked. His infamous crime was recorded in print in London and sold across the country, providing a whole new audience access to this scandalous tale.[1]

Like killer-mothers, fathers were not supposed to kill their children and could easily be demonised in print for doing so. However, the effective condemnation of a father's actions was more complex than for mothers. The killing itself was not enough to prove their wickedness: they had to kill without provocation in an extreme manner or, as in this case, kill several of their children at once if they were to receive the same kind of condemnatory language as killer-mothers. Men were expected to be violent and to correct family members physically. A jury would need to be convinced that they were acting in excess of this permissible violence, and *with malicious intent*, before they could thoroughly condemn them. Mothers who killed found it difficult to escape accusations of malice; fathers were never perceived in such uncomplicated ways.

The largest percentage of murdered children were killed by their mother or father. However, parents were not the only source of danger, just as today mothers are not the prime source of our fears for children. Today, children are perceived as more at risk from strangers lurking in the shadows than from either one of their parents. Modern stranger-danger is defined as partly sexual and always to do with a psychological disorder. In these scenarios, the stranger is usually white and male. Even unmarried mothers, although still demonised (albeit in different ways), are not portrayed as being as threatening as these external, random killers of children.

The reality, of course, is quite different. Children are most at risk from abuse by family members and death in simple traffic accidents. These facts are well known and still the fear of stranger-danger persists. Parents are still considered sacrosanct protectors of children. Those that assault or abuse their children are considered unnatural monsters without qualification. In a murder case, while the family always heads the suspect list, it is not danger from within the home that is universally feared. This was just as true of two-parent families in early modern England. Both now and then, we have to accept that danger *can* come from within the idealised family, while it was *invariably* expected from without.

Although in the early modern period unmarried mothers were especially targeted by the law for the perceived risk they posed to children (and, of course, because of their sexual misbehaviour), other people killed children and were prosecuted for this in court. Strangers and those *in loco parentis*, such as a master and mistress, did abuse and kill children, albeit occasionally. But if assault was known to come from these sources, and the potential danger of violent men was well acknowledged, these sources of danger were never given the same legislative focus as killings by unmarried mothers.

'Excessive correction' was a very real danger, but it was never perceived as the kind of systemic threat to children that the unmarried mother was to her illegitimate infant. In addition, child murder did not create the same kinds of drama or hysteria that it does now. Although considered a heinous and wicked act, it was thought no more wicked than many other types of killing. It was quite permissible to beat a child, especially one who had been intransigent or wilful. Parents and masters alike were expected to keep their charges under control and to punish them for their misdeeds. While it was unacceptable to kill a child in the process, the act could be interpreted as no more than manslaughter if the master had a favourable jury and argued his case convincingly. The killing of a child occurred in a complex social and cultural environment that we need to try to decode in order to understand.

In the first place, a child victim was not always considered to be entirely innocent. Children were seen as needing firm guidance to ensure they turned into socially appropriate adults. The point of physical correction was to limit their desire to sin and to promote obedience, hard work and deference – all crucial facets of early modern society. Small misdemeanours and sins were perceived as leading to bigger and more destructive things. The 'cycle of sin' was quoted from most scaffold speeches by felons who warned that failure to attend church or be obedient would lead directly to their own ignominious end. In this way, not all violence towards children was abusive. Instead it could be corrective, inflicted for the child's own good. A child who was old enough to leave home and go into service in another house and under different guardians was quite old enough to obey the rules of his or her new household. The beatings they may have been subjected to have to be viewed in the context of early modern society as permissible and even desirable violence.

Such views on violence did not extend to beating infants, however. Despite theological disagreement on the origin of an infant's soul, newborns were most often considered as archetypal victims, as yet uncorrupted by the world,[2] and the killing of such innocents was viewed as the ultimate in barbarism, for there could not be a more unequal conflict. After the newborn babe was washed clean of original sin its soul was considered to be pure. It could not provoke its parent, and should inspire only love from them.[3] These perfect child-victims were so well-known a stereotype that their innocence tended to be implied rather than explicitly described. The victims were seldom presented as characters with distinctive identities; rather they were implicitly constructed as passive victims of a terrible outrage. In theory, they were the ultimate innocent victims, whose assault was incomprehensible and whose killing was profoundly wicked.

Despite this pervasive subtext of innocence, illegitimate infants were not universally welcomed or protected and their unnatural deaths did not always lead to a public outcry. Their very identity as victims was problematic. Although infants may have been briefly described by their sex, they were not explicitly portrayed as innocent and were seldom presented as individuals. One reason for this lies in the nature of the 1624 act, which, as we have seen, was partly a response to widespread anxiety about bastardy, in which perceptions of a rise in illegitimacy rates sparked economic, religious and social concerns. Illegitimate children were symbols of sin, had little legal status, were unable to inherit property and were often deprived even of a certain name. As such, the infant was a significant social problem and an additional financial pressure on often poor communities, as well as being the embodiment of sexual sin. Such concerns multiplied with Puritanism and with theological debates about the potential influence parents had over an infant's soul.[4] No infant was born completely innocent, but was until baptism bathed in original sin. A child who died before its baptism – for whatever reason – was condemned to an unconsecrated burial and to damnation.

Many murdered infants, however, were not described as innocent, helpless or even, in many cases, as infants at all, especially when the child was illegitimate. In Yorkshire in 1667 Ann Crisby described the infant body she had found as 'something that affrighted her'.[5] In other cases, the bodies were described as lumps of flesh or as looking like a dog. The victim was dehumanised by these descriptions into flesh without soul or individuality. In some cases such a description may have been apt as it related to miscarried foetuses. However, the narrative power of such a denial of shape and meaning had an additional potency we cannot ignore. Illegitimate infant-victims were publicly mourned for, but were seldom wanted, despised and considered to be unclean while also conceptually pure. They seldom had their innocence articulated beyond the formal record.

In many ways stories of infanticide made the illegitimate infant an un-victim. Although legally murdered, the newborn otherwise bore a striking resemblance to the unborn foetus, and was seldom depicted as having a unique personality or features. Instead, it was generically defined, often without even a gender to differentiate it. A foetus had its identity thoroughly limited in infanticide stories, as until birth it had neither form nor sex. Nor did it have any legal status, making it impossible to murder. Despite this, unborn children inspired widespread concern and affection. If not a crime, abortion was a sin, and the foetus was commonly considered to be alive once it could move in the womb at quickening.[6] However, just as its life was always contingent on its mother, its identity was defined solely in terms of its parentage: its legitimacy affected its public image. Regardless of these limitations, the foetus had a narrative presence, often existing at the heart of the tale and fundamental to the action.

In stories in which a pregnant woman was killed, the foetus played a profound role in the tale, highlighting the mother's vulnerability. An assault on a pregnant woman was always described in a distinctive manner. The unborn infant was clearly used to build a picture of innocence and indefensible assault.[7] The role of the unborn was far from generic, however. Although ostensibly lacking identity, the foetus was clearly judged by contemporaries. A foetus had resonance, which an early modern audience would be clearly aware of. It had a status that the community could swiftly identify.

An example of the role of the unborn subject can be found in a printed tale from London in 1684. The pamphlet recorded the murder of the pregnant Mrs Kirk by her husband Edmund. They had been married only a few weeks when Edmund killed his wife by beating her black and blue with a cane and cutting her throat 'from one Ear to another'. Mrs Kirk's pregnancy underlined both her maternity and the illicit sexuality she must have engaged in before her marriage. Indeed, it was her swollen belly that incited the attack. The pamphleteer carefully recorded that the victim-mother was with (illegitimately conceived) child 'which probably she was before Marriage' and that the marriage had been a forced one.[8] Both the mother and the foetus were effectively constrained in this tale, and yet they were central to the story. Mrs Kirk was reduced to the carrier of a disputed infant. She was not given a name of her own and was symbolised in the text only as an illegitimate mother and the passive victim of her husband's rage. The foetus defined her immorality and provoked marital discord, which was the antithesis of the role it would play in less contested marriages.

As legitimacy or illegitimacy was a foetus's prime defining characteristic, the identities of the unborn were essentially binary. A legitimate foetus carried none of the stigma of an illegitimate one. In fact, a legitimate pregnancy was generally perceived as a joyful event. After all, the condemnation involved in infanticide related to the circumstances of the birth and not to broader questioning of the value of children or of childhood innocence. Consequently, the killing of a legitimate foetus was symbolic of a wicked undermining and betrayal of the family. In a pamphlet tale of murder from 1680 John Marketman was described as 'Committing a horrible and Bloody Murther upon the Body of his wife that was big with Child when he stabbed her'. He was drunk and extremely jealous of her, which led him into violence. The infant was hardly mentioned in the text but was omnipresent from the first as a symbol of their marriage and fertility as well as the future of their family. All these symbols were slain with Mary by the destructive act of her husband.[9] The death of the infant was not a crime and so was of tangential significance, and mentioned only as it related to the legally and textually more important death of the mother, Mary. Its death represented the marriage and maternity the killing had destroyed.

There was thus a distinctive kind of 'child' murder that played on legal definitions of life, in that it involved the killing of a foetus in the womb. Life did not legally occur until an infant had fully emerged from the birth canal. Neither abortion nor killing while in the process of birth (although somewhat difficult to prove) was illegal. However, there were a series of assaults that were loudly decried as murderous crimes, despite their involving attacks and killings of unborn children. Although the outcry was loud and persistent, this unusual genre of crimes did not receive the special legislative attention that infanticides received. This may have been because the number of crimes was relatively low. However, before 1624 the recorded incidence of infanticide was low, increasing only after the statute became law. Assaults on pregnant women that led to the death of their unborn children may have been presented far more often if this crime had been perceived as more than a common assault on the mother.

It was certainly not that popular concerns excluded these victims. Assaults involving the targeting of the bellies of married pregnant women, and the subsequent death of their foetus, caused discernible tensions and communal disquiet. Between 1685 and 1720 in Westminster alone eighty-seven cases of this type of killing were presented to the court. Although far from statistically significant, such numbers do indicate a popular interest in prosecuting this crime.[10] The deliberate targeting of the stomachs of obviously pregnant women suggests a common subtext of hostility towards fertility and a determination to injure the infant (and maybe the mother). Such assaults on fertility struck at the heart of the family. In many ways this crime was about expressing power over the future of an enemy's family. The victim – the unborn infant – was in fact a symbolic victim. It had no personality of its own – it was not even considered to be alive – but it did have the potential to increase a family and provide joy. This is why unborn children were targeted. They offered a low risk way of attacking the whole family and placing its future in jeopardy.

Several assaulted mothers prosecuted their cases in court, crying 'murder', even though such an act was not legally seen as any more than common assault. In 1697 in Yorkshire David Mitchell beat up pregnant Ann Midgeley when he was drunk and, her husband argued, 'unhuman'. The infant was born prematurely and quickly died from a bruise it supposedly had on its head.[11] Jane Lovegrove was also brought to miscarriage and near death in 1694 in London when Thomas Bedingfield pushed 'her on the side of the belly in a Quarrel'.[12] The female victims clearly presented these assaults as deliberate attacks on their infants and their own lives. When Alice Kay's twin boys were killed by the persistent stone throwing of William Backhouse, she clearly told the women who attended her subsequent labour that she held William responsible for the deaths of her twins and that she would not forgive him for so deliberate an act.[13]

Although, according to the law, the assault on the mother was the only legitimate crime that had been committed, the subsequent death of the infant was always presented as the more significant event. The mothers were clear that what they had experienced was in fact murder. In 1669 in Yorkshire John Holt seriously assaulted Frances Mountaine, by accosting her while she was out riding and snatching her bridle and her switch. He then took hold of her foot and proceeded to sexually molest her. She said that John:

> Endeavouring to throw his hand up her coats and pinched her by the belly, and bruised her belly she being great with child, Immediately after plucked open her waistcoat and pinched her by that breast and also bruised her breast.

This is clearly a story of sexual assault, and one that another witness corroborated with a similar tale. However, it is also a story of murder, in which the foetus Frances was heavily pregnant with died six weeks later. Two further deponents gave evidence relating to the birth and the death of the child. Isabell Popleton saying that 'the child she was delivered on was very black and bruised on the right side, And that the said Frances Mountaine did absolutely say that the bruise and blackness which was on the child's side did come by the pinches that John Holt ... did give'.[14] John's earlier sexual assault had previously remained unprosecuted. Only when a foetus died as a result of the assault, which was not a homicide under English law, were John's actions given formal legal attention.

While it was common for such assailants to claim they had meant no harm, their acts were popularly read as crimes. These popular concerns were, however, unaddressed in law. When women prosecuted their assailants, they wanted to publicly accuse them of the murder of their infants. A steady stream of prosecutions did occur, in which the death and/or miscarriage of a foetus was described in these terms. The death of the infant was not described as accidental, but as a murder deliberately wrought by the malicious actions of a third party. These prosecutions seldom achieved their aim of a murder conviction, though, and no special legislative tool was crafted to deal with these popular concerns, despite popular disaffection with this exemption.

Strikes at the pregnant belly of a married woman were an assault on her fertility, her family and even, potentially, her life. Assailants and their female victims clearly understood the subtext to their attacks. In 1655 in Skipton in Yorkshire Elizabeth Catterall claimed that William Hodgson stopped her in the street and 'Laid his hand upon her Belly and griping it fast in his hand told her that he thought she would be as big as Benson wife'.[15] Elizabeth later miscarried. Despite William's denials, the witnesses considered this to be a case of unnatural death akin to homicide. When Margaret Wainnopp confronted burglars late at night in her home in 1666 she claimed they hit her with a pistol and ran a sword into her belly. Although not pregnant, she had recently given birth. The burglars struck at a soft target of her large belly, while another threatened to kill her small child. This robbery was an assault on more than the family's money – it hit at the very core of their existence.[16]

Despite repeated presentations, the courts refused to interpret these crimes as homicide. In London in 1694 Jonathan Easden boasted of his assault on the heavily pregnant Ann Roberts. He said that he had attacked her because she owed him money, calling her 'an ill woman, and a Bawd', even though others declared she was of good repute.[17] Ann later miscarried. Despite his confession, Jonathan was acquitted. The courts simply did not perceive the death of Ann's infant to be murder. Despite intense popular concerns, these assaults were not criminalised. Foetuses were legitimate and socially valued, but remained unprotected until birth. Clear judgements were being made about the legal status of the foetus and infant that did not always agree with popular opinion.

Just as foetuses did not fit the criteria for victims of murder in this period, so fathers seldom fitted the expected profile of child-killers. As the Devon-shire killings made clear, murderous fathers were described as unusual and distinctively extreme. Men were known to be violent; as noted, it was an expected and accepted part of their character and identity. There were cases of fathers killing their children, especially when they were angry. However, such men were no more especially condemned for their violence towards children than they were for their violence in broader society. Men were perceived as being naturally and almost instinctively violent. It was this, so it was believed, rather than the perverse desire to kill their progeny that probably led to a child's death.

Indeed, despite constant monitoring of their involvement, fathers were peripheral to the killing of infants. These men were not considered innocent because of their sex; they were simply marginal to a crime widely perceived to be female. Women were interrogated about the role their lovers had played in instigating such crimes, but men were never the main focus of the narratives. Frequently, fathers and other men acted as mere ancillaries to female wickedness. When Mary Norsen tried, in 1696, to blame her lover for the murder, she could not completely remove herself from culpability. She told the court that immediately after her labour she had passed the infant onto its father 'But what he did with it she could not tell'.[18] However, she still played a key role in the death. The man's peripheral role could be advantageous and many men simply denied being the father, which was easy to achieve as the evidence was not written on their bodies. Despite steep financial penalties for fathering a bastard and despite the impact sexual immorality had on male reputations, fathers were seldom seen as socially dangerous. The malicious killing of infants was simply not a male crime.[19]

The distance fathers had from infant killings allowed them to present unique defences. When yeoman Andrew Waterlow gave evidence about the death of his newborn infant in 1682 he claimed he had not known that his servant, Susanna Watkin, was pregnant. However, he could neatly refute any motive for killing by stating that if he had known he would have married her.[20] This meant that fathers could act with greater subtlety. As historian Keith Wrightson argued, men could kill infants by employing neglect in the form of infanticidal nurses.[21] Such cases seldom came to court, and they did not receive special legislative scrutiny. The actions of William Jordan towards his illegitimate child demonstrated how problematic such a crime could be, conducted as it was at so great a distance. In 1647, William sent his infant out to nurse, moving him from one place to another every few weeks. He used his servant to move the baby and apparently had no further direct contact with the child. The child died in 1649 shortly after another move, though his cause of death was unclear. In this case, William was bound over to answer for the killing at the assizes.[22] His actions in moving the child repeatedly were seen as suspicious. However, in many other cases, the father may not have been suspected at all.

Fathers of older, legitimate children tended to kill more overtly, but even here the legitimacy of their actions was always clearer than that of mothers. It was acceptable for a man to be violent on occasion. Men were popularly perceived as being intemperate and at times unpredictable. These tendencies were not expected to disappear or be transformed when they became parents. Maternity rigidly defined female actions in ways paternity was never expected to. When, in 1668 in York, William Atkinson killed his small daughter, he presented his actions to the court as accidental. He said he had struck the child by mistake while trying to hit his wife. William's mother-in-law argued that William had been violent towards her; but no one argued that he had acted with deliberation.[23]

As the Devonshire case shows, pamphlet accounts only focused on the more sensational cases of paternal violence. Printed stories represented most fatherly violence in similar ways to depositions, when they emphasised the father's right to physically correct his children. In a tale from 1678 an unnamed father was described as 'naturally of a cruel dogged Temper, and always immoderately severe to this child, [and who] got up in a rage to look after him, and was seen walking furiously that way with a huge Cudgel.' His twelve-year-old son was later found viciously beaten, although his father denied he was responsible. An examination of the corpse showed that the child's extensive wounds overlaid many old injuries. In similar cases a mother would have expressed self-condemnation for her inappropriate acts. This father did not. He was described as 'too Excessive [in] Correction', but rather than being executed, was burnt on the hand for man-slaughter.[24] Unlike judgements of murderous mothers, his extreme act was not seen as warranting the death sentence. It was presupposed that fathers, like all men, had violent elements in their nature, often outside their control. While it was natural for women to nurture, fathers were not expected to be kind. Acceptance of the basic violent nature of men meant they were unaffected by the duality women experienced.

Both in print and in court a father had a discernible identity outside his paternity. His actions were therefore frequently linked to personal frustrations unrelated to his children. In 1664 in Northumberland Richard Foster declared 'that the last child that his wife had borne unto him was a devil, and he had thrown it into the fire and burnt it'. Even so, he acted not out of a frustration borne from concern or for its sustenance, like the mothers described earlier, but from a more general malaise. Richard killed a child he saw as a threat.[25] In such cases, fathers maintained a distance from their children in physical, emotional and psychological terms that women were seldom allowed. Becoming a father did not transform perceptions of a man's nature. A father was first and foremost a man, and a man could be harsh, excessive and intemperate. These facets of his identity were not celebrated; rather, they were usually widely condemned, but they did explain any excessive reaction he may have towards his child.

Although parents were the prime source of danger towards children, other members of the community killed children. As today, deliberate murder represented only a small proportion of child-deaths. However, unlike our modern terror of the threat of people outside the family, child-killings by strangers and neighbours never excited the kind of interest that murder by mothers received. Indeed, there was a startling consistency of interpretation regarding child-killers. Those who were most feared, and who were responsible for the majority of child murders in this period, were those who were acting as *parents* to the children, *in loco parentis*.

When young William Beane was brutally beaten in 1671 he clearly identified his master as the wrongdoer, before dying of his wounds. He said that Christopher Dalton had beaten him and had brought him to his end. Christopher did not deny the beating, but he did deny its consequence. He said he:

> doth confess That he tied the said William Beane's heels together in Regard he had bunched him with his Feet And did tie him up in a Tree by the Heels But not above a foot from the Ground, And denies, And denies [sic] that he did him any violence that might occasion his death.[26]

Despite the extremity of the assault, Christopher clearly saw his punishment of his servant's disobedience as just. The court may have been less forgiving, but it may well have chosen to interpret the violence as over enthusiastic rather than malicious. As we have seen, men were expected to be violent and to correct, and so any criticism of a master's violence needed to be based on such extreme actions no one could justify them in court. In a printed session paper from 1669 the terrible beating inflicted by the master was clearly stated to have been on 'no just offence'. Richard Sandford's master had repeatedly beaten him on the head with a broomstick and then with ropes, leaving him naked and cold on the floor to die.[27] That the killing was criminal was not in doubt; whether it was murder or manslaughter was.

At the same time, and like murderous mothers, the women who killed the children they were responsible for were always presented as sensational killers. Although mistresses and mothers had the same rights to chastise their charges as husbands and fathers, female violence was always seen as unnatural and extreme. Women who killed children were described as cruel mothers, and their crimes linked to a distortion of this most highly regarded feminine role. When Elizabeth Hazard killed her grandchild in Cheapside in 1659 she was called 'The Unnatural Grandmother', a title which generalised her wickedness. The author stated 'That in stead of nourishing, and cherishing that which comes at first from her own Loins, she so unwoman like and unnaturally hath now destroyed'. Like the murderous mothers described earlier, her crime was more than just killing; it was a betrayal of her maternal identity. The text concluded that she was:

> more like an Infernal Hag then the mother or Grandmother of children, without any fear or remorse of conscience, catches the poor harmless child as it lay in a sweet slumber, up in her wretchless arms, thinking to knock the brains out.[28]

It was Elizabeth's identity as a grandmother-killer that made this case so terrible. Only a depraved, unnatural mother could hear the whispers of the devil or could put their own needs above those of the child.[29] To act in such a way was to invert social notions of appropriate feminine identity.

Links between women and inappropriate maternity extended well beyond the biological family. When connected to children, women were always defined in terms of maternity. It was, after all, one of the prime characteristics of the early modern feminine identity. When wet nurse Mary Anderson killed eight-week-old Hannah Jones in 1699 her actions were defined as 'wickedly incensed' against a 'poor Harmless and Innocent Babe'. Mary was driven to distraction by Hannah's crying and feared it would awake her own infant. So, in a moment of madness, she drowned her. Mary did not confess to the crime until three years later, but the pamphlet argued that in the intervening period she had tried to kill her own child in a similar manner, making her a cruel mother, both to her own child and *in loco parentis*.[30]

Not all women were considered to be killers, as to kill was the act of an extreme, unnatural or isolated woman. However, all female killers of children were likened to murderous mothers. Although unusual and peripheral women, these killers represented the potential of women to harm maliciously and secretly. Popular conceptions of femininity always included the possibility that women could become unreasonably violent and strike out with malice. Most women, especially those safely ensconced in the legitimacy of marriage and constrained and policed by their husband, father or other women, did not act violently. But it was believed that there was always the potential for some to do so, making wickedness rather than innocence a more credible narrative when women were accused.

In 1654 Jane Scales was accused of killing a month-old infant using a complicated form of poisoning. It was reported that Jane entered the house of Alice Lund, the child's wet-nurse. Mary, Alice's child, deposed that Jane killed using a perversion of the female desire to nurture, by feeding the infant a substance taken from a piece of white paper. After this the infant grew suddenly sick 'and presently the said child did purge both upwards and downwards very Filthy matter both white and yellow'. Jane claimed she had fed the child some sugar, but the narrative efforts of several witnesses clearly implicated her in the crime.[31] Similar narratives can be found in cases in which women were believed to harm via witchcraft. Children and animals were the prime targets for harm by *maleficium*, with anxious parents attributing frightening illnesses to supernatural causes. Like the case of Jane Scales, narratives of deliberate murder were constructed around likely suspects. Even the act of passing an apple to a child by a suspected woman could lead to a serious accusation of wrongdoing.[32] As popular literature indicated, all women *potentially* posed a threat to children – even though most women *actually* did not.

Early modern people were not only conscious of socially constructed notions of fixed gender identities, but made explicit use of these categories to direct trial verdicts. Jane Cowper used a novel defence in 1682 to deflect an infanticide accusation by constructing an elaborate story in which her mistress, Margaret Mason, physically restrained her before killing her newborn twins. Jane told an extraordinary tale in which she claimed Margaret refused to allow her to call for help and 'said if she cried out she would stab her'. According to the story Jane was passive and dominated by Margaret; and the characterisation of Margaret as wicked was completed with the statement that she 'had been in Ireland and said she had put children on spear points there'. Jane's information was well disseminated, as all the other witnesses recounted the same tale.

However, these claims were not accepted without question. Despite her protestations, Jane's role remained suspect and she was described as reacting violently to questioning before the birth. One midwife said she was reluctant to enter the house alone to examine Jane for fear of threats to her life, while another claimed she had been called a lying whore and a thief for suspecting Jane. Dorothy Lister said she encountered Jane before the birth and said 'Thou art with child and Jane called her whore and said she was not and beat her this deponent with her own hat'.[33] In this tale notions of femininity and innocence clashed. The central females fought to retain an acceptable identity in an essentially bipolar arena. Jane's narrative cleverly attempted to prove her innocence by placing Margaret at the centre of the tale, while she took up an ancillary stance. At the same time, the other witnesses deliberately contextualised this tale by defining Jane as violent. It was a clear-cut struggle, and one it was essential to engage in, since, in early modern terms, women were either good or bad, innocent or guilty. Possession of an appropriate identity could make a critical difference to the verdict.

On occasion, killers who embody the modern concern of the lone stranger preying on the young can be found in early modern court cases. These killers were often considered to be wicked, but their crimes were not singled out as a specific cause of concern. There were no special laws to deal with men from outside the family who targeted children. Neither was there any discernible outcry in the press specifically about the nature, motive or character of these killers. While young unmarried mothers were effectively and repeatedly demonised, men – even from outside the family or complete strangers – were not subject to the same levels of vitriol or suspicion.

Psychological explanations for assaults were seldom made. While in modern cases of abduction or murder, sexual motives are swiftly suspected, revelations of sexual desire or contact were seldom made in this period. This is not to say that sexual desires to dominate and to penetrate young bodies did not exist. In 1699 two young apprentice boys told a London court how their master had committed buggery on their bodies while they were all out of the country, 'after which he threatened to murder ... [both of them] in case ... [they] revealed it'.[34] Although buggery was a felony, making an accusation had serious implications for the victim as well as the accused, since the victim of a rape could be at equal risk of prosecution and punishment. It is likely that many cases existed in which the boys – or girls – involved remained silent about their abuse, and without this evidence, any subsequent death could have been read in the same way as the cases of 'excessive correction' – as misfortune rather than sexual perversion.

Other equally alarming cases of assaults by strangers were recorded, involving extreme and unwarranted cruelty. Although there was no outcry about the threat of single men to the nation's children, certain men could be suspected of misdeeds. In 1675 in Yorkshire Alice Outwaite told of two men who had come to her alehouse. One man was forty or fifty years of age, while the other was only seventeen. Both men were strangers to her, but she claimed to be instinctively suspicious and to dislike them. The younger man was sick and the older one tended to him assiduously, but she refused them lodging 'by reason of their often whispering'. Her suspicions were clear and were directed towards both men rather than purely towards the older man. Other witnesses were also suspicious. The boy, John Sill, was later found dead. Robert became the immediate and only suspect. However, there was no subtext of especial cruelty or sexual impropriety.

Despite the suggestive suspicions, the case was treated simply as a murder, like many others.[35]

Only a small number of assaults were linked to strangers. Of these, a large proportion were coupled with robbery or the furtherance of another crime. When John Buchan stabbed and killed thirteen-year-old William Taylor in 1658, in Yorkshire, his action was primarily linked to his theft of a horse. John was essentially a thief who reacted to the presence of another by killing him. He was not presented as a danger to children outside this practice.[36] Other attacks by strangers were not so easily categorised. In 1666 Thomas Bell told of an unprovoked assault by Edward Ruddocke on himself and around fourteen young male friends. The group of boys went into a wood near Ruddocke's home to search for a young ash tree to cut down as a maypole. They were undoubtedly high-spirited and even rowdy – although no such evidence was presented to the court. In the midst of their enjoyment a gun was discharged by an incensed Ruddocke, and one of the boys, William Knagge, was killed. Two men then revealed themselves to the boys, and Ruddocke apparently said, 'ho rogues ho rogues … it is more fit you were in your beds then here at this time of night'. The two men may well have been poachers and the subsequent death of the boy unintentional, albeit still murder under the law as it was committed in the course of another 'crime'. However, Ruddocke's final statement to Thomas Bell indicated hostility and even a more sinister motive for the killing. He asked if there were more boys and enquired after their location. He then said that the dead William would act as 'an example for all the rest'. His reaction to the boys and to his subsequent killing of one of them was far from benign.[37]

Although men unrelated to their victims were responsible for killing a significant proportion of murdered children, they were never as vilified as women were. In fact, their killings were often termed accidental or the result of manslaughter rather than murder. The horror of the crime was diminished by the gender of the killer. These male crimes were not considered to be especially 'cruel' acts, but the everyday killings of children. Significant numbers of children were beginning to be killed on the road in vehicular accidents. Although indicted for their negligent acts, the male killers of these sometimes quite small children did not invoke undue hostility. In London in 1692 carman John Jellis knocked down a five-year-old boy in Newgate Street. Passers-by held John until a constable arrived, but no one told a tale in which malice was invoked.[38] This killing was clearly accidental, if a function of Jellis's aggressive driving style. But killings of this kind were not quantified and the killers were not executed, although some were tried for their carelessness. These child victims did not have their deaths avenged; they were not the children the law chose to protect.

Crimes involving deliberation were not always considered to be murders, especially if the crime was linked to uncontrollable male anger. In 1683 in London Philip Johnson was tried for the murder of eighteen-month-old John Hill. Philip had been drinking in John's parents' alehouse when John's mother refused to give him a private room. He returned the next day to smash windows, during which he deliberately hit the child with a stick and killed him. The court found that Philip had acted without premeditated malice, despite the gap between the insult and the revenge, and convicted him only of manslaughter, although recommending transportation.[39]

Likewise, when thirteen-year-old William Giles was killed by a neighbour, Jeremy Nelson, he was prosecuted for his act, but his violence was not presented as extraordinary. William told his master that Jeremy had beaten him with a stick. Jeremy contended that he had done so because William had acted mischievously in putting pins in the ground to trip unwary passers-by. He claimed that he warned William to stop, but he would not, so he physically chastised him. Although such an unrelated man would not have legal duties (or rights) to so physically punish, his actions would not necessarily have been criticised. Death was not an acceptable outcome, but any member of the community (male and sometimes female) could be legally excused for hitting out at provocative and disorderly children.[40] Although these crimes were as individually terrible as those involving women *in loco parentis*, the language of condemnation women habitually received in court and in print was noticeably absent.

Child-killings were not the simple tales of innocence corrupted and wicked desires fulfilled that they have now become. The child – even from birth – was not viewed as being always, unquestionably innocent. Its definition depended on the marital status and perceived morality of its mother, and the value of its death depended on the current bogey(wo)men pursued by the state. Children were not protected equally in this society: some killings were downplayed and others fell outside the remit of the law. Clearly not all were murders – vehicular homicide, for example, lacked the malice needed to make it a crime. Attacks on the bellies of pregnant women were clearly malicious and yet remained unencompassed by the law. Only certain children were protected by the law, and often it was not the *victim* of the killing that the law aimed to defend. Child-killings were based on the text and subtext of gender identities, in which unacceptable mothers and excessively violent fathers were judged and punished accordingly. Such crimes were never about the child-victim or the infant alone. They were means to an end of a state and locality determined to order and police their unmarried women.

10

Brawling and Duelling

In 1659 two Yorkshiremen, John Feurvely and Nicholas Poole, quarrelled. Poole quickly demanded 'satisfaction', by which he meant he wanted to engage in a physical fight to resolve the dispute and avenge the insults that had been exchanged. In this instance one witness claimed she heard a third man spur the two on by telling one of the combatants, 'thou art a man fight it out'. The two men fought enthusiastically and viciously, until one man was unable to continue and the fight stopped. This man, John Feurvely, later died of his wounds and Nicholas Poole was left to defend his actions while on trial for his life.

Despite the extreme consequences of this fight, it should not be seen as exceptional. Men were expected to be publicly violent in such circumstances. The fight that followed was spontaneous and, unlike some descriptions of elite duels, proceeded without formal regulation. However, it was not a conflict without honour. Feurvely fell during the conflict and Poole closed in on him, an action that met with a cry from an onlooker of 'You cowardly dog'. Poole replied by saying 'Thou art in my mercy but I will not hurt thee'.[1] Although he had fought his opponent furiously, Poole indicated that he understood the unspoken 'rules of engagement' and the unacceptability of striking a man when he was down. Poole later claimed he had no idea how Feurvely died, as he said he had not struck him and had desisted when he fell down.

This fight, like the majority of conflicts between men, was ambiguous. It was disorderly and disruptive while also seen as natural and even honourable. Its meaning shifted as it progressed. It was at times a spontaneous brawl, with no rules or regulation, and at other times it was constrained by popular concepts of honour and fighting etiquette. Even now, male violence is categorised by onlookers and judges in relation to its fairness and how it conforms to notions of order and acceptable violence. Men were expected to fight as equals and inequities in age, strength or weapons were disapproved of and would have affected how people interpreted the conflict. Onlookers may not have physically intervened but few fights occurred without any kind of structure. If they did, the community could display its displeasure via their evidence in court and informal censure. This fight, like many all-male conflagrations, crossed genres and legal definitions. It can be seen as both manslaughter and murder, and even at times self-defence. It was a duel and a brawl as it had both formal and informal moments. Fights were complex occasions that local people would have had to substantially unpick in order to fully interpret. Of course, how they interpreted it – before and during a trial – had a real impact on the verdict and punishment inflicted.

Early modern men were perceived as prone to violence, and were explicitly linked to hotter tempers, shorter fuses and a strong desire to fight. This imagined connection pervaded early modern literature and prescriptive texts, and can even be seen in the legal structure. As we have seen, not all male violence was unacceptable. Socially defined as the defenders of families, communities and nations, men represented the saviours of society and functioned as its policemen. They regulated their wives, servants and children and were further desired to overlook and constrain the behaviour of their neighbours. However, they could also be considered the biggest threats to social harmony, life and limb.[2] Male violence was both criticised and tacitly accepted, making definitions of this violence highly unstable in this period.

Although violence occurred every day it was by no means experienced equally within communities or even by the (mostly) men involved. Other factors like work, family and status, and a range of demographic and natural forces, played as great a role in determining social harmony. Despite being statistically the most disruptive of criminals, men were not collectively demonised by contemporaries. Most male aggression was understood as a key part of masculinity and, as such, was far from extraordinary. Violent masculinity was interpreted in disparate and sometimes contradictory ways. Its reception depended on the context of the crime and the nature of the audience. The meaning of violence was therefore far from certain.[3]

Male violence could be directed at household members, with women the prime victims. When the victim changed, the entire meaning ascribed to the violence also shifted. Violence towards a wife, for example, was always considered to be partially acceptable – albeit circumscribed by rules governing motivation and degree of chastisement. However, as the wife was identified as weaker and more dependent partner, extreme violence could be more heavily criticised than that that occurred in other contexts. At the same time, violence between males of approximately the same age and status was viewed differently. This was seen as much more of a battle of equals and often required the willing participation of both parties to occur at all. One participant may have been considered more culpable – in provoking or insisting on conflict – but few men were considered to be as helpless or as passive as wives. Male violence was most prolific when it was directed at other men. In such homosocial assaults men were acting to define and maintain their maleness, although the action changed with the status, age and individual identity of the men involved. In any case, early modern masculinity should be seen as intimately connected to violence, albeit violence that was subject to careful definition and a sliding scale of nuance.

This is not to imply that early modern men were endemically violent, or that this was a society plagued by disorder. Assault was by no means the only, or indeed the first, response of men to tense or difficult situations. Most violence occurred in specific contexts or as a last resort. On occasion a physically threatening or damaging response was felt necessary to ensure the protection of property, name, family and even of a life. But there were other equally well-used means for dealing with insults or threats. A threatening word or stance could sometimes be enough to deflate a difficult situation. If not, then arbitration, conducted by friends, neighbours, the priest or constable, could ensure a dispute was resolved peacefully. Court action for defamation could be undertaken to challenge an insult, and civil actions could resolve conflicts over property. Peaceful, non-physical and non-life-threatening responses were thus available to early modern men, with tried and trusted mechanisms for resolving disputes legally and equitably. These processes were often used: it is easy to forget in a study of violence, that in most cases violence was by no means either the norm or, for many men, even the preferred option.

Even when men were violent their actions were only scantily reported in the press and received relatively light punishments in court. It was, after all, considered normal male behaviour to fight. Therefore little public fuss was made when this expected activity occurred. This is in contrast to the intense focus pamphlets directed on to the relatively infrequent killings by women, as wives and mothers, servants and children of their masters and parents; and on other early modern scapegoats, like robbers (who, although mostly male, formed a distinct sub-category). These silences provide insight into how crime and especially violence was socially constructed. Although as dangerous as more demonised assaults, male violence was substantially down played. It was only the exceptional and the excessive that were publicly displayed; only the unusual and extreme violent act that transgressed local norms was extensively criticised.[4]

These facts notwithstanding, men were disproportionately violent. Nearly 90 per cent of homicides (excluding infanticides) had male defendants.[5] Likewise, men were protagonists in most assault cases, as assailants and as victims. In 80 per cent of cases in which a male was accused of homicide, another man was the victim,[6] male violence was always viewed as complex and as needing nuanced reading. Women were defined in binary terms, as either passive, chaste, and therefore 'good', or as violent, sexual and so 'bad'. Men were never viewed in this clear-cut way. Their violence was unacceptable as well as understood and legally excused. In most cases the sheer inequality of the murder of a child by its parent or the secret poisoning of a husband by his wife did not apply in cases of male brawls. Men were the fundamental source of order within the patriarchal state. As the heads of households, they had a duty to keep order. They were even permitted to (moderately) beat their wives and household members to ensure their obedience. These same men made up local militias and would be expected to fight to protect their communities, co-operate in a hue and cry or fight for their country. Violence was seen as naturally male, and at times necessary to fulfil the man's social roles. Although this acceptable civic violence had to exist within the confines of state power, popular and legal tacit acceptance of male violence was a clear and fundamental part of early modern mentalities.[7]

It is clear that the public violence to which men were most prone was socially contentious. Increasingly, civic and religious authorities were concerned about public expressions of violence. The law clearly outlawed assault, and the courts harshly punished those guilty of extreme acts and of homicide. Violence was commonly associated with passion and a lack of control and was therefore discouraged in young elite men, who were strictly disciplined to restrain any unseemly passions. Homicide rates were high in this period, although in steady decline.[8] Anxiety about public violence was therefore pervasive. This fundamental element of masculinity was as contentious and as actively prosecuted as it was played down in court.

Although masculinity was linked to violence, not all men were violent in the same ways. Some men were habitually violent, while others made a conscious effort to avoid all kinds of conflict, resorting only to violence in their own defence. The rest were violent only on occasion, when they had been drinking or as part of a sudden conflict. Violent behaviour can also be linked to lifecycle, with young men eagerly practising violence as part of their mantle of masculinity, and old men avoiding conflict. It is more difficult to make distinctions based on marital status, however, as few of the men involved had this noted in their depositions. Nevertheless, social standing clearly impacted on decisions about violence. The court was more lenient towards the elite. It may have been that these men engaged in violence less often, although there is no evidence of this. It is more likely that they were just prosecuted less often for violent crimes.

It is clear that some men eagerly embraced violence and considered it to be a fundamental part of their lives. Such men could be dangerously unpredictable at times, but they were usually well known in their communities.

In Yorkshire in 1674 Edward Dawson took it upon himself to force a fellow drinker to pay a bill, although he had no official role in the running of the alehouse. Edward was, according to one witness, 'in everyone's esteem a man of very bad fame and behaviour'. Witnesses noted that while no one had asked him to intervene, he enthusiastically used excessive force on this occasion.[9] Likewise, in St Brides in London in November 1693, three men were indicted for the murder of Henry Hutton. Witnesses reported that the men had 'agreed amongst themselves to kill the first man they should meet'.[10] The men killed Hutton with their swords after mistaking him for the alehouse keeper who had refused them entry. These men were unpredictable, brutal and quite unconcerned with hiding their crimes. Even so, printed sources tended not to express these crimes in terms of broad social dislocation. Although these men represented examples of more extreme and undesirable forms of early modern masculinity, they were also a constant and even expected presence.

For adolescents, violence played a quite different role. Young men and boys were often keen to assert their strength and their masculinity in a public forum. The social meaning of this violence was distinctive. Manhood began 'roughly by 25 or 28' and was waning by fifty.[11] However, men and boys under twenty-five were aware of the parameters of masculinity and certainly of the overt displays of power that were a fundamental part of it. Adolescence was a distinctive period in which characteristics of adulthood were learnt and practised.[12] The violence of young apprentice-men took the form of rough play and apparently lacked malicious intent, but there was an inherent danger in these violent pastimes, which was very much the point of such violence and the learning curve of those boys. London apprentice Thomas Foster argued, in 1676, that he threw a 'great stone' at James Cope 'in jest'. Another boy added that 'before that all three of them had been throwing of stones'. The friendly conflict and rough jest led to James's death.[13] Likewise, William Blaynners accidentally killed his fellow young servant Mary Jackson when he toyed with a fowling piece. He said 'as he was pulling the cock up it slipped from him ... [and] it went off'. When he saw that Mary had been hit he ran from the house terrified by the consequences of his act.[14]

Most often the conflicts of young men aped adult forms of violence, and the young men appeared to learn masculinity by replicating the flamboyant excesses of public fighting. These adolescents were eager to establish their maleness; something that was vital to their adult identity.[15] In Holborn in 1676 two apprentice surgeons, Henry Tyzack and Stephen Tucker, were drawn into a conflict over a gambling dispute. Tucker called Tyzack a cheat, and so Tyzack's friend, Cherry, arranged a meeting at the fencing school.

The two principal combatants and friends ('seconds') took their swords and entered the fencing school to fight. This was obviously an acceptable place for such conflicts, as the men had immediately known where to go. The fight did not just involve the two principals: all four men engaged in conflict, with one friend, John Draponteare receiving a head wound. Henry Tyzack was more seriously wounded and died three days later.[16] Despite the energy they committed to developing their proto-masculinity, this fight was hidden from their probably more socially conforming (and older) male employers.

Youth, and a probable lack of understanding of the moral consequences of their proto-masculine acts, were often considered to be mitigating factors in such cases and encouraged the court or community to be more lenient. As in all homicides, it was the intention behind the action that was critical in deciding what kind of crime had been committed. Young men who had engaged in rough play in which no malice could be identified were often acquitted or convicted of a lesser crime. In London in 1676 one thirteen-year-old apprentice stabbed and killed his friend after a quarrel. The boys had argued, the pamphlet said, 'about cutting their Apron-Strings', implying they had disagreed about their proto-masculinity and relative social status. However, the judge told 'the Jury to consider whether the boy understood what he had done or not, he being but thirteen years and a month old, the Jury afterwards brought him in guilty of Man's Slaughter'.[17]

On the other hand, where malice was felt to be present little mercy was shown whatever the age of the defendant. When fourteen-year-old Joseph Dyson was executed for highway robbery and attempted murder his crime was reported at length, primarily due to his age. A pamphlet referred to John as 'a little boy about 14 years of age ... young in years but old in wickedness'.[18] He was tried and executed as an adult for a crime that was seen as deliberately malicious. By defining him as wicked, the jury clearly distinguished his actions from those other less malicious young men. Because his violence was motivated by robbery and was not about mutual involvement or the protection of honour, his action was far more critically interpreted. No distinction was made between him and a similar adult killer.

In records peppered with bad-tempered males who were swift to retaliate physically, even-tempered men who avoided conflict were as remarkable as excessively brutal or young killers. While such men were seldom described in print, they were avidly defended in court as simply not the type of men who would act in an antisocial manner. They are also the men that the study of homicide alone can only underestimate. Non-violent men were rarely seen in court records of violence. However, on occasion local people explicitly informed the court of their goodness as a defence from an accusation of killing. In 1648 in Yorkshire fifty-four men signed a petition protesting the previous good reputation of Roberte Camme, who was accused of stabbing Nathan Normanton in the street. Roberte was, they petitioned:

> generally reputed amongst us a very honest man of good life and conversation amongst his neighbours, no Alehouse haunter, nor given to brablinge or quarrelling, But a very peaceable man and of a quiet disposition, a good Churchman and forward in religion, and religious duties, a man very industrious and painful in his vocation and calling whereby he maintained his wife and five small children in good order and fashion according to his degree and calling.

Even the local coroner signed this petition.[19] Generally the petitioners in such cases did not argue over the details of the conflict, over who struck the first blow or on previous malice, but they simply contended that these men did not possess violent traits.

Despite these distinctive cases, the majority of male violence involved mainstream men whose aggression was not distinctive, and who engaged with men of similar status, profession and social standing. They killed people they lived near to, and worked or socialised with. Violent male behaviour can be consistently found across social strata. It was the behaviour of gentlemen, yeoman, tradesmen and labourers, and, although there were few inter-status conflicts, the propensities to violence, and its acceptability as a form of male expression, were features held in common. Ordinary men fought other ordinary men in battles that few felt to be extraordinary. Small anomalies like age or history of violence were seldom enough to warrant extra lines of print or fulfil the requirements of salacious pamphlets. In fact, it was often the bad luck of happening to die that distinguished an everyday fight (which was still a crime but relied on the willingness of the victim to prosecute) from a homicide.

Male violence was so complex that contemporaries had to divide men into identifiable diagnostic groups to ensure they reacted appropriately to the level of violence and the perceived disorder that had occurred. This process of comprehension was both legal and cultural, as violence was variously analysed and labelled 'criminal' or 'acceptable', 'honourable' or 'disorderly'. Unlike female violence, where almost any aggressive action was interpreted in simple terms as 'good' or 'bad', male violence was deconstructed by the courts and contemporaries to discover its precise 'meaning' and social threat.

Within the legal system there was a desire to punish malefactors but also a determination to excuse certain kinds of male violence. Popular attitudes towards male defendants influenced judicial decisions, which in turn affected the application of the law. Definitions of culpability were slippery and informed by social and cultural concerns.[20] The law on homicide was stratified in this period, and male crimes fell somewhere between excusable homicide (including self-defence), manslaughter and culpable homicide (murder).[21] The dividing line between these categories of killing was fine and ultimately rested on the decision of the jury in court. However, there were enormous differences in the punishments inflicted. Although women were acquitted more often than men, the range of potential interpretations for a male crime was uniquely broad. These categories were, of course, legislatively open to women, but cultural conceptions of femininity linked women with violence only in the worst of scenarios, that of malicious intent. Although a small number of women may have fitted the criteria for manslaughter or self-defence convictions, there is little evidence of their benefiting from them.

In any case, the criteria for self-defence and manslaughter were predicated upon male examples. Self-defence was defined as a forced violent response after an attack, which was incompatible with femininity. Women were expected to receive such assaults passively, not to be able to defend themselves. Manslaughter referred to a battle of equals resulting from hot anger. This type of sudden, uncontrolled violent response was not one socially or legally associated with women. A woman was perceived as unlikely to be able to protect herself from a man, with her only defence being flight. Such a passive response was seen as understandable in a woman, while an active, violent response was not, making either self-defence or manslaughter unrealistic options for a female defendant.

Since men were expected to be violent, it was actually more problematic to construct a case in which a man was unquestionably culpable of murder. For men, a murder verdict depended on subjective decisions about the scale of the crime and the intentions of the killer. Deliberate crime or killings in the course of another felony (like robbery) were clearly classified as murder. However, most male killings were variations on mutual conflicts. This meant that the killing could fit into any of the three legal categories of homicide, with distinctions resting on juridical and judicial decisions alone.[22] As a consequence, factors like inequality in the conflict, or in the weapons used, the character of both defendant or victim and their past relationship were fundamental to a trial's outcome. Murder was not a clear-cut category, but contingent on detailed decisions made by jurors about individual cases. Consequently, the stories told about the crime in court were critically important, as was the spin witnesses gave them.

Excusable homicide covered both a killing by a legal official in pursuit of a felon and self-defence. These pleas were often based purely on the credibility of a defendant's story. Both were closely monitored crimes, as they in effect allowed someone to 'get away' with murder. Defendants tended not to make direct pleas, but rather used their stories to clearly imply their stance. These complex narratives had to meet very strict criteria, however. To justify a plea of self-defence the defendant had to have resisted fighting, have been literally backed into a corner and to have acted only at the last moment to preserve his own life; he could not have claimed to have struck out of anger or with any kind of forethought.

A case from Yorkshire in 1669 provides a clear example of a precise and credible self-defence tale. Adam Bland described how he had killed James Strangewayes after a pleasant and friendly evening together. James had been drinking and Adam claimed he was suddenly assaulted, saying:

> Mr Strangewayes started up upon a sudden and drew his sword and swore God damn him he would kill him [Adam] if he would not fight him and with that made a pass at him which he avoided by leaping Back till he came with his back against a ... cupboard (being against the wall at the furthest side of the room) and then the said Mr Strangwayes made a second pass which he put by and got a strike in the knee with Mr Strangewayes sword, and the said Mr Strangewayes made a third violent pass at him which he put by with his left hand and having his sword (for his defence) pointed against Mr Strangewayes he run himself upon it by which he believes he received his wound.[23]

This carefully constructed tale met all the necessary criteria for a self-defence plea, and, since the other witnesses helpfully concurred, would undoubtedly have been accepted.

Few other attempts to build a self-defence narrative went as smoothly, however. The courtroom was often a battleground in which witnesses in pursuit of justice competed over the interpretation of events. Aware of the importance of their words, witnesses and defendants carefully constructed their statements. An example of this can be found in the case relating to the killing of George Phillips by Christopher Little in Yorkshire in 1663. Christopher met up with George on the moor and said George and his friends taunted him with the fact that he had to walk while they rode. He claimed George hit him for no reason. In response, Christopher 'threw him down and held him down by his arm desiring him to be quiet'. He let him go, but George attacked him again, and Christopher said he told the company 'thou seeist how civilly I use thy comrade and might abuse him if I would I desire you to take him and free me of him'. He then claimed to remember no more about the incident.

Unfortunately for Christopher, the other witnesses were reluctant to allow him to explain away his actions. Instead of provocation and assault, they claimed they saw a fight in which Christopher fully participated and even had the upper hand. George's friend, Thomas Bankes, described the fight in detail and added that, as he died, George said that Christopher had threatened to kill him five days before. This story effectively challenged Christopher's by emphasising his willing participation in the fight and by suggesting he had acted with malice.[24] As with the majority of homicides, this crime potentially fitted all the available homicide categories. A self-defence verdict would have been purely subjective in this case and based on unrecorded details such as character, appearance and how the evidence was presented on the day. However, the jury could just as easily have decided this was a case of murder.

Manslaughter was less rigidly defined in law as it relied on more subjective decisions about mutuality, anger and intent. The criminal mitigation manslaughter offered had been developed in the sixteenth century by judicial decision and relied on two clear conditions. Firstly, the defendant must not have intended to kill his victim, and secondly he must have acted in hot anger. Hot anger meant an immediate violent response to physical provocation, although sometimes insults were accepted as a cause. Provocation received the most attention in this period, as juries considered how extreme the temptation to be violent was and how reasonable it was to expect restraint. Women were not (and are not) legally or culturally believed to feel hot anger, and provocation was seldom related to female violence.[25] Female anger was seen as cold and calculated. In other words, women were predisposed to malice and therefore murder, while the uncontrollability in men, which the civic authorities and local people often feared, in part excused their actions and reduced their punishment.

Ideas about the (un)acceptability of male violence were not openly discussed. Despite its criminal nature, certain male violence was commonplace. The printed sessions tended to refer only briefly to conflicts which were clearly defined as mutually engaged in. In 1676 in London, a short printed report of a homicide case stated only that a gentleman had killed his friend after both had been drinking hard. The conflict consisted of a sudden quarrel that was resolved with swords. The pamphlet recorded that there had been no previous malice and did not address the legitimacy of the act itself.[26] However, the brevity of the record, the lack of comment on the manslaughter conviction and the absence of hyperbole of any kind is revealing of a level of acceptance. Unless further extraneous and unusual detail could be added, a case in which two men fought on equal terms seldom received much attention in session papers. By giving male conflicts limited coverage, these pamphlets effectively normalised this type of violence by deliberately separating it out from other, more deviant crimes.

At times witnesses made deliberate efforts to direct the verdict to either murder or manslaughter, by heightening perceptions about the culpability of the accused. Victimhood did not sit easily with common interpretations of masculinity. While women were prescriptively passive, a man was supposed to be able to defend himself. However, conflicts were not always fair, so with skill, and a friendly jury, a fight could be shifted from a mutual battle to an unprovoked assault. Even so, few deponents implied that the victim had been powerless. A male victim of an assault was usually quick to engage his attacker and could frequently emerge as the victor (and the killer) of the man who had attacked him, which seldom occurred when a woman was assaulted. Judicial distinctions were made according to the scale and swiftness of the victim's response.

An excellent example is provided by the case of John Swan in Yorkshire in 1668. Witness Jaine Brooks used her evidence to suggest the blameless role played by her dead lodger in his own death by saying that 'he was very sober and pleasant in his discourse and she is verily persuaded that he had no intention to fight at that time for that he carried only a little sword by his side not fit for such a purpose'. Her servant concurred by saying that 'Mr Swan was a Civil man and not given to quarrel for any thing he knows or ever heard'.[27] Neither described John Swan as helpless. They merely asserted that he had no obvious intention to fight at that time.

In terms of the application of the law, the acceptability of male violence was predicated on several subjective and interconnected categories. These included the intentions of the killer, the equality of the fight and the relative status of the combatants. Decisions about the value of a crime and the judicial and communal response to it were highly contingent. Invectives about the wickedness of the violence were clearly presented, with pamphleteer and witness alike distinguishing between male actions. Acceptable levels of masculine violence were not explicitly debated in print or in court. Instead, popular and legal decisions were based on subjective views of appropriate male behaviour. Certain violence was more regularly perceived to be criminal. In particular, assaults on social superiors by their inferiors were often celebrated and infamous crimes.

A trial at the Old Bailey, in which the murder of a worthy knight by two 'villainous' persons was presented, shows how status impacted on the portrayal of a crime. One pamphlet presented an especially condemnatory view of the gravity of the offence, saying 'The Gentleman upon whom this assassination was committed was a person of good worth, a handsome noble Estate, young in years, and likely to have proved very useful and serviceable to his Country and Generation'.[28] The attack on this paragon was later described as 'insolency', with the two accused men's malice and lies as the only cause of the affray. The two men were described as being caught due to the intervention of providence. An attorney set a hue and cry in motion after he had overheard a tale about a different crime, but it was these criminals that were eventually captured. The intervention of providence provided the readers with a metaphor for a society out of joint and neatly demonstrated how reprehensible the act was considered by God and man.

Legal decisions about culpability were not the only ones made. Conceptual distinctions based on status and the perceived orderliness of male violence were also made by contemporaries and by modern historians. Although seldom found in depositions, these categorisations of conflict can be seen in other prescriptive texts. In particular, violence was divided into two seemingly opposite categories, duels and brawls. Duels are usually described by historians as high status, honourable and mutually undertaken events. It has often been argued that duelling was the conceptual opposite of the unregulated violence of the brawl. A duel was supposedly more refined and highly regulated, its function a physical restoration of apparently fragile male honour. Death was seldom the intention or the outcome of a duel, with 'first blood' widely acknowledged as settling the dispute and, strangely enough, even leading the combatants into a closer relationship. Early modern men and women were aware of the language and putative structure of duels as well as the broader meanings of this violence. Conversely, the term 'brawl' has been used historically to invoke a disorderly kind of violence. Unlike the high status duel, the brawl was the arena of the common man. Although both parties willingly participated, the term implied this was not a planned engagement. It was said to be violence for violence's sake, without formal structures or honour.[29]

In reality, distinctions between a duel and a brawl were seldom as un-complicated, and nor were they the only ways of defining a violent act. Injudicious use of either of these terms can create confusion and, in par-ticular, be misleading about the levels of awareness, planning and participation of both parties in the conflict. Individual acts of violence were actually understood in a more flexible manner. Until the mid-eighteenth century, duels were seldom orderly, pre planned events as they lacked the formal and sometimes written rules of later generations, leaving them almost indistinguishable from brawls.[30]

Conversely, an examination of low status conflicts shows brawls to have been more orderly and rule-bound than the term itself suggests.[31] Ordinary men fought to defend their honour as much as those of high status did. Their rules of engagement could be as strict as duels purported to be, with rules about not interfering with the parties (if the initial attempts to part them and prevent the conflict failed), while at the same time these were passionate and spontaneously violent conflicts.[32] Indeed, ritual played a clear role in English brawls. Fights can be seen as 'a carefully staged set of

symbolic gestures, with complex ritual meanings'.[33] It is certainly the case
that order was palpable in early modern homicides, if only momentarily.
Most conflicts began in a semi-formal way with an insult and response. In
1650, soldier Captain William Barcroft, and excise master William Shaw
'fell at some words about their manhood'. The two men therefore 'appointed
the field', and although they then seemed to grow more friendly, later that
evening Shaw killed Barcroft.[34] Their anger, which they had tried to regulate
had apparently overwhelmed them.

Witnesses were also aware of the social nuances of engagement and their
potential to get out of control. In 1672 in Chatten in Yorkshire Andrew
Carr and James Swinhoe were initially prevented from fighting by friends,
despite a written challenge having been issued. Richard Henderson said that
the morning after the two men had quarrelled:

> suspecting some mischeifs ... [He] came up Anthony Dunstalls Garden [and
> found them with] drawn swords fighting, and he [Richard] reached upon Mr
> Carr and soon parted them without any harm done.

He took both men inside and gave them a drink and considered the matter
closed. Later that afternoon, however, he heard a woman cry that:

> two men were fighting in Garden so he run in to the said Garden and did find
> James Swinhoe and Mr Carr swords drawn and Robert Gray with them and the
> said James Swinhoe being wounded in the arm did I help to bring him in to the
> said Dunstall and he further sayth that he bled to death of that wound as he
> believes.[35]

Richard Henderson made every effort to prevent the violence, while Robert
Gray, another bystander, was described as having fully participated in the
conflict. Their perceptions about the necessity of the battle obviously differed, as would those of many in their community.

It is too simplistic, however, to define physical violence in a one-dimensional manner, whether as ritualised and meaningful or spontaneous and
brutal. Rather than duels and brawls representing opposing categories for
early modern violence, most conflicts were an active mixture of order and
disorder, ritual and chaos. Circumstances disarranged and transformed
planned conflicts into a multiplicity of shifting meanings. In 1675 in the
Duke's Playhouse on Shaftesbury Avenue, Sir Thomas Armestrong and
Jervis Scroope, esquire, fought until Scroope's died. The pair had obviously
previously been good friends, and, as witnesses said, even on the evening
of the conflict they had constantly been together and were very 'merry'.
However, Armestonge stated that Scroope soon grew abusive and challenged
Armestronge to a fight, which he at first refused 'conceiving it to be the

effects of drink'. Scroope then pursued Armestronge with a drawn sword until Armestronge responded.

Armestronge, one witness argued, tried to defer the fight until the morrow, as was traditional, no doubt hoping his old friend would calm down in the intervening period and call the fight off. All attempts at persuasion failed, and one good friend, Armestronge, was forced to draw against another, Scroope, and kill him.[36] Like the conflict of Feurvely and Poole, at different moments this fight fulfilled all the categories of homicide in law and had elements of a duel and a brawl. It was both spontaneously brutal and governed by popular and social conventions.

To define male conflicts successfully in this period we need to blur categories and distinguish less sharply between behaviour types. Conflicts were seldom perceived simply. Duels and brawls were not distinctive, and neither were the gentry any more likely to be orderly than working men. If we deny the disorder of physical violence by over-rationalising it, it loses part of its meaning. Violence, and especially homicide, was, partly at least, disorderly, messy, uncontrolled and unpleasant, and we must not forget this. However, disorder existed in concert with an overarching sense of order. Deponents were aware that the final assignment of a category was the role of the court. The conflicts they described simply were complex and decisions about them depended on the context and history of the central relationship. Discrete categories strain to encompass individual cases. To define conflicts in unambiguous terms drains them of their vitality. Violence was, at once, orderly and disorderly, expected and unexpected. Categories of violence need to be flexible, and male violence is revealing of early modern masculinity precisely because it was so amorphous. Violence was inherent in a broad range of masculinities, albeit subject to differing interpretations.

Nevertheless, that much socially destructive male violence was normalised is intriguing and somewhat difficult to explain. The legislative leniency shown to men was made up for in the higher proportion of convictions they received. However, even then, benefit of clergy could be easily sought (in manslaughter cases) to reduce punishment. It seems trite to say that patriarchy was acting to protect men generally, while allowing specific, dangerous men to be convicted, but this is a probable explanation, if only of the broader early modern mindset. It is also clear that apart from a few civic and religious leaders few wholeheartedly linked male violence with broad social threats, unless the perpetrators were members of archetypally dangerous groups, like soldiers. A woman who killed her husband was clearly treasonous, a mother who murdered, unnatural; and either could be devilish. Violent husbands, fathers or neighbours on the other hand were not widely regarded as threatening or wicked. Instead, they were seen as dangerous individuals who had to be controlled but not judged collectively. Despite their dominance in crime, men were never universally conceived as systemic social threats.

In reality, male violence existed in a continuum. At one end was the acceptable and normal violence of a good man, who defended his household, his parish and his country, who pursued criminals as needed and who disciplined his wife, servants and children well. At the other end was the cold-blooded and malicious killer. In between were the more common and everyday interpretations of masculinity, of rowdiness, or occasional misbehaviour, of public drinking and fighting and even of lesser forms of killing. All female violence was unequivocally criticised, but male violence was often viewed as natural, honourable and even desirable. Nevertheless, it was problematic to clearly distinguish between acceptable and unacceptable male violence. Social and legal notions were often in conflict. Being a good man meant being simultaneously obedient to the state and maintaining the potential for violence; being both passive and potentially aggressive. This ambiguity meant there was no clear line in the sand, and therefore male juries in a masculine courtroom had to rely on the minutiae of detail in each case to make a judgement. Even killing was not always 'wrong' enough to warrant the full wrath of the law, with some offenders only slightly punished, especially in manslaughter cases.[37] It was in secret juridical judgements that decisions about the nature of acceptable masculinity were made and challenged every day.

In 1693, two Dutch soldiers in Leeds were sufficiently provoked by a large group of local men to respond by openly killing their prime tormentor in broad daylight.[38] This assault, although not unique, was extraordinary – not in terms of its violence but of the context in which it occurred.

Only the occasional angry or alienated man would risk fighting in daylight. In fact, most daytime confrontations were cautious and partially hidden, as in 1693 in the North Riding of Yorkshire, when John Sparrow chose to throw a stone to wound Mr Sutton, rather than assault him more personally. Although he was attacked at 9 am, only the victim saw the stone thrower, and so only he could identify him as the culprit in court.[39] The daytime street was otherwise an unlikely space for inter-male violence. Indeed, witnesses indicated that they were far more shocked at displays of aggression on the open street than they were by similar but more discrete violence.[40]

The importance of an appropriate space for a conflict was well understood. Male violence was not deliberately disguised, but it did (mostly) occur in masculine spaces from which women were largely excluded. Most men were far more comfortable fighting in the gloom of alehouses, dark or partially hidden streets, fields and other open ground. These spaces were neither completely hidden nor were they in the midst of the community. The more masculine the site was perceived to be, the more unfettered the aggression became.

Physical violence was usually an attempt to resolve private disputes, not to provide gladiatorial displays for general amusement. Men fought in spaces where few females were recorded as being, and where few actually witnessed the violence.[41] Although violence could enhance male reputations, nearly all participants perceived it as socially disruptive. Therefore, the majority fought in places and at times where their activities could be easily disguised. Their violence occurred on the edges of public life and away from the bustling streets. Such spaces had an additional purpose: they prevented intervention and minimised the chance of attracting witnesses. Darkness and semi-privacy must have aided escape and, to some extent, prevented detection, which allowed the full and unfettered reign of certain violent masculinities.

The meaning attached to early modern spaces was far from consistent. The way spaces were used shifted throughout the day, and hence, the meaning and the level of danger inherent to that space. Their gender composition could also be transformed. For example, the household had multiple uses, acting as an informal alehouse, a place of congregation for neighbours and a workspace. A home was seldom an exclusively private space. Neighbours, relations and even strangers could easily gain access, and often felt they had a right to enter, be hospitably received, and monitor the activities of the occupants in order to criticise their behaviour or their familial structure. Households were both male and female to fluctuating degrees, with their compositions distinctive and changing with individual occupants.

Time had special effects on the interpretation of a space. Fights frequently occurred at night, with the cover of darkness adding another dimension of privacy and a different context to the bustling daytime streets.[42] After all, when violence occurred in well-lit mixed sex spaces, with bystanders ready and willing to intervene, the conflict seldom reached mortal proportions. Night transformed the composition of the streets, changing respectable mixed sex areas into dangerous, male-dominated and threatening places. Groups of men appeared to roam about the night-time streets, visiting alehouses and meeting other men after working hours. An insult delivered at night, away from civilised daytime society, would receive a harsher and swifter response. Even legal officials were quick to act more violently in this context, and several watchmen were described in depositions as suddenly and mortally wounding men with little provocation.[43]

Time provided another key ingredient in male violence. It was not only night-time that proved dangerous, although it was certainly a more volatile time than any other. Conflicts were arranged for the early morning in quiet outlying spaces, partially in the hope that in the sober daylight the men would limit their aggression, and partly to construct a normative context for the brawls. In common with the night-time, early mornings were less populated and less possessed by broader society than other times.

Although all spaces could be dangerous, certain areas were repeatedly linked to male violence. Workplaces were prime sites for inter-male conflict. In both enclosed rooms and larger, more open spaces, like fields, men jostled with work mates and rivals alike to establish and maintain their relative positions in the crucial micro-environments. Certain men quarrelled over the quality of another's work, their dexterity or over their wider reputations, literally and figuratively scuffling over public portrayals of their manhood.[44] In 1673, James Burn told John Swan that he 'was not fit to be a plowdriver if he could not keep the oxen in the farrow'. He later demanded that John re-yoke the oxen and when John refused, James claimed he 'boxed' his ears. This type of violent response was intended to demean the other party and clearly establish workplace power relationships. On this occasion, however, the beating was severe and John Swan later died.[45]

Tempers could just as easily overheat in a predominantly male workroom. In Yorkshire in 1724 four tailors gathered in Mary Shaw's house. Although Mary and her daughter were present, they described themselves as on the edge of the group and as doing a different sort of work. A quarrel swiftly escalated when Isaac Lister called Christopher Smith a liar. When he repeated the accusation, Christopher threw shears across the room in his direction, but added that they did not touch Isaac. Then 'Lister took the same shears and threw them back with great violence'. He missed Christopher so he attacked another tailor, William Robinson, stabbing him in the neck.[46] After he had killed, Isaac fled. Women were quite peripheral to these battles. Although not all men conducted such physical struggles for supremacy in their everyday spaces, for those that did violence allowed them to display their masculinities in largely homosocial arenas.

The most prominent contexts for displays of violence, however, were alehouses and informal drinking houses. Inns and drink featured in a large number of male conflicts, and although many were fought outside an inn, on the night-time street or in alleyways, deponents were keen to add the context of the alehouse and the implications it and alcohol conveyed to their stories of male homicides. Alehouses were not exclusively male spaces, as women served, drank and entered to locate their husbands, but evidence from depositions shows inns to be fundamentally spaces for male interaction and male pursuits, for drinking, gambling, gossiping, fighting, and occasionally killing.

Drink had a multiplicity of meanings in early modern England, and this ambiguity of definition can consistently be seen in depositions. Like violence, the meaning of a drink and its interpretation by a jury was a complex matter. On one hand, alcohol was used as a form of shorthand for the particular circumstances in which the violence should be interpreted. The location of the alehouse and the act of drinking were usually noted in tales about the brawl, providing an implicit context in which violence was omnipresent. An alehouse had harsh rules of behaviour, which a jury and society would have immediately recognised, although not necessarily condoned. Indeed, under the law, being drunk aggravated rather than mitigated a crime (this was not always the case in practice, however).[47] Mentioning alcohol gave the expectation of an extreme situation in which sudden violence was not uncommon. The men who frequented alehouses were presented as people who swiftly took violent offence. A comment that may have produced an action for defamation on a doorstep would usually produce an assault in an alehouse or the surrounding dark alleyways.

Although the alehouse provided a logical masculine context for the display of violent passions, it was the occupants, rather than the space, that perpetuated this meaning. Different alehouses supported distinctive levels of violence, depending on the clientele. Each would be occupied by like-minded men, who would have understood the violent subtexts of their specific location. Many disputes would have been drunk away. Nevertheless, regulars would have had extensive experience of drunken men acting excessively. After an incident, it was these like-minded individuals who would have been called as witnesses. Therefore, it is their interpretation of the normality or extremity of events that was the dominant discourse in court.

Drink allowed the blurring of boundaries and made it easier to act in a disreputable manner. In January 1674 in London, innkeeper Amos Childe described Edward Byfeild as repeatedly demanding drinks after he had refused to serve him. Edward grew quarrelsome and fought Amos in a conflict that led to Edward's death.[48] The popular link of drink and violence may have positively attracted certain men to alehouses. Alehouse conflicts were strikingly ferocious, and the additional risk of entering into a fight in such a context is a consistent subtext to this violence. Alehouses were not constantly disorderly, but aggression was omnipresent and almost accepted as permissible. This danger must have been fully comprehended by early modern men, as to an extent it was created by their violent actions.

In many instances an alehouse acted as an effective meeting ground for the resolution of a dispute. In 1642 in Leeds a long-standing conflict was concluded with a group alehouse brawl. At first, the incident appeared to be a simple quarrel over ale. Jackson and Holmes quarrelled over paying for drinks and 'fell at some words'. Holmes hit Jackson 'whereupon Jackson upon a sudden drew his dagger and stabbed Holmes upon which stab he died instantly'. However, Jackson told a different tale. He said that Holmes had threatened to kill him on their next meeting, and was therefore claiming that he had acted in direct response to this explicit threat.[49]

The positioning of activities like gambling within alehouses heightened their potential for violence. Men played cards and placed wagers, all in the convivial surroundings of the inn. Even if the wager was placed elsewhere, gambling proved a consistent topic of conversation in an alehouse, often causing violent disputes. Card playing was a frequent companion activity to drinking, and often provoked tension. A violent dispute arose out of a game of 'hazard' in 1677 in London. Charles Seymour was playing dice with some others in the inn and had lost about 6d ... When he asked for a loan to continue playing the tapster refused and gave him 'ill language'. Insults flew, and pots and candlesticks soon followed. Repeatedly gambling, especially in the context of drinking, was described as an incitement to anger, causing quarrels and leading to upsets, with the potential for a violent conclusion present even in the most apparently good humoured company.

Despite its potential for danger and physical threat, drinking had other equally pervasive cultural meanings; alehouses can never be read uncritically as purely violent spaces. Alcohol was as much about friendliness and conviviality as it was about conflict. The alehouse was a central meeting place for local men, a site of good humour and good company.[50] Deals were settled there, and drinks exchanged to display good faith. A drink could also signify the end of a quarrel and restoration of friendship.[51] John Lister highlighted this practice in his defence. He claimed that he had wrestled with the victim for exercise, and stressed that no malice ever existed. The fact that the two had shared a drink after the wrestling was supposedly illustrative of their friendship.[52] Alcohol could be used to imply conviviality and a definite absence of malice, or at least convey mixed meanings in which hot anger rather than cold malice reigned. In 1671, in Cumberland, John Wildrish explained his violence towards a fellow servant by saying that they had quarrelled 'and cussed several times and being both drunk with Brandy'. Unlike most other defendants he tried to further excuse his actions by claiming that 'he was so drunk that he was not sensible of what he did'.[53] His action would not have been excused but the court, and the community, would have clearly understood the context of the conflict, and may have limited his culpability to manslaughter.

It is also clear that the weapons used in male homicide cases had as many meanings as the space in which the crime occurred. The ways in which a weapon was used, how and when it was drawn were all described in detail in court. The meaning behind weapons such as swords was clearly aggressive, while other implements had more ambiguous meanings. Knives had a domestic purpose, for cutting food or tobacco, and so could be legitimately kept in a pocket and thereafter used in a fight without implying a deliberate intent to harm. Likewise, fists and most blunt instruments successfully implied sudden and hot anger. In 1649 Thomas Hason killed William Aplay using his carpenter's rule. Thomas claimed that he was hard at work when William arrived and they quarrelled over some wood. When William struck him with a blade, Thomas responded by striking out with the carpenter's rule he was holding, rather than a weapon he had pre-selected for its ability to harm.[54] The accessibility of a weapon and its primary function all impacted upon the broader story of the conflict. The more ordinary the method of killing, the greater the mitigation in court.

On the other hand, a drawn sword was distinctively aggressive and, by its very nature, to display such a weapon thus indicated an intention to kill or maim. In Bentley, Yorkshire, in 1656, the question of who drew, when and why proved central to the description of the conflict. Barnabas Elcocke hit Samuell Pickeringe's dog with a cane while on Samuell's land. An enraged Samuell said he ran inside to get a rod but on seeing his sheathed sword took that instead and returned to attack Barnabas. Samuell's wife tried to restrain Samuell and prevent him 'offering violence' to Barnabas, so she grabbed at the sword, accidentally pulling it from its sheath. Samuell then used it to stab Barnabas to death. Samuell's maidservant deliberately described the drawn sword as pure mischance. Barnabas's wife saw things differently and stressed the inequality of the fight by deliberately juxtaposing her husband's 'little cane' against Samuell's 'naked sword'. However, the witnesses carefully placed the weapon, in this case a sword, in context. The speed at which the weapon had been drawn and the responses of the opponent to the escalation of the conflict were always factors. So potent were weapons as images of malicious intent that if a sword was not drawn by its owner but used sheathed as a club, its meaning shifted again, becoming less sinister. By choosing not to draw, the combatant signalled he had had no desire to kill.

Guns were the most ambiguous weapons in homicide cases, with their meaning shifting with the context of the crime. Contrary to initial impressions, guns actually implied friendship, conviviality and an absence of malice, and were seldom linked to deliberate murders. Although, almost as exclusively masculine as swords and linked to such male endeavours as war and hunting, guns were seldom described as having been discharged in anger. Men who were shot while hunting were often killed by friends, usually as a result of a misfiring gun. Firearms attracted masculine interest, drawing men together to use the weapon in social pursuits or to gather to discuss the gun and tell tall tales. In some places men were habitually armed when they went out poaching together; this only added to the comradely subtext of these weapons.[55] In 1678 in Yorkshire several men gathered together in the garden of an alehouse to gaze at Thomas Digby's pistol and tell war stories. One witness described the care and awe with which the gun was treated, saying 'so it past from one hand to another only to be looked at and Mr Digby told them it was charged and ... desired him not to discharge it for he had never another bullet but one besides that which was in it'.[56] One of the men did accidentally discharge the weapon and killed Digby. However, the implication of the tales was that the killing had been accidental, as the group had been friendly throughout.

Motivation was as central to male crime as the context and perceived orderliness of the engagement. Although motive was sometimes revealed in cases involving female defendants, it was far more regularly discussed in male cases. This was not just due to the large number of male crimes. In male cases, motive was examined to see if provocation had occurred or if the conflict was equally and mutually engaged in. The plethora of legal responses to male crimes made the motive of the defendant essential evidence. Women were only either innocent or guilty of murder. Their crimes were seldom considered in terms of manslaughter or self defence, and so their reasons for acting were never as relevant.

Although we cannot know what went on in the hearts and minds of combatants, certain records allow insight into the kind of words, insults and provocative actions that led to conflicts, providing us with a map of the kind of issues that inspired violent responses. Outside of familial violence, male conflicts were driven primarily by anxieties about possessions and status: men battled over the ownership of goods and land and violently resisted perceived slurs. Indeed, self-interest, property and money frequently fragmented early modern communities. Property defined social identity in the early modern period, and it certainly influenced status, and so the protection of property through the law or independent action was a fundamental concern.

These concerns were by no means exclusively male. Some property disputes inspired heated conflicts, involving large groups of people. In 1649 in York two interested groups fought for several days in 'contentions, furies, and batteries' over the ownership of a parcel of land. Margaret Greswicke, the victim's wife, said that the accused and two other men had threatened her husband and James Parkin, and that various men and a woman attacked them and pulled their cattle out of a field. This dispute went on for some time until William Hobson hit her husband with a hedge stake 'on the left side of his head, which caused his brains to come forth at his mouth and nose'.[57] Such violent affrays were not uncommon, and, although not exclusively male affairs, men were the main aggressors in such large-scale conflicts.

Disputes over small parcels of land could be as bitter and as deadly as those conducted over large estates. Although again not limited to men, such disputes often involved male protagonists. All encroachments were viewed as serious threats to status and authority and received responses ranging from legal to violent. Men had to publicly defend their status so that their credibility was not indelibly eroded. Fences (and especially the enclosure of land) were fraught issues. Property can be seen as an extension of male space, and therefore male honour, with the defence of the land and goods being about defending a sense of self, public image and local standing. Popular masculinity required that a man show his ability to fully defend his property from even the smallest encroachment. When James Hargreaves repaired and rebuilt a wall in his garden in Yorkshire in 1648 his actions incensed his neighbour William Pollard and provide us with an excellent example of small property conflicts. Pollard said the wall was not on Hargreaves's land and threatened him if he did not stop building there. When Hargreaves did not stop Pollard pulled down part of the wall in anger. Hargreaves and his wife then reportedly threw stones at Pollard and physically attacked him, in defence of their property. The two men fought, hitting each other, leaving Hargreaves fatally wounded.[58]

Male honour had very specific meanings in violent conflicts. It revolved around notions of strength, power, possessions, but also a man's good name and his refusal to show fear. Men were as concerned with publicly preserving their honour as defamed wives were with protecting their sexual honour in the ecclesiastical courts. A good name was crucial to male status, and a challenge to this name could not easily be ignored. Consequently, some men fought over relatively minor issues. In 1718 in St Brides in London, Mr Quinn and William Bowen fell into conflict. Robert Martin was in the tavern with them and described their behaviour. He said that they came in to drink 'and during that time Mr Bowen and Mr Quinn were very merry and jocuse with each other, without any sign of anger on either side and that they being bragging of each others performances on the stage'. The two men then disagreed about who played the part of 'Jackamore' the best, and a bet was placed. The earlier good humour began to dissipate. 'Mr Bowen [said] in a jocuse manner to Mr Quinn, he was worthless Rogue, but that he himself was an honest … man and went home in good time to his family'. Quinn objected and said the reverse was true, and other insults followed until, 'Mr Quinn accusing Bowen of drinking the Duke of Ormands health, and at another time refusing to Drink it Mr Bowen then seemed to be angry, and said he could not bare it'. Later on, the two fought more literally and Bowen was fatally wounded.[59]

Insults to a man's good name and his ability to control his space were commonplace causes of violence. A man's reputation as variously brave, honest, reputable or powerful was almost a tangible commodity in business terms and in terms of his everyday life. His masculinity was being challenged when an insult questioned his character, his social status and authority. However, to interpret the precise impact of an insult is very difficult. So much of the harm of a verbal attack depended on the context, rather than the content, of a slur and on the attitude of the man insulted. Some insults that led to violence seem very mild at first glance. Reading the provocative exchanges recorded in depositions cannot fully recapture the tone of voice used by the abuser or the body language of the combatants. The oblique references to wild, provoking speech frequently seen in witness statements hides much of the tension and passion of an exchange.

However, occasionally there is a reference in depositions that provides insight into the presentation of insults, and the theatricality of provocation. Some men's deliberate aggravation of a tense situation undoubtedly increased the probability of a physical conflict. When, in 1654, Yorkshiremen Jervis Sheppard and Isacke Waterhouse quarrelled in an alehouse over a half crown debt, Jervis followed his lengthy verbal assault on Isacke by untrussing his breeches and announcing he was going outside to relieve himself. Jervis may have been intentionally challenging Isacke to follow him outside to fight, since his going outside was a clear and recognisable invitation to do so. However, Jervis fuelled the already highly tense situation when he reportedly said to Waterhouse 'thou may Follow me and thou wilt dry my tail or words to that effect'.[60] The reference to defecation, and the clear insult it relayed, heightened the quarrel and, ultimately, led to Jervis's death. We can only speculate, though, on the unrecorded visual posturing that may have accompanied Jervis's insulting invitation.

Nevertheless, a complete picture of the meaning of an insult is elusive because most often the previous relationship of the quarrellers is not revealed in the records. The insult may seem mild out of context, but could represent the last in a series of insulting words and gestures, or be presented in a particularly inflammatory way. Thus, a crucial subtext of these quarrels is ultimately hidden from us. In addition, the location in which the insult occurred probably significantly impacted upon how the offensiveness of the words was received. Words expressed in an alehouse, the site of repeated male violence, could have an added mockery attached to them. It would have been more difficult to ignore words given in this context than elsewhere, as an alehouse held a concentrated composite of local men, all of whom could have eagerly absorbed the insult and its response. Like women insulted before their neighbours and so forced to go to law to re-establish their good name, men had to be willing to physically rebut derogatory words in order to keep their reputation intact. However seemingly inconsequential the insult, its potency in provoking a lethal engagement was linked to the circumstances of its delivery.

Whatever the trigger, a challenge to fight could not easily be ignored. Although conduct literature defined courage as an exclusively noble virtue, early modern men from all social groups were concerned to display their courage when pressed.[61] Many defendants argued that they had made significant efforts to avoid engaging in physical and verbal conflicts, with various defendants claiming, for the court's benefit, that the other (dead) party had been more aggressive. In 1683 at Tower Hill in London two soldiers quarrelled about one of their lieutenants. One, John Hillon, 'fell thereupon in a passion and called Mr Crown [the other soldier] Rascal and coward and both drew their swords'. A third man intervened, but Hillon would not desist 'And the said Mr Hillon urged Mr Crown to go out and give him satisfaction but Mr Crown declined it and desired him to be quiet'. Crown, in his deposition, indicated he then received a final and effective provocation. He said Hillon declared that 'he would fight' and 'urged this Examinant extremely saying he would post him for a coward if he refused it, and forced this Examinant ... out of the Tower'.[62] For a soldier the label 'coward' would have questioned his ability to fight, his bravery and even the name of his company. A challenge avoided could seriously impact upon a man's credibility, standing and name. This was a risk Peter Crown, and many other men, were patently unwilling to take, choosing to fight and risk the legal, social and personal consequences rather than backing down and losing face.

This domination of male conflicts by local concerns needs to be clarified. Although religion and politics formed part of the language of insult, they were usually presented as specific insults to particular men. When Catholics and foreigners were jeered as untrustworthy, this was partly an expression of general ideas about racial and religious tolerance, and partly about insulting individuals. Likewise, since throughout the early modern period a man could still be called upon to act as a physical protector of his community, the link between violence and politics may have felt natural to many. However, quarrels based on political disagreements were seldom found, and when they did occur they tended to be simplistic defences of faction. Political viewpoints were mixed with large quantities of alcohol until they became extreme, physical conflicts that required a violent resolution, although the ideas themselves tended to be simply expressed. In Halifax in 1648 John Goodbourne apparently exclaimed to William Swaine:

> they are all knaves that ever fought against the king to which the said William Swaine answered Knave if thou say so again I will throw a bowl of wine in thy face to which the said Goodbourne replied If I have offended let it fall and I have done yet I will not eat my words for I say they are knaves that ever fought against the king.[63]

William Swaine would not 'let it fall' and instead violently responded to John Goodbourne's words. Principles and politics inspired violence in men who were defining the boundaries of their masculinity by attacking anything that impinged upon it. However, in these fights, political ideas were infinitely simplified and revolved around the individual.

Similarly, sex and female honour were only tangential causes of male violence, despite playing a key role in the construction of early modern social ideologies and even in the formation of maleness. Men often paraded their masculinity before other men by discussing their sexual conquests and their virility in marriage and by displaying their overt control over women.[64] The need to control women was culturally strong in this society, with sex and sexual conflicts subjects of intense interest generally. Writing on defamation cases has focused on how vital a woman's sexual reputation was, and how damage to this reputation could affect views of a woman's honesty, her status, the identity of her children and her husband's good name. Even the general insult 'whore' could have a dramatic impact if not countered in the courts.[65] However, few instances of sexual slurs and insults can be seen in homicide depositions. When, in 1667, Matthew Patteson called Matthew Collison's wife 'a whore' and Collison 'a cuckold', witnesses were describing an almost unique trigger to violence.[66] When similar terms were occasionally used in other conflicts, they were only fleetingly mentioned and appear to have played only a small role in the escalating conflict.

Sexual jealousy played a more prominent role in conflicts, albeit in a small proportion of cases. The men involved did not quarrel over the details of their wives' sexual reputations, and terms like 'whore', 'whoremonger' and 'cuckold' seldom appeared in descriptions of the insults leading up to a violent conflict (although they were regularly used in defamation cases). They appeared more likely to fight over a challenge to their right to the possession of their wives. Indeed, men threatened other men by claiming they could take wives away. In this context, the kind of sexual jealousy that led to violence was akin to the protectiveness and concern to maintain ownership described in other kinds of property dispute.

This was the case when Henry Beecroft lost his temper after a suggestive comment was made about his wife in an alehouse. Josephe Walton reportedly told Beecroft 'Thou hast a fair wife, [and] if I could get you dead I would have her'. Other witnesses claimed that Henry, angered by this statement, picked up an iron pick, and attempted to strike Josephe. The blow was minor, but apparently later led to Josephe's death.[67] Sexual ribaldry made a more distinctive appearance in 1688 when John Butterworth and two strangers asked Henry Illingworth if he would sell his wife to them. Henry said that he would and one of the strangers paid him a deposit of 12d ... Henry apparently promised he would deliver her to the stranger and refuse to have her back, but Henry's wife, who had been present, left the tavern at this point and the disappointed stranger demanded his deposit back from her husband. Henry refused, but offered to buy 6d. worth of drink. A struggle ensued, in which John Butterworth's ale cup struck and injured Henry, apparently leading to his death.[68]

The fact that so few cases appear to have had sexual quarrels as their motivation is perplexing. What was it about property that could invoke territorial responses that insults to wives did not? As sexual insults were reportedly so common, their under-representation in the homicide records is intriguing. It could be that sexual insults have merely been hidden from our eyes by deposition-givers, who failed to accurately report the context of the violence, perhaps out of a sense of loyalty or propriety. This seems highly unlikely given the frequency and detail with which such insults were reported in other courtrooms, and the otherwise oft-present theatricality with which homicide evidence was presented.

On the other hand, perhaps sexual ribaldry was so common that it no longer led to conflict in all male contexts, although, again, the injury ascribed to such comments in other contexts makes this improbable. It seems far more likely that insults concerned with female sexual honour were made directly to the woman concerned rather than via the husband. It is possible that sexual honour needed to be defamed in a specific female social context, that is, from a doorstep, in the marketplace and in front of the appropriate audience – other women – for such comments to be effective. The damage inflicted by the insult depended on who overheard its delivery. Reconstructing female sexual honour would not then be a masculine task, but a delicate, linguistic endeavour, involving a respectable legal verdict. Whatever the explanation, it seems that men were more concerned by threats to their personal space and possessions than by threats to the reputation of their wives, daughters or sisters. Although they were keen to defend their personal boundaries from encroachments, masculinity was very differently defended to femininity. In particular, outward symbols of wealth and authority were given far more importance than the second-hand sexual honour provided by female relations.

Male conflicts were perceived to be complex and as nuanced as they were frequent. Men were expected to be violent – it was a regular and normal part of everyday life. However, they were not allowed to act maliciously or to plan an assault: such would be considered as much an act of murder as if committed by a woman. Nevertheless, men's actions, their intentions and even the context of their crime were thoroughly analysed before a judgement was made. The link between men and violence meant that this most disruptive sex was often legally and socially protected from excessive censure for their actions. Male violence was considered disorderly and often undesirable, but it was not broadly feared. This is probably because it did not threaten everyone in the community equally. Rather, male violence was homosocial and it occurred in male spaces and in male contexts to fulfil an especially male sense of honour. Such violence was primarily about masculinity – a vital commodity for an early modern man to assert.

Male violence was also broadly understood. Indeed, the acceptance of 'natural' male propensities to violence actually led to the mitigation of penalties for manslaughter and self-defence. Women seldom received such mitigation, with acquittal being the only option to avoid capital punishment. Male violence was never so simply and uncritically judged.

11

The Usual Suspects

In 1681 Thomas Thynn, one of the richest men in England, was killed in his own coach on the open highway. Although it seemed like a simple highway robbery, investigators quickly became convinced that this prominent Whig politician had been deliberately targeted by blood-thirsty killers. Three Germans were eventually arrested and tried for the crime. Their supposed master, Count Connigsmark, was also tried as an accessory for instructing them to kill Thomas Thynn. The count was acquitted, but the other men were convicted of the crime.

These three strangers were accused of killing Thynn over a dispute he had had with their master over a woman. They may have been ordered to kill him or acted for other reasons. The stories relating to this crime leave their motives unclear. However, they did fulfil popular stereotypes about unprincipled and dangerous foreigners, and in the myriad tales told about this crime, were linked to papists and Jesuits. Whether or not they were in fact Catholics, they were considered as dangerous as these sources of universal concern.

This murder caused a furore, with countless printed elegies, ballads and illustrated broadsheets being published to bemoan Thynn's death and most importantly to use the killing as an example of the terrible state of the nation. Pamphlet after pamphlet decried the streets as unsafe, and declared that criminals were hiding everywhere ready to strike. One, entitled *Hew and Cry after Blood and Murther*, described what it saw as the grim reality of everyday life in contemporary England. It said:

> In the last end o'th' Iron Age we live,
> A Brother won't a Brother now forgive:
> But for some slight affront or weak offence,
> With Sword or Pistol he is hurried hence ...

> So impious and so vile now Men are grown,
> As never in our Age before was known;
> Who cann't but go or Ride the Streets in fear,
> When we have Bravo's and Banditti here?

> Under our English cloth men must wear Buff,

> A Coat of Mail, or Armor Pistol-Proof,
> For fear of some revenge from Jilting drabs,
> Or else for Friendships or Religion stabs;
> Poison, or Bullet, fraud, or force they take,
> Both for reveng and for Religion's sake.[1]

This ballad replicated what was being said in print and in sermons across the country throughout the early modern period. When it made explicit reference to a widespread national terror of murder and disorder, it was actually referring to a constant state of concern which had existed for hundreds of years, and continues to this day.[2] Even now people believe they live in the most lawless of all times and that in the past life was better, people friendlier and more peaceful. Crime rates fluctuate and people are therefore sometimes correct in their comments, but the concern itself is omnipresent (whether or not statistics prove it warranted). Levels of fear fluctuate according to individual experience and personality, but in general terms the perception of danger always existed. Individuals could be fearful of assault in their communities and even in their own homes – and if they were fearful there were a number of bogeymen for them to choose from.

This is not to say that early modern people lived in constant fear of attack. However, there was a general feeling of concern especially in relation to specific groups or types of criminal. In addition, there were sporadic moments of intense anxiety, usually in the aftermath of a particular incident, such as the murder of Thomas Thynn. The household may have been a prime focus for murder texts in early modern England, but it was far from the only source of anxiety. Everyday fractures between individuals and small groups disrupted good relations and involved the entire community in the restoration of more common order. The community we have been discussing in terms of perceived threat and its resolution encompassed the immediate and everyday – the geographic area of the parish, neighbours and customers – as well as any newcomers and strangers who entered into it.

Despite the disruption of the Civil War and occasional enclosure and food riots, crime was the biggest source of disorder in the early modern world. Most communities saw themselves as orderly and well policed, disrupted only by moments of crime, which they swiftly dealt with using appropriate methods of justice. Fear of disorder, crime and mayhem did not necessarily relate to actual experiences. Imagination was often a far more effective restraint as well as a far more fertile source of concerns. The bogeymen people feared may well have committed some crime but their actions were interpreted out of all proportion to their activities. That they were feared the most does not make them the most prolific of criminals

– or even of killers – only the most notorious and terrifying ones conceived of in this historical period. As such, we should see stories about homicide as complex tales about fear, brutality, justice and order. They are revealing of a generic terror of potential violence and of specific reactions to crimes; they were terrifying and reassuring at the same time, stories of wickedness in which the killers were (usually) caught and harmony restored. The horrors recorded were not new, albeit subject to fluctuating anxieties.

The source of fears remained remarkably consistent across this period, and included robbers, strangers and perpetrators of hidden assaults. These were the omnipresent and dangerous criminals. Robbers and hidden assailants were perceived as the enemies within: they were believed to be someone known to the victim who had disguised their activities while plotting the downfall of their neighbours. Like the much feared witch, these criminals were the antithesis of community spirit. In many ways these concerns matched common experience – disputes and feuds were inevitably with neighbours rather than strangers. As today, ordinary people often disliked and resented the people they knew the best – with a neighbour who hid their true animosity and malicious nature usually considered the most dangerous.

This did not stop people fearing the unknown. Strangers were always considered suspect, especially foreigners. Indeed, new variations were added over time. The early modern period saw specific concerns developing, which were reflected in new kinds of fears. Papists became a favourite target, as plots like that of Guy Fawkes in 1605 were uncovered and still more were greatly feared to have remained undiscovered. Later on, with civil war raging, soldiers became a new enemy to order and prosperity – and even to life and limb – and therefore became targets of rhetoric and some accusation. The disorder and disruption of the seventeenth century generally highlighted public anxiety and augmented fears that already existed with specific new terrors.

While we know about general early modern concerns, we can rarely know how *individuals* read tales of crime and plotting. Likely responses ranged from indifference to awe and even terror. Like horror stories today, such tales both perpetuated and eased terror. They can also provide intriguing insights into perceptions of communal order by highlighting concerns. Fears were distinctly individual, but public stories needed to express horror in terms that the audience understood and respected. Violence was not experienced in a uniform manner, as it shifted with the imagination of the participant and onlooker. However, fear has a historic specificity that meant most would recognise generic stories of terror, even if they did not personally subscribe to them.[3]

None of the records can provide unambiguous insights into early modern people. As direct accounts, depositions provide our best opportunity to discover how ordinary people viewed crime, even though one has to remember that they were not designed for the collection of emotions or for descriptions of fear. On the other hand, pamphleteers preferred dramatic and sometimes fantastic stories, which were certainly more widely disseminated than depositions and provided greater opportunity to express fear, making them to an extent a popular viewpoint. However, pamphlets were often the work of an individual and at most represented the views of a small group. Many printed accounts represented a distinct moralising agenda that many contemporaries would not have agreed with.[4] Pamphlets certainly increased the fear of certain crimes by publicising them, and may even have created new fears. Nevertheless, taken together these sources give us an insight into the many ways in which early modern people perceived crime, although neither holds the monopoly on defining terror. That these sources do not always agree provides a good opportunity to study the fluctuations of early modern fears.

Questions about the orderliness of early modern society and the propensity of early modern man to violence have inspired and intrigued historians over the last few decades. Lawrence Stone had argued that homicide rates in the sixteenth and seventeenth centuries were 'five to ten times higher than those today'.[5] His vision is of a hellish, violent and disrupted society in which violence was expected and to some extent the norm. Although this may have been the case (at times) in other European societies, it is an exaggeration of life in early modern England.[6] His statistics have been persuasively challenged by a number of historians, who argue that this is an unfair depiction.[7] Indeed, statistics alone cannot convey the experience of living in this society. Homicide had a greater impact, in terms of notoriety and of terror, than bare statistics allow.

Communities frequently united against common foes. Strangers, foreigners and criminals were perceived as sources of habitual disruption and crippling debt, and so were viewed as dangerous. These invaders of harmony were frequently subjects of anxious pamphlets. Stories about purveyors of disorder hidden within the very fabric of society were pervasive. Systemic wickedness was linked with certain groups of people. Indeed, society was depicted as constantly threatened, from within and without, by a collection of robbers, soldiers, foreigners and papists. Although such actors were not the main sources of murderous violence in this period, pamphleteers were excited by crimes in which the villain was predictably wicked, and popular fears were perpetuated by a series of scare stories. The alleged killers came from the most commonly feared social groups, against whom ordinary people consistently defined themselves. These 'others' were sometimes strangers, sometimes temporary residents and sometimes neighbours who explicitly refused to accept social rules of behaviour. Whatever their threat, they were a clear source of overt, communal fears.

Even so, the strangers described in early modern homicide stories were not the ones we might have expected. Vagrants, for example, had been a source of public wrath for many years and were routinely watched, arrested and prosecuted for a range of crimes, most notably theft.[8] However, there were few instances of vagrants being blamed for homicides. Generic fictional culprits were accused of a range of crimes, like theft or illicit sex, where names like 'Jack England' identify them as vagrants or unknown suspects.[9] However, few fictional culprits can be found in homicide records, as it was neighbours who were more often accused. In fact, with the exception of the vagrant, there were few true strangers at all, especially in rural communities. People had a remarkable knowledge of those who shared their society and their everyday lives.[10] Even though a large proportion of any community would have been made up of migrant workers on annual contracts,[11] most people could be traced through previous contacts with a place, leaving few that were absolutely unknown. Although less true in urban areas, most communities could easily identify strangers. Indeed, once identified, many went out of their way to find out what they could about the newcomer. Assimilation was one way of circumventing and deflating local concerns about an individual.

Despite being scapegoats and sources of contemporary concern, strangers, papists and vagrants *et al.* were not constant targets of malicious accusations in cases of violence. In fact, these distinctive and notoriously bad people were actually less often suspected than we would suppose. Though considered dangerous, they were seldom perceived as killers. In fact, killers were actually seldom considered to be psychologically distinctive from the rest of the community, but commonly believed to have started from the same moral position as other members of society: a murderer was not preordained, but chose to be wicked.[12] It was a fundamental of early modern justice that anyone could be culpable of even the worst crimes – and most of the time people felt more threatened by a neighbour with whom they had had a particular quarrel than someone from a generically dangerous group.

The statistics agreed that a killer was more likely to be a neighbour or family member than a stranger, solider or secret papist. Danger came from well-known and often well-anticipated sources, although this knowledge failed to limit concerns about strangers. Any threat by these outsiders was regularly taken out of all proportion. Nevertheless, when it came to making accusations, people were realistic about who was the likely source of murderous activity. Strangers and invidious insiders were much feared, but it was the close friend and neighbour who were consistently suspected and most often accused.

Crime stories were ostensibly told with moral motives to discourage wickedness. Trials were held publicly and stories permitted to be printed in order to spread the word and warn about the kind of wickedness that led to crime. People were supposed to learn from others' crimes and punishments, much in the way they were supposed to learn from sermons. Many printed texts began with biblical quotations that made reference to the heinous nature of a sin, before ending with confession and execution, allowing a public cleansing of the wickedness the crime represented. To this end, the motive of the killer was critical information, as was the killer's barbarous nature and admitted congress with the devil. These elements would be used to assess the nature of the crime, be it self-defence, manslaughter or murder.

Not all justifications were accepted at face value, as can be seen in a case from 1677 in London, when a husband killed a stranger who had tried to stop him publicly beating his wife. The husband claimed to be 'so incensed' at the fair and gentle words of the stranger that he instantly killed him, arguing he had been provoked. The court deemed this 'A poor excuse!' and convicted him of murder.[13] Even a killing in which little motive was apparent would still have been recorded, with the actions placed in a broader religious and moral context for the audience. In 1699 Edward Scales confessed to killing the child Ann Hazelcroft in London 'without any reason'. Edward told the court that he had returned from sea and wasted his money on a whore. He was wandering the streets penniless when he killed Ann, a complete stranger. He explained his act only by saying he was 'upon a desperate design'.[14] Desperation was a mortal sin, and it was clearly his rejection of God and common morality that inspired his terrible action. It was believed that his undermining of social and godly order could only be put right by an abject scaffold confession.[15] His rejection of God and his sudden wickedness would have inspired fear in contemporaries and horror from the reading public.

Whatever the publicly professed motivation for printing murder stories, to strike terror was the underlying aim of all such tales.[16] Random brutality was not excluded from texts, with greater emphasis always placed on the most fear-inducing types of crime. A proportion of texts existed without an overt moral framework, which made them low on comforting structure, but high on drama. In a 1691 robbery the murdered bodies of three women were found lying in pools of blood in their own home. Their murders were described in meticulous detail, although no suspect had been apprehended. The pamphleteer imaginatively reconstructed the scene through the eyes of the woman who found the bodies. He said she found the door open and entered only to find general disorder and three bodies. Mrs Sarah Hodges was 'most barbarously murthered in her naked Bed, her throat being cut, and the right side of her Head cut, and her Skull broke'. The writer speculated that a hammer had probably been the murder weapon. He described the mutilations inflicted on Elizabeth Smith, the lodger. She had been stabbed in her ear and about her head, her hands had been bound and she was also naked and 'that she lays as it were swimming in her Blood'. Finally, the body of Hannah Williams, the maid, was described as one on which the villains had 'vended their fury in a large measure' by cutting her throat and stabbing her repeatedly.[17]

This was a pure and unresolved horror story, which mixed informing the public with a desire to entertain. Terror sold pamphlets and received wide-eyed attention at trials. Although ostensibly designed to educate and prevent crime, tales of murder also titillated and terrified. After all, publishers were in the business of selling stories, and no one bought large numbers of moral tracts. Just as we are attracted to murder stories today, early modern people wanted to read or hear about horrible crimes. In the process, the narratives constructed and maintained public and private fears about violence.

Robbery backed with violence was the prime 'scare story' of the early modern period. No other kind of tale received as much printed attention or was so consistently told in such detailed and bloodthirsty terms. Although highwaymen were often glamorised and even hero worshipped, more every-day robbers were universally reviled.[18] The purple prose such criminals inspired was linked to the doubly wicked nature of their actions. Not only did these criminals break open secure houses or violate personal safety to steal – they killed their victims. Such tales were an extension of fears of the danger from within that we saw in the context of household and domestic murders. Robber-killers were suspected to be people the victim knew well, which led to households examining themselves and the wider neighbourhood minutely. These were some of the most effectively de-monised of killers. There was no possible explanation for their crime, no acceptable provocation, no circumstances in which contemporaries could imagine that they too could have acted in such a way. In general terms, the degree of outrage a killing incurred depended on how fair the assault was perceived to be.[19] Robbery with violence was considered amongst the most unfair, which only added to the vicarious thrill, making these stories highly saleable commodities.

Robbery was a felony, and although many more thieves achieved acquittals at the assizes than murderers, burglary or thefts involving weapons or intimidation were viewed very dimly.[20] Robbers were especially fearsome because they were described as striking suddenly against sleeping or defenceless householders, using superior weapons and brutality even in the face of capitulating victims. In a 1679 pamphlet an archbishop was robbed and killed at gunpoint on the highway by two men he had previously had arrested for debt. One of the killers was described as 'a vile person, who had nothing of good in him, and was scarce admitted to the society of sober-men'.[21] This was not an unusual depiction. These criminals were portrayed as endemically wicked, as men who preyed on the law-abiding and used a cover of respectability to hide their true natures.

Such was the public fear of robbery and appetite for horror stories that fantastic tales could be repeated in the courtroom, without a demand for corroborating evidence. In 1682 in Leeds Hester Webster retold an extraordinary tale about burglary and mayhem, which she claimed was told to her one night in Dublin. She freely admitted that the couple who had originally narrated the story were not witnesses to the crime, making her evidence third-hand (at least). However, her tale was so dramatic, and had such an impact on those who heard it privately recounted, that she was instructed to repeat it in front of local justices.

Hester's tale concerned the household of a Mr Scurre that had been set upon by an indeterminate number of robbers a few days previously. The robbers sealed all the exits to the house and proceeded to the bedroom of an old woman. She cried out at the invasion, and her son came down with a knife to defend her. After a struggle, in which two of the robbers were possibly mortally wounded, Scurre was cornered and struck with an axe. His dead body was thrown on to the bed along with his mother's corpse. The assailants then encountered another far more dramatic potential victim. Hester said:

> there was a pretty young woman, she begged her life of them and told them she would be racked in pieces before she would tell of them if they would spare her life. The man did grant her her life, but there was a woman [assailant there], she could not grant her her life, but chopped off her head.[22]

The house was then set on fire to hide the evidence.

Hester mimicked the language and escalating narrative twists of printed media. She was telling a dramatic tale of wickedness and murder, into which she incorporated gendered notions on the brutality of dominant women and the helplessness of good and innocent women. This was a clear expression of the popular power of the thrilling robbery-murder story. Hester was both terrified and attracted by the tale. Although the Yorkshire courts would have had no jurisdiction over Irish crimes, such was the narrative strength of this case that it had to be seen to receive formal attention.

Stories of old servants or defenceless women set upon and killed by robbers were ever popular in print, as the protagonists added the pathos of the innocent victim to an already salacious tale. A 1674 pamphlet told the story of the 'horrible bloody' murder of 'an ancient retainer' to a wealthy family. Esquire Bluck, the householder, and most of his servants went to Hertfordshire, leaving their Holborn house in the sole care of an old woman. On the day that the family was due to come back to town, a milk woman discovered the old woman slain. Little was known about the killers, but the pamphleteer argued the victim had probably known her assailants, as she would not have let in strangers, which would have explained why she had been killed rather than tied up.[23]

Although the known-but-secret killer added an extra dimension of fear to these scare stories, it was the stoic innocence of the victim that made these into especially heinous crimes. In 1680, a burglary and killings in Grays in Essex led a pamphleteer to describe the culprits as 'Monsters in human shape'. At 10pm five men in seamen's uniforms broke into the house. All the inhabitants were women – the mistress, her sixteen-year-old daughter and a maidservant. The mistress fled to raise the alarm, while the robbers broke open chests, trying to steal as much as they could. At the same time 'with impious hands bereaved them [the maid and the daughter] of their Lives by giving them several mortal wounds'.[24] The vulnerability of the victims added to the pathos of the tale, emphasising the brutality of the terrifying killers.

Pamphlets frequently made a dramatic link between involvement in violence and in other crime. Just as thieves were often assumed to be perfectly capable of violence, other seemingly passive crimes were felt to engender desperate violence and general wickedness. In a 1673 pamphlet a family conspiracy was reported, in which several male family members acted together to kill another family member's wife. The unnamed wife had married into the Alsop family. She was a widow 'of good credit and competent Estate, with 3 children'. James and his wife were very happy; although the pamphleteer considered that they were too fond of the 'amorous marriage bed'.

One day, the new wife saw other family members clipping coins – an act of high treason in this period. Clipping involved the pinching off of small pieces of genuine coin to be melted down to provide a commodity to sell or turn into new, forged coins.[25] The wife mentioned what she had seen to her family, and the conspirators felt she could not be trusted. Said to be inspired by Satan, they decided to kill her, making two unsuccessful attempts before they succeeded. The wife clearly suspected their intentions, as she refused to consume a drink they had given her, telling her child she feared poisoning. However, like the good and dutiful wife she was, she did not run away or call for help from her neighbours, merely waiting passively for them to act. The conspirators were nevertheless resolute, and after telling the neighbours that she had gone away, one entered her room, 'with a black Gown on, and a vizard on his Face, with a candle in one hand, and a naked knife in the other'. He cut her throat and then removed a pane of glass to make it appear as if robbers had killed her. He then raised a hue and cry.

Neighbours and local legal officials thoroughly investigated this crime, and swiftly decided that the killer had to have come from inside the house since, providentially, a whole and unbroken cobweb was found on the inside of the window. The search also turned up the mask (with a convenient bloody thumbprint) and some clipped money. The killers were detected and effectively *unmasked* by the efforts of their neighbours. This was not the end of the family's attempts to avert justice though, as:

> A Notable Stratagem is set on foot (as 'tis supposed) to clear him [one of the men accused] of the Fact: for a report was raised that some Highwaymen had confessed they robbed the house, and killed the woman.[26]

However, following the tradition of morality tales and public punishment stories, they were unsuccessful in their attempts to cheat justice, and all the conspirators were convicted and duly executed.

Like all pamphlet stories of unusual crimes, the drama described seems incredible, but the horror and fear expressed were palpable. Although the killers were members of the wife's new family, their hidden identity as treasonous criminals was the most terrible element of this crime. It was their secrets that she suffered for, and their strange 'otherness' as desperate criminals that led to their accepting the temptation of the devil and killing her in cold blood. Although set in the midst of a wicked and criminal family, the wife was praised for her good name and obedient nature. She may have been cruelly murdered in the tale, but the storytellers ensured that she was depicted in glowing terms for posterity.

That robbery and murder seldom appeared in such dramatic terms in depositions confirms how disproportionately flamboyant the printed reports were. A reputation for theft was damning, but murder itself was always the prime focus in court. Few of the robbery-with-murder stories that exist in the archives used the same language of horror seen in pamphlets. This is partly because the legal purpose of depositions was not the recording of feelings but the collection of facts. Nevertheless, the simplicity of a father's description of his son's killing and the theft of two much needed horses in West Audesley in Yorkshire in 1651, seems excessively calm. John Jagger said of the incident 'a man unknown slew his son (as he thinketh) and cast him in a ditch bottom in a corn close where he was found his head being severed from his body'.[27] The bare facts of the incident in this and many other cases were all that were recorded. Robber-killers were feared by their law-abiding neighbours, but they were few in number and only inspired extreme terror as the generically wicked attackers of printed tales. Individual crimes were always more complex than the highly fictionalised tale of outrage and horror.

Even so, terror comparable to that in the pamphlet accounts can be seen in other kinds of depositions for crimes that also mixed loss of goods and money with violence and murder. In these cases the homicides were linked to extortion. Armed men who purported to be legal officers took money in return for not pursuing an often unseen warrant. They approached a household when the husband was away or when the householders were isolated from their neighbours. They told of a warrant they supposedly held and threatened to 'arrest' the male householder and take him to gaol. Even a genuine arrest could be a very violent and dangerous experience. Bailiffs, watchmen and constables seldom approached unarmed and they often acted violently from the start to ensure compliance. It was certainly an unpleasant experience most would pay to avoid. This was, of course, how the extortion worked – the 'officer' would demand a payment to 'forget' the warrant and leave the household alone. In light of their isolated position and their apt fear of what they would physically endure if 'captured', many paid up.

Such tales seldom appeared in print, but unlike robbery these crimes were described in detail in depositions and so provide insight into the abject terror the victims experienced. They were sophisticated narratives, in which the weak were assaulted in questionable acts of justice. These were not the secret crimes of pamphlet robbers, but face-to-face assaults. The stories told were essentially about relative strength and weakness. The sense of terror felt by the victims was intense. Rural victims were especially vulnerable to the extortion tactics of both real and bogus legal officials, and many such tales exist in the Yorkshire archives: geographic remoteness from others and from the forces of the law helped to victimise rural dwellers.

A particularly illuminating case comes from Knottingley in Yorkshire from 1670. Three men, who claimed to be bailiffs, held a small community hostage. Witness John Simpson said that the three men came to his house claiming to have a warrant, and demanded 20d., which his wife paid. They returned later that day making a claim of a different suit against him and demanded a further 6d. 'but never showed him any writ they had though he desired to see it'. Several other men made similar complaints of warrants that the bailiffs refused to show and of extortionate fees. Fran Strickland paid 4s. 4d. and then a further 3s. 6d. to escape a supposed arrest. Thomas Simpson said they demanded 6s. 8d. from him and, when he refused to pay, one of his attackers threatened him with two pistols. William Denby likewise claimed that 'for fear of danger he was forced to pay him'.[28] The male victims were not aggressive or armed, and were referred to in similar terms to their wives as plausible, weak victims. The three aggressors admitted to the courts that they were not bailiffs, and, with one villager seriously injured and one dead from this episode alone, these were certainly dangerous men whom the villagers were right to fear.

Even legitimate legal officials were often accused of using unnecessarily brutal force when arresting suspects. On occasion, officials significantly injured or even killed those they apprehended – so that despite their official status, they were sources of fear and concern. The people they arrested had sometimes not yet been tried and yet many complained that they were treated with unwarranted force. This cannot have been the only way in which suspects were treated, but it was a common and, for many, a very real fear. In 1685 Susanna Greateheade was badly beaten by two bailiffs who had come to arrest her husband. Susanna tried to stop the men injuring her husband but they beat her, her mother, her father and her sister, and ended up by killing her.[29] Likewise, in London in 1698 Ann Andersby was killed when she tried to stop an arrest. She claimed she approached the officer 'in a peaceable manner and entreated him not to take her husband'.[30] In response, he threw her down and struck her in the belly with his cane. There were a series of stories which were remarkably similar to this, in which the (male) legal official was presented as oppressive, while their (female) victims were unarmed.

On the other hand, men were generally portrayed as clashing somewhat more equally. Robert Thompson, a Sheriff's officer, and his assistant tried to enter the house of John Walker by deception. John claimed Robert came to the house 'and desiring to light a pipe of tobacco there pretending they were going up Hull river to shoot some fowl'. The suspicious householder refused to allow them in, and barricaded the doors. When the bailiffs tried to force their way in, John Walker shot him, as he believed they were a danger to him.[31] Unlike female victims of potential encroachment, John reacted violently. Although other men were not necessarily so aggressive or so successful, the defence of one's home was perceived as a core masculine duty.

There were, of course, many more cases in which pursued criminals became unreasonably violent and attacked the official who had come to arrest them. Policing order was far from a safe occupation, with many criminals violently determined not to be apprehended. In 1677 in Cumberland Cuthbert Musgrave stabbed Thomas Hodgson when he said he would arrest him.[32] Similarly, when George Wilson stopped Will Casson in the street with mention of a writ, Casson reacted badly. He drew his sword and reportedly said 'there is too many such rogues as thou', and beat George with his rapier.[33]

Although we do not have the verdicts in these cases, it is unlikely that a jury would have viewed the motivation for such actions as self-protection if the bailiff were genuine, since a lethal attack on an officer of the law was legally considered to be murder. In 1682 in London, two men and a woman were found guilty of murdering a bailiff's follower who had come to arrest one of their mothers.[34] The silence of pamphlets may be explained by the inherent ambiguity at the heart of this and most other extortion cases. Although a popular source of disquiet, these were not the simple and easily replicated tales that robberies were. It was not always immediately apparent who the victim was or even if the violence (on either side) was legitimate. Loopholes in the law added to the tension. Killing a legal official in pursuit of his duty was always construed as murder, while killing by an official in pursuit of an arrest was justifiable homicide and automatically pardoned.[35] The lines of legal culpability and cultural notions relating to a personal responsibility to defend the family and the home overlapped and the line was too blurred to allow these more problematic conflicts to become mainstream tales of terror.

Robbers were far from the only sensationalised criminals though, as other somewhat predictable villains appeared regularly in printed tales, and, to a lesser extent, in depositions. As we have seen, throughout the early modern period soldiers, foreigners and papists were at various times considered to be major threats to peace and prosperity. These were the scapegoats of early modern thought, constructed as the enemies within, who brought devastation and threatened to destabilise order at every level.[36] Although communities saw these groups as a substantial danger, such scapegoats played only a peripheral, albeit interesting, role as killers. The kinds of terror such individuals posed were magnified by hysterical preconceptions.

Soldiers are a prime example of both alienation and misrepresentation. They were generally men from outside the community, living away from their homes and families and quartered with people they did not know and who resented their presence. Their often antisocial behaviour, and the costs quartering imposed upon the community, led locals to despise them.[37] They were known to be drunken and to be quick to fight. They were also a danger to local women as they were fond of fornicating, and left their illegitimate children behind them for the parish to care for (and of course to pay for). Consequently, it is not inconceivable that these men may have felt isolated from the society they inhabited, while growing close to members of their unit. Soldiers did fight regularly, provoked by even slight insults. They fought members of their own unit, other companies of soldiers and men from the wider community. This is why they became the narrative embodiment of disorder, both in and out of print. At the same time, these men were instantly recognisable and therefore avoidable. Their unpredictability was not surprising. Most soldiers were feared before they had acted in any way inappropriately.

Soldiers had a terrible reputation for violence, which was exacerbated by their familiarity with weapons and printed descriptions of their exploits.[38] If the combatant was a soldier, the fact would have been clearly stated in court, possibly because it allowed contemporaries to make clear assumptions about his propensity for violence. In York in 1646 Roger Todd denied confessing to involvement in an earlier crime. The victim was a Captaine Beckwith, and clearly a soldier. Roger, on the other hand, identified himself as a labourer and said:

> that he is not, nor ever was a soldier, that he hath lived about a year at Towthrop, [and that he had for 9 years worked at] husbandry, as hedging ditching mowing ploughing and such like labour by day for wages.

Considering he was giving evidence in a case in which he was accused of a capital crime, he provided a lot of extraneous information about his occupation to the courts, which other deponents rarely did. He was obviously concerned with the need to establish a respectable identity, especially one that had little to do with soldiering.[39]

Soldiers most often fought with other soldiers, over regimental honour or from a mutual desire for violence. In York in 1686 seven soldiers from two different regiments clashed outside an alehouse after a quarrel. Although two men were slain, another soldier claimed that 'he does not believe the said Absolom Anderson had any malice or prejudice against the persons that happened to be slain'.[40] The fight itself was mutually engaged in out of high spirits. In 1677 in London three fellow soldiers went out for the evening drinking. They reportedly all got on well, until late in the evening Captains Sellwood's and Cranehall's tempers started to fray. Servant Joanna Dionys said a third soldier tried to get the two men to 'be quiet', but '[Sellwood] swore Gods blood he would not and ran at him [Cranehall] again and so soon as he had hit him, Mr Cranehall vomited blood.'[41]

A soldier's honour could be swiftly offended. In fact, even a small disagreement could become disproportionately meaningful in this regard.

Honour was vital currency for men and many felt it was worth fighting for.[42] In 1641 two troopers fought in Darfield in York. One of the troopers, Charles Younge, spent some time searching out his pre-arranged opponent, John Stonehouse, as he did not know where John was billeted. At first John refused to come down to fight, saying he wanted to sleep and had other things to do than 'meet an ass'. However, he soon changed his mind. William Bartram, also a soldier, tried to prevent the two fighting as he feared 'mischiefe'. Bartram took Younge's sword to prevent the conflict, and threatened to dishonour him in the eyes of their lieutenant over the incident. Younge begged him to be lenient, so Bartram returned his sword, and Younge immediately used it to run Stonehouse through.[43] Such violence was intense and to an extent pervasive, but it remained largely contained within soldierly ranks.

Nevertheless, the multiple strains upon the local-and-soldier relationship did occasionally translate into violence. Local people often resented soldiers because of the disruption and expense their quartering imposed on the parish. Soldiers tended not to integrate well and could be domineering. In Lymsworth in York in 1648 two soldiers attacked three local men. A simple request for directions swiftly degenerated into violence. However, tensions other than the immediate quarrel clearly existed. The soldiers felt other locals had treated them badly, which led them to strike out, apparently suddenly.[44]

The uneasy and antagonistic relationship between locals and soldiers, and the forced financial drain and social imposition soldiers represented, formed a powder-keg of repressed hostility, ready to go off with the right provocation. These tensions were more explicitly expressed in 1648, when a soldier killed John Oldfield after an outburst of anger in an inn. John was reported to have said 'We must help to winter you, and you are all ways oppressing us, and said you shall drink with me and offered him [the soldier] drink, but gave it to another man'.[45] John obviously felt the social and financial disruption caused by the presence of the soldiers was too much for his community to bear, so he taunted the soldier and deliberately provoked a conflict. In this tale, the local was the aggressor, but in other early modern narratives the image of the oppressive and brutal soldier who was a threat to local resources, order and certain masculine identities, was potently woven into stories about these kinds of conflict.

Most fights between locals and soldiers actually replicated the patterns of violence of ordinary men. The context of the violence was similar, with alehouse and night-time streets favoured locations. The same 'rules' of engagement and attitudes to fairness were employed. Indeed, in reality, most soldiers were no more violent than the average man. Nevertheless, as they were armed, trained and outsiders, soldiers were often perceived as a larger threat to local society than they really were. There was a real difference between what they did and what they were believed capable of doing. A local man described his fight with, and killing of, two soldiers in a mass bar brawl in Aldgate in 1691. He claimed he was drinking with his brother when John Smith, a 'certain soldier ... Being a pretty tall lusty man', stopped him and started a quarrel.[46] The soldier's size and perceived experience in conflict were factors in the assault that the defendant felt were integral to explaining why he had responded as violently as he did.

Soldiers brought an air of disorder into communities, and their reputations suffered accordingly. In one case, in 1647 in Doncaster, an unnamed soldier was killed after he had broken into a private house and demanded drink. The householders were terrified by his potential to harm, and so the husband drew his sword in fear and killed the man.[47] In fact, soldiers caused relatively little violent disruption in their adoptive communities, and were responsible for only a small proportion of homicides. Given the large numbers of men quartered in strange places (especially in the seventeenth century), the actual incidence of violent death was relatively small.[48] There were no dramatic swings in the levels of violence over this period, and in spite of their reputations, only a small number of soldiers appeared before the assizes as killers. Although some would have been prosecuted in military courts, the relatively small number tried at the assizes is significant. It also reveals the difference between perception of danger and its actuality. It could be that the general public was aware of the threat soldiers potentially represented, and that the incidence of homicides by soldiers was low simply because ordinary people avoided engaging these dangerous fellows. Their threat was real, but at least it was overt. Unlike the masked robber, soldiers were known to be unpredictable and so the crimes they committed were never surprising.

Foreigners, too, were enduring sources of suspicion and of perceived threat. In post-Reformation England, though, a new terror had emerged, which mixed this fear of foreigners with a wholehearted suspicion of papists. 'Papist' was the colloquial, and generally insulting, term for English Catholics. Considered to be the ultimate hidden threat, it was believed they were determined to overthrow all that was good and free, and would attempt to plunge England into the hands of the Antichrist.[49] Foreigners had always been feared for similar reasons, as they also represented threats to sovereignty and power, so together, foreigners and papists were perceived as constantly plotting disaster and widespread disorder. They were repeatedly described with stereotypical characteristics that most would have found plausible. Like soldiers, even before they acted violently, papists and foreigners were considered to have a greater propensity for violence and for brutality than ordinary citizens. Therefore, they provide us with the best examples of collective fear to be found in homicide records.

England experienced fluctuating, but intensely divisive religious tensions throughout this period. Papists were prime targets of concern, with several high-profile murders attributed to them.[50] At moments tensions became extreme and popular anxieties spilled into homicide texts. One such moment was the crisis of 1678–1681, when twenty-four people were executed after wild accusations of a popish plot to overthrow the king and reinstate Catholicism.[51] Political tensions undoubtedly heightened fears, leading to a spate of anti-papist stories. In a 1680 pamphlet John Bodnam, 'A Notorious Papist', was accused of killing Hereford JP Robert Pye, an eminent Protestant. Pye was incensed by Bodnam's refusal to take an oath, and decided to arrest him. The pair fought and Pye was badly wounded, dying eighteen days later. The language used to define this quarrel was inflammatory. The incident was seen from the start of the text as a conspiracy. The author questioned, 'Whether it be Folly or Madness for the Papists to give such a bloody Experiment of their Cruelty … One would think that it were an Article of the Roman Catholick Faith to murther Protestant Justices of the Peace'.[52] Bodnum was defined solely by his religion as 'an obstinate and violent Papist' or the 'Papistical Butcher', while the magistrate was called eminent or valiant. The story concluded by opining that, 'We have lost an Industrious and Valiant Magistrate; the Papists only a loose base Butcherly Villan'.[53]

Such tales were not limited to pamphlet accounts. Indeed, when prominent magistrate Sir Edmondbery Godfrey was murdered in 1678, his death was immediately blamed on papists. Three men were convicted and two were executed on the strength of suspicion, dubious report and a broader fear of the threat of Catholics. In this case, the murder was supposedly arranged to hide a larger papist plot, so it fitted well with broader suspicions of a systemic Catholic assault. Also, as the victim was prominent and his murder politically sensitive, such an accusation apparently made sense – the plotter would more likely target someone of high social standing, after all.[54]

The prominence of this case and the judicial approval it gave to suspicions of papists was considerable. However, despite the virulence of this story, tales accusing papists appeared only occasionally and never matched those in which robbers featured as the prime narrative villains. Papists were more often encountered in political or religious texts, only sporadically spilling into criminal literature at moments of extreme stress. In London, also in 1678, when a man named Powell disappeared and was believed dead, the only factor that aroused his neighbours' and friends' suspicions was the fact that he had recently associated with papists. Samuell Browne said Powell told him the man he did business with was a Catholic and that he had dreamed that they would kill him. Browne added that Powell had claimed 'that he heard his name was in their black list'. Mary Cleevely confirmed that Powell had been anxious about his associates, but had believed he was safe as 'God was above the Devil'.[55] These witnesses clearly felt that the shadowy men with their devilish religion had caused Powell's disappearance. There is no way of knowing how seriously such accusations were taken. It may have been that the witnesses were universally disbelieved. However, it does show how popular belief could shape evidence and affect those suspected of a crime.

Jews were another early modern scapegoat, who occasionally appeared in murder stories as highly distinctive killers. However, cases involving Jews were even rarer than those involving papists. Some may have loathed and feared Jews, but this did not translate into solid criminal accusations. As with Catholics, such stories were built on supposition and rumour rather than definite evidence of criminal activity. In 1674 in London, a pamphlet reported a midwife's account of a murder of a Jewish woman, committed by her father soon after the birth of her illegitimate child. The story has several fictive elements – the midwife, the victim and the father were not named and the midwife claimed she did not know where the crime occurred, as she was brought to the site by sedan chair at night. Even more suggestively, no body seems to have been found. However, the story does display an anxiety about the strange practices of Jews and, in particular, their harsh attitude to illicit sexuality.

Our sympathy in this tale is directed towards the unmarried and pregnant daughter. Her illicit sexuality was not criticised; rather, as in eighteenth century seduction narratives, she was presented as the victim of a great wrong 'by a Gentleman who pretended love to her'. The birth was attended by six masked men, all apparently Jewish, in a clear inversion of the usual all-female ritual of birth. The mockery of normative birthing practices was completed when the men proceeded to murder the new mother. The woman had been aware of her impending fate, reportedly telling the midwife that 'when she was delivered, she must be Burned in that fire that was below, within an hour'.[56] The midwife claimed she heard the woman's dying screams as she left the building. Without names, the characters were identified only as stereotypes, with their religion the prime feature of the story. Such tales were uncommon, but the occasional dark and frightening tales that do exist implied that wickedness was a function of Jewishness, and that it was seldom seen not because of its infrequent occurrence but due to obsessive secrecy.

Killings by foreigners appeared somewhat more frequently in homicide stories, but were never seen as part of a broad plot, like that usually associated with papists. In these stories, foreignness simply translated into suspicious behaviour and a propensity for extreme violence. Indeed, such distinctive inhabitants were easily singled out. In Fenchurch Street in London in 1699 Richard Brown attacked Bridget Wells in the coffee-house in which she worked and 'was calling the said Bridgett Wells whore and bitch and several ill names, whereupon she replied that she was no more a Scotch bitch than he was or words to that effect'.[57] Brown's insults targeted her gender and her sexuality, but they were also directed towards her race. Bridget later died of her wounds.

Scottishness invoked particularly dangerous passions in Yorkshire, as the proximity of the Scots and the history of conflict motivated widespread hatred and xenophobia. The line between acceptable defence and unacceptable aggression was difficult to draw, especially for soldiers or members of local militias. In 1648 William Rawson told how he and William Shaw were on their way to musters when they met a man who told them there were Scottish soldiers on the hill. After rushing to meet these enemies, fierce fighting ensued between the four soldiers and the two men, which resulted in William Shaw being stabbed in the back. When Shaw accused the soldiers of murder as he lay bleeding they apparently replied 'they did not weigh it, for he was a rogue that lay in the woods to rob men as they passed by'.[58] The two men attacked the four soldiers thinking they were Scottish, and the soldiers struck back as they feared their attackers were robbers – a perfect example of the interplay of fear and violence. Each saw what they wanted to see.

Defence of one's community could spill over into simple crime, as hatred distorted the duty to protect. In a dramatic example of spontaneous rage, soldier Thomas Tutin attacked Ann Iongate, an old Scottish woman. Tutin was a stranger to Iongate and had just come back from fighting in a legitimate battle. He and his fellow soldiers met the old woman on the road in Yorkshire, and, on learning she was Scottish, searched her and stole her money. Moments later she was dead. Although none of the soldiers admitted seeing her killed, some reported Tutin's confession to the killing soon afterwards. John Barton said:

> Thomas Tutin did then say that he had killed her and that she was a Scotch woman, and that the women in Scotland had murdered many English and said that he would kill more of them, if they came his way.[59]

The other soldiers corroborated this evidence, saying they had tried to restrain Tutin.

This cold-blooded killing was perceived as inappropriately brutal even by the battle-hardened soldiers present. Although hatred of the Scots was legitimate in battle, it was seen as inappropriate and criminal in the context of an old female victim. The theft only served to underline the felonious nature of the crime. This was an evocative tale in which a tension existed between Ann's alien nationality and her familiarity as a resident, as well as between Thomas's identity as a fit, male soldier and hers as an old, defenceless woman. Ann has no direct voice in these tales, but she was not one-dimensional. Her age and her gender were omnipresent in the tale and prevented her being defined purely by her Scottishness.

Individual foreigners were consistently viewed as far greater threats than they actually were. In court they were seen as naturally brutal, since foreign ethnicity was linked to violence in the minds of many contemporaries. In most cases the distinction between the violence of foreigners and that of local men was that witnesses were seldom interested in excusing the crime of a foreigner. Foreigners were infrequently assisted in court, or supported in print. Their violence was not depicted as normal, necessary or provoked; the definition implied by their race was perceived as all encompassing. Often the only ambiguity expressed in such cases derived from the defendant's own words. When Frenchman John de Fountain killed Hamond Jones in 1689 in Yorkshire after they had quarrelled about the feeding of horses, witnesses referred to de Fountain as 'the Frenchman', and described him as having acted in a sudden violent manner. However, in his statement to the court via an interpreter, de Fountain said that he acted to prevent Jones beating an old Frenchman. He said Jones had wounded him first with a drawn sword, calling him a 'French dog'. But none of the other deponents felt inclined to support his self-defence claim in their evidence. He was defined purely by his nationality and portrayed as exclusively culpable for the disorder.[60]

It seems clear that courtroom perceptions about the generic brutality of foreigners could mean they were unfairly judged and severely punished. When Irish trooper Rynian Scot was attacked by the drunken Thomas Story in an alehouse, his words of self-defence were considered in terms of his Irishness. Scot said that when Story heard 'there was an Irishman in the room he sent for him'. Scot claimed he refused to fight with Story and had tried to leave the inn, but Story pulled a gun, presumably to attack Scot. He only succeeded in killing himself, however. Two witnesses gave evidence about Scot, saying 'he always had the character of a civil fair conditioned man'.[61] Despite this vote of confidence, the jury were not sympathetic and found that Scot had been the aggressor and was guilty of manslaughter, rather than self-defence.

Despite the emphasis pamphleteers placed on danger groups, most crimes were committed by neighbours. These conflicts dominated courtroom narratives and caused intense concern. People knew that when a crime was committed, the likely source of the trouble was someone they knew well. Neighbours may not have been generally feared, but the kinds of danger they represented were acknowledged. Unlike crimes within the family, neighbourly violence was not understood via notions of duty or by a responsibility to chastise. Other than law enforcement officers and the hue and cry, no one had rights to physically restrain or assault other community members. Indeed, public violence and disorder were rigorously challenged and collectively opposed within communities.

Even so, neighbours could act as invidiously as the masked robber and the sensational domestic killer to disrupt good order. Neighbours, family members and friends were always the first to be suspected of a homicide, and violence from neighbours was neither surprising nor unusual. Despite this, murderous neighbours were often excluded from printed accounts of crime and appeared to rate low on national scales of terror. The concern such conflicts caused was qualitatively different from that caused by robbers and strangers. Neighbours were also more likely to be acquitted of their crimes than receive exemplary punishment.[62] They were treated with a subtlety alien to depictions of crimes by papists, foreigners or robbers, and although feared, their names and crimes were not subjects of national debate.

We need to accept that early modern communities were not always harmonious, but spaces in which conflicts both festered and erupted suddenly, and in which disruptive clashes between individuals regularly occurred. People did not experience community life uniformly, with some finding support in like-minded individuals, and others finding censure and even ritual humiliation. Communities could fragment at moments of stress, leaving members feeling alienated. William Swinyard certainly felt isolated from his neighbours when, in 1667 in Kirkegate in Yorkshire, he found himself a victim of a stang riding. 'Riding the stang' was a ritual form of public humiliation in which an individual was mocked in a stylised performance.[63] Edmond Wharfe said that William was agitated, because 'they are riding the Stang for me this night, he [Wharfe] replied never heed them'. William was obviously being punished for a perceived transgression and had become an outcast in his own society.

Barthol Shearburne described a great company of people processing down the street making lots of noise, and said that William grew increasingly agitated during the ritual and eventually took a loaded weapon, shot randomly into the crowd and killed two people. William reportedly then exclaimed 'if they be not dead I wish they were for I shot with a full resolution to kill forty if I could'. Clare Fysh also testified to William's words, saying 'Yes said he, they ride the stang for me, but I'll (meaning the said William Swinyard) will speed some of them, although they wore golden chains about their necks'. His wife concurred with his antisocial sentiments. Neighbour Isabell Marshall said she heard Swinyard's wife say '(by God) that if he (meaning her husband[)] would not discharge the gun she would and swore again the same oath'.[64] William and his wife were alienated from, and mocked by, their community, and he retaliated by indiscriminately shooting his gun.

Our conception of community needs to incorporate elements of casual violence if it is to reflect early modern reality. In Northumberland in 1669 William Gresham and Thomas Robinson fought and Thomas was killed. Although the two did not know each other, William was sure that Thomas had stolen a horse's halter from him five years earlier, and so he and two of his friends brutally beat him to death with staves and their fists.[65] In London in 1690 Richard Merrideth grew angry when guard John Pascall refused to let him pass. The two had very short tempers and a witness stated that the angry Richard said 'I'll give it you, and with that thrust the end of the scabbard (the sword being in it) into the right eye of John Pascall'.[66]

Violence appears to be omnipresent in these tales, and a casual disregard for one's neighbours emerges as a subtext to all such disagreements. In a case from 1666 an apothecary was presented as uninterested in the care of his patient. According to the complainant, Joseph Booth, John Smith neglected Robert Morehouse's wound shamefully, and when Joseph complained, instead of John acting more competently he refused to attend to the victim further, saying 'Let him Rot'. John also refused to allow another apothecary to attend to the patient, saying 'no, they should have been more Civil to me'. Joseph blamed his friend's death on John's neglect and his 'unwholesome salves'.[67]

Accounts of moments of chaotic violence and extreme reactions litter assize records. Quarrels between strangers sometimes broke out over such minor matters that we have a fleeting sense of the disorderly society Lawrence Stone portrays. Even close neighbours and friends could let themselves be overwhelmed by their anger and strike out using the nearest weapon to hand. In Yorkshire in 1684 neighbours Roger Preston and John Holderness quarrelled over the ownership of the sheep Roger was then taking home. Insults and bad language were exchanged before Roger hit John with his hand, on which John grabbed hold of a sheep and clubbed Roger over the head with it, causing his death.[68] The suddenness of the violence in this conflict and the speed with which John reached for his 'weapon' were facets seen in a plethora of similar homicide cases.

Not all assaults threatened communal order equally, and it was the unpredictable assault that was often presented as more shocking and extreme than other kinds of dispute. Some of the most unpredictable violence involved clashes between unrelated men and women, who, even when close neighbours, had little social contact, although they would almost certainly know each other by name and reputation. Nevertheless, the records show that occasionally men would fatally assault women they hardly knew for minor or undisclosed reasons. Widow Margarett Hill was beaten to death by Henery Thompson in 1662 in Lancaster, in an assault lasting two hours. Henery's wife and another woman watched, hidden, fearful and unable to help until he left the scene. The witnesses described Margarett as a 'poor old widdow', and one, Anne Ashmore, said Henery beat Margarett so violently that she 'cried lamentably out'. Her age and her gender were deliberately mentioned to present her as helpless and innocent of blame for the assault. Although Henery claimed Margarett incited his response by insulting his sister, her failure to defend herself, or to act in any way other than as a victim, made the pathos of her assault more acute. Indeed, when Anne recounted how Henery called Margarett a witch, she said he 'gave her not over until he made [her] kneel down of her knees and ask him Forgiveness'. Then he killed her.[69] Neither woman felt able to stop Henery. Their fear of him and his dominance over them was complete.

Such casually violent acts were not everyday occurrences, but neither were they unfamiliar events. It was the extremity of the act and the passivity of the victim that distinguished these from more acceptable, pardonable violence. Nevertheless, being passive and female certainly did not protect women from brutal men. When Londoner Simon Durrant battered a woman to death he claimed his actions had been mild and even jocular. In his explanation 'he pleaded that her dancing was with her own consent, and as for the rest it was but a Frolic, and he intended no harm'.[70] Likewise, when Elinor Cutherberson was attacked in Cumberland in 1669, a witness stated that 'Henry Blemise did beat her and put his knees upon her belly or heart, and did thrust her breasts with his heel'.[71] She watched the violence but did not intervene, possibly as she was unsure of the context. Such men were clear threats to social harmony. However, since their violence was unexpected, it required careful consideration before it could be condemned.

Community tensions could be extreme and of long standing. Self-professed enemies would have significantly disrupted order long before their violent conflict appeared on the legal record. Such parties were always the first to be suspected of violent crime, with witnesses keen to give evidence against them concerning their long-held, bitter relationship with the victim. Malice was critical evidence in the early modern courtroom as it allowed the jury to distinguish between murder and manslaughter, and so was fundamental to the construction of justice and order. All discord was clearly noted. When Mathew Laidley and Jeffrey Robson fought in 1698 in Northumberland and Mathew subsequently died, John Aynsley claimed Jeffrey had said, a year earlier that 'he would be a block in the said Mathew Laidleys way as long as he lived'. Several other witnesses gave similar evidence of discord, with one describing a physical assault with a ladle two or three years earlier. All the witnesses agreed that there was an old but relevant history of dislike at the core of this case.[72]

In some cases the animosity was extreme and the consequent disorder ingrained in the community. In 1649 in Skipton in Yorkshire Francis Holden claimed he had acted in self-defence when he struck William Waineman. Evidence from witnesses indicated that this was not the first fight between the two. The conflict seemed to involve the entire family, and Elizabeth Holden, Francis's mother, was reported as having said 'if any of the mason kind had their finger hurt by any Waineman there should not be a Waineman left a live in Craven'. Thomas Alcocke likewise heard Elizabeth make a threat when she reportedly said to her son 'Thou hath not killed him, but if any other of the Wainemans set of thee if thou kill not then thou shall have none of my bread'.[73] To Elizabeth, familial honour was more important than community order. She encouraged her son to perpetuate the quarrel, even though this undermined acceptable communal desires for order.

However, it would be unfair to classify early modern society as wholly disorderly. After all, it was the explicit function of the courts to transform violence and restore communal harmony through open legislative decisions. Public trials and judgements were ingrained in the English legal system for this very reason. To maintain the impression of openness that underlay this judicial system, all unnatural deaths, even those the coroner had judged accidental, were pursued through the court system. The intention was to present a public image of rigorous justice being done, even in the most implausible of cases: even friendship did not mean that murder was unthinkable, with foul play frequently investigated in cases of sudden death. When Hugh Berry died after a public handball game the authorities checked for foul play, despite a lack of witnesses or marks on the corpse. Although the game was friendly, Hugh's sudden death was thoroughly and openly investigated to ensure justice was seen to be done.[74]

An absence of malice and lack of intent to harm were just as clearly stated in court as animosity. Friendship could be an important factor in refuting malice. As Zachary Babington had argued in his advice to grand jurors, a sudden assault should be defined as manslaughter rather than murder.[75] This did not mean automatic exemption from suspicion, though. In Holborn in 1694 Thomas Toothall killed his friend in a tavern after an escalating argument about cricket. William Redman started to vigorously insult his erstwhile friend, Thomas, calling him 'Rascall, Villan, son of a whore and gave him other scurrilous Language, upon which this Examinant [Toothall] begged of him to be quiet, yet he continued his Railing and followed this Examinant over to Lether Lane'. Thomas finally lost his patience and struck his friend with a naked sword, killing him outright.[76] True friendships were always mentioned in these cases. When, in 1674 in York, Jonathan Jennings killed George Asylaby he told the court they had been 'very kind and intimate friends'. Jonathan claimed that George had sent for him to meet him in a field. He had willingly complied, but when he arrived George pulled a sword and, for no apparent reason, attacked him. He claimed he struck his good friend purely in self-defence.[77]

Some killings were explicitly related to friendship and were depicted as cases of pure misfortune. In 1664 in Westmoreland, John Dent was shot by John Winter, his good friend. The shooting was neither an expression of anger nor the result of a fight: it was caused by high spirits. John Winter was in an alehouse and had been charging his gun while he waited for his friend to arrive. When Dent did arrive, Winter apparently stood and said 'Rogue, is this a time of night to come at', before shooting his friend in the side, killing him. However, witnesses concurred that Winter had acted in a 'jesting manner' and had not intended to hurt his friend.[78] Likewise, John Gledhill killed his friend James Birkeheade while wrestling in the open air. Gledhill claimed he had not intended to hurt his friend, saying 'that all was done in love'. Although both men had been drinking, there were no harsh words and no history of disagreements between them.[79]

In fact, stories of killing in error reveal the critical distinctions made between types of killing. All killers, whatever their motivation, were publicly tried and judged. However, defendant's tended to frame accidental killings in terms of shock and disbelief. This shock neatly expressed both a lack of familiarity with the consequence of violence and an absence of intention to kill. The killers were relying on their self-confessed (but often confirmed) orderliness to redefine their intentions and make them honourable. When William Morton killed fellow servant Mary Scholefield in 1725 he expressed anguish and surprise. According to one witness, after the shot, William raced into the room where his victim lay and said 'Have I hurt thee Molly if I have I am sorry for it'. The attending physician added his view of the killing to his report on the wounds saying 'he [William] had unluckily shot a woman with a Gun which he did not believe was charged'. Even the victim concurred, telling her mother before she died that it had all been done in jest.[80]

John Walker went further in his display of contrition for his unintended shooting. He told the court that Frances Coroler, his victim, 'was a very kind neighbour. And one that he always loved and never intended any harm to him or any man living'.[81] Guns were highly volatile in this period and accidents were therefore likely occurrences. A jury would be sympathetic and find misfortune if the circumstances were right, although all fatal accidents were seriously investigated. In 1676 a young man was arraigned and tried for murder at the Old Bailey. He and two other boys had killed a man when they had thrown stones at him at Clerkenwell Green. After the trial, however, the pamphleteer decided 'it was his hard misfortune to be too good a marks man'.[82] The jury decided that he had not committed murder, and was guilty only of manslaughter.

Moments of disorder can be revealing of an essentially orderly society and of the durability of communal structures. Crime was not endemic. Communities were heavily policed not necessarily because disorder reigned but to ensure order remained. The kind of violence pamphlets most often chose to represent was not the most frequent kind. Neighbours were a prime source of violence and danger, and their disorderly actions were taken seriously and feared locally. Nevertheless, in their relative silence on such assaults, pamphlets acknowledged the ambiguity with which such crimes were perceived within communities. Although vigorously prosecuted, local killers were portrayed as less dangerous than the robber or the soldier.

As I have shown, violence between neighbours was variously interpreted on a scale from extreme to accidental. However, it was all seen as triggered from personal motives and specific circumstances. Usually both victim and killer had engaged in a confrontation or quarrel, thus denying the victim the innocent, uninvolved and undeserving persona so valued for the drama and pathos it offered printed records. After all, when both parties consented to an essentially equal engagement, the incident ceased to be an unprovoked assault by a nefarious other that could have affected anyone. The more open and personal the conflict the less likely it was to spark national concern.

Prejudice has always existed, and there have always been groups who are hated, feared or overly suspected of crime. The logically corollary of this should have been a large number of accusations and trials of these groups, but this did not occur in homicide cases. The fear certainly existed, but there was a real disparity between the 'usual suspects' and the believed source of most murderous disorder. Neighbours were the first to be suspected and the most regularly accused, as in spite of their prejudice towards

Catholics, robbers and soldiers, most realised that it was those they knew who represented the real source of most violence. This did not affect the object of early modern fears. People did not start fearing their neighbours or family members simply because they formed the largest threat. Fear is not based on experience, but imagination. The usual suspects did not quantitatively top the list of potential killers, but they did terrify and threaten in the imaginations of early modern people. And it was this terror that shaped stories and prejudice, if not homicide indictments.

12

Serial Killers and Sex Crimes

In 1675 seven corpses were discovered in the garden of a former inn in Gloucestershire. The new owner of the property, a blacksmith, found the bodies after he had started to dig out the foundations for an anvil in his garden. On breaking the soil 'he found the bones and part of the flesh of a man buried there'.[1] He immediately alerted his neighbours, who assisted him in uncovering the remaining bodies, which all lay in the same part of the garden and were in varying states of decay.

After the initial discovery the process of uncovering the rest of the corpses was relatively quick. The pamphleteer tells us that:

> they in short time found the Skeletons or Bones of seven several persons, the bodies or flesh of them were much consumed, yet some of them had certain remnants of woollen and linen Garments remaining, whereby it might be perceived that they were buried in their Clothes.[2]

The scene was as horrific for these individuals as it would be for us today. These were ordinary people faced with uncovering a mass grave. The neighbours were clearly shocked at their awful discovery. Yet their involvement did not stop there: as well as uncovering the corpses and reporting the matter, they also had a duty and a desire to pursue justice. This was something they took very seriously and so the hunt for the killer and for proof of guilt began in earnest.

The former innkeepers were quickly suspected of being the perpetrators of these crimes. In fact, the couple were apparently perfect candidates for such suspicions. The man was identified as a Cromwellian soldier and the woman as Scottish. This combination of popular stereotypes drew on nationality, profession and politics to create the perfect amalgam of heartless brutality. Both the accused represented recognisable stereotypes of unusual and excessive wickedness that those reading or hearing the story would be able to swiftly recognise.

The two suspected killers were so stereotypically bad that they are undoubtedly exaggerations of a real couple, or even entirely made up by the pamphleteer. The couple were not named in the pamphlet, which adds a further sense of unreality to the text. Indeed, we cannot know whether or not the crime occurred as described. It may be only an embellished account of a series of killings, or totally untrue. As no court records exist in this case, it is impossible to know with any kind of certainty. However, even if it did not occur as stated (or even at all), the fact that the story was still told in print indicates a contemporary level of concern about the *kind* of crime and killers described. Such tales were part of popular culture and were told to warn of wickedness and inspire fear. Like horror stories today, they were experienced as plausible tales which addressed real concerns. They cannot be read purely as fiction. They had a broader resonance.

In fact, the local people in this case had been suspicious of the former innkeepers' activities for some time, albeit without any real proof of wrongdoing. Their inn was in a reasonably favourable location but locals always perceived their trade to be 'small and inconsiderable'. However, the neighbours noted that, 'contrary to all expectations, they began to thrive again, furnishing their house rarely well with all sorts of household goods, and convenient Utensils'. This was very suspicious, and the neighbours would undoubtedly have believed that the money came from some kind of illegal activity – if one they had yet to uncover.

It is here that we get the first glimpse of the pamphlet's explanation for the murders (and probably how this crime was popularly rationalised). The motivation was greed – the intention was really only to steal. The couple's unexplained wealth together with the newly recovered bodies was highly suggestive – so much so that the pamphleteer spelt out the nature of these suspicions very clearly, saying 'that this spring tide of Fortune was swelled with blood, and his Gaines raked together with the Barbarous hands of Robbery and Murther'.[3] According to the tale, the murders occurred over several years, and with them the wealth of the couple grew exponentially. In fact, the couple gained so much from their killings that they moved into a bigger house, selling their old property to the blacksmith. This was when the bodies were revealed. Despite the crimes having taken place over such a long time span, the storyteller was quick to absolve local people of culpability in the crime, and for not having discovering it earlier. He declared that the locals had not 'the least suspition or mistrust of the unhappy truth'. They simply had not been aware of what was going on.

Nevertheless, the former innkeepers were suspected of the killings as soon as the bodies were uncovered. This was partly because they had owned the property and partly because of their isolated (and undoubtedly) wicked natures and what appeared to be a clear motive. Even so, the courts would still have required proof that a crime had occurred and that they had been the perpetrators. No eyewitnesses apparently existed, but another type of proof was (rather conveniently) forthcoming. On examination of the bodies a murder weapon was found on which was engraved the name of the soldier-innkeeper whom everyone already suspected. This tangible proof of his culpability was undoubtedly a 'legal fiction' which allowed the pair to be proven guilty. If the case was based in fact, and was tried in court, then it is possible that entirely different evidence would have been presented. However, the drama of the engraved knife added to this already salacious tale. Some may even have read the fortuitous finding of the knife as an act of God, believing that providence had intervened to prevent the murderers from escaping justice.

Despite being presented as clearly wicked and fearsome, the innkeeping couple were not described as sadists, nor was wickedness considered enough to explain their crime. Rather, the tale implies they had simply (and even mundanely) killed for the cash. There was no suggestion that they had enjoyed it; the psyche was viewed differently in the past, and little attention was paid to the psychological desire to kill. Indeed, there was scant medical knowledge of the kind of mental categories modern profilers and police use to discuss certain killers. Contemporaries regarded killing as wicked and terrifying, but not as something that only psychologically distinctive people were prone to. It was thought that anyone could kill, and anyone could be tempted into wickedness at any time. Although the Gloucestershire crime terrified contemporaries, by linking it to robbery, people could easily understand why the couple had acted in such extreme ways. And at the very least, this meant that the neighbours could have made some sense of the fearsome crime they had uncovered.

The crime itself was clearly the work of what we would now identify as a serial killer. Both the husband and wife were accused of perpetrating the killings, and would probably have been tried and even executed together. No distinction was made between their roles. Although modern experience suggests lone men are the most common suspects in serial murders, predatory couples are far from unknown. In the absence of other evidence we have to take the accusation of the pair at face value and assume they were jointly culpable of the killings. As mentioned earlier, the killings may never have occurred, although it is likely the story was at least based on a real case. This, of course, makes a difference to how we understand this story. However, it does not have to be significant in terms of the history of serial killing, since this was far from the only tale concerning multiple, odd or sexually motivated crime. Therefore we can put aside the question of the 'reality' of the tale (which is interesting but not vital to an analysis of this crime) and consider something just as valid – how this story of multiple killing differed from one about a single murder.

In modern terms the distinction is plain. Serial killers, mass murderers and sexually motivated or psychotic killers are easily recognisable as the most significant sources of modern terror. These are the killers we fear the most, despite being aware of the tiny statistical risk they pose. Like early modern people, we are more likely to be killed by people we know well. Indeed, our risk of being killed by a family member is generally higher than that that existed in this period.[4] Yet we continue to be obsessed with the unlikeliest of all kinds of killers.

Today, multiple murderers and sexually motivated criminals have a consistently high profile. They appear on the front pages of newspapers and on the headlines of news reports – honours seldom accorded to humble, domestic murderers. These assailants are also given glamorous pseudonyms while their real identities are being sought, and the pseudonyms often remain popular after capture and can remain more famous than their real names. To modern eyes, serial killers are seen as distinctive in psychological and even genetic terms. Early modern commentators would not have agreed. They would happily label a killer 'wicked', but this was wickedness anyone could attain. Evil was not determined by unseen social or behavioural forces, but was linked to God and the hereafter. To act wickedly was to succumb to the temptation of the devil.

Modern paranoid fantasies concerning the danger of sadistic strangers and serial killers were almost entirely absent in this period. While it is true that such crimes occurred rarely, infrequency of occurrence had not stopped murderous robbers becoming common bogeymen. Mass murderers, psychotic and sexually motivated killers were seldom feared as contemporaries did not perceive them to be different from other murderers. Such crimes were considered wicked, but there was little of the associated hysteria we have now. Multiple murders were considered to be as wicked as individual ones. It was the initial act of malice that determined the response, not the number of corpses accumulated.

The question of why such crimes were not especially condemned is intriguing. It could be that such crimes were considered implausible, as indeed relatively few mass killings survive in legal records. With vastly different conceptions of the psyche, early modern people may not have interpreted the threat of multiple killers as universal. On the other hand, people may not have made connections between individual crimes and, if they did, such killers may have proved impossible to apprehend. This would certainly impact upon the recorded numbers of such criminals. All we know for certain is that killings for sexual or sadistic motives by strangers were only reluctantly presented in this period; and planned, large-scale and serial crimes were only rarely recorded in printed texts and depositions. The prime source of modern fears was entirely under-represented and apparently little feared in the early modern period.

This is not to say that wild and excessive perceptions of crime were not formulated in this period. Although witch belief in England can never really be described in terms of a craze, it certainly was pervasive in the sixteenth and seventeenth centuries and the cause of multiple trials. Many were convicted on highly suspect evidence relating to muttered curses and devil's marks found on their bodies. Witches were even believed capable of murder. The last English assize trial for witchcraft did not take place until 1712.[5] With this in mind, the fact that psychotic killings did not cause panic or broad social concern in this period, despite being clearly recorded in the archives, needs explanation.

It is true that fear is difficult to trace in the past (as it is today), since individual responses to violent reports differed. However, perceptions of danger were always historically specific, and this specificity is somewhat easier to uncover. People would have known what was commonly feared within their society – what was plausible, what was a frequent cause of concern and how certain crimes were broadly interpreted as worse than others. Individuals may not have shared these concerns, but they existed in a cultural context in which such concerns were regularly expressed.

That early modern fears could include witches while they seemingly ignored serial killers is intriguing. The occurrence of serial, mass and sexually motivated crimes has to be examined for explanations of these silences. The perpetrators of such crimes existed; they were caught, prosecuted and even executed. But they left no indelible impression on communal beliefs – they did not become one of society's deepest fears. However, to understand why this is, we have to study a fear that was not apparent, and concerns that did not occur. Although such a study will necessarily have to be speculative, it will be suggestive of differences between modern and early modern perceptions of crime and of the relative and culturally specific nature of fear.

A good way to begin this study is to review the kinds of unusual crime that were recorded. We know about odd, serial or sexually motivated crime from the witnesses who discussed it or from the pamphlets that recorded it. There may be, of course, many similar crimes that have not been recorded, partly because the witnesses did not notice that they were unusual or because the records of these crimes have been lost. Therefore we can never know how many crimes occurred that could be categorised in these ways. Nevertheless, that some existed is suggestive of further undiscovered crimes, although it is unlikely that the so-called 'dark figure' of undiscovered crime was disproportionately large.[6] Despite the unreliable nature of the statistics, we can still discuss these partially hidden crimes through the stories told about them.

Although reasonably infrequent, records indicative of psychosis and sexually motivated crime exist – men stalking women, luring them into quiet places and killing them, for example. But cases were effectively minimised by common assumptions that the killer was well known to the female victim, and that she played a significant role in causing her assault. When Edmund Audley stalked Hannah Bullevant in London in 1698 his actions were attributed to his specific malice towards Hannah, 'supposing ... that she had some way injured, pinched or wronged him in bearing Testimony against him'. The writer did not explain what this previous incident was, but did say 'he dogg'd her, for some time together, from place to place for a conveniency to execute his Bloody Design'. He pursued her and attempted to shoot her. He missed at first, but when she tried to escape 'he pulled forth another [gun], and shot her quite through the Head, her Brains being shattered to pieces'. A man in the crowd then arrested Edmund.[7] Although the murder was described as terrible, the crime was linked specifically to Hannah, with no corollary decrying female safety generally.

Early modern audiences were always highly suspicious of crimes potentially involving sex. As in the case of Hannah Bullevant, these crimes were seen as innately personal. Indeed, the female victim was always suspected and her character was tried along with the defendant. When Mary Bush was slain in London in 1678, as a consequence of a violent sexual assault, all the medical professionals who examined her body could tell the court was that sex had led to her death. Midwife Anne Hempstall said she 'is very confident that ... Mary Bush hath been entered very lately by a man in the way of carnal copulation and that [she] ... will certainly lose her life by means of the penetration aforesaid'.[8] Although she must have been brutally attacked to suffer such mortal injuries, the crime was not identified as rape and murder because her role and sexual resistance had not been established. Until they knew for certain that she had *not* consented, the assumption would always be that she had – however violently her body had been treated.

If such a victim could be shown to have been immoral, she was mercilessly criticised in print. In some cases her immorality was described as contributing towards – and even being the cause of – her death. In an undated pamphlet from Leeds a young man was described as killing his married lover by 'cutting her Tongue and her eyes out of her Head, her Throat being Cut from Ear to Ear; and after all this, being not satisfied, rips her open, and takes a child out of her Womb, laying it down by her side'. Although she had been brutally slain, the repeating chorus warned only against murder and adultery. The woman's own sexual deviance, in engaging in adultery, was clearly portrayed as a determining factor in her death. The brutality of the killing was shocking but was related to her sinfulness as much as the man's depravity. Indeed, the story concluded by warning wives to:

> Take warning by this womans fall;
> Don't yeild to flattering speeches fair;
> And of lewd young-men have a care.[9]

The pamphleteer was concluding that this female victim ultimately had to take the blame for her own death. Most contemporaries would probably have agreed with this assessment. As a consequence, the crime against her was downplayed and her killer's role minimised.

'Unusual' killers were pursued as vigorously as all assailants. However, despite a wealth of potential, the unusual factors in these cases were not emphasised in the stories told about them. Although references can be found in court records, they were not prominently displayed in the evidence and do not seem to have inspired printed repetitions. Widow Dorothy Smith was found dead on her bed at home in 1688 in Yorkshire after she had been missing for ten days. Neighbours immediately suspected that Dorothy's lover, Ralph Poyson, had killed her: William Langley reported he had heard Ralph say 'that if Dorothy did report that he was a suitor to her that he would burn her or do her a mischief.'[10] There was strong evidence to suggest they were right to suspect him, as several witnesses recalled that Ralph had threatened to kill Dorothy if she revealed their relationship.

Katherine Poyson, Ralph's mother, confirmed suspicions when she told the court that, despite his claim, he had not been home on the evening Dorothy went missing. Although the town felt sure of his guilt, they did not dwell on the strange aspects of this case: Elizabeth Smyth said that the body had been found apparently laid out ready for burial 'with her coats folded on her breast and bare from the breast downwards'. She further suggested an additional crime had occurred, saying she did 'verily believe she was Ravished and also murdered'. The odd and the sexual aspects of the crime do not seem to have drawn special attention, with only the personal relationship of the pair scrutinised. The rape and post-mortem actions of the killer were largely ignored.

These distinctive criminals were seemingly little feared, with only a select few receiving attention from pamphleteers. Such crimes would certainly have been differently defined today, and any ritual or strange obsessions of the killer seen as an integral part of the crime. Those eventually accused may have caused disquiet for some time, and so made clear and unsurprising suspects. Even so, reports do not note previously odd behaviour, quite unlike the historic reports to be found in domestic killings, when evidence about past behaviour was felt to be vital evidence.

In most cases the 'odd' crime was simply described, with few commenting on how it differed from other murders. A good example can be found in a disturbing case from 1658 in Yorkshire. William Keath killed Margery Brambery on a public highway before, oblivious to onlookers, removing some of her clothes. William clearly committed the crime, as one deponent, Milcah Browne, said he called her over and said:

> Come Milcah I have killed the witch now and said she would never milk kine [cows] more) and I looking towards him did see Margery Brambery lying under the said William Keath his feet and the said Keath bowing down towards her, and doing something at her head, and chopping his hands downward.

Milcah took advantage of his distraction to run for help.[11]

Another passer-by, Edward Humphrey, also saw the dead body by the gates and 'William Keath ... busy about her feet, as if he had been pulling of her shoes'. Humphrey was too afraid to approach William but watched him. He said William told him the woman was dead and subsequently threw her milking stool down the hill, saying 'Devil gather up thine own'. William then wandered off singing. Once he had moved away, Humphrey moved nearer to the corpse and said he 'did find it was Margery Brambery who lay all bloody and her blood did then run down the hill and highway, and the said woman her left leg was bare above her knee'. William Temple added to the mystery and possible symbolism of the killing by saying that when he saw the corpse he observed she was:

> dead in her own gate stead with much blood running from her, and she had four or five wounds in her throat, and one was in the midst of her throat, and the wounds did seem to have been with a knife, and her head cloths were all or most off, and her head and face were all bloody, and her shoes were cut off her feet.

Although the witnesses clearly expressed their deep fear of William, the causes of his behaviour and his possible motivation were never discussed. He was presented only as anomalous and not as a representative of a broader murderous trend.

In fact, some notable exceptions apart, few multiple killings were publicly identified. We cannot know therefore how many actually occurred. Indeed, we cannot certainly know that the sexually motivated cases already seen were the only murders committed by each killer. The simple fact was that early modern people did not think in terms of multiple killings. They did not look for similar crimes, unless they had persuasive reasons for doing so. Of course, comparison over even relatively short distances may not have been possible, due to the fragmented nature of the legal system and informal organisation of the policing system.[12] Nor did pamphlets tend to draw parallels between crimes, presenting only linked killings when any other conclusion was impossible. Murder was seldom abstracted from the personal. Individual quarrels provoking violence were the norm, with multiple killings proving a real conceptual problem for early modern people.

Of course, some multiple killings were identified. This was usually because they occurred at the same time as each other or, as in the Gloucestershire case, the bodies were found together. Servants who targeted their entire household were obvious sources of this kind of accusation. Indeed, it seems clear that when Mary Taylor poisoned an entire pot of ale for general consumption in Samuel Fish's house she intended to have a random and potentially mass impact. The inquisition limited her crime by concluding that her intention had been the murder of Samuel alone and that the tabler, George Braviner, was actually killed in error. Nevertheless, one deponent declared that the beer pot the poison was placed in was 'for the use of the family' and that at least two other people had drunk from it and become very ill. Another deponent stated that Mary had spoken to her in the street before the poisoning and said 'she hoped to see (within a short time) some of her enemies fall'. The coroner's inquisition concluded that she had acted with malice, but failed to fully present the potentially mass nature of the killing. The punishment would have been the same whatever implication had been drawn. Nevertheless, the coroner was obviously keen not to speculate about Mary's potential to cause mass deaths.[13]

Even if the mass potential of this crime had been acknowledged, the killer would not have been especially vilified. With the exception of treason, a felony was the worst possible kind of crime, and as this received the death penalty, there was really no worse kind of punishment that could be inflicted. Of course, if this crime had been considered to be distinctively wicked, such killers could have received the spectacular and unusual form of execution that those who committed petty treason received. However, from the earliest development of murder law, multiple malicious killings had failed to be identified as especial kinds of killings, warranting a separate form of punishment.[14]

Crimes that we consider to be indicative of real wickedness and to be beyond the pale of ordinary people were never considered to be any more wicked in the past than individual killings. It was not until the later nineteenth century and notable crimes, like the Ripper murders, that such killings were considered to be separate and linked to particular kinds of psychosis. It is only when this distinction is made that the crime becomes a distinctive activity and a singular source of modern terror. In a world in which all minds were considered to be capable of violence and wickedness, distinguishing between categories of killers was simply neither possible nor practical.

It is clear that there was a real dissonance between what people feared and what actually happened. Not all hidden killers became the focus of pamphlet hyperbole or public panic. For a crime to be considered as truly terrifying to the majority of people, the victim had to be portrayed as passive and blameless in the conflict. This often precluded crimes involving sex, as the woman's role in such crimes was always questioned and her innocence unclear to the early modern audience. When a crime was considered to have been provoked by its victim, it lost the capacity to terrify generally. Ordinary people felt that they need not fear sexual assault or death if they had not directly incited a criminal. The publicity a crime received was directly linked to how likely a crime was perceived to affect people indiscriminately.

Fear is difficult to define as it related to individual reactions and sensitivities. As such, it was governed neither by the frequency and moral simplicity of printed tales, nor by the statistical likelihood of a victim's intimate relationship with their attacker. Fear derived partly from the experience of crime and partly from a separate perception of danger that had little to do with criminal realities. Fear was thus a specific product of its times, and the absence of fear (or at least the special public protestation of that fear) provides intriguing information on priorities and values. Serial and sexual killers were not singled out essentially on account of their normative status. Unlike papists and witches, ordinary men were not constructed as sources of collective fear and mortal terror in this period, and their actions were considered to be neither especially demonically inspired nor a systemic threat. Occasional cases of extreme and unusual violence did not lead to their redefinition, and largely failed to incite widespread terror. Male criminals who existed outside archetypal violent categories were not considered as anything more than isolated cases of wickedness.

13

Punishment

Until now we have been considering how murders were investigated and how crimes were solved. However, the process that followed a trial was just as vital to the regulation of justice. It was not enough for justice to be done – it had to be seen to be done and local people had to participate in this process. Popular involvement was required in English criminal cases far more often than it was on the continent, where the inquisitorial system of justice meant that magistrates decided who to accuse and trials were held in secret. Expert witnesses – notably doctors – were employed by the justice to investigate crime and comment on it. Although these men were undoubtedly learned, such elite direction of trials substantially eroded popular participation in the trial system and in justice.

As I have shown, in England such popular distance from the process of justice was neither desired nor achieved. Ordinary people had to present criminals to the courts if they wanted them to be prosecuted. They had to speak out in court – and sometimes even pay for the justice they sought. Bodily evidence was provided by doctors, but it was paid for by individuals, not the state, and ordinary people could voluntarily supply similar kinds of testimony. The whole process of trial that has been discussed revolved around ordinary people – whom they accused, what they thought about the crime and how this affected what they said in court.

The process of deciding on guilt and on punishment was just as much a public and communal matter. Admittedly it was not the whole community who heard evidence and decided on guilt, but it was the representatives of the community, in the form of the jury. While the jury were all male and were made up of people with a certain level of property, they acted as representatives of the whole locality. Their decision was essentially very simple: they decided between guilt and innocence.

Once this decision was made, the judge imposed punishment. In homicide cases, his choices were limited. Felony law was quite rigid, and death was the only penalty that could be imposed, even for (what seem like) lesser felonies like theft. The connection between conviction and death was something people were very aware of; in particular, the jury would thoroughly understand the relationship between their pronouncement of guilt and the public execution that was likely to follow. This connection may have sometimes led them to acquit guilty defendants whom they did not believe deserved to die.

In fact, it was the desire to circumvent the harsh punishment of felony that led to the development of the law of manslaughter. In manslaughter cases, the conflict was seen as mutual and as sudden and uncontrolled. Unlike murder, it was not legally predicated on malice, so judges and juries alike were determined to impose a lesser sentence. A series of sixteenth century judicial decisions enshrined in law the principle that the punishment for manslaughter, while still a felony, could be commuted from death to branding. In this case, the law itself shifted to accommodate the mitigation. Although the crime was still tried as murder, the jury could decide that it had in fact been manslaughter, which allowed the judge to mitigate the punishment.[1]

In other types of crime, the law itself remained rigid. In fact, the only way to mitigate the punishment was for the jury to convict of a lesser crime (especially in theft cases, where they would undervalue the goods involved to allow them to impose a lighter sentence) or by simply acquitting the defendant. This sometimes happened even when the defendant was plainly guilty of the crime as charged, but the jury felt they were undeserving of further punishment.

Once a conviction for felony had been secured, however, the punishment imposed was left to the judge. Manslaughter was technically still a felony and could receive a death penalty, although it was mostly murder convicts that received this harsh punishment where homicide was concerned. If (and when) the death penalty was imposed, the court would be sombre. In fact, a ritual of sentencing would be performed to demonstrate the gravity of the punishment. The judge would put a black headcloth over his wig, which was a symbol of the terminal nature of the punishment to follow.[2] Everyone in court would be quite clear what was going to happen.

The death penalty (for crimes other than treason) was hanging. English executions tended not to resort to the drama of continental executions, where convicts could be broken on the wheel or elaborately publicly tortured for days. However, hanging was not a neat or fast method of death. On average, a hanging could take thirty to forty-five minutes. Unlike the executions of the nineteenth and twentieth centuries, there was no sudden drop and swift breaking of the neck. Hanging in this period involved slow strangulation, during which convicts traditionally 'danced' on the end of the rope as they struggled to breathe, and only slowly succumbed to strangulation. Relatives were aware of the long and horrific struggle their loved one faced. This was why close relations or friends would often charge to the scaffold and pull vigorously on the dancing convict's legs, in the hope of speeding the death and easing the torment of their friend.[3]

Petty treason was the only kind of murder to invoke a special and distinctive kind of execution and was a verdict reserved for those who killed people they had a legal duty to obey. It was mainly applied to wives who killed their husbands and servants who killed their masters. Female convicts were burnt at the stake and men were hanged, drawn and quartered. This may not have occurred in every case, although the law did stipulate that this special form of execution should be applied. Women were spared the ordeal of being hanged, drawn and quartered to avoid the indecency of having their bodies revealed. However, most executioners and the crowd saw death by burning as an extreme and terrible end. In many cases, the executioner quietly garrotted the woman at the stake, before burning her corpse – this was seen as the merciful and moral approach.[4] Often the crowd were unaware of the early death and, even if they were, the spectacle of burning the body publicly would still have had the required impact: burning, though rare, was a sensational, public warning to women to behave and obey their husbands.

Local people were expected to play an active role in the punishment process. In the first place, they were expected to come and witness this visitation of justice. Scaffolds were built on the edge of communities but were supposed to be places of assembly, places where people could *see* justice being done. In fact the whole process of execution became ritualised, with each of those involved playing a familiar role for the waiting crowd. Historians have compared executions to theatrical experiences in which the convict in particular was aware of the role they were expected to play and how this would be received by the crowd.[5]

In most cases the condemned were expected to be penitent and to sermonise on their repentance and on their own wickedness. Essentially this was a form of confession, in which the condemned acknowledged what they had done and warned others to be more law-abiding and obedient. Confession was not a requirement of English law, but it was desired by the crowd attending an execution. It not only confirmed to the audience that the accused had been guilty (and deserving of punishment), but it provided a performance that the crowd thoroughly expected. A prisoner dragged to the scaffold unwillingly, refusing to repent, ignored convention and was considered to have died a shameful death. Those convicted knew what was expected of them – and that their confession was also supposed to ease their way into heaven. For many, dying a good death remained more important than resisting or claiming innocence.

Despite the simplicity and rigidity of the law in these matters, execution was not the only response to a guilty verdict. Before judgement was passed, the judge asked the defendant if they had an *allocutus* – or a 'what can you say to avoid the death penalty' speech'.[6] There were three main mitigations that could be claimed at this point: benefit of clergy, pregnancy or pardon.[7] Benefit of clergy was originally designed for clerks in orders, but, by the fourteenth century, was being used to mitigate a felony conviction. From the sixteenth century, the courts were able to extend this mitigation to lay men with the ability to read. Convicted men who pleaded benefit of clergy were given a biblical verse to read, but as this 'neck-verse' rarely changed, criminals could learn it by heart and then pretend to read it. After 1706, recitation was not longer considered necessary,[8] but until then this 'legal fiction' had allowed those convicted of manslaughter and lesser thefts to escape the death penalty and receive a non-mortal punishment.

Convicted prisoners could only claim this mitigation once, and were branded on the hand with a mark indicating they had been granted leniency.[9] This supposedly prevented the claiming of benefit of clergy on multiple occasions. However, the judge determined the heat of the brand and could allow it to be applied cold, which left no mark. Clergy was made partially available to women after 1623, with full equality existing from 1691.[10] Murder cases, however, were always exempted from benefit of clergy, and as few women qualified for manslaughter, due to cultural perceptions about the absence of a link between sudden violence and femininity, in terms of homicide, clergy remained a male mitigation of an essentially male crime.

Female punishments for crime were more usually mitigated by claims of pregnancy. On 'pleading the belly' a woman would be examined to see if she were truly pregnant. A 'jury of matrons' would be assembled, often married women and midwives in the court at the time, who would physically examine the convicted felon for signs of pregnancy. Such knowledgeable women had long held formal and semi-formal legal roles as arbiters of female bodies. If a pregnancy was detected and the child perceived to be 'quick' (that is, alive and moving), the execution would be stayed. Although officially only a deferral, in practice maternity often totally freed the defendant; and few post-natal convicts were subsequently executed.[11]

The final mitigation possible was a pardon, which was available equally to both sexes. Derived from notions of kingly mercy, the pardon was supposedly an arbitrary and random show of mercy. In practice, pardons were more often allocated to those of wealth and status, and often took the form of voluntary transportation, which removed the social problem from the affected area without having to resort to execution.

All these methods of mitigation were well used and popular. In fact, only about 10 per cent of those convicted were executed. Felons were dispersed by favour, mitigation, transportation and forced labour.[12] Although harsh, the law was applied flexibly, and, despite rising indictment rates, convictions remained static across this period.[13] Indeed, new methods for dealing with convicts were developing, which provided additional options other than execution. From the middle of the seventeenth century, judges started to transport criminals. Transportation, although preferable to hanging, could be harsh: the ships were crowded and could be affected by epidemic disease. The trip was long and often hazardous. If the convict survived, life in the new world was also tough. In the seventeenth century, this new world was America; by the eighteenth century the American colonists objected to the shipments and convicts were sent instead to Australia to build the colonies' infrastructure and work on plantations. There were few comforts and often little law and order.

The transportation of convicts was often privately funded and the workers became indentured to private individuals and companies in the new world, where they would act as labourers in hostile and sometimes dangerous environments. This meant that men were always more favoured, and women and the old often rejected. Although judges could order transportation, if the company would not take the convicts, they were left in prison for a while, and some were even quietly released. Generally though, as transportation physically removed the criminal, it solved the immediate social problem. However, few sentences of transportation were for life. Most were for seven years and many returned at that point, or indeed, illegally returned early.[14]

Transportation gave judges and juries further options to punish without killing. Many eagerly responded to this opportunity, and although many crimes still led to execution, transportation was increasingly favoured. In a society with few other choices, this was the best chance of a convict remaining alive. Although prisons existed in the early modern period, they were used as holding cells before trials and prior to execution: it was not until the eighteenth century that they were used solely as a place of punishment.[15]

Whatever the sentence, be it death or some lesser punishment, convicted persons were not quickly forgotten. Many, indeed, were immortalised in print, and those who had committed particularly scandalous crimes were remembered in ballads, nursery rhymes, pictures and playing cards. Some became nationally renowned for their wickedness and the extremity of their violence. Some felons even became popular heroes, although this occurred less often with murderers than it did with other kinds of criminal. Even if a killer did not become famous, local people would have undoubtedly remembered what they had done and would have used this knowledge to remind their families of the resulting disgrace. In many cases the crime was impossible to forget as the dead body was sentenced to be hung in chains from the gibbet while it decomposed.

The point of punishment was that people watched it; the point of a guilty verdict was that people remembered it. This was part of the punishment – that everyone knew and used it against the criminal and the criminal's family. However, crime was also remembered to deter further criminals. The point of visiting justice on criminals was not only to punish but to warn others. The community did not believe all killers should die – and many had their crimes substantially mitigated. However, the community did want to prevent a recurrence and so the courtroom and the scaffold became prime locations for the theatre of justice and its public outcome.

Notes

Notes to Introduction

1. J. H. Baker, *Introduction to English Legal History*, Butterworth, 1990, p. 602.
2. Zachary Babington, *Advice to Grand Jurors in Cases of Blood*, London, 1676, pp. 104–5.
3. Baker, *Introduction*, p. 601.
4. Baker, *Introduction*, p. 601 and J. M. Kaye, 'The Early History of Murder and Manslaughter', *Law Quarterly Review*, 83, 1967.
5. See Chapter 13, below, for further discussion of this and other mitigations.
6. Baker, *Introduction*, p. 602.
7. J. S. Cockburn, *A History of the English Assizes*, Cambridge University Press, 1972, p. 3.
8. Cockburn, *A History*, pp. 51–4 and p. 66.
9. J. H. Baker, 'Criminal Courts and Procedure at Common Law, 1550–1800', in J. S. Cockburn (ed.), *Crime in England, 1550–1800*, Methuen, 1977, p. 24.
10. Cockburn, *A History*, p. 127.
11. Cockburn, *A History*, p. 66.
12. Baker, 'Criminal Courts', p. 33.
13. Cockburn, *A History*, p. 121.
14. A medieval tool to force appearance by monetary penalty.
15. Cockburn, *A History*, p. 122.
16. Baker, *Introduction*, p. 575.
17. Cockburn, *A History*, p. 127.
18. Cynthia Herrup, *The Common Peace: Participation and the Criminal Law in Seventeenth-Century England*, Cambridge University Press, 1987, p. 144.
19. Herrup, *Common Peace*, p. 153.
20. John Beattie, *Crime and the Courts in England, 1660–1800*, Princeton University Press, 1986, pp. 85–97.
21. 88 per cent of infanticide convicts were hanged, as opposed to only 65 per cent of murder convicts. Herrup, *Common Peace*, p. 168.
22. Cockburn, *A History*, p. 109.
23. Beattie, *Crime*, p. 78.
24. Baker, 'Criminal Court', p. 41, and Barbara Shapiro, *Probability and Certainty in Seventeenth-Century England*, Princeton University Press, 1983.
25. Mark Jackson, *New Born Child Murder: Women, Illegitimacy and the Courts in Eighteenth-Century England*, Manchester University Press, 1996; Toni

Bowers, *The Politics of Motherhood: British Writing and Culture, 1680–1760*, Cambridge University Press, 1996.

26. Frances Dolan, *Dangerous Familiars: Representations of Domestic Crime in England, 1550–1700*, Cornell University Press, 1994, p. 18.
27. Helena Kennedy, *Eve was Framed: Women and British Justice*, Vintage, 1993.
28. See Peter Lake, 'Deeds against Nature: Cheap Print, Protestantism and Murder in Early Seventeenth-Century England', Kevin Sharpe and Peter Lake (eds), *Culture and Politics in Early Stuart England*, Macmillan, 1994 and Peter Lake with Michael Questier, *Antichrist's Lewd Hat: Protestants, Papists and Players in Post-Reformation England*, Yale University Press, 2002.
29. For further discussion see, Frances Dolan, *Whores of Babylon*, Cornell University Press, 1999, and Brian Levack, *The Witch-Hunt in Early Modern Europe*, Macmillian, 1987.
30. Cynthia Herrup, 'Law and Morality in Seventeenth-Century England', *Past and Present*, 106, 1985, p. 107.
31. Indictments were formulaic lists of those formally accused. Recognizances were formal agreements to attend court and give evidence or a large fine would be imposed upon the witness and (usually) two others who had agreed to guarantee their attendance.
32. Cockburn, *A History*, p. xii.
33. See Charles Gray (ed.) Sir Matthew Hale, *The History of the Common Law of England*, University of Chicago Press, Chicago, 1971.
34. Dolan, *Dangerous Familiars*, p. 9.
35. Dolan, *Dangerous Familiars*, p. 11.

Notes to Chapter 1: Investigating Crime

1. PRO, Assi 45/5/7/82–92.
2. PRO, Assi 45/2/1/22.
3. CLRO, London Sessions, December 1677. It is unknown if this is the same Elizabeth Cellier as the infamous Popish Midwife. (See Frances Dolan, *Whores of Babylon*, Cornell University Press, 1999, ch. 4).
4. A 'Tyburn ticket' secured an exemption from prosecution in some cases. In this case, it allowed the holder to avoid their legal duty to act as policemen, without fear of conviction for their negligence. J. J. Tobias, *Crime and Police in England*, Gill and Macmillan Ltd, 1979.
5. PRO, Assi 45/8/2/57–61.
6. CLRO, London Sessions, January 1693.
7. My survey of depositions shows that there were 936 female witnesses out of a total of 2732 (drawn from the Assi 45 records and London Sessions, 1640–1730).
8. See Carol Wiener, 'Is a Spinster an Unmarried Woman?', *American Journal of Legal History*, 1970. In my analysis, women gave 936 depositions out of a sample of 2732 individual depositions (drawn from both the London sessions and Northern assize circuit).

9. Laura Gowing, *Domestic Dangers*, Oxford University Press, 1998, ch. 7.

10. PRO, Assi 45/4/3/2.

11. PRO, Assi 45/4/3/87.

12. See Cynthia Herrup, *The Common Peace: Participation and the Criminal Law in Seventeenth-Century England*, Cambridge University Press, 1987, for a broader discussion of this change.

13. *The Arraignment, Tryal, Conviction and Condemnation of Henry Harrison*, London, 1691, pp. 24–5.

14. PRO, Assi 45/11/2/232–5 and CLRO, London Sessions, December 1678.

15. CLRO, London Sessions, March 1677.

16. CLRO, London Sessions, May 1697.

17. PRO, Assi 45/1/5/74–7.

18. PRO, Assi 45/5/1/2–3.

19. E. P. Thompson, *Customs in Common*, Merlin Press, 1991, ch. 7.

Notes to Chapter 2: Supernatural Sleuths

1. Ronald Sawyer, '"Strangely Handled in all her Lyms": Witchcraft and Healing in Jacobean England', *Journal of Social History*, 22, 1989, p. 471.

2. PRO, Assi 45/3/1/242–4.

3. Peter Lake, 'Deeds against Nature: Cheap Print, Protestantism and Murder in Early Seventeenth-Century England', in Kevin Sharpe and Peter Lake (eds), *Culture and Politics in Early Stuart England*, Macmillan, 1994, p. 267, and Michael Hunter, *The Occult Laboratory: Magic, Science and Second Sight in Late Seventeenth-Century Scotland*, Boydell Press, 2001.

4. Lake, 'Deeds', p. 274.

5. See Lake, 'Deeds' and Alexandra Walsham, *Providence in Early Modern England*, Oxford University Press, 2001.

6. Walsham, *Providence*, p. 99. See also p. 3.

7. Natalie Zemon Davis, *Fiction in the Archives: Pardon Tales and their Tellers in Sixteenth-Century France*, Polity Press, 1987, p. 4.

8. *A Strange and Wonderfull Discovery of a Horrid and Cruel Murther Committed Fourteen Yeares Since upon the Person of Robert Eliot of London*, n.p., 1662, p. 3.

9. See Brian Levack, *The Witch Hunt in Early Modern Europe*, Macmillan, 1987, and Ian Bostridge, *Witchcraft and its Transformations, 1560–1750*, Clarendon Press, 1997.

10. Bostridge, *Witchcraft*, p. 242 and p. 154.

11. PRO, Assi 45/1/5/38–9.

12. J. H. Marshburn and A. R. Velie, *Blood and Knavery: A Collection of English Renaissance Pamphlets and Ballads of Crime and Sin*, Farleigh Dickinson University Press, 1973, p. 78.

13. Walsham, *Providence*, p. 86.

14. PRO, Assi 45/7/1/78–80.

15. PRO, Assi 45/11/3/81–2.
16. PRO, Assi 45/5/5/31–40.
17. PRO, Assi 45/7/2/9.
18. Robert P. Brittain, 'News, Notes and Queries: Cruentation in Legal Medicine and in Literature', *Medical History*, 9, 1965.
19. PRO, Assi 45/5/5/55–9.
20. PRO, Assi 45/9/2/44–52a.
21. PRO, Assi 45/5/7/55–8. Malcolm Gaskill has a different view of this case. See *Crime and Mentalities in Early Modern England*, Cambridge University Press, 2000, p. 232.

Notes to Chapter 3: Bodies

1. *The Tryal of Spencer Cowper Esq*, London, 1699; *An Account of the Full Tryal and Examination of Spencer Cooper*, London, 1699; *A Dialogue between a Quaker and his Neighbour in Hertfordshire*, London, 1699; *The Case of Mrs Mary Stout, Widow*, London, 1699; *The Hertford Letter*, London, 1699.
2. Beverley Adams, 'The Body in the Water: Religious Conflict in Hertford, 1660-c. 1702', London University PhD Thesis, 2000.
3. Thomas Forbes, *Surgeons at the Bailey: English Forensic Medicine to 1878*, Yale University Press, 1985, p. 91 Mark Jackson, 'Suspicious Infant Deaths: The Statute of 1624 and Medical Evidence at Coroners' Inquests', in Michael Clark and Catherine Crawford (eds), *Legal Medicine in History*, Cambridge University Press, 1994, p. 80 (both on hydrostatic tests); Michael Clark and Catherine Crawford, 'Introduction' in Michael Clark and Catherine Crawford (eds), *Legal Medicine in History*, Cambridge University Press, 1994, p. 9.
4. My survey of depositions (1640–1730) shows that in London fifty professionals gave evidence in sixty-four cases and in Yorkshire seventy-one professionals testified in 163 cases.
5. In 92 cases out of a total of 163.
6. For Yorkshire this is 137 cases involving women out of a total of 163 that mentioned bodily testimony. In London, the figure is 30 out of 64 cases.
7. Barbara Shapiro, *Probability and Certainty in Seventeenth-Century England*, Princeton University Press, 1983 and *A Culture of Fact*, Cornell University Press, 2000, p. 13.
8. J. D. Havard, *The Detection of Secret Homicide: A Study of the Medico Legal System of Investigation of Sudden and Unexplained Deaths*, Macmillan, 1960, p. 1, and Catherine Crawford, 'Legalising Medicine: Early Modern Legal Systems and the Growth of Medico-Legal Knowledge', in Michael Clark and Catherine Crawford (eds), *Legal Medicine in History*, Cambridge University Press, 1994, p. 94, pp. 102–3.
9. Peter Linebaugh, 'The Tyburn Riot against the Surgeons', in Douglas Hay, Peter Linebaugh, John Rule, Edward Thompson and Carl Winslow (eds), *Albion's Fatal Tree*, Penguin, 1977, pp. 109–17.

10. Thomas Laqueur, *Making Sex: Body and Gender from the Greeks to Freud*, Harvard University Press, 1990, pp. 73–5.
11. Crawford, 'Legalising', p. 106.
12. Shapiro, *Culture*, ch. 1.
13. Forbes , *Surgeons*, p. 21.
14. Malcolm Gaskill, 'Attitudes to Crime in Early Modern England with Special Reference to Witchcraft, Coining and Murder', Cambridge University PhD Thesis, 1994, p. 262.
15. Shapiro, *Probability and Certainty*, ch. 5.
16. Similar arguments have been made relating to scientific evidence by Steven Shapin. See *A Social History of Truth: Civility and Science in Seventeenth-Century England*, University of Chicago Press, 1994.
17. On the masculinising of medicine, see Adrian Wilson, *The Making of Man-Midwifery: Childbirth in England 1660–1770*, Harvard University Press, 1995.
18. PRO, Assi 45/4/2/55–60.
19. Adams, 'Body in the Water', p. 278.
20. Richelle Munkhoff, 'Searchers of the Dead: Authority, Marginality and the Interpretation of Plague in England, 1574–1665', *Gender and History*, 11, 1, 1999.
21. Laura Gowing, 'The Haunting of Susan Lay', *Gender and History*, August 2002.
22. PRO, Assi 45/12/3/8–13.
23. PRO, Assi 45/15/4/86–7.
24. Roy Porter, *Mind-Forg'd Manacles*, Athlone Press, 1987, pp. 111–14.
25. PRO, Assi 45/7/2/69–70.
26. PRO, Assi 45/15/2/29–30 and PRO, Assi 45/4/3/20–3.
27. Roy Porter, *Disease, Medicine and Society in England, 1550–1860*, Cambridge University Press, 1993, p. 11.
28. PRO, Assi 45/15/2/73–82.
29. PRO, Assi 45/17/1/61.
30. PRO, Assi 45/8/1/172–182.
31. *A True Narrative of the Proceedings*, London, January 1676, p. 6.
32. PRO, Assi 45/6/1/149–150.
33. PRO, Assi 45/5/1/61–8.
34. CLRO, London Sessions, July 1678.
35. PRO, Assi 45/10/2/124–6.
36. PRO, Assi 45/15/2/21–4.
37. PRO, Assi 45/13/2/83–5.
38. PRO, Assi 45/6/2/50–4.
39. CLRO, London Sessions, October 1677.
40. CLRO, London Sessions, February 1693.
41. *Hertford Letter*, p. 26.
42. *Hertford Letter*, p. 25.
43. Adams, 'The Body in the Water'.
44. PRO, Assi 45/1/3/51.
45. PRO, Assi 45/17/3/17–27.

46. CLRO, London Sessions, January 1675.

47. PRO, Assi 45/15/1/79–81.

48. PRO, Assi 45/14/2/23–5.

49. *The Tryal of Spencer Cowper*, p. 36.

Notes to Chapter 4: Infant Corpses

1. PRO, Assi 45/9/1/119–124.

2. My survey of deposition records (1640–1730) shows that 93 of the 227 cases of medical testimony related to infanticides. In total there are 132 infanticide cases out of 707 homicides.

3. Ninety-three cases out of 132.

4. Mark Jackson, *New Born Child Murder: Women, Illegitimacy and the Courts in Eighteenth-Century England*, Manchester University Press, 1996, p. 87.

5. *The Proceeding on the King and Queens Commissions*, London, September 1690.

6. PRO, Assi 45/9/3/77–8.

7. PRO, Assi 45/11/1/42–6.

8. PRO, Assi 45/11/1/82–5.

9. See both Thomas Forbes, 'A Jury of Matrons', *Medical History*, 32, 1988; and James C. Oldham, 'On Pleading the Belly: A History of the Jury of Matrons', *Criminal Justice History*, 1985.

10. PRO, Assi 45/12/4/88–9.

11. PRO, Assi 45/5/7/73–7.

12. PRO, Assi 45/10/1/118–120, and PRO, Assi 45/10/3/195–8.

13. PRO, Assi 45/3/2/184.

14. PRO, Assi 45/11/1/82–5.

15. CLRO, London Sessions, February 1692.

16. PRO, Assi 45/15/4/1.

17. A *feme covert* was a married woman. After marriage, a woman had no legal identity or right to own any property until after her husband's death. Amy Erickson, *Women and Property in Early Modern England*, Routledge, 1993, and Tim Stretton, *Women Waging Law in Elizabethan England*, Cambridge University Press, 1998.

18. CLRO, London Sessions, 1677.

19. PRO, Assi 45/7/1/71–4.

20. *News from Newgate*, London, September 1673, pp. 4–5.

21. Mark Jackson, 'Suspicious Infant Deaths: The Statute of 1624 and Medical Evidence at Coroners' Inquests', in Michael Clark and Catherine Crawford (eds), *Legal Medicine in History*, Cambridge University Press, 1994, pp. 67–70.

22. PRO, Assi 45/18/5/53–71.

23. CLRO, London Sessions, February 1696.

24. PRO, Assi 45/15/4/1.

25. PRO, Assi 45/9/2/112.

26. PRO, Assi 45/10/3/105–8.

27. CLRO, London Sessions, September 1682.

28. CLRO, London Sessions, April 1700.

29. PRO, Assi 45/10/1/59–61.

30. PRO, Assi 45/10/3/14–5.

31. PRO, Assi 45/7/1/12–4.

32. PRO, Assi 45/6/2/14–5.

33. Catherine Crawford, 'Legalising Medicine: Early Modern Legal Systems and the Growth of Medico-Legal Knowledge', in Michael Clark and Catherine Crawford (eds), *Legal Medicine in History*, Cambridge University Press, 1994, p. 91.

34. PRO, Assi 45/13/2/96–103.

35. PRO, Assi 45/13/2/105–8.

Notes to Chapter 5: Husbands and Wives

1. John Taylor, *Divers Crabtree Lectures*, 1639, pp. 73–4, as cited in Elizabeth Foyster, 'A Laughing Matter? Marital Discord and Gender Control in Seventeenth-Century England', *Rural History*, 1993, p. 11.

2. I also discuss this case in 'Deconstructing Murder in Seventeenth-Century England: The Case of Marie Hobry' in 'Heroes and Villians of Seventeenth-Century England', *Seventeenth-Century Journal*, forthcoming (2004).

3. *A Hellish Murder Committed by a French Midwife on the Body of her Husband Jan 27 1687*, London, 1687. Italics represent speech.

4. Ann Louise Shapiro, *Breaking the Codes: Female Criminality in Fin de Siècle Paris*, Stanford University Press, 1996, p. 25; Meg Arnot and Cornelie Usbourne, 'Why Gender and Crime: Aspects of an International Debate', *Gender and Crime in Modern Europe*, UCL Press, 1999, p. 27; Frances Dolan, *Dangerous Familiars: Representations of Domestic Crime in England, 1550–1700*, Cornell University Press, 1994, p. 4.

5. See *A Hellish Murder* and *A Cabinet of Grief: Or a French Midwife's Miserable Moan for the Barbarous Murther Committed upon the Body of her husband*, London, 1688.

6. PRO, Assi 45/10/1/169–171.

7. See illustrations for the three playing cards depicting Marie Hobry's crime, entitled *Orange Cards* or *The Glorious Revolution of 1688*, dated 1689, Courtesy of the Worshipful Company of Makers of Playing Cards (Guildhall Library).

8. *A Hellish Murder*, p. 11.

9. See Frances Dolan, *Whores of Babylon*, Cornell University Press, 1999.

10. *A Hellish Murder*, p. 21.

11. See illustrations for 'A Representation of the Bloody Murder Committed by Mary Aubry, a French Midwife, which was Burnt to Death the 2nd Day of March 1687/8', Guildhall Library, Corporation of London.

12. Margaret Hunt, 'Wife Beating, Domesticity and Women's Independence in Eighteenth-Century London', *Gender and History*, 4, 1, 1992, p. 16.

13. Quoted in Margaret Hunt, 'Wife Beating', p. 25.
14. William Heale, *An Apologie for Women*, Oxford, 1608.
15. Ilana Ben Amos, *Adolescence and Youth in Early Modern England*, Yale University Press, 1994, p. 154.
16. See Hunt, 'Wife Beating' and Susan Amussen, '"Being Stirred to Much Unquietness": Violence and Domestic Violence in Early Modern England', *Journal of Women's History*, 6, 2, 1994.
17. Joy Wiltenburg, *Disorderly Women and Female Power in the Street Literature of Early Modern England and Germany*, University Press of Virginia, 1992, p. 95.
18. 'Couragious Anthony: A Relation of a Dreadful Combat between Bonny Anthony and his Wife', W. Geoffrey Day (ed.), *The Pepys Ballads*, iv, Brewer, 1987, p. 146.
19. 'Hen-Peckt Cuckold: Or the Cross-Grained Wife', *Pepys Ballads*, p. 129.
20. Diane Purkiss points out the gender of authors is highly ambiguous in early modern pamphlets, especially in comic stories. The female perspective in this ballad undoubtedly came from a male author.
21. 'The Wife's Answer to the Hen Peckt Cuckolds Complaint', *Pepys Ballads*, p. 135.
22. *My Wife will be my Master: or The Married-Man's Complaint against his Unruly Wife*, London, 1679. Text as in original document (including spelling).
23. 'The Scolding Wife, or the Poor Man's Lamentation of his Bad Market in Chusing him a Wife', 1689, *Pepys Ballads*, p. 136.
24. PRO, Assi 45 10/3/88–95
25. Amussen, 'Being Stirred'.
26. PRO, Assi 45/17/2/70.
27. PRO, Assi 45/12/2/147–150.
28. Laura Gowing, *Domestic Dangers: Women, Words, and Sex in Early Modern London*, Oxford Studies in Social History, Oxford University Press, 1998, p. 207.
29. PRO, Assi 45/5/5/55–9.
30. Also noted by Walker, 'Crime, Gender', p. 79.
31. *News from the Sessions: Or, the Whole Tryal of George Allen the Butcher who Murdered his Wife in the Fields behind Islington*, n.p., 1675, p. 4.
32. PRO, Assi 45/1/4/13.
33. Natalie Davies, *Fiction in the Archives: Pardon Tales and their Tellers in Sixteenth-Century France*, Polity Press, 1987, p. 82.
34. PRO, Assi 45/4/3/73–4.
35. *The Bloody Husband and Cruell Neighbour or A True Historie of Two Murthers Lately Committed in Laurence Parish in the Isle of Thanet in Kent*, London, May 1653, p. 3.
36. PRO, Assi 45/2/1/35–6.

Notes to Chapter 6: Disrupted Households

1. CLRO, London Sessions, January 1677.
2. Lawrence Stone, *The Family, Sex and Marriage in England, 1500–1800*, Weidenfeld and Nicolson, 1977.
3. Paul Griffiths, *Youth and Authority: Formative Experiences in England, 1560–1640*, Clarendon Press, 1996.
4. PRO, Assi 45/13/2/83–5.
5. PRO, Assi 45/7/2/69–70.
6. PRO, Assi 45/18/7/1–4.
7. See Laura Gowing, 'The Haunting of Susan Lay', *Gender and History*, August 2002.
8. PRO, Assi 45/10/2/22–3.
9. *An Exact Relation of the Bloody and Barbarous Murder, Committed by Miles Lewis and his Wife, a Pinmaker upon their Prentice*, London, 1646, p. 2.
10. PRO, Assi 45/10/2/22–3.
11. Gowing, 'The Haunting'.
12. PRO, Assi 45/15/4/31A.
13. *Cruel and Barbarous News from Cheapside in London*, n.p., 1676, p. 4.
14. *God's Justice against Murther or the Bloody Apprentice Executed*, London, 1668.
15. PRO, Assi 45/18/1/48–50.
16. PRO, Assi 45/9/3/92–4.
17. See Ilana Krausman Ben-Amos, *Adolescence and Youth in Early Modern England*, Yale University Press, 1994.
18. Laura Gowing, 'The Haunting '.
19. PRO, Assi 45/15/3/97.
20. PRO, Assi 45/14/3/11–16.
21. PRO, Assi 45/10/1/152–5.
22. Douglas Hay, 'Poaching and the Game Laws on Cannock Chase', in Douglas Hay, Peter Linebaugh, Cal Winslow, John Rule and Edward Thompson (eds), *Albion's Fatal Tree*, Penguin, 1975, and Dan Beaver, '"Bragging and Daring Words": Honour, Property and the Symbolism of the Hunt in Stowe, 1590–1642', in Michael Braddick and John Walter (eds), *Negotiating Power in Early Modern Society*, Cambridge University Press, 2001.
23. PRO, Assi 45/5/1/61–8.
24. CLRO, London Sessions, October 1690.
25. PRO, Assi 45 5/1/48–54.
26. PRO, Assi 45 8/2/86–7.
27. PRO, Assi 45 12/4/85.
28. PRO, Assi 45 18/3/31–2c

Notes to Chapter 7: Poison: A Woman's Weapon

1. PRO, Assi 45/7/1/152 and 7/1/169–171.
2. Cynthia Herrup, *The Common Peace: Participation and the Criminal Law in Seventeenth-Century England*, Cambridge University Press, 1987, p. 172.
3. Malcolm Gaskill, 'Attitudes to Crime in Early Modern England with Special Reference to Witchcraft, Coining and Murder', Cambridge University PhD Thesis, 1994, p. 209.
4. Frances Dolan, *Dangerous Familiars: Representations of Domestic Crime in England, 1550–1700*, Cornell University Press, 1994.
5. See Keith Thomas, *Religion and the Decline of Magic*, Harmondsworth., Penguin, 1978.
6. *Horrid News from St Martins or Unheard of Murder and Poyson: Being a True Relation how a Girl not Full 16 Years of Age Murthered her own Mother*, London, 1677, p. 1.
7. PRO, Assi 45/3/1/242–4.
8. PRO, Assi 45/5/2/90–1.
9. See Ilana Krausman Ben-Amos, *Adolescence and Youth in Early Modern England*, Yale University Press, 1994.
10. PRO, Assi 45/8/2/129–132.
11. PRO, Assi 45/14/2/139–141.
12. CLRO, London Sessions, February 1691.
13. CLRO, London Sessions, December 1692.
14. PRO, Assi 45/6/2/50–4.
15. PRO, Assi 45/16/5/12–6.
16. Gaskill has a less positive view of female medical deponents, see Gaskill, 'Attitudes to Crime', p. 262.
17. PRO, Assi 45/16/1/39–41.
18. *Muther, Murther*, London, 1641.
19. PRO, Assi 45/6/2/50–4.

Notes to Chapter 8: Murderous Mothers

1. *Newes from the Dead or a True and Exact Narration of the Miraculous Deliverance of Anne Greene*, London, 1651.
2. See Mark Jackson, *New Born Child Murder: Women, Illegitimacy and the Courts in Eighteenth-Century England*, Manchester University Press, 1996, introduction. Laura Gowing, 'Secret Births and Infanticide in Seventeenth-Century England', *Past and Present*, 156, August 1997, pp. 88–9. Peter Hoffer and N. E. H. Hull, *Murdering Mothers: Infanticide in England and New England, 1558–1803*, New York University, 1981, p. x, and Frances Dolan, *Dangerous Familiars: Representations of Domestic Crime in England, 1550–1700*, Cornell University Press, 1994, p. 131. Keith Wrightson, 'Infanticide in Early Seventeenth-Century England', *Local Population Studies*, 1975. John Beattie, *Crime*

and the Courts in England, 1660–1800, Princeton University Press, 1986, pp. 117–124.

3. John Beattie, *Crime and the Courts in England, 1660–1800*, Princeton University Press, 1986, p. 118, and Steve Hindle, *The State and Social Change in Early Modern England, 1550–1640*, Macmillan Press, 2000, p. 162. Herrup puts the conviction rate at 88 per cent. Cynthia Herrup, *The Common Peace: Participation and the Criminal Law in Seventeenth-Century England*, Cambridge University Press, 1987, p. 168.

4. 21 James I, c. 27. Quoted in Hoffer and Hull, *Murdering Mothers*, p. 20. Analysis of earlier attitudes to illegitimacy can also be found in Jackson, *New Born Child Murder*, amongst others.

5. See Peter Laslett, Karla Oosterveen and Richard Smith (eds), *Bastardy and its Comparative History*, Edward Arnold, 1980, and Vanessa McMahon, 'Desire, Sex and Consequences: Women, Gender and the Bawdy Courts in Late Sixteenth and Early Seventeenth-Century England', Royal Holloway MA Dissertation, 1995.

6. Quoted in Hoffer and Hull, *Murdering Mothers*, p. 20.

7. From Bernard Mandeville, *The Fable of the Bees*, quoted in Jackson, *New Born Child Murder*, p. 113.

8. CLRO, London Sessions, April 1700.

9. PRO, Assi 44/6.

10. Toni Bowers, *The Politics of Motherhood: British Writing and Culture, 1680–1760*, Cambridge University Press, 1996, p. 94.

11. *The Proceedings on the King and Queen's Commissions*, London, October 1690, p. 1.

12. G. R. Quaife, *Wanton Wenches and Wayward Wives: Peasants and Illicit Sex in Early Seventeenth-Century England*, Croom Helm, 1979. See also Richard Adair, *Courtship, Illegitimacy and Marriage in Early Modern England*, Manchester University Press, 1996, p. 72.

13. PRO, Assi 45/13/2/14–6.

14. For example, Dolan, *Dangerous Familiars*, p. 14, and Peter Lake, 'Deeds against Nature: Cheap Print, Protestantism and Murder in Early Seventeenth-Century England', in Kevin Sharpe and Peter Lake (eds), *Culture and Politics in Early Stuart England*, Macmillan, 1994, p. 264. Such debates are also implicit in Jackson, *New Born Child Murder*, p. 11, and Hoffer and Hull, *Murdering Mothers*, p. 143 and p. x.

15. See Gowing, 'Secret Births' for discussion of the role of mistresses.

16. Hoffer and Hull, *Murdering Mothers*, p. 124.

17. Wrightson, 'Infanticide', p. 19 and Hoffer and Hull, *Murdering Mothers*, p. 145.

18. V. A. C. Gatrell, *The Hanging Tree: Execution and the English People 1770–1868*, Oxford University Press, 1994.

19. *Newes from the Dead*, p. 2–3.

20. *Newes from the Dead*, p. 5. Spelling as in original text.

21. *Newes from the Dead*, p. 4.

22. *Newes from the Dead*, p. 14.

23. PRO, Assi 45/6/2/112.

24. PRO, Assi 45/7/1/10.

25. PRO, Assi 45/13/2/105–8.

26. CLRO, London Sessions, January 1704.

27. PRO, Assi 45/7/2/117–9.

28. PRO, Assi 45/8/1/70–2.

29. CLRO, London Sessions, January 1674.

30. PRO, Assi 45/9/2/112.

31. CLRO, London Sessions, July 1677.

32. PRO, Assi 45/17/2/137–8.

33. Ulinka Rublack, *The Crimes of Women in Early Modern Germany*, Clarendon Press, 1999, pp. 181–2.

34. PRO, Assi 45/9/1/119–124.

35. PRO, Assi 45/10/2/32 a and b.

36. PRO, Assi 45/9/3/45–8.

37. PRO, Assi 45/18/5/53–71.

38. PRO, Assi 45/9/3/77–8.

39. PRO, Assi 45/8/2/80.

40. PRO, Assi 45/10/1/149–150, PRO, Assi 45/17/2/129 and PRO, Assi 45/10/2/113–114 respectively.

41. Gowing, 'Secret Births', p. 99.

42. PRO, Assi 45/11/2/154–5.

43. *News from Newgate*, London, 1673, p. 2.

44. Gowing, 'Secret Births'. See also Bowers, *Politics of Motherhood*.

45. Also suggested by Joy Wiltenburg, *Disorderly Women and Female Power in the Street Literature of Early Modern England and Germany*, University Press of Virginia, 1992, p. 145.

46. Gowing, 'Secret Births' and Linda Pollock, 'Childbearing and Female Bonding in Early Modern England', *Social History*, October 1997, p. 297.

47. Gowing, 'Secret Births', p. 99.

48. PRO, Assi 45/18/3/2, PRO, Assi 45/16/5/130–1, and PRO, Assi 45/10/1/84 respectively.

49. PRO, Assi 45/13/3/105.

50. CLRO, London Sessions, September 1718.

51. For similar arguments on degradation in these records, see Regina Schulte, *The Village in Court: Arson, Infanticide and Poaching in the Court Records of Upper Bavaria, 1848–1910*, Cambridge University Press, 1994, pp. 104–5.

52. PRO, Assi 45/6/1/54–6.

53. See Gowing, 'Secret Births', p. 108.

54. PRO, Assi 45/18/2/31–33.

55. Similar motives are noted in Deborah Symonds, *Weep Not for Me: Women, Ballads and Infanticide in Early Modern Scotland*, Pennsylvania State University Press, 1997.

56. PRO, Assi 45/1/4/50–1.

57. PRO, Assi 45/16/5/67–8.

58. PRO, Assi 45/10/1/59–61.

59. PRO, Assi 45/5/3/108–15.

60. Cynthia Herrup, *The Common Peace: Participation and the Criminal Law in Seventeenth-Century England*, Cambridge University Press, 1987, p. 144.

61. *News from the Sessions House in the Old Baily*, London, April 1675, p. 3.

62. *The Proceedings on the King and Queen's Commissions*, London, September 1690, p. 1.

63. Bowers, *Politics of Motherhood*, p. 94.

64. Beattie, *Crime*, pp. 117–124, Jackson, *New Born Child Murder*, introduction, and Adair, *Courtship*, p. 62.

65. See Bowers, *Politics of Motherhood*, p. 114.

66. *The Proceedings on the King and Queens Commissions*, London, December 1691.

67. PRO, Assi 45/13/2/3–5.

68. Jackson, *New Born Child Murder*, p. 110.

69. *Blood for Blood, or Justice Executed for Innocent Bloodshed*, London, 1670, p. 15.

70. PRO, Assi 45/9/3/17.

71. PRO, Assi 45/3/2/55–6.

72. PRO, Assi 45/10/2/86–92a.

73. CLRO, London Sessions, December 1719.

74. *The Proceedings on the King and Queen's Commissions*, London, July 1693.

75. PRO, Assi 45/6/2/3–5.

76. *A True and Perfect Account of the Proceedings*, London, January 1674, pp. 2–3.

77. *Blood for Blood*, sermon/prelude.

78. PRO, Assi 45/8/1/61.

79. PRO, Assi 45/1/2/9.

80. *The Distressed Mother: or, Sorrowful Wife in Tears*, London, 1690, p. 2.

81. For further discussion, see Thomas Forbes, 'A Jury of Matrons', *Medical History*, 32, 1988, and James C. Oldham, 'On Pleading the Belly: A History of the Jury of Matrons', *Criminal Justice History*, 1985.

Notes to Chapter 9: Child-Killers

1. *Bloody News from Devonshire*, London, 1694, p. 1.

2. See Philip Almond, *Heaven and Hell in Enlightenment England*, Cambridge University Press, 1994, pp. 4–24, for debate on the theological state of the infant.

3. Frances Dolan, *Dangerous Familiars: Representations of Domestic Crime in England, 1550–1700*, Cornell University Press, 1994, p. 141.

4. Almond, *Heaven*, p. 24.

5. PRO, Assi 45/9/1/128–130.

6. G. R. Quaife, *Wanton Wenches and Wayward Wives: Peasants and Illicit Sex in Early Seventeenth-Century England*, Croom Helm, 1979, p. 118.

7. See Jennine Hurl, '"She Being Bigg with Child is Likely to Miscarry": Pregnant Victims Prosecuting Assault in Westminster, 1685–1720', *London Journal*, 1999.

8. *A Full and True Relation of a Most Barbarous and Dreadful Murther*, London, May 1684.

9. *The True Narrative of the Execution of John Marketman*, London, 1680.

10. Hurl, 'She Being Bigg with Child', p. 19.

11. PRO, Assi 45/17/2/71.

12. CLRO, London Sessions, August 1694.

13. PRO, Assi 45/9/1/9–12.

14. PRO, Assi 45/9/3/41–2. Miranda Chaytor also discusses this case in Miranda Chaytor, 'Husband(ry): Narratives of Rape in the Seventeenth-Century', *Gender and History*, 7, 3, 1995.

15. PRO, Assi 45/5/2/38–43.

16. PRO, Assi 45/8/1/13–5.

17. *The Proceedings on the King and Queen's Commissions of the Peace*, London, April 1694, pp. 3–4.

18. PRO, Assi 45/17/2/75.

19. Steve Hindle, *The State and Social Change in Early Modern England, 1550–1640*, Macmillan Press, 2000, p. 160; Wrightson, 'Infanticide'; and Laura Gowing, 'Ordering the Body: Illegitimacy and Female Authority in Seventeenth-Century England', in Michael Braddick and John Walter (eds), *Negotiating Power in Early Modern Society: Order, Hierarchy and Subordination in Britain and Ireland*, Cambridge University Press, 2001.

20. PRO, Assi 45/13/2/96–103.

21. Wrightson, 'Infanticide', p. 16.

22. PRO, Assi 45/3/1/100–1.

23. PRO, Assi 45/9/1/1–8.

24. *Strange and Lamentable News from Dullidg–Wells*, London, 1678, pp. 5–6.

25. PRO, Assi 45/7/1/78–80.

26. PRO, Assi 45/10/1/33.

27. *Inquest After Blood Being a Relation of the Several Inquisitions of All That Have Died by Any Violent Death in the City of London*, 1670, London.

28. *The Unnatural Grandmother*, London, 1659, p. 7.

29. Toni Bowers, *The Politics of Motherhood: British Writing and Culture, 1680–1760*, Cambridge University Press, 1996, pp. 93–4.

30. *Concealed Murther Reveild*, London, 1699, p. 2.

31. PRO, Assi 45/5/2/90–1.

32. PRO, Assi 45/1/5/38–9.

33. PRO, Assi 45/13/2/27–32.

34. CLRO, London Session, Feb 1699.

35. PRO, Assi 45/11/2/232–5.

36. PRO, Assi 45/5/5/5.

37. PRO, Assi 45/8/1/158.

38. CLRO, London Sessions, February 1692.

39. *The True Proceedings of the Sessions*, London, April 1683.
40. PRO, Assi 45/16/2/43–5.

Notes to Chapter 10: Brawling and Duelling

1. PRO, Assi 45/5/6/65–70.
2. See Dan Beaver, '"Bragging and Daring Words": Honour, Property and the Symbolism of the Hunt in Stowe, 1590–1642', in Michael Braddick and John Walter (eds), *Negotiating Power in Early Modern Society*, Cambridge University Press, 2001.
3. Beaver, 'Bragging', p. 163.
4. Alex Shepard, 'Meanings of Manhood in Early Modern England, with Special Reference to Cambridge, *c.* 1560–1640', Cambridge University PhD Thesis, 1998, p. 12.
5. My survey of homicide depositions between 1640 and 1730 showed that in Yorkshire, 414 cases out of 461 and in London 102 cases out of 114 had male defendants. If infanticide cases are excluded the figure is 89–90 per cent. John Beattie, *Crime and the Courts in England, 1660–1800*, Princeton University Press, 1986, p. 97; Robert Shoemaker, 'Reforming Male Manners: Public Insult and the Decline of Violence in London, 1660–1740', in Tim Hitchcock and Michele Cohen (eds), *English Masculinities, 1660–1800*, Longman, 1999, p. 133. In addition, Cockburn's statistics indicate that between 86 and 91 per cent of all suspected felons were men. J. S. Cockburn, *Calendar of Assize Records for the Home Circuit* (5 vols), HMSO, 1989.
6. My survey shows that 415 cases out of 516 were of men killing other men (aggregate of London and Yorkshire cases, excluding infanticide).
7. See Victor Stater, *High Life, Low Morals: The Duel that Shook Stuart Society*, John Murray, 1999; Shepard came to the same conclusions in 'Meanings of Manhood', p. 153.
8. Shoemaker, 'Reforming Manners?', p. 136; Lyndal Roper, 'Blood and Codpieces: Masculinity in the Early Modern German Town', *Oedipus and the Devil: Witchcraft, Sexuality and Religion in Early Modern Europe*, Routledge, 1994; Pieter Spierenberg, 'Knife Fighting and Popular Codes of Honor in Early Modern Amsterdam', in Pieter Spierenberg (eds), *Men and Violence: Gender, Honor, and Ritual in Modern Europe and America*, Ohio State, 1998; Elizabeth Foyster, 'Boys will be Boys? Manhood and Aggression, 1660–1800', in Tim Hitchcock and Michele Cohen (eds), *English Masculinities, 1660–1800*, Longman, 1999, pp. 154–47; Stone, 'Interpersonal Violence', pp. 28–9. See also Spierenberg, 'Knife Fighting', p. 106.
9. PRO, Assi 45/11/2/75–78.
10. CLRO, London Sessions, December 1693.
11. Shepard, 'Meanings of Manhood', p. 38.
12. Paul Griffiths, *Youth and Authority: Formative Experiences in England, 1560–1640*, Clarendon Press, 1996, introduction.

13. CLRO, London Sessions, April 1676.
14. PRO, Assi 45/14/3/11–16.
15. Shepard, 'Meanings of Manhood', p. 12.
16. CLRO, London Sessions, June 1676.
17. *A True Narrative of the Proceedings*, London, January 1676, p. 5.
18. *News from Tyburn, or the Confession and Execution of the Three Bayliffs*, London, December 1675, pp. 4–5; London Sessions, October 1675; and *A True Narrative of the Proceedings at Session House in the Old Baily*, London, August 1675.
19. John Brige appears on the signatory list and this seems to be in the same hand as the 'John Brige' signature of the coroner. PRO, Assi 45/2/2/18–20.
20. Garthine Walker, 'Crime, Gender and Social Order in Early Modern Cheshire', Liverpool University PhD Thesis, 1994, p. 113.
21. Beattie, *Crime*, pp. 74–140.
22. See Walker, 'Crime and Gender', p. 128.
23. PRO, Assi 45/9/3/7. Other examples of such narratives: PRO, Assi 45/2/1/158–160, and PRO, Assi 45/2/1/281–2.
24. PRO, Assi 45/6/3/86–94.
25. See Natalie Zemon Davis, *Fiction in the Archives: Pardon Tales and their Tellers in Sixteenth-Century France*, Polity Press, 1987.
26. *A True Narrative of the Proceedings at the Sessions House in the Old Baily*, London, March 1676/7.
27. PRO, Assi 45/9/1/41–51.
28. *News from Fleet Street or the Last Speech and Confession of the Two Persons Hanged there for Murther*, London, October 1675, p. 1. See also *A Narrative of the Proceedings at the Sessions House in the Old Baily*, London, October 1675.
29. Elizabeth Foyster, *Manhood in Early Modern England: Honour, Sex and Marriage*, Longman, 1999, p. 178; Ute Frevert, 'The Taming of the Noble Ruffian: Male Violence and Duelling in Early Modern and Modern Germany', in Pieter Spierenberg (ed.), *Men and Violence: Gender, Honor, and Ritual in Modern Europe and America*, Ohio State, 1998; Pieter Spierenberg, *The Broken Spell: A Cultural and Anthropological History of Preindustrial Europe*, Macmillan, 1991, ch. 7; Edward Muir, *Ritual in Early Modern Europe*, Cambridge University Press, 1997, ch. 4; Alan Macfarlane, *The Justice and the Mare's Ale*, Basil Blackwell, Oxford, 1981; Cockburn, 'Patterns of Violence' and Beattie, *Crime*, ch. 3; Spierenberg, 'Knife Fighting'; Donna Andrew, 'The Code of Honour and its Critics: the Opposition to Duelling in England, 1700–1850', *Social History*, 5, 1980; Andrew, 'Duelling'; Foyster, *Manhood*, p. 179 and Beattie, *Crime*, p. 92.
30. Frevert, 'The Taming', p. 39; and Spierenberg, 'Introduction'.
31. Shepard, 'Meanings of Manhood', p. 140.
32. Spierenberg, 'Knife Fighting'.
33. Shoemaker, 'Reforming Manners?' and Shepard, 'Meanings of Manhood', pp. 169–170.

34. PRO, Assi 45/3/2/154–7.
35. PRO, Assi 45/10/2/40–3.
36. CLRO, London Sessions, September 1675.
37. For example, the judge decided how hot the 'M' brand would be. He could decide it would be cold, leaving no mark and causing no pain.
38. PRO, Assi 45/16/3/32–40.
39. PRO, Assi 45/16/3/77.
40. See PRO, Assi 45/9/2/149–154.
41. Shepard, 'Meanings of Manhood', p. 187.
42. Robert Shoemaker, 'Public Spaces, Private Disputes: Conflict on the Streets of London, 1660–1800', unpublished paper at Streets of London conference, December 1999.
43. PRO, Assi 45/10/2/10–6.
44. Shepard, 'Meanings of Manhood', p. 12.
45. PRO, Assi 45/11/1/49–50.
46. PRO, Assi 45/18/1/48–50.
47. J. H. Baker, *Introduction to English Legal History*, Butterworth, 1990, p. 598.
48. CLRO, London Sessions, January 1674.
49. PRO, Assi 45/1/4/23–7.
50. Roper, 'Blood and Codpieces', p. 110.
51. See Foyster, 'Manhood', p. 178.
52. PRO, Assi 45/11/2/159.
53. PRO, Assi 45/10/1/152–5.
54. PRO, Assi 45/3/1/82–3.
55. Douglas Hay, 'Poaching and the Game Laws on Cannock Chase', in Douglas Hay, Peter Linebaugh, Cal Winslow, John Rule and Edward Thompson (eds), *Albion's Fatal Tree*, Penguin, 1975.
56. PRO, Assi 45/12/2/127–131.
57. PRO, Assi 45/3/1/95.
58. PRO, Assi 45/2/2/107–110.
59. CLRO, London Sessions, May 1718.
60. PRO, Assi 45/5/2/101–5.
61. Shepard, 'Meanings of Manhood', Ch. 1.
62. CLRO, London Sessions, October 1683.
63. PRO, Assi 45/3/1/84–6.
64. Foyster, *Manhood*, p. 5.
65. Discussion of the dynamics of insults can be found in Laura Gowing, *Domestic Dangers: Women, Worlds, and Sex in Early Modern London*, Oxford Studies in Social History, 1998; and Shoemaker, 'Reforming Male Manners'.
66. PRO, Assi 45/9/1/23–4.
67. PRO, Assi 45/2/2/9–11.
68. PRO, Assi 45/15/2/21–4.

Notes to Chapter 11: The Usual Suspects

1. *Hew and Cry after Blood and Murther or an Elegie on the Most Barbarous Murther of Thomas Thinn Esq*, London, 1681, p. 1.
2. See Lincoln Faller, *Turned to Account: The Forms and Functions of Criminal Biography in Late Seventeenth-Century England*, Cambridge University Press, 1987, pp. 83–4.
3. Penny Roberts and William Naphy (eds), *Fear in Early Modern Society*, Manchester University Press, 1997.
4. Steve Hindle, *The State and Social Change in Early Modern England, 1550–1640*, Macmillan Press, 2000, pp. 142–3.
5. Lawrence Stone, 'Interpersonal Violence in English Society, 1300–1980', *Past and Present*, 103, 1983, p. 25. See also, Lawrence Stone, 'A Rejoinder', *Past and Present*, 1985.
6. Malcolm Greenshields, *The Economy of Violence in Early Modern France: Crime and Justice in the Haute Auvergne, 1587–1664*, Pennsylvania State University Press, 1994.
7. The main contributors to this debate are: Alan Macfarlane, *The Justice and the Mare's Ale*, Basil Blackwell, 1981; J. A. Sharpe, 'Debate: The History of Violence in England: Some Observations', *Past and Present*, 105, 1985; J. S. Cockburn, 'Patterns of Violence in English Society: Homicide in Kent, 1560–1985', *Past and Present*, 130, 1991; Keith Wrightson, 'Two Concepts of Order: Justices, Constables and Jurymen in Seventeenth-Century England', in John Brewer and John Styles (eds), *An Ungovernable People: The English and their Law in the Seventeenth and Eighteenth-Centuries*, Hutchinson, 1980.
8. Hindle, *The State*, p. 128, p. 146; J. A. Sharpe, *Crime in Early Modern England*, Longman, 1984, p. 103; Cynthia Herrup, *The Common Peace: Participation and the Criminal Law in Seventeenth-Century England*, Cambridge University Press, 1987, p. 172.
9. Cockburn, 'Patterns', 1991; and see Vanessa McMahon, 'Desire, Sex and Consequences: Women, Gender and the Bawdy Courts in Late Sixteenth- and Early Seventeenth-Century England', Royal Holloway MA Dissertation, 1995.
10. Susan Amussen, *An Ordered Society*, Blackwell, 1988.
11. Sharpe, *Crime*, 1984, p. 74.
12. Faller, *Turned to Account*. See his analysis of pamphlets for further examples.
13. *A Caution to Married Couples: Being a True Relation How a Man in Nightingale Lane Having Beat and Abused his Wife Murthered a Tubman*, London, 1677, p. 7.
14. CLRO, London Sessions, April 1699.
15. See J. A. Sharpe, '"Last Dying Speeches": Religion, Ideology and Public Execution in Seventeenth-Century England", *Past and Present*, 107, 1985, or Thomas Laqueur, 'Crowds, Carnival and the State in English Executions, 1604–1868', in A. L. Beier, David Cannadine and James Rosenheim (eds), *First Modern English Society*, Cambridge University Press, 1989.

16. Peter Lake, 'Deeds against Nature: Cheap Print, Protestantism and Murder in Early Seventeenth-Century England', in Kevin Sharpe and Peter Lake (eds), *Culture and Politics in Early Stuart England*, Macmillan, 1994.

17. *Murther upon Murther: Being a Full and True Relation of a Horrid and Bloody Murther*, n.p. 1691, p. 2.

18. Faller, *Turned to Account*, pp. 117–127.

19. Herrup, *Common Peace*, p. 172.

20. John Beattie, *Crime and the Courts in England, 1660–1800*, Princeton University Press, 1986, pp. 140–198.

21. *A True Relation of What is Discovered Concerning the Murther of the Archbishop of St Andrews, and What Appears to have been the Occasion Thereof*, London, 1679, p. 2.

22. PRO, Assi 45/13/2/59.

23. *A True Relation of the Horrible Bloody Murther and Robbery Committed in Holbourn ... The Murther Committed on the Body of one Widdow Brown*, n.p., 1674, p. 1.

24. *A Strange and Wonderful Account of a Most Barbarous and Bloody Murder*, n.p., 1680, p. 3.

25. Alan Macfarlane describes this process clearly in *The Justice and the Mare's Ale*, Basil Blackwell, Oxford, 1981.

26. *Treason and Murther: or The Bloody Father-in-Law*, Essex, 1673.

27. PRO, Assi 45/4/1/102–5.

28. PRO, Assi 45/10/1/58.

29. PRO, Assi 45/14/2/75–83.

30. CLRO, London Sessions, October 1698.

31. PRO, Assi 13/1/131.

32. PRO, Assi 45/12/2/60b.

33. PRO, Assi 45/10/1/23–4.

34. *A Full and True Account of the Proceedings at the Sessions of Oyer and Terminer*, London, April 1682.

35. Beattie, *Crime*, p. 79.

36. See Frances Dolan on Catholics in *Whores of Babylon*, Cornell University Press, 1999.

37. Peter Linebaugh, 'The Tyburn Riot against the Surgeons', in Douglas Hay, Peter Linebaugh, John Rule, Edward Thompson and Carl Winslow (eds), *Albion's Fatal Tree*, Penguin, 1977. In these cases, it was sailors who were prolifically prosecuted, pp. 85–6.

38. *The Military Memoirs of Captain George Carleton for the Dutch War*, 1672, London, 1728, pp. 42–3.

39. PRO, Assi 45/1/5/63.

40. PRO, Assi 45/15/1/1–3.

41. CLRO, London Sessions, March 1677.

42. Dan Beaver, ' "Bragging and Daring Words": Honour, Property and the Symbolism of the Hunt in Stowe, 1590–1642', in Michael Braddick and John Walter

(eds), *Negotiating Power in Early Modern Society*, Cambridge University Press, 2001, p. 165.

43. PRO, Assi 45/1/3/57. Duels are more fully discussed in ch. 10.

44. PRO, Assi 45/2/2/12–3.

45. PRO, Assi 45/2/1/111–2.

46. CLRO, London Sessions, December 1691.

47. PRO, Assi 45/2/1/93–97.

48. Cockburn, 'Patterns', 1991, p. 96.

49. See Peter Lake, 'Anti Popery: The Structure of a Prejudice', in Richard Cust and Ann Hughes (eds), *Conflict in Early Stuart England*, Longman, 1989; and John Scott, 'England's Troubles: Exhuming the Popish Plot' in Tim Harris, Paul Seaward and Mark Goldie (eds), *The Politics of Religion in Restoration England*, Blackwell, 1990.

50. For example, Thomas Thynn and Sir Edmond Bury Godfrey.

51. See Dolan, *Whores of Babylon*.

52. *A True Relation of a Late Barbarous Assault Committed upon Robert Pye Esq*, n.p., January 1680, p. 3.

53. *A True Relation*, p. 4.

54. There are a whole series of pamphlets concerning this murder. For example, *Sir Edmondbery Godfrey's Ghost*, London, 1678.

55. CLRO, London Sessions, December 1678.

56. *A Strange and Horrible Relation of a Bloody and Inhumane Murther Committed on the Body of a Jewish Woman*, London, 1674, back of frontispiece.

57. CLRO, London Sessions, December 1699.

58. PRO, Assi 45/2/2/168–9.

59. PRO, Assi 45/4/1/174–5.

60. PRO, Assi 45/15/3/28.

61. PRO, Assi 45/13/1/106–8.

62. Cynthia Herrup, *The Common Peace: Participation and the Criminal Law in Seventeenth-Century England*, Cambridge University Press, 1987, pp. 149–50.

63. See Martin Ingram, 'Ridings, Rough Music and Mocking Rhymes in Early Modern England', in Barry Reay (ed.), *Popular Culture in Seventeenth-Century England*, Croom Helm, 1985.

64. PRO, Assi 45/8/2/113–5.

65. PRO, Assi 45/9/2/59, 171–3.

66. CLRO, London Sessions, February 1690.

67. PRO, Assi 45/8/1/103.

68. PRO, Assi 45/14/1/72–3

69. PRO, Assi 45/6/3/154–5.

70. *The Proceedings on the King's Commissions of the Peace*, London, October 1687, pp. 1–5.

71. PRO, Assi 45/8/2/8.

72. PRO, Assi 45/17/3/17–27.

73. PRO, Assi 45/2/1/125–8.

74. PRO, Assi 45/12/4/36–7.
75. Zachary Babington, *Advice to Grand Jurors in Cases of Blood*, London, 1676, pp. 104–5.
76. CLRO, London Sessions, January 1694.
77. PRO, Assi 45/11/2/142–6.
78. PRO, Assi 45/7/1/231–6.
79. PRO, Assi 45/9/2/55–8.
80. PRO, Assi 45/18/3/18–20.
81. PRO, Assi 45/1/4/59–61.
82. *News from the Session House in the Old Bailey*, London, April 1676, p. 8, and CLRO, London Sessions, April 1676.

Notes to Chapter 12: Serial Killers and Sex Crimes

1. *The Bloody Innkeeper or Sad and Barbarous News from Glocestershire*, London, 1675, p. 4. This case is also discussed in Bernard Capp, 'Serial Killers in Seventeenth-Century England', *History Today*, March 1996.
2. *The Bloody Innkeeper*, p. 5.
3. *The Bloody Innkeeper*, p. 4.
4. A survey of depositions from 1640–1730 from London and Northern Assize sources indicates that 26 per cent of all homicide cases involved family members as the killers. These records are far from complete, but such a figure is suggestive of common levels of crime. Modern sources indicate that men are killed by family at a slightly lower rate to the early modern figure (21 per cent). Women are far more often killed by family or lover, though, with 68 per cent of cases being classified in this way. House of Common Research Paper, 99/56, *Homicide Statistics*, 27 May 1999, p. 17.
5. Michael Braddick, *State Formation in Early Modern England, 1550–1700*, Cambridge University Press, 2000, p. 150.
6. The phrase 'dark figure' is widely used by criminal historians and refers to the unknown number of crimes that were committed and never discovered.
7. *True Valour*, London, 1698, p. 2.
8. CLRO, London Session, July 1678.
9. *Inhumane and Cruel Bloody News from Leeds in Yorkshire*, n.p., n.d.
10. PRO, Assi 45/9/2/102.
11. PRO, Assi 45/5/5/31–40.
12. J. J. Tobias, *Crime and Police in England*, Gill and Macmillan Ltd, 1979.
13. PRO, Assi 45/14/2/139–141.
14. J. H. Baker, *Introduction to English Legal History*, Butterworth, 1990, p. 584.

Notes to Chapter 13: Punishment

1. J. M. Kaye, 'The Early History of Murder and Manslaughter', *Law Quarterly Review*, 83, 1967.

2. J. H. Baker, 'Criminal Courts and Procedure at Common Law, 1550–1800', in John Cockburn (ed.), *Crime in England, 1550–1800*, Methuen, 1977, p. 42.

3. See V. A. C. Gatrell, *The Hanging Tree: Execution and the English People 1770–1868*, Oxford University Press, 1994.

4. A. D. Harvey, 'Burning Women at the Stake in Eighteenth-Century England', *Criminal Justice History: An International Annual*, 11, 1990.

5. See Thomas Laqueur, 'Crowds, Carnival and the State in English Executions, 1604–1868', in A. L. Beier, David Cannadine and James Rosenheim (eds), *First Modern English Society*, Cambridge University Press, 1989, and J. A. Sharpe, '"Last Dying Speeches": Religion, Ideology and Public Execution in Seventeenth-Century England', *Past and Present*, 107, 1985.

6. J. H. Baker, 'Trial by the Book? Fact and Theory in the Criminal Process, 1558–1625', J. H. Baker (eds), *Legal Records and the Historian*, Royal Historical Society, 1978, p. 41.

7. There are examples of 'plea bargaining' for types of theft etc; although this may have occurred in terms of manslaughter, it was often unrecorded and unrecoverable.

8. J. H. Baker, *Introduction to English Legal History*, Butterworth, 1990, p. 587.

9. Baker, 'Trial by Book', p. 41.

10. Cynthia Herrup, *The Common Peace: Participation and the Criminal Law in Seventeenth-Century England*, Cambridge University Press, 1987, p. 47, and J. A. Sharpe, *Crime in Early Modern England*, 1550–1750, Longman, 1984, p. 67.

11. See James C. Oldham, 'On Pleading the Belly: A History of the Jury of Matrons', *Criminal Justice History*, 1985, and Thomas Forbes, 'A Jury of Matrons', *Medical History*, 32, 1988.

12. J. S. Cockburn, *A History of the English Assizes*, Cambridge University Press, 1972, p. 127.

13. John Beattie, *Crime and the Courts in England, 1660–1800*, Princeton University Press, 1986, p. 97.

14. Beattie, *Crime and the Courts*.

15. See Michel Foucault, *Discipline and Punish: The Birth of the Prison*, Peregrine Books, 1979.

Bibliography

UNPRINTED SOURCES

Corporation of London Record Office

London Session Papers, 1648–1730. *Sessions Reviewed*: 1648, 1664, 1665, 1668, 1670, 1673, 1674, 1675, 1676, 1677, 1678, 1679,1680, 1681, 1682, 1683, 1684, 1685, 1686, 1687, 1688, 1689, 1690, 1691, 1692, 1693, 1694, 1695, 1696, 1697, 1698, 1699, 1700, 1701, 1702, 1703, 1704, 1705, 1706, 1707, 1708, 1709, 1710, 1711, 1712, 1713, 1714, 1715, 1716, 1717, 1718, 1719, 1720, 1721, 1722, 1723, 1724, 1725, 1726, 1727, 1728, 1729, 1730.

Guildhall Library

Microfilm of Session Papers, from 1670.
MIC CAB 4.5 Seventeenth and Eighteenth century Trials.

Public Record Office, The National Archives

Assi 44 – indictment records, Northern Assize Circuit. *Record Boxes Reviewed*: 1, 2, 3, 4, 5, 6, 7, 8, 9, 10, 11,12, 13, 14, 15, 16, 17, 18, 19, 20, 21, 22.
Assi 45 – Depositions, Northern Assize Circuit. *Record Boxes Reviewed*: 1/2, 1/3, 1/4, 1/5, 2/1, 2/2, 3/1, 3/2, 4/1, 4/2, 4/3, 5/1, 5/2, 5/3, 5/4, 5/5, 5/6, 5/7, 6/1, 6/2, 6/3, 7/1, 7/2, 8/1, 8/2, 9/1, 9/2, 9/3, 10/1, 10/2, 10/3, 11/1, 11/2, 11/3, 12/1, 12/2, 12/3, 12/4, 13/1, 13/2, 13/3, 14/1, 14/2, 14/3, 15/1, 15/2, 15/3, 15/4, 16/1, 16/2, 16/3, 16/4, 16/5, 17/1, 17/2, 17/3, 18/1, 18/2, 18/3, 18/4, 18/5, 18/6, 18/7

PRINTED SOURCES

William Allen, *Killing No Murder: Briefly Discoursed in Three Questions*, n. l., 1689.
Zachary Babington, *Advice to Grand Jurors in Cases of Blood*, London 1676.
Chadwick-Healey, *British Trials, 1660–1900*, Microform, 1990–2001.
A Cabinet of Grief: Or a French Midwife's Miserable Moan for the Barbarous Murther Committed upon the Body of her husband, London, 1688.
A Caution to Married Couples: Being a True Relation How a Man in Nightingale Lane having Beat and Abused his Wife Murthered a Tubman, London, 1677.

A Compleat Narrative of the Tryal of Elizabeth Lillyman found Guilty of Petty Treason and Condemned at the Sessions of the Old Bayly, London, 1675.

A Dialogue Between a Quaker and His Neighbour in Hertfordshire, London, 1699.

A Full and True Account of the Proceedings at the Sessions of Oyer and Terminer, London, April 1682.

A Full and True Account of the Proceedings at the Sessions of Oyer and Terminer, London, June 1682.

A Full and True Account of the Tryal, Examination and Proceedings Against Mr John Maugridge, a Kettle Drummer, who was on Saturday the 14th December ... for the Murther of Captain Cope on the Guard at the Tower, London, 1705.

A Full and True Relation of all the Proceedings at the Assizes Holden at Chelmsford, London, 1680.

A Full and True Relation of a Most Barbarous and Dreadful Murther Committed on the Body of Mrs Kirk, London, May 1684.

A Full and True Relation of the Examination and Confession of W Barwick and E Mangall, n.p., 1690.

A Full and True Relation of the Murther of Doctor Urthwait, n.p., 1688.

A Full Relation of a Barbarous Murther Committed upon the Body of Esq. Beddingfield by Mr Barney, London, 1684.

A Great and Wonderful Discovery of the Bloudy Villans, and Inhumane Murtherers, Committed to Newgate and Other Places, Since that Great and Lamentable Fire at Mr Delann's House, London, 1663.

A Hellish Murder Committed By a French Midwife on the Body of Her Husband Jan 27 1687, London, 1687.

A Hew and Cry after Blood & Murther or an Elegie on the Most Barbarous Murther of Thomas Thinn Esq., London, 1681.

A Matchless Murder, London, 1681.

A Most Execrable and Barbarous Murder done by an East Indian Devil, London, 1641.

An Account of a Most Horrid and Barbarous Murther and Robbery Committed on the Body of Captain Brown, Shrewsbury, 1694.

An Account of the Apprehending and Taking of John Davis and Philip Wake, London, 1700.

An Account of the Apprehending and Taking of Mr John Robinson and William Criss for the Murther of Mrs Mary Robinson, London, 1696.

An Account of the Arraignment, Tryal, Escape and Condemnation of the Dog of Heriots Hospital in Scotland, London, 1682.

An Exact Account of the Daily Proceedings of the Commisioners of Oyer and Terminer at York, London, January 1663.

An Account of the Discovery and Seizing of Mr Harrison and Mr R – – – on the Account of the Murther of the Late Dr Clench, London, 1690.

An Account of the Examination of Capt Holland Before a Committee of Lords upon the Murther of the Earl of Essex, n.p., n.d.

An Account of the Full Tryal and Examination of Spencer Cooper, London, 1699.

An Account of the Manner, Behaviour and Execution of Marie Aubry who was Burnt to Ashes in Leicester Fields, on Friday the 2d Day of March 1687, London, 1687.

An Account of the Proceedings at the Sessions, London, October 1683.

An Account of the Tryals of Several Notorious Malefactors for Murders, Fellonies, Burgaries, London, 1682.

An Account of the Whole Proceedings at the Sessions, London, July 1683.

An Exact Account of the Daily Proceedings of the Commissioners of Oyer and Terminer at York, Dublin, 1663.

An Exact Narrative of the Bloody Murder and Robbery Committed by Stephen Eaton, Sarah Swift, George Rhodes and Henry Prichard Upon the Person of Mr John Talbot Minister, London, 1669.

An Exact Relation of the Barbarous Murder Committed on Lawrence Caddel a Butcher, who was Buryed Alive, London, 1661.

An Exact Relation of the Bloody and Barbarous Murder, Committed by Miles Lewis and his Wife, a Pinmaker upon their Prentice, London, 1646.

An Impartial Account of the Misfortunes that Lately Happened to the Right Honourable Philip Earl of Pembroke and Montgomery, London, 1680.

A Narrative of the Proceedings at the Session House of the Old Bailey, July 1675.

A Narrative of the Proceedings at the Sessions House in the Old Baily, London, October 1675.

A Narrative of the Proceedings at the Sessions House in the Old Baily, London, April 1680.

A Reply to the Hertford Letter: Wherein the Case of Mrs Stouts' Death is more particularly considered, London, 1699.

A Sad and Dreadful Account of a Most Unusual and Barbarous Murther Committed Upon the Body of the Wife of One William Langstaff, London, 1689.

A Strange and Horrid Murther Committed in White-Fryers upon Mr John Blackston, London, 1684.

A Strange and Horrible Relation of a Bloody and Inhumane Murther Committed on the Body of a Jewish Woman, London, 1674.

A Strange and Wonderful Account of a Most Barbarous and Bloody Murder, n.p., 1680.

A Strange and Wonderfull Discovery of a Horrid and Cruel Murther Committed Fourteen Yeares Since Upon the Person of Robert Eliot of London, n.p., 1662.

A Succinct Narrative of the Bloody Murder of Sir Edmondbury Godfrey, October 12 1678, London, 1683.

A True Account from Chichester concerning the Death of Habin the Informer, London, 1682.

A True Account of the Behaviour, Confession & Last Dying Speeches, n.p., 1681.

A True Account of the Horrid Murther Committed Upon his Grace the Late Lord Archbishop of Saint Andrews, London, 1679.

A True Account of the Prisoners Executed at Tyburn, London, May 1684.

A True Account of the Proceedings Against the Criminals at the Assizes, London, 1685.

A True Account of the Proceedings on the Crownside at this Lent Assize, London, 1683.

A True Account of the Robbery and Murder of John Stockden a Victualler in Grub Street, London, 1698.

A True and Genuine History of the Two Last Wars against France and Spain, London, 1741.

A True and Impartial Account of the Cruel and Bloody Murther, Committed Upon the Body of Thomas Thin, London, 1682.

A True and Perfect Account of the Proceedings, London, January 1674.

A True and Perfect Relation of Three Inhumane Murders, Committed by William Blisse Alias Watts of the Parish of Mims, London, 1672.

A True and Sad Account of a Barbarous Bloody Murther Committed upon the person of John Mulleny, London, 1685.

A True and Wonderful Relation of a Murther Committed in the Parish of Newington, the 12th Day of this Present January By a Maid who Poisoned Herself and Cut the Throat of a Child, London, 1681.

A True Copy of the Paper Delivered by James Clough who was Executed on Friday Last at Tyburn, London, 1680.

A True Narrative of the Proceedings at Session House in the Old Baily, London, August 1675.

A True Narrative of the Proceedings at the Session House in the Old Baily, December 1675.

A True Narrative of The Proceedings, London, January 1676.

A True Narrative of the Proceedings, 14th January 1676.

A True Narrative of the Proceedings, 17th January 1676.

A True Narrative of the Proceedings at the Sessions House in the Old Baily, London, March 1676/7.

A True Narrative of the Proceedings, London, December 1676.

A True Relation of a Late Barbarous Assault Committed upon Robert Pye Esq., n.p., January 1680.

A True Relation of All Bloody Murthers that have been Committed in and about the Citie, London, 1677.

A True Relation of the Execution of John Smith Alias Ashburnham (for murder), London, 1684.

A True Relation of the Horrible Bloody Murther and Robbery Committed in Holbourn ... The Murther Committed on the Body of One Widdow Brown, London, 1674.

A True Relation of the Most Horrible Murther Committed by Thomas White of Lane Green … Upon the Body of his Wife Mrs Dorothy White, n.p., 1682.

A True Relation of the Names and Suspected Crimes of Prisoners Now in Newgate to be Tried for their Lives, n.p., n.d.

A True Relation of What is Discovered Concerning the Murther of the Archbishop of St Andrews, And What Appears to have been the Occasion Thereof, London 1679.

A Warning for Bad wives or the Manner of the Burning of Sarah Elston who was Burnt to Death at Stake, London, 1678.

Blood for Blood, or Justice Executed for Innocent Bloodshed, London, 1670.

Bloody News from Chelmsford, Oxford, 1668.

Bloody News from Clarkenwell, Being a True Relation of a Horrid Murther Committed by John Mason upon Gregory Reeves, London, 1661.

Bloody News from Devonshire, London, 1694.

Bloody News from St Albans Being a Perfect Relation of a Horrible Murder, London, 1661.

Bloody News from Shrewsbury Being a True and Perfect Relation of a Horrible Villan by Name Thomas Reynolds, London, 1673.

Concealed Murther Reveild Being a Strange Discovery of a Most Horrid and Barbarous Murther, that was Committed in St Catharines Lane near Tower Hill, London, 1699.

Cruel and Barbarous News from Cheapside in London, n.p., 1676.

God's Justice against Murther or the Bloudy Apprentice Executed, London, 1668.

Great and Bloody News from Farthing Ally in St Thomas's Southwark or the True and Faithfull Relation of a Horrid and Barbarous Murther, n.p., 1680.

Great and Bloody News, from Turnham Green, or a Relation of a Sharp Encounter Between the Earl of Pembrook, and his Company … with the Constable and the Watch, London, 1680.

Great News from Hertfordshire Being a Particular Account of a late Engagement Between a New Gang of Highwaymen and Several of the Country People near Barnet, London, 1691.

Hold Your Hands Honest Men, London, n.d.

Horrid News from St Martins or Unheard of Murder and Poyson Being a True Relation how a Girl not Full 16 years of Age Murthered her own Mother, London, 1677.

Inhumane & Cruel Bloody News from Leeds in Yorkshire, n.p., n.d.

Inquest after Blood Being a Relation of the Several Inquisitions of all that have Died by any Violent Death in the City of London, London, 1669.

Misery upon Misery: A More Full and Particular Relation of the Present Sad and Deplorable Condition of Elizabeth Farrington, n.p., n.d.

More bloody News from Essex: Or a True Account of the Lamentable Murder of a Poor Woman Big with Two Children, on the Highway, London, 1677.

Murther, Murther or a Bloody Relation how Anne Hamton ... By Poyson Murthered her Deare Husband, London, 1641.

Murther Unparall'd: Or an Account of the Bloudy Murther of Thomas Thin, London, 1682.

Murther upon Murther. Being a Full and True Relation of a Horrid and Bloody Murther, n.p., 1691.

Murther Will Out Or an Unrighteous Discharge, No Security to the Murtherer, n.p., 1662.

My Wife will be my Master. Or, The Married-Man's Complaint against his Unruly Wife. London, 1679.

News from Fleet Street or the Last Speech and Confession of the Two Persons Hanged There for Murther, London, October 1675.

News from Islington, or the Confession and Execution of George Allin, Butcher, who now Hangs in Chains, London, 1674.

News from Newgate, London, September 1673.

Newes from the Dead Or a True and Exact Narration of the Miraculous Deliverance of Anne Greene, London, 1651.

News from the Sessions House in the Old Baily, London, April 1675.

News from the Session House in the Old Bailey, London, April 1676.

News from the Sessions: Or, the Whole Tryal of George Allen the Butcher who Murdered his Wife in the Fields Behind Islington, n.p., 1675.

News from Tyburn, London, September 1674.

News from Tyburn, Or the Confession and Execution of the Three Bayliffs, London, 1675.

News from Tyburn, or the Confession and Execution of the Three Bayliffs, London, December 1675.

News from Tyburn, London, April 1676.

None But the Sheriffs Ought to Name and Return Jurors to Serve in Inquests Before Commissioners of Oyer and Terminer, London, 1681.

Sad and Bloody Newes from Yorkshire Being a True Relation of a most strange Barbarous and Cruel Murther, London, 1663.

Sad and Dreadful News from Dukes Place near Aldgate or a True Account of a Barbarous and Unnatural Self Murder Committed by Dorcas Pinkney, London, 1686.

Sad and Dreadful News from Kings Street in Westminster, or A most lamentable Relation of the Untimely End of the Lady Philip, London, 1684.

Strange and Bloody News from Fetter Lane Being a True Relation of the murder of Percy Wiseman Esq. of Essex, London, 1684.

Strange and Horrible News which Happened Betwixt St John's Street and Islington ... by One Sir Sander Duncomes Beares on the Body of his Gardener, London, 1642.

Strange and Lamentable News from Dullidg–Wells, London, 1678.

Strange and Wonderful news from Lincolnshire or a Dreadful Account of A Most Inhumane and Bloody Murther, London, 1679.

Sad Newes from Blackwall Being a True Relation of the Bloody Designe of Simon Man ... [who] Burned the Good Ship ... [killing 58 men], London, 1641.

Sad News from Ratcliff Being a Full and True Relation of a Horrid and Bloody Murder, London, 1691.

Strange News from Stratton in Cornwall: Or a True Relation of a Cruel Bloody Murder Committed by one JR upon his own father, London, n.d.

The Arraignment, Tryal, Conviction and Condemnation of Henry Harrison, London, 1691.

The Bawdy House Tragedy: or the Mischief that Attends Lewd Company. Being an Impartial Account of the Barbarous Murther of Mrs Mary Duckenfield, London, 1698.

The Black Book of Newgate or an Exact Collection of the Most Material Proceedings at the Sessions in the Old Baily, London, 1677.

The Bloody Husband and Cruell Neighbour or A True Historie of Two Murthers Lately Committed in Laurence Parish in the Isle of Thanet in Kent, London, May 1653.

The Bloody Innkeeper or Sad and Barbarous News from Glocestershire, London, 1675.

The Bloody Lover or Barbarous News from Glocester, n.p., 1673.

The Bloody Murtherer Discovered or A True Relation of the Examination and confession of John Rendor, n.p., 1674.

The Careless Curate and the Bloudy Butcher, n.p., 1662.

The Case of Mrs Mary Stout, Widow, London, 1699.

The Cruel French Lady or a True and Perfect Relation of the Most Execrable Murthers Committed by a French Lady, London, 1673.

The Distressed Mother: or, Sorrowful Wife in Tears, London, 1690.

The Hertford Letter, London, 1699.

The History of Mrs Jane Shore Concubine to K. Edward the Fourth, n.p., 1688.

The Lamentation of Mr Pages Wife of Plimouth, London, n.d.

The Matchless Murder, London, n.d.

The Memoirs of Captain George Carleton, London, 1743.

The Military Memoirs of Captain George Carleton for the Dutch War, 1672, London, 1728.

The Penitent Murderer: Or and Exact and True Relation Taken from the Mouth of Mr William Ivy (Lately Executed), London, 1673.

The Proceedings at the Sessions at the Old Bailey, London, 1679.

The Proceedings of the King and Queens Commissions, London, October 1680.

The Proceedings of the King and Queens Commissions, London, August/September 1682.

The Proceedings of the King and Queens Commissions, London, December 1684.

The Proceedings of the King and Queens Commissions, London, January 1685.

The Proceedings of the King and Queens Commissions, London, February 1685.

The Proceedings of the King and Queens Commissions, London, July 1685.

The Proceedings of the King and Queens Commissions, London, December 1685.

The Proceedings of the King and Queens Commissions, London, May 1686.

The Proceedings of the King and Queens Commissions, London, January 1686/7.

The Proceedings on the Kings Commissions of the Peace, London, October 1687.

The Proceedings of the King and Queens Commissions, London, January 1687/8.

The Proceedings of the King and Queens Commissions, London, March 1687/8.

The Proceedings of the King and Queens Commissions, London, October 1687.

The Proceedings of the King and Queens Commissions, London, February 1688.

The Proceedings of the King and Queens Commissions, London, October 1688.

The Proceedings of the King and Queens Commissions, London, October 1689.

The Proceedings of the King and Queens Commissions, London, January 1690.

The Proceedings of the King and Queens Commissions, London, February 1690.

The Proceedings of the King and Queens Commissions, London, April/May 1690.

The Proceedings of the King and Queens Commissions, London, September 1690.

The Proceedings on the King and Queens Commissions, London, October 1690.

The Proceedings of the King and Queens Commissions, London, April 1691.

The Proceedings of the King and Queens Commissions, London, September 1691.

The Proceedings on the King and Queens Commissions, London, December 1691.

The Proceedings of the King and Queens Commissions, London, June/July 1692.

The Proceedings of the King and Queens Commissions, London, December 1692.

The Proceedings of the King and Queens Commissions, London, April 1693.

The Proceedings of the King and Queens Commissions, London, May/June 1693.

The Proceedings on the King and Queens Commissions, London, July 1693.

The Proceedings of the King and Queens Commissions, London, October 1693.

The Proceedings on the Kings and Queens Commissions, London, April 1694.

The True Narrative of the Proceedings at the Assizes Holden at Kingstone-upon-Thames for the County of Surry, London, 1680.

The Unnatural Grandmother or a True Relation of a Most Barbarous Murther Committed by Elizabeth Hazard ... on her Grand Childe, London, 1659.

The Sufferers Legacy to Surviving Sinners: Edmund Kirk's Dying Advice to Young Men, n.p., 1684.

The True Narrative of the Confession and Execution of the Three Prisoners at Kingston upon Thames, London, March 1679.

The True Narrative of the Execution of John Marketman, London, 1680.

The True Narrative of the Proceedings at Surrey Assizes, London, July 1679.

The True Narrative of the Proceedings at the Assizes Holden for the County of Surrey, London, March 1679.

The True Narrative of the Proceedings at the Sessions House in the Old Bailey, London, January 1680/1.

The True Narrative of the Proceedings at the Sessions House in the Old Bailey, London, October 1680.

The True Narrative of the Proceedings at the Sessions House in the Old Bailey, London, April 1681.

The True Narrative of the Proceedings at the Sessions House in the Old Bailey, London, n.d. (probably 1682/3).

The True Narrative of the Proceedings at the Sessions for London and Middlesex, London, June 1679.

The True Narrative of the Proceedings at the Sessions for London and Middlesex, London, December 1679.

The True News from Tyburn, London, December 1674.

The True Proceedings at the Sessions for London and Middlesex, London, 1679.

The True Proceedings of the Sessions Begun at the Old Bayly, London, April 1683.

The True Proceedings of the Sessions, London, April 1683.

The True Relation of the Tryals at the Sessions of Oyer and Terminer, London, n.d.

The Tryal and Condemnation of Col Adrian Scrope ... who Sate as Judges Upon our Late Soveraigne Lord King Charles, London, 1660.

The Tryal and Condemnation of Several Notorious Malefactors at a Sessions of Oyer and Terminer Holden for the City of London, London, April 1681.

The Tryal and Condemnation of Several Notorious Malefactors at a Sessions of Oyer and Terminer Holden for the City of London, London, July 1681.

The Tryal of Spencer Cowper Esq., London, 1699.

Treason and Murther or the Bloody Father-in-law Being a True and Perfect Relation of a Horrible Murther Committed at Ham, near Stratford in Essex on the wife of James Aslop by her Husbands Father and Brother, London, 1673.

True Valour, London, 1698.

SECONDARY SOURCES

Richard Adair, *Courtship, Illegitimacy and Marriage in Early Modern England*, Manchester University Press, 1996.

Beverley Adams, 'The Body in the Water: Religious Conflict in Hertford, 1660-c1702', London University PhD Thesis, 2000.

Philip Almond, *Heaven and Hell in Enlightenment England*, Cambridge University Press, 1994.

Susan Amussen, '"Being Stirred to Much Unquietness": Violence and Domestic Violence in Early Modern England', *Journal of Women's History*, 6, 2, 1994.

Susan Amussen, *An Ordered Society: Gender and Class in Early Modern England*, Blackwell, 1988.

Susan Amussen, 'Gender, Family and the Social Order, 1560–1725', in Anthony Fletcher and John Stevenson (eds), *Order and Disorder*, Cambridge University Press, 1985.

Donna Andrew, 'The Code of Honour and its Critics: The Opposition to Duelling in England, 1700–1850', *Social History*, 5, 1980.

Meg Arnot and Cornelie Usbourne, 'Why Gender and Crime: Aspects of an International Debate', *Gender and Crime in Modern Europe*, UCL Press, 1999.

J. H. Baker, 'Criminal Courts and Procedure at Common Law, 1550–1800', in John Cockburn (ed.), *Crime in England, 1550–1800*, Methuen, 1977.

J. H. Baker, 'Trial by the Book? Fact and Theory in the Criminal Process, 1558–1625', in J. H. Baker (ed.), *Legal Records and the Historian*, Royal Historical Society, 1978.

J. H. Baker, *Introduction to English Legal History*, Butterworth, 1990.

T. Barnes, 'Examination Before a Justice in the Seventeenth-Century', *Somerset and Dorset Notes and Queries*, Vol. 27, 1955–60.

John Beattie, *Crime and the Courts in England, 1660–1800*, Princeton University Press, 1986.

Dan Beaver, '"Bragging and Daring Words": Honour, Property and the Symbolism of the Hunt in Stowe, 1590–1642', in Michael Braddick and John Walter (eds), *Negotiating Power in Early Modern Society*, Cambridge University Press, 2001.

Ilana Krausman Ben-Amos, *Adolescence and Youth in Early Modern England*, Yale University Press, 1994.

William Blackstone, *Commentaries on the Laws of England*, Clarendon Press, 1765–69.

Ian Bostridge, *Witchcraft and its Transformations, 1560 – 1750*, Clarendon Press, 1997.

Toni Bowers, *The Politics of Motherhood: British Writing and Culture, 1680–1760*, Cambridge University Press, 1996.

Michael Braddick, *State Formation in Early Modern England, 1550–1700*, Cambridge University Press, 2000.

Michael Braddick and John Walter, 'Introduction. Grids of Power: Order, Hierarchy and Subordination in Early Modern Society', in Michael Braddick and John Walter (eds), *Negotiating Power in Early Modern Society*, Cambridge University Press, 2001.

Mark Breitenberg, *Anxious Masculinity in Early Modern England*, Cambridge University Press, 1996.

John Brewer and John Styles (eds), *An Ungovernable People: The English and their Law in the Seventeenth-and Eighteenth-Centuries*, Hutchinson, 1980.

Robin Briggs, 'Women as Victims? Witches, Judges and the Community', *French History*, 5, 4, 1991.

Robert P. Brittain, 'News, Notes and Queries: Cruentation in Legal Medicine and in Literature', *Medical History*, 9, 1965.

Helen Brock and Catherine Crawford, 'Forensic Medicine in Early Colonial Maryland, 1633–83', in Michael Clark and Catherine Crawford (eds), *Legal Medicine in History*, Cambridge University Press, 1994.

Peter Burke, 'The Art of Insult in Early Modern Italy', *Culture and History*, 2, 1987.

Bernard Capp, 'Serial Killers in Seventeenth-Century England', *History Today*, March 1996.

Charles Carlton, 'The Widows Tale: Male Myths and Female Reality in Sixteenth- and Seventeenth-Century England', *Albion*, 10, 2, 1978.

N. Caston, 'Criminals', in Natalie Davis and Arlene Farge (eds), *A History of Women*, III, Harvard University Press, 1993.

Miranda Chaytor, 'Husband(ry): Narratives of Rape in the Seventeenth-Century', *Gender and History*, 7, 3, 1995.

Maria Cioni, 'The Elizabethan Chancery and Women's Rights' in D. Guth and J. McKenna (eds), *Tudor Rule and Revolution*, Cambridge University Press, 1982.

Michael Clark and Catherine Crawford, 'Introduction', in Michael Clark and Catherine Crawford (eds.), *Legal Medicine in History*, Cambridge University Press, 1994.

J. S. Cockburn, *A History of the English Assizes*, Cambridge University Press, 1972.

J. S. Cockburn, 'Early Modern Assize Records as Historical Evidence', *Journal of the Institute of Archivists*, Vol. 5, 1974–7.

J. S. Cockburn, 'The Nature and Incidence of Crime in England 1559–1625: A Preliminary Survey', in J. S. Cockburn (ed.), *Crime in England, 1550–1800*, Metheun, 1977.

J. S. Cockburn, 'Trial by the Book? Fact and Theory in Criminal Process, 1558–1625' in J. H. Baker (ed.), *Legal Records and the Historian*, Royal Historical Society, 1978.

J. S. Cockburn, *Calendar of Assize Records for the Home Circuit*, (5 vols), H. M. S. O., 1989.

J. S. Cockburn, 'Patterns of Violence in English Society: Homicide in Kent, 1560–1985', *Past and Present*, 130, 1991.

Catherine Crawford, 'Legalising Medicine: Early Modern Legal Systems and the Growth of Medico-Legal Knowledge', in Michael Clark and Catherine Crawford (eds), *Legal Medicine in History*, Cambridge University Press, 1994.

Catherine Damme, 'Infanticide: The Worth of an Infant under the Law', *Medical History*, 22, 1978.

Natalie Davis, *Fiction in the Archives: Pardon Tales and their Tellers in Sixteenth-Century France*, Polity Press, 1987.

Natalie Davis, *Society and Culture in Early Modern France*, Polity Press, 1998.

W. Geoffrey Day (ed.), *The Pepys Ballads*, IV, Brewer, 1987.

Frances Dolan, *Dangerous Familiars: Representations of Domestic Crime in England, 1550–1700*, Cornell University Press, 1994.

Frances Dolan, *Whores of Babylon*, Cornell University Press, 1999.

Vivien Brodsky Elliott, 'Single Women in the London Marriage Market: Age, Status and Mobility, 1598–1619', in R. B. Outhwaite (ed.), *Marriage and Society*, London, 1981.

G. R. Elton, 'Introduction: Crime and the Historian', in J. S. Cockburn (ed.), *Crime in England, 1550–1800*, Methuen, 1977.

Amy Erickson, *Women and Property in Early Modern England*, Routledge, 1993.

Doreen Evenden, 'Mothers and their Midwives in Seventeenth-Century London', in Hilary Marland (ed.), *The Art of Midwifery: Early Modern Midwives in Europe*, Routledge, 1993.

Lincoln Faller, *Turned to Account: The Forms and Functions of Criminal Biography in Late Seventeenth-Century England*, Cambridge University Press, 1987.

Valerie Fildes (ed.), *Women as Mothers in Pre-Industrial England*, Routledge, 1990.

Anthony Fletcher, *The Outbreak of the English Civil War*, Edward Arnold, 1991.

Anthony Fletcher and Peter Roberts (eds), *Religion, Culture, and Society in Early Modern Britain: Essays in Honour of Patrick Collinson*, Cambridge University Press, 1994.

Anthony Fletcher, *Gender, Sex and Subordination in England, 1500–1800*, Yale University Press, 1995.

Anthony Fletcher and Steven Hussey, *Childhood in Question: Children, Parents and the State*, Manchester University Press, 1999.

Thomas Forbes, 'Inquest into London and Middlesex Homicides, 1673–1782', *The Yale Journal of Biology and Medicine*, 50, 1977.

Thomas Forbes, *Surgeons at the Bailey: English Forensic Medicine to 1878*, Yale University Press, 1985.

Thomas Forbes, 'A Jury of Matrons', *Medical History*, 32, 1988.

Michel Foucault, *Discipline and Punish: The Birth of the Prison*, Peregrine Books, 1979.

Elizabeth Foyster, 'A Laughing Matter? Marital Discord and Gender Control in Seventeenth-Century England', *Rural History*, 1993.

Elizabeth Foyster, 'Boys will be Boys? Manhood and aggression, 1660–1800', Tim Hitchcock and Michele Cohen (eds), *English Masculinities, 1660–1800*, Longman, 1999.

Elizabeth Foyster, *Manhood in Early Modern England: Honour, Sex and Marriage*, Longman, 1999.

Ute Frevert, 'The Taming of the Noble Ruffian: Male Violence and Duelling in Early Modern and Modern Germany', in Pieter Spierenburg (ed.), *Men and*

Violence: Gender, Honor, and Ritual in Modern Europe and America, Ohio State, 1998.

Malcolm Gaskill, 'Attitudes to Crime in Early Modern England with Special Reference to Witchcraft, Coining and Murder',Cambridge University PhD Thesis, 1994.

Malcolm Gaskill, 'Reporting Murder: Fiction in the Archives in Early Modern England', *Social History*, 23, 1, 1998.

Malcolm Gaskill, *Crime and Mentalities in Early Modern England*, Cambridge University Press, 2000.

V. A. C. Gatrell, *The Hanging Tree: Execution and the English People 1770–1868*, Oxford University Press, 1994.

James Buchanan Given, *Society and Homicide in Thirteenth-Century England*, Stanford University Press, 1977.

Laura Gowing, 'Secret Births and Infanticide in Seventeenth-Century England', *Past and Present*, 156, 1997.

Laura Gowing, *Domestic Dangers: Women, Words, and Sex in Early Modern London*, Oxford University Press, 1998.

Laura Gowing, 'The Haunting of Susan Lay', *Gender and History*, August 2002.

Laura Gowing, 'Ordering the Body: Illegitimacy and Female Authority in Seventeenth-Century England', in Michael Braddick and John Walter (eds), *Negotiating Power in Early Modern Society: Order, Hierarchy and Subordination in Britain and Ireland*, Cambridge University Press, 2001.

Charles Gray (ed.) of Sir Matthew Hale, *The History of the Common Law of England*, The University of Chicago Press, 1971.

Malcolm Greenshields, *The Economy of Violence in Early Modern France: Crime and Justice in the Haute Auvergne, 1587–1664*, Pennsylvania State University Press, 1994.

Paul Griffiths, *Youth and Authority: Formative Experiences in England, 1560–1640*, Clarendon Press, 1996.

P. E. H. Hair, 'A Note on the Incidence of Tudor Suicides', *Local Population Studies*, 1970.

P. E. H. Hair, 'Notes and Queries: Homicide, Infanticide, and Child Assault in Late Tudor Middlesex', *Local Population Studies*, 9, 1972.

William Hale (ed.), *A Series of Precedents and Proceedings in Criminal Causes, Extending from the Year 1475–1640*, Bratton Publishing, 1973.

A. Jams Hammerton, 'The Targets of 'Rough Music': Respectability and Domestic Violence in Victorian England', *Gender and History*, 3, 1, 1991.

Barbara Hanawalt, 'The Female Felon in Fourteenth-Century England', *Viator, 5, 1974.

A. D. Harvey, 'Burning Women at the Stake in Eighteenth-Century England', *Criminal Justice History: An International Annual*, 11, 1990.

David Harley, 'Provincial Midwives in England: Lancashire and Cheshire, 1660–1760', in Hilary Marland (ed.), *The Art of Midwifery: Early Modern Midwives in Europe*, Routledge, 1993.

David Harley, 'The Scope of Legal Medicine in Lancashire and Cheshire, 1660–1760', in Michael Clark and Catherine Crawford (eds), *Legal Medicine in History*, Cambridge University Press, 1994.

David Harley, 'Political Post-Mortems and Morbid Anatomy in Seventeenth-Century England', *The Society for the Social History of Medicine*, 7, 1, 1994.

J. D. Havard, *The Detection of Secret Homicide: A Study of the Medico Legal System of Investigation of Sudden and Unexplained Deaths*, Macmillan, 1960.

Douglas Hay, 'Poaching and the Game Laws on Cannock Chase', in Douglas Hay, Peter Linebaugh, Cal Winslow, John Rule and Edward Thompson (eds), *Albion's Fatal Tree*, Penguin, 1975.

Cynthia Herrup, 'Law and Morality in Seventeenth-Century England', *Past and Present*, 106, 1985.

Cynthia Herrup, *The Common Peace: Participation and the Criminal Law in Seventeenth-Century England*, Cambridge University Press, 1987.

Steve Hindle, 'The Shaming of Margaret Knowsley: Gossip, Gender and the Experience of Authority in Early Modern England', *Continuity and Change*, 9, 3, 1995.

Steve Hindle, *The State and Social Change in Early Modern England, 1550–1640*, Macmillan Press, 2000.

Tim Hitchcock, *English Sexualities, 1700–1800*, Macmillan, 1997.

Peter Hoffer and N. E. H. Hull, *Murdering Mothers: Infanticide in England and New England, 1558–1803*, New York University, 1981.

Clive Holmes, 'Women: Witnesses and Witches', *Past and Present*, 140, 1993.

Geoffrey L. Hudson, 'Negotiating for Blood Money: War Widows and the Courts in Seventeenth-Century England', in Jenny Kermode and Garthine Walker (eds), *Women, Crime and the Courts in Early Modern England*, UCL Press, 1994.

Margaret Hunt, 'Wife Beating, Domesticity and Women's Independence in Eighteenth-Century London', *Gender and History*, 4, 1, 1992.

Michael Hunter, *The Occult Laboratory: Magic, Science and Second Sight in Late Seventeenth-Century Scotland*, Boydell Press, 2001.

Jennine Hurl, '"She Being Bigg with Child is Likely to Miscarry": Pregnant Victims Prosecuting Assault in Westminster, 1685–1720', *London Journal*, 1999.

Martin Ingram, 'Ridings, Rough Music and Mocking Rhymes in Early Modern England' and 'The Reform of Popular Culture? Sex and Marriage in Early Modern England', in Barry Reay (ed.), *Popular Culture in Seventeenth-Century England*, Croom Helm, 1985.

Martin Ingram, *Church Courts, Sex and Marriage in England, 1570–1640*, Cambridge University Press, 1987.

Mark Jackson, *New Born Child Murder: Women, Illegitimacy and the Courts in Eighteenth-Century England*, Manchester University Press, 1996.

Mark Jackson, 'Suspicious Infant Deaths: The Statute of 1624 and Medical Evidence at Coroners' Inquests', in Michael Clark and Catherine Crawford (eds), *Legal Medicine in History*, Cambridge University Press, 1994.

Ann Rosalind Jones, 'Nets and Bridles: Early Modern Conduct Books and Sixteenth-Century Women's Lyrics', in Nancy Armstrong and Leonard Tennenhouse (eds), *The Ideology of Conduct*, Methuen, 1987.

J. M. Kaye, 'The Early History of Murder and Manslaughter', *Law Quarterly Review*, 83, 1967.

Helena Kennedy, *Eve was Framed: Women and British Justice*, Vintage, 1993.

Peter King, 'Punishing Assault: The Transformation of Attitudes in the English Courts', *Journal of Interdisciplinary History*, 1996.

Walter King, 'Punishment for Bastardy in Early Seventeenth-Century England', *Albion*, 1978.

Peter Lake, 'Anti Popery: The Structure of a Prejudice', in Richard Cust and Ann Hughes (eds), *Conflict in Early Stuart England*, Longman, 1989.

Peter Lake, 'Puritanism, Arminianism and a Shropshire Axe-Murder', *Midland History*, 1990.

Peter Lake, 'Deeds against Nature: Cheap Print, Protestantism and Murder in Early Seventeenth-Century England', in Kevin Sharpe and Peter Lake (eds), *Culture and Politics in Early Stuart England*, Macmillan, 1994.

Peter Lake with Michael Questier, *Antichrists Lewd Hat: Protestants, Papists and Players in post Reformation England*, Yale University Press, 2002.

Thomas Laqueur, *The Making of the Modern Body*, University of California Press, 1987.

Thomas Laqueur, 'Crowds, Carnival and the State in English Executions, 1604–1868' in A. L. Beier, David Cannadine and James Rosenheim (eds), *First Modern English Society*, Cambridge University Press, 1989.

Thomas Laqueur, *Making Sex: Body and Gender from the Greeks to Freud*, Harvard University Press, 1992.

Peter Laslett, 'Introduction: Comparing Illegitimacy Over Time and Between Cultures', in Peter Laslett, Karla Oosterveen and Richard Smith (eds), *Bastardy and its Comparative History*, Studies in Social and Demographic History, Edward Arnold, 1980.

Peter Laslett, 'The Bastardy Prone Sub Society', in Peter Laslett, Karla Oosterveen and Richard Smith (eds), *Bastardy and its Comparative History*, Studies in Social and Demographic History, Edward Arnold, 1980.

Peter Laslett, Karla Oosterveen and Richard Smith (eds), *Bastardy and its Comparative History*, Edward Arnold, 1980.

Beverly Lemire, 'The Theft of Clothes and Popular Consumerism in Early Modern England', *Journal of Social History*, 24, 1990.

Bruce Lenman and Geoffrey Parker, 'The State, The Community and the Criminal Law in Early Modern Europe', in V. A. C. Gattrell, Geoffrey Parker and Bruce Lenman (eds), *Crime and the Law: The Social History of Crime in Western Europe Since 1500*, Europa, 1980.

Brian Levack, *The Witch-Hunt in Early Modern Europe*, Macmillian, 1987.

David Levine and Keith Wrightson, 'The Social Context of Illegitimacy in Early Modern England', in Peter Laslett, Karla Oosterveen and Richard Smith (eds), *Bastardy and its Comparative History*, Studies in Social and Demographic History, Edward Arnold, 1980.

Peter Linebaugh, 'The Tyburn Riot against the Surgeons', in Douglas Hay, Peter Linebaugh, John Rule, Edward Thompson and Carl Winslow (eds), *Albion's Fatal Tree*, Penguin, 1977.

Peter Linebaugh, 'The Ordinary of Newgate and His Account', in J. S. Cockburn (ed.), *Crime in Egland, 1550–1800*, Methuen, 1977.

Michael Macdonald, *Mystical Bedlam: Madness, Anxiety, and Healing in Seventeenth-Century England*, Cambridge University Press, 1981.

Alan Macfarlane, 'Review of Stone's "The Family, Sex and Marriage"', *History and Theory*, 18, 1979.

Alan Macfarlane, 'Illegitimacy and Illegitimates in English History', in Peter Laslett, Karla Oosterveen and Richard Smith (eds), *Bastardy and its Comparative History*, Studies in Social and Demographic History, Edward Arnold, 1980.

Alan Macfarlane, *The Justice and the Mare's Ale*, Basil Blackwell, Oxford, 1981.

Hilary Marland, 'Introduction', in Hilary Marland (ed.), *The Art of Midwifery: Early Modern Midwives in Europe*, Routledge, 1993.

J. H. Marshburn and A. R. Velie, *Blood and Knavery: A Collection of English Renaissance Pamphlets and Ballads of Crime and Sin*, Farleigh Dickinson University Press, 1973.

Kate McLuskie, ''Tis But a Woman's Jar: Family and Kinship in Elizabethan Domestic Drama', *Literature and History*, 9, 1983.

Vanessa McMahon, 'Desire, Sex and Consequences: Women, Gender and the Bawdy Courts in Late Sixteenth and Early Seventeenth Century England', Royal Holloway MA Dissertation, 1995.

S. F. C. Milsom, *Historical Foundations of the Common Law*, Butterworth, London, 1981.

Edward Muir, *Ritual in Early Modern Europe*, Cambridge University Press, 1997.

Edward Muir and Guido Ruggerio (eds), *History From Crime*, John Hopkins University Press, 1994.

Richelle Munkhoff, 'Searchers of the Dead: Authority, Marginality and The Interpretation of Plague in England, 1574–1665', *Gender and History*, 11, 1, 1999.

James C. Oldham, 'On Pleading the Belly: A History of the Jury of Matrons', *Criminal Justice History*, 1985.

James C. Oldham, 'Truth Telling in the Eighteenth-Century English Courtroom', *Law and History Review*, 12, 1, 1994.

Darren Oldridge, *The Devil in Early Modern England*, Sutton, 2000.

Margaret Pelling, 'Thoroughly Resented? Older Women and the Medical Role in Early Modern London', in Lynette Hunter and Sarah Hutton (eds), *Women, Science and Medicine, 1500–1700*, Sutton, 1997.

T. F. T. Plucknett, *Edward I and Criminal Law*, Cambridge at the University Press, 1960.

Frederick Pollock and Frederic Maitland, *History of English Law: Before the Time of Edward I*, II, Cambridge University Press, 1911.

Linda Pollock, 'Childbearing and Female Bonding in Early Modern England', *Social History*, October 1997.

Roy Porter, *Mind-Forg'd Manacles*, Athlone Press, 1987.

Roy Porter, *Disease, Medicine and Society in England, 1550 –1860*, Cambridge University Press, 1993.

Wilfred Prest, 'Law and Women's Rights in Early Modern England', *The Seventeenth-Century*, 6, 1991.

Mary Prior, 'Wives and Wills, 1558–1700', in J. Chartres and D. Hey (eds), *English Rural Society, 1500–1800*,

Diane Purkiss, *The Witch in History: Early Modern and Twentieth-Century Representations*, Routledge, 1996.

Diane Purkiss, 'Material girls: The Seventeenth-Century Woman Debate', in Clare Brant and Diane Purkiss (eds), *Women, Texts and Histories, 1575–1760*, Routledge, 1992.

G. R. Quaife, *Wanton Wenches and Wayward Wives: Peasants and Illicit Sex in Early Seventeenth-Century England*, Croom Helm, 1979.

Philip Rawlings, *Crime and Power: A History of Criminal Justice, 1688–1998*, Longman, 1999.

Penny Roberts and William Naphy (eds), *Fear in Early Modern Society*, Manchester University Press, 1997.

Hyder Rollins (ed.), *A Pepysian Garland: Black Letter Broadside Ballads of the Years, 1595–1639*, Cambridge University Press, 1922.

Michael Roper and John Tosh, 'Introduction: Historians and the Politics of Masculinity', in Michael Roper and John Tosh (eds), *Manful Assertions*, 1991.

Lyndal Roper, *Oedipus and the Devil: Witchcraft, Sexuality and Religion in Early Modern Europe*, Routledge, 1994.

Ulinka Rublack, *The Crimes of Women in Early Modern Germany*, Clarendon Press, 1999.

Ronald Sawyer, '"Strangely Handled in all her Lyms": Witchcraft and Healing in Jacobean England', *Journal of Social History*, 22, 1989.

Regina Schulte, *The Village in Court: Arson, Infanticide and Poaching in the Court Records of Upper Bavaria, 1848–1910*, Cambridge University Press, 1994.

John Scott, 'England's Troubles: Exhuming the Popish Plot' in Tim Harris, Paul Seaward and Mark Goldie (eds), *The Politics of Religion in Restoration England*, Blackwell, 1990.

Steven Shapin, *A Social History of Truth: Civility and Science in Seventeenth-Century England*, University of Chicago Press, 1994.

Ann Louise Shapiro, '"Stories More Terrifying than the Truth Itself": Narratives of Female Criminality in Fin De Siecle Paris', in Meg Arnot and Cornelia Usbourne (eds), *Gender and Crime in Modern Europe*, UCL Press, 1999.

Ann Louise Shapiro, *Breaking the Codes: Female Criminality in Fin De Siecle Paris*, Stanford University Press, 1996.

Barbara Shapiro, *Probability and Certainty in Seventeenth-Century England*, Princeton University Press, 1983.

Barbara Shapiro, *A Culture of Fact*, Cornell University Press , 2000.

J. A. Sharpe, *Crime in Early Modern England, 1550–1750*, Longman, 1984.

J. A. Sharpe, 'Debate: The History of Violence in England: Some Observations', *Past and Present*, 105, 1985.

J. A. Sharpe, '"Last Dying Speeches': Religion, Ideology and Public Execution in Seventeenth-Century England", *Past and Present*, 107, 1985.

J. A. Sharpe, 'Witchcraft and Women in Seventeenth-Century England: Some Northern Evidence', *Continuity and Change*, 6, 2, 1991.

W. J. Sheehan, 'Finding Solace in Eighteenth-Century Newgate', in J. S. Cockburn (ed.), *Crime in England, 1550–1800*, Metheun, 1977.

Alex Shepard, 'Meanings of Manhood in Early Modern England, with Special Reference to Cambridge, c1560–1640', Cambridge University PhD Thesis, 1998.

Robert Shoemaker, *Prosecution and Punishment: Petty Crime and the Law in London and Rural Middlesex, 1660–1725*, Cambridge University Press, 1991.

Robert Shoemaker, 'Reforming Male Manners: Public Insult and the Decline of Violence in London, 1660–1740', in Tim Hitchcock and Michele Cohen (eds), *English Masculinities, 1660–1800*, Longman, 1999.

Robert Shoemaker, 'Public Spaces, Private Disputes: Conflict on the Streets of London, 1660–1800', unpublished lecture at Streets of London conference, 17.12.99.

Pieter Spierenberg, *The Broken Spell: A Cultural and Anthropological History of Preindustrial Europe*, Macmillan, 1991.

Pieter Spierenburg, 'How Violent were Women? Court Cases in Amsterdam, 1650–1810', *Crime, Histoire & Societes*, 1, 1, 1997.

Pieter Spierenberg, 'Knife Fighting and Popular Codes of Honor in Early Modern

Amsterdam', and 'Masculinity, Violence, and Honor: An Introduction', in Pieter Spierenberg (ed.), *Men and Violence: Gender, Honor, and Ritual in Modern Europe and America*, Ohio State, 1998.

Victor Stater, *High Life, Low Morals: The Duel that Shook Stuart Society*, John Murray, 1999.

Lawrence Stone, *The Family, Sex and Marriage in England, 1500–1800*, Weidenfeld and Nicolson, 1977.

Lawrence Stone, 'Interpersonal Violence in English Society, 1300–1980', *Past and Present*, 103, 1983.

Lawrence Stone, 'A Rejoinder', *Past and Present*, 105, 1985.

Tim Stretton, *Women Waging Law in Elizabethan England*, Cambridge University Press, 1998.

Deborah Symonds, *Weep Not for Me: Women, Ballads and Infanticide in Early Modern Scotland*, The Pennsylvania State University Press, 1997.

E. P. Thompson, *Customs in Common*, Merlin Press, 1991.

J. J. Tobias, *Crime and Police in England*, Gill and Macmillan Ltd, 1979.

D. E. Underdown, 'The Taming of the Scold: The Enforcement of Patriarchal Authority in Early Modern England', in Anthony Fletcher and John Stevenson, *Order and Disorder in Early Modern England*, Cambridge University Press, 1985.

Amanda Vickery, 'Golden Age to Separate Spheres? A Review of the Categories and Chronology of English Women's History', *The Historical Journal*, 36, 2, 1993.

Garthine Walker, 'Crime, Gender and Social Order in Early Modern Cheshire', Liverpool University PhD Thesis, 1994.

Garthine Walker, 'Women, Theft and the World of Stolen Goods', in Jenny Kermode and Garthine Walker (eds), *Women, Crime and the Courts in Early Modern England*, UCL Press, 1994.

Garthine Walker, 'Rereading Rape and Sexual Violence in Early Modern England', *Gender and History*, 1998.

Alexandra Walsham, *Providence in Early Modern England*, Oxford University Press, 2001.

Michael Weisser, 'Crime and Punishment in Early Modern Spain', in VAC Gattrell, Geoffrey Parker and Bruce Lenman (eds), *Crime and the Law: The Social History of Crime in Western Europe Since 1500*, Europa, 1980.

Carol Wiener, 'Is a Spinster an Unmarried Woman?', *The American Journal of Legal History*, 1970.

Carol Wiener, 'Sex Roles and Crime in Late Elizabethan Hertfordshire', *Journal of Social History*, 8, 4, 1974–5.

Adrian Wilson, *The Making of Man-Midwifery: Childbirth in England 1660–1770*, Harvard University Press, 1995.

Joy Wiltenburg, *Disorderly Women and Female Power in the Street Literature of Early Modern England and Germany*, University Press of Virginia, 1992.

Andy Wood, *The Politics of Social Conflict: The Peak Country, 1520–1770*, Cambridge University Press, 1999.

Keith Wrightson, 'Infanticide in Early Seventeenth-Century England', *Local Population Studies*, 1975.

Keith Wrightson, 'Two Concepts of Order: Justices, Constables and Jurymen in Seventeenth-Century England', in John Brewer and John Styles (eds), *An Ungovernable People: The English and their Law in the Seventeenth- and Eighteenth-Centuries*, Hutchinson, 1980.

Keith Wrightson, 'The Nadir of English Illegitimacy in the Seventeenth-Century', in Peter Laslett, Karla Oosterveen and Richard Smith (eds), *Bastardy and its Comparative History*, Studies in Social and Demographic History, Edward Arnold, 1980.

Index